New Participatory Dimensions in Civil Society

This book examines citizen engagement in contemporary democratic politics and the development of new participatory forms. Based on empirical information gathered from citizens, activists and organizations, it examines the changing face of democratic participation.

Advanced democracies are 'plagued' by the complex problem of basing political decisions on the active engagement of citizens and citizens' organizations. Although the benefits of an active citizenry appear great, the reality is that most citizens positively embrace a relatively marginal role in organized politics. The conventional activist – citizens as active members engaged in voluntary associations and collective decision making – seems to be replaced by passive supporters and donors or ephemeral or episodic democratic participators. This volume aims to address several issues at the core of this transformation: the rise of chequebook participation, the growing attractiveness of individualized forms of participation and the increasing relevance of professional expertise.

Looking beyond the traditional single focus on participation or on organizations in isolation, the book innovatively examines the empirical link that can be established between actual developments in democratic participations and the organizational framework in European countries.

New Participatory Dimensions in Civil Society is essential reading for students and scholars of democracy, participation, civil society, politics and sociology.

Jan W. van Deth is Professor of Political Science and International Comparative Social Research at the University of Mannheim, Germany.

William A. Maloney is Professor of Politics and Head of Politics in the School of Geography, Politics and Sociology at Newcastle University, UK.

Routledge/ECPR studies in European political science
Edited by Thomas Poguntke
Ruhr University Bochum, Germany on behalf of the European Consortium for Political Research

The Routledge/ECPR Studies in European Political Science series is published in association with the European Consortium for Political Research – the leading organization concerned with the growth and development of political science in Europe. The series presents high quality edited volumes on topics at the leading edge of current interest in political science and related fields, with contributions from European scholars and others who have presented work at ECPR workshops or research groups.

1 **Regionalist Parties in Western Europe**
   Edited by Lieven de Winter and Huri Türsan

2 **Comparing Party System Change**
   Edited by Jan-Erik Lane and Paul Pennings

3 **Political Theory and European Union**
   Edited by Albert Weale and Michael Nentwich

4 **Politics of Sexuality**
   Edited by Terrell Carver and Véronique Mottier

5 **Autonomous Policy Making by International Organizations**
   Edited by Bob Reinalda and Bertjan Verbeek

6 **Social Capital and European Democracy**
   Edited by Jan van Deth, Marco Maraffi, Ken Newton and Paul Whiteley

7 **Party Elites in Divided Societies**
   Edited by Kurt Richard Luther and Kris Deschouwer

8 **Citizenship and Welfare State Reform in Europe**
   Edited by Jet Bussemaker

9 **Democratic Governance and New Technology**
   Technologically mediated innovations in political practice in Western Europe
   Edited by Ivan Horrocks, Jens Hoff and Pieter Tops

10 **Democracy without Borders**
   Transnationalisation and conditionality in new democracies
   Edited by Jean Grugel

11 **Cultural Theory as Political Science**
Edited by Michael Thompson, Gunnar Grendstad and Per Selle

12 **The Transformation of Governance in the European Union**
Edited by Beate Kohler-Koch and Rainer Eising

13 **Parliamentary Party Groups in European Democracies**
Political parties behind closed doors
Edited by Knut Heidar and Ruud Koole

14 **Survival of the European Welfare State**
Edited by Stein Kuhnle

15 **Private Organisations in Global Politics**
Edited by Karsten Ronit and Volker Schneider

16 **Federalism and Political Performance**
Edited by Ute Wachendorfer-Schmidt

17 **Democratic Innovation**
Deliberation, representation and association
Edited by Michael Saward

18 **Public Opinion and the International Use of Force**
Edited by Philip Everts and Pierangelo Isernia

19 **Religion and Mass Electoral Behaviour in Europe**
Edited by David Broughton and Hans-Martien ten Napel

20 **Estimating the Policy Position of Political Actors**
Edited by Michael Laver

21 **Democracy and Political Change in the 'Third World'**
Edited by Jeff Haynes

22 **Politicians, Bureaucrats and Administrative Reform**
Edited by B. Guy Peters and Jon Pierre

23 **Social Capital and Participation in Everyday Life**
Edited by Paul Dekker and Eric M. Uslaner

24 **Development and Democracy**
What do we know and how?
Edited by Ole Elgström and Goran Hyden

25 **Do Political Campaigns Matter?**
Campaign effects in elections and referendums
Edited by David M. Farrell and Rüdiger Schmitt-Beck

26 **Political Journalism**
New challenges, new practices
Edited by Raymond Kuhn and Erik Neveu

27 **Economic Voting**
Edited by Han Dorussen and Michaell Taylor

28 **Organized Crime and the Challenge to Democracy**
Edited by Felia Allum and Renate Siebert

29 **Understanding the European Union's External Relations**
Edited by Michèle Knodt and Sebastiaan Princen

30 **Social Democratic Party Policies in Contemporary Europe**
Edited by Giuliano Bonoli and Martin Powell

31 **Decision Making within International Organisations**
Edited by Bob Reinalda and Bertjan Verbeek

32 **Comparative Biomedical Policy**
Governing assisted reproductive technologies
Edited by Ivar Bleiklie, Malcolm L. Goggin and Christine Rothmayr

33 **Electronic Democracy**
Mobilisation, organisation and participation via new ICTs
Edited by Rachel K. Gibson, Andrea Römmele and Stephen J. Ward

34 **Liberal Democracy and Environmentalism**
The end of environmentalism?
Edited by Marcel Wissenburg and Yoram Levy

35 **Political Theory and the European Constitution**
Edited by Lynn Dobson and Andreas Follesdal

36 **Politics and the European Commission**
Actors, interdependence, legitimacy
Edited by Andy Smith

37 **Metropolitan Governance**
Capacity, democracy and the dynamics of place
Edited by Hubert Heinelt and Daniel Kübler

38 **Democracy and the Role of Associations**
Political, organizational and social contexts
Edited by Sigrid Roßteutscher

39 **The Territorial Politics of Welfare**
Edited by Nicola McEwen and Luis Moreno

40 **Health Governance in Europe**
Issues, challenges and theories
Edited by Monika Steffen

41 **Republicanism in Theory and Practice**
Edited by Iseult Honohan and Jeremy Jennings

42 **Mass Media and Political Communication in New Democracies**
Edited by Katrin Voltmer

43 **Delegation in Contemporary Democracies**
Edited by Dietmar Braun and Fabrizio Gilardi

44 **Governance and Democracy**
Comparing national, European and international experiences
Edited by Yannis Papadopoulos and Arthur Benz

45 **The European Union's Roles in International Politics**
Concepts and analysis
Edited by Ole Elgström and Michael Smith

46 **Policy-making Processes and the European Constitution**
A comparative study of member states and accession countries
Edited by Thomas König and Simon Hug

47 **Democratic Politics and Party Competition**
Edited by Judith Bara and Albert Weale

48 **Participatory Democracy and Political Participation**
Can participatory engineering bring citizens back in?
Edited by Thomas Zittel and Dieter Fuchs

49 **Civil Societies and Social Movements**
Potentials and problems
Edited by Derrick Purdue

50 **Resources, Governance and Civil Conflict**
Edited by Magnus Öberg and Kaare Strøm

51 **Transnational Private Governance and its Limits**
Edited by Jean-Christophe Graz and Andreas Nölke

52 **International Organizations and Implementation**
Enforcers, managers, authorities?
Edited by Jutta Joachim, Bob Reinalda and Bertjan Verbeek

53 **New Parties in Government**
Edited by Kris Deschouwer

54 **In Pursuit of Sustainable Development**
New governance practices at the sub-national level in Europe
Edited by Susan Baker and Katarina Eckerberg

55 **Governments, NGOs and Anti-Corruption**
The new integrity warriors
Edited by Luís de Sousa, Barry Hindess and Peter Larmour

56 **Intra-Party Politics and Coalition Governments**
Edited by Daniela Giannetti and Kenneth Benoit

57 **Political Parties and Partisanship**
Social identity and individual attitudes
Edited by John Bartle and Paolo Belucci

58 **The Future of Political Community**
Edited by Gideon Baker and Jens Bartelson

59 **The Discursive Politics of Gender Equality**
Stretching, bending and policy making
Edited by Emanuela Lombardo, Petra Meier and Mieke Verloo

60 **Another Europe**
Conceptions and practices of democracy in the European social forums
Edited by Donatella Della Porta

61 **European and North American Policy Change**
Drivers and dynamics
Edited by Giliberto Capano and Michael Howlett

62 **Referendums and Representative Democracy**
Responsiveness, accountability and deliberation
Edited by Maija Setälä and Theo Schiller

63 **Education in Political Science**
Discovering a neglected field
Edited by Anja P. Jakobi, Kerstin Martens and Klaus Dieter Wolf

64 **Religion and Politics in Europe, the Middle East and North Africa**
Edited by Jeffrey Haynes

65 **New Directions in Federalism Studies**
Edited by Jan Erk and Wilfried Swenden

66 **Public Policy and the Media**
The interplay of mass communication and political decision making
Edited by Sigrid Koch-Baumgarten and Katrin Voltmer

67 **Changing Government Relations in Europe**
From localism to intergovernmentalism
Edited by Michael J. Goldsmith and Edward C. Page

68 **Political Discussion in Modern Democracies**
A comparative perspective
Edited by Michael R. Wolf, Laura Morales and Ken'ichi Ikeda

69 **Dominant Political Parties and Democracy**
Concepts, measures, cases and comparisons
Edited by Matthjis Bogaards and Françoise Boucek

70 **The Political Representation of Immigrants and Minorities**
Voters, parties and parliaments in liberal democracies
Edited by Karen Bird, Thomas Saalfeld and Andreas M. Wüst

71 **The Role of Governments in Legislative Agenda Setting**
Edited by Bjørn Erik Rasch and George Tsebelis

72 **Administrative Reforms and Democratic Governance**
Edited by Jean-Michel Eymeri-Douzans and Jon Pierre

73 **Puzzles of Government Formation**
Coalition theory and deviant cases
Edited by Rudy B. Andeweg, Lieven De Winter and Patrick Dumont

74 **New Regionalism and the European Union**
Dialogues, comparisons and new research directions
Edited by Alex Warleigh-Lack, Nick Robinson and Ben Rosamond

75 **Politics of Religion in Western Europe**
Edited by François Foret and Xabier Itcaina

76 **Ageing Populations in Post-industrial Democracies**
Comparative studies of policies and politics
Edited by Pieter Vanhuysse and Achim Goerres

77 **New Participatory Dimensions in Civil Society**
Professionalization and individualized collective action
Edited by Jan W. van Deth and William A. Maloney

Also available from Routledge in association with the ECPR:
Sex Equality Policy in Western Europe, *Edited by Frances Gardiner*; **Democracy and Green Political Thought**, *Edited by Brian Doherty and Marius de Geus*; **The New Politics of Unemployment**, *Edited by Hugh Compston*; **Citizenship, Democracy and Justice in the New Europe**, *Edited by Percy B. Lehning and Albert Weale*; **Private Groups and Public Life**, *Edited by Jan W. van Deth*; **The Political Context of Collective Action**, *Edited by Ricca Edmondson*; **Theories of Secession**, *Edited by Percy Lehning*; **Regionalism Across the North/South Divide**, *Edited by Jean Grugel and Wil Hout*.

New Participatory Dimensions in Civil Society

Professionalization and individualized collective action

Edited by Jan W. van Deth and
William A. Maloney

LONDON AND NEW YORK

First published 2012
by Routledge
2 Park Square, Milton Park, Abingdon, Oxfordshire OX14 4RN

Simultaneously published in the USA and Canada
by Routledge
711 Third Avenue, New York, NY 10017
First issued in paperback 2014

Routledge is an imprint of the Taylor & Francis Group, an informa business

© 2012 Selection and editorial matter, Jan W. van Deth and William A. Maloney; individual chapters, the contributors

The right of Jan W. van Deth and William A. Maloney to be identified as the authors of the editorial material, and of the authors for their individual chapters, has been asserted in accordance with sections 77 and 78 of the Copyright, Designs and Patents Act 1988.

All rights reserved. No part of this book may be reprinted or reproduced or utilized in any form or by any electronic, mechanical or other means, now known or hereafter invented, including photocopying and recording, or in any information storage or retrieval system, without permission in writing from the publishers.

Trademark notice: Product or corporate names may be trademarks or registered trademarks, and are used only for identification and explanation without intent to infringe.

British Library Cataloguing in Publication Data
A catalogue record for this book is available from the British Library

Library of Congress Cataloging in Publication Data
New participatory dimensions in civil society: professionalization and individualized collective action/edited by Jan W. van Deth and William A. Maloney.
    p. cm. – (Routledge/ECPR studies in European political science; 77)
    Includes bibliographical references and index.
    1. Political participation–European Union countries–History–21st century. 2. Civil society–European Union countries–History–21st century. I. Deth, Jan W. van. II. Maloney, William A.
    JN40.N48 2012
    323′.042094–dc23
                                                            2011027427

ISBN 978-0-415-58893-5 (hbk)
ISBN 978-1-138-80236-0 (pbk)
ISBN 978-0-203-14273-8 (ebk)

Typeset in Times New Roman
by Wearset Ltd, Boldon, Tyne and Wear

Contents

List of figures xiii
List of tables xiv
List of contributors xv
Acknowledgements xix

1 **Introduction: democracy, professionalization and participation** 1
JAN W. VAN DETH AND WILLIAM A. MALONEY

PART I
Professionalization and democratic politics 13

2 **How to domesticate civil society by public–private partnerships: evidence from German local health policy** 15
MATTHIAS FREISE

3 **Entrepreneurial participation in international local politics: the case of Marseilles, European Capital of Culture for 2013** 27
NICOLAS MAISETTI

4 **New issues, new forms of action? Climate change and environmental activism in Britain** 46
CHRISTOPHER ROOTES

5 **The professionalization of the EU's civil society: a conceptual framework** 69
SABINE SAURUGGER

xii *Contents*

6   The democratic contribution of professionalized representation   84
    WILLIAM A. MALONEY

7   Professionalized supply-side mobilization: are financial
    contributors 'meaningful participants'?   97
    GRANT JORDAN

PART II
Changing democratic engagement   113

8   New modes of participation and norms of citizenship   115
    JAN W. VAN DETH

9   A remedy for unequal participation? How welfare states
    impact on social and political engagement   139
    ISABELLE STADELMANN-STEFFEN

10 Peripheral participants: the activation of the politically less
    engaged in advanced democracies   157
    ELINE A. DE ROOIJ

11 Surrogates for the underrepresented? Ideology and
    participatory inequality in personal and professional
    political action   178
    TOM W.G. VAN DER MEER

12 The stability of individualized collective action: results of a
    panel study among Belgian late adolescents   197
    ELLEN QUINTELIER AND MARC HOOGHE

13 Youth participation from the top down: the perspectives of
    government and community sector decision makers in
    Australia   212
    ARIADNE VROMEN

14 Conclusions: professionalization and and individualized
    political action?   231
    WILLIAM A. MALONEY AND JAN W. VAN DETH

    References   243
    Index   265

Figures

8.1	Use of individualized modes of political participation (boycotting) in Austria, Britain, Finland, West Germany, Italy, Netherlands, and Switzerland	119
9.1	Social and political volunteering of low and high income individuals respectively	143
9.2	Interaction between welfare state policy and individual civic engagement	147
9.3	Marginal effect of low income on social and political volunteering respectively	152
10.1	Typology of peripheral and core political participants	162
10.2a	Type of participant	163
10.2b	Type of participant	163
10.3	Percentage of all participants that are peripheral (by whether there was a national election and/or a major political issue on the agenda in a country)	164
10.4	Percentage of all participants that are peripheral (by the percentage of urbanization in a country)	165
10.5	Percentage of all participants that are peripheral (by the mobilization score of a country)	167
10.6	Percentage of all participants that are peripheral (by GNI per capita in US$1,000 of a country)	167
11.1a	Participatory inequalities along policy lines: voting	187
11.1b	Participatory inequalities along policy lines: contacting	187
11.1c	Participatory inequalities along policy lines: demonstrate	188
11.1d	Participatory inequalities along policy lines: civic action	188
11.1e	Participatory inequalities along policy lines: membership interest association	189
11.1f	Participatory inequalities along policy lines: membership activist association	189

Tables

4.1	Membership of selected environmental NGOs	49
4.2	Leading British ENGOs	50
6.1	UK campaign groups' income source and most important source	89
8.1	Forms of participation in Austria, Britain, Finland, West Germany, Italy, Netherlands, and Switzerland	120
8.2	Forms of participation in Europe	123
8.3	Explorative structure of political participation in Europe	125
8.4	A typology of individualized and organized modes of participation	127
8.5	Types of participation in Europe	128
8.6	Antecedents of types of participants	130
8.7	Main characteristics of participants in Europe	133
9.1	Overall context effect of welfare state policy on social and political volunteering	149
9.2	Group-specific welfare state effects on social and political volunteering	150
10.1	Two level logistic regression model predicting being a peripheral participant	172
11.1	Left–right position and policy preferences	185
11.2	Explaining six forms of participation by ideology, extremism, and perceived distance	192
11.3	Explaining the ideology effects on six forms of participation by policy positions	193
12.1	Frequency of participation acts	203
12.2	Types of activists	205
12.3	Logistic regression for four types of participants	207
12.4	Multinomial regression for different participation types	208
13.1	Three levels of young people's participation in decision making	213
13.2	Comparing participation mechanisms used by service providers to engage young people	222
13.3	Young people's involvements in types of decision-making processes	223
13.4	Identifying themes in youth participation discourses	225

Contributors

Eline A. de Rooij is a Postdoctoral Prize Research Fellow of Nuffield College, University of Oxford. Her main research interests are in the field of political sociology and concern electoral and non-electoral political behaviour; as well as the political integration and participation of (ethnic) minority and marginal groups. Currently her main research project explores the causes and consequences of changes in the nature of political involvement in advanced democracies, which includes a study of immigrant political participation. A second research project (with Donald Green) examines campaign effects on voter registration and turnout of marginalized groups, among which Native Americans, through a series of field experiments. She has published in the *Annual Review of Political Science* and the *European Sociological Review*.

Matthias Freise is a research associate at the Department of Political Science in Münster. Previously, he was the supervisor of the research group 'European Civil Society and Multilevel Governance' at Münster University. His research interests include civil society theory, third sector research, European multilevel governance and interest representation. He is co-editor of the series 'European Civil Society' at Nomos Publishers. Recent publications include *A Panacea for all Seasons? Civil Society and Governance in Europe* (Baden-Baden: Nomos, 2010).

Marc Hooghe is Professor of Political Science at the University of Leuven (Belgium) and an Invited Professor at the University Lille-II (France). His main research interests are political participation, social capital and social cohesion.

Grant Jordan, Department of Politics and International Relations, University of Aberdeen. Grant Jordan's first book *Governing Under Pressure* (with Jeremy Richardson, Oxford: Wiley) was published in 1979. They are now revisiting the idea of policy community that it floated – to argue that the competing idea of 'majoritarianism' poorly fitted the UK in the 1970s and fits even less well today. This belief in the centrality of British consensus and consultation is most thoroughly advanced in *Engineers and Professional Self Regulation* (Oxford: Clarenden Press, 1992) and with William Maloney in 'Accounting for Sub Governments: Explaining the Persistence of Policy Communities, *Administration and Society*, 1997.

Nicolas Maisetti is a PhD student in Politics at the University of Paris 1 Panthéon-Sorbonne (France) and member of the Centre Européen de Sociologie et de Science Politique de la Sorbonne (CESSP-Sorbonne). His Master dissertation was about municipal foreign policy and state restructuring (2007). His thesis is about the internationalization of the city of Marseilles through a case study of urban projects. His research fields are international relations, urban governance, international political economy and political sociology. Recent publications include 'La Coopération décentralisée aux échelles du territoire marseillais: un réseau politique local international?' in *Les Cahiers de la Coopération décentralisée* (Vol. 2, August 2010).

William A. Maloney is Professor of Politics and Head of Politics in the School of Geography, Politics and Sociology, Newcastle University (UK). His main research interests are in the areas of interest group politics (internal and external dynamics), social capital, political involvement and nonparticipation. He has published extensively in these areas and his recent publications include *Civil Society and Activism in Europe: Contextualising Engagement and Political Orientation* (co-edited with Jan W. van Deth, London: Routledge, 2010), *The Politics of Organized Interests in Europe: The State of the Art*, a special issue of *West European Politics* (December, 2008), vol. 31 no. 6 (co-edited with Jan Beyers and Rainer Eising), *Civil Society and Governance in Europe: From National to International Linkages* (co-edited with Jan W. van Deth, Cheltenham: Edward Elgar, 2008) and *Interest Groups and the Democratic Process: Enhancing Participation?* (co-authored with Grant Jordan; Houndmills etc.: Palgrave, 2007).

Ellen Quintelier is postdoctoral researcher of the Research Foundation Flanders. Her research interests lie in political behaviour, political sociology and comparative politics. More specifically, she focuses on the inequality of political participation patterns and political socialization agents. Her work has been published in *European Union Politics*, *Political Studies* and the *Journal of Ethnic and Migration Studies*.

Christopher Rootes is Professor of Environmental Politics and Political Sociology and Director of the Centre for the Study of Social and Political Movements at the University of Kent, Canterbury, England. His recent research, mostly funded by the European Commission, has been on environmental protest, movements and NGOs, the global justice movement and public contention over waste management facilities. He is Editor in Chief and Chair of the Editorial Board of the journal *Environmental Politics*, a member of the editorial boards of *Mobilization* and *Social Movement Studies* and was convener of the ECPR Standing Group on Green Politics (1997–2007). Among other publications, he has edited *The Green Challenge: The Development of Green Parties in Europe* (with Dick Richardson; London: Routledge, 1995),

Environmental Movements: Local, National and Global (London: Routledge, 1999), *Environmental Protest in Western Europe* (Oxford: Oxford University Press, 2003, 2007), *Acting Locally: Local Environmental Mobilizations and Campaigns* (London: Routledge, 2008) and *Environmental Movements and Waste Infrastructure* (with Liam Leonard; London: Routledge, 2010). He is currently working on an investigation of participation in protest demonstrations, and on a book on environmental movements.

Sabine Saurugger, PhD (Sciences Po Paris) is Professor of Politics at the Institut d'Etudes Politiques de Grenoble and Research fellow at the Centre of Public Policy, Political Action and Geography (PACTE), Grenoble. Recent publications include *Le choix rationnel en science politique: Approches critiques* (with Mathias Delori and Delphine Deschaux-Beaume; Rennes: Presses Universitaires de Rennes, 2009) and *La science politique de l'Union européenne* (with Paul Magnette and Céline Belot, Paris: Economica, 2008), as well as articles in *West European Politics, Political Studies, Comparative Politics, Journal of European Public Policy, Journal of Comparative Policy Analysis, French Politics, Revue Française de Science Politique* and *Swiss Revue of Political Science*. She currently works on theories and concepts of European integration, as well as the relationship between interest groups and democracy in the European Union.

Isabelle Stadelmann-Steffen is post-doctoral researcher at the Universities of Konstanz (Germany) and Bern (Switzerland). Her main research interests concern comparative politics, welfare state research, civic engagement and empirical methods. Together with Markus Freitag she constitutes the research team for the Swiss Volunteering Survey (Schweizer Freiwilligen-Monitor) within the Research Centre Civil Society and Social Capital at the University of Konstanz. Since 2008 she has been co-director of the empirical methods standing group of the Swiss Political Science Association. Her most recent publications include *Swiss Volunteering Survey 2010* (with Richard Traunmüller, Birte Gundelach and Markus Freitag; *Schweizer Freiwilligen-Monitor 2010*, Zurich: Seismo, 2010), 'Social Volunteering in Welfare States: Where Crowding out should Occur' (*Political Studies*, 2011, forthcoming) and 'Dimensions of Family Policy and Female Labour Market Participation: Analysing Group-specific Policy Effects' (*Governance*, Vol. 24, No. 2, 2011, forthcoming).

Jan W. van Deth is Professor of Political Science and International Comparative Social Research at the University of Mannheim (Germany). His main research areas are political culture (especially social capital, political engagement and citizenship), social change and comparative research methods. He was Director of the Mannheim Centre for European Social Research (MZES), convener of the international network Citizenship, Involvement, Democracy (CID) of the European Science Foundation and Book Series Editor of the Studies in European Political Science of the European Consortium for

Political Research (ECPR). He is a Corresponding Member of the Royal Netherlands Academy of Arts and Sciences (KNAW) and national coordinator of the German team for the European Social Survey. Recent publications include *Civil Society and Activism in Europe: Contextualising Engagement and Political Orientation* (co-edited with William Maloney; London: Routledge, 2010) and 'Civicness, Equality, and Democracy: A "Dark Side" of Social Capital?' special issue of the *American Behavioral Scientist*, Vol. 53, No. 5 (co-edited with Sonja Zmerli).

Tom W.G. van der Meer is Assistant Professor at the Department of Political Science of the University of Amsterdam. He is a member of the Amsterdam Institute for Social Science Research (AISSR) and the Institute for Migration and Ethnic Studies (IMES). He has published on various fields of interest: citizen participation in associational and political life; political trust; party systems and party system change (at the elite and electoral levels); ethnic diversity and social capital; and the use and abuse of quantitative research methodology.

Ariadne Vromen is an Associate Professor in the Department of Government and International Relations at the University of Sydney, Australia. She has a long-standing interest in political participation, especially young people's engagements, and Internet based politics. She is currently completing a book on new forms of participation.

Acknowledgements

Drafts of most of the contributions to this volume were presented at the Joint Sessions of Workshops of the European Consortium for Political Research in Lisbon, Portugal, 14–19 April 2009. As conveners of this workshop we had the opportunity to discuss new developments in research on participation and civil society with a number of outstanding experts in these areas. Participants at the meetings were: Georg Aichholzer, Doris Allhuter, Luigi Ceccarini, Francesco Forno, Matthias Freise, Kersty Hobson, Peter John, Grant Jordan, Nicolas Maisetti, Irene Martín Cortés, Michele Micheletti, Emanuele Polizzi, Ellen Quintelier, Liz Richardson, Christopher Rootes, Sabine Saurugger, Isabelle Stadelmann-Steffen, Eric Uslaner and Ariadne Vromen. We are very grateful for their willingness to share their knowledge with the workshop participants and to discuss problems and prospects of research in a rapidly changing area.

For each of the two main perspectives discussed at the workshop – new modes of participation and professionalization of associations – we selected the most relevant papers presented. There were other papers presented that were of a very high quality, but did not neatly fit the thematic concern of this volume. All the chapters have been subject to detailed revisions and we are grateful for the comments from two anonymous referees that helped improve the quality of the various contributions. In order to strengthen the main argument of the volume we invited Eline A. de Rooij and Tom W.G. van der Meer to contribute two additional chapters on the basis of their empirical research on political participation. We thank them not only for their willingness to contribute very interesting chapters to this volume, but especially for their willingness to finish these contributions in a very short period of time.

The production of an edited volume with contributions by a numbers of scholars from various countries can only be completed with the help of many people. First, we would like to thank the ECPR for giving us the opportunity to organize a workshop at the Joint Sessions and for taking care of the administrative tasks involved. Second, we are very grateful to Thomas Poguntke who, as the ECPR Book Series Editor, was enthusiastic about our volume and provided us with many useful suggestions. Finally, student assistants Benjamin Engst, Jasmina Islamovic, Sarah Odrakiewicz and Anne-Kathrin Weber (University of Mannheim) very patiently spent a great deal of time transforming the pile of papers, edited chapters, tables, figures and references into a consistent manuscript. We are very grateful to all those people who shared their expertise, time and friendliness in such generous and unconditional ways with us – it is only this kindheartedness which makes working on a volume like this for a long time so rewarding.

Jan W. van Deth, Mannheim
William A. Maloney, Newcastle
April 2011

1 Introduction
Democracy, professionalization and participation

Jan W. van Deth and William A. Maloney

"Some do and some do not"

By now Abraham Lincoln's assurance that "government of the people, by the people, for the people, shall not perish from the earth" seems to have materialized with about half of the world population living under democratic rule. Yet the challenges of these political systems are immense. Democracies are continuously beset by the complex problem of basing political decisions on active engagement of citizens and citizens' organizations. From an instrumental point of view, citizens' participation is required to articulate interests and demands and to arrive at decisions based on these interests and demands. From this perspective government "for the people" can be obtained only "by the people". Developmental approaches do not emphasize results of decision-making processes. Instead participation is primarily required to enable citizens to develop their social and human capacities. From a developmental perspective government "by the people" is identical to government "of the people". Irrespective of the position one adopts it is clear that the democracy label loses its currency if political decisions and decision-making processes are not based on citizens' participation.

The recognition that citizens' participation is indispensible for any vibrant democracy is undisputed. For example, Lorentzen and Hustinx (2007: 105) refer to the *civic trinity* – i.e. to be a *good citizen* one should "actively participate in one's community ... care for others in the community, and ... advance common interests by public debate and involvement". They note however, that the *civic trinity* has been

> replaced by more specialist participant roles whose ties to the collective and organizational bases of civil society are increasingly tenuous and nonexclusive. The active participant has been replaced by the consumerist and/or passive citizen. 'Finally, the citizen role shifts from a mediated engagement, channelled through conventional collective representation, to a new kind of monitorial citizenship' (Schudson, 1998).
>
> (ibid.)

Accordingly, debates do not focus on the necessity of citizens' democratic engagement, but on the *amount* and *modes* of participation. First, not all modes of participation are viewed as enriching or supporting democracy or indeed as democratically acceptable. To be democratically compatible participation should be inherently consent oriented and non-violent in character. Second, the idea that the more participation there is the higher the quality of democracy is somewhat naive and overlooks the potential hazards of unrestrained political involvement among large parts of the population, or the use of unrestricted modes of participation that threaten the rights of other citizens. In their seminal discussion of the relationship between democracy and voting Berelson *et al.* (1954) highlighted the functional democratic requirement of a

> balance between total political war between segments of the society and total political indifference to group interests of that society ... With respect to group or bloc voting, *as with other aspects of political behaviour*, it is perhaps not unfortunate that "some do and some do not".
>
> (320, emphasis added)

In this view a lack of political participation is not depicted as a shortcoming of democracy as long as activism and apathy are mixed – an idea most famously developed further by Almond and Verba (1963) in their concept of a "civic culture". As Katz (1997: 72) argued: "Participationist democracy does not require that everyone participate in every decision, merely that everyone participate regularly in some area and that all people can participate fully in any area in making decisions that affect themselves and their community." Accordingly, a vibrant and vital democracy, then, does not require active or passionate political engagement of each and every citizen, but a general willingness to participate as well as active involvement every once in a while.

Although these requirements of individual citizens are rather modest, the reality is that most citizens don't find political involvement attractive. Many citizens very willing embrace a passive role in organized politics – eschewing direct and active political involvement in favour of chequebook participation (Hayes, 1986) – i.e. paying *professionals* to represent their interests. These two developments are congruent and mutually supportive. An emancipated and individualized citizenry increasingly rejects conventional, organized modes of political participation and prefers – if active – loosely organized or spontaneous forms of action, which do not require many resources or initiatives. At the same time the professionalization[1] process continues apace via a rapidly growing number of political action committees, social movements and pressure groups. Strømsnes *et al.* (2009: 393) highlight:

> From the beginning of the 1980s we see a gradual organisational change. Organizations became more professionalised, specialised and centralised (Tranvik and Selle 2005). Many voluntary organisations changed their view on membership and gave less priority to organizational democracy. The new organisations adopted market logics and cooperated more frequently with market actors.

These organizations increasingly rely on professionally trained staff with expertise in several areas – e.g. recruitment, marketing, law, lobbying, science and management. The professionalization of staff went hand-in-glove with technological advancements – e.g. computerized databases, direct mail, telemarketing, automated payments, donations and contributions via text messaging, the Internet and more recent forms of social media (blogs, facebook and twitter). Even when these organizations seek to mobilize members there approach is not broad brush, but "scientifically" targeted. Miller (2009: 14) notes that while bodies such as the "National Federation of Independent Businesses segments its members into categories and recruits them for political action based on perceived likelihood of assent". Groups such as the Sierra Club "also stratifies its members for purposed of political mobilization".

The reluctance of individualized citizens to get involved seems to be wholly matched by the offer of professional organizations to act as their agent. In fact, this lack of enthusiasm might even be based on the availability of professional help. If we view this in "market" terms, then these political entrepreneurs can be seen as having identified a viable market and are supplying goods to meet a demand. In other words, the spread of "checkbook participation" and the rise of a "protest business" (Jordan and Maloney, 1997) are flipsides of the same coin. This volume aims to address several issues at the core of these parallel developments: the continuing attractiveness of individualized forms of participation, the rise of chequebook participation and the increasing relevance of professional expertise for organizing political action. Do professionalization and individualization develop differently under different circumstances? Are they causally related, complementary or mutually supportive? Most importantly: are they mutually compatible in democratic political systems?

Individualization and professionalization

There are several paradoxes at the heart of democratic politics that directly follow from the need to base political decisions on the active engagement of citizens and citizens' organizations. While concurrently groups abound,[2] citizens prefer to be passive spectators, or use the market and other seemingly private or non-political arenas as venues for action. The conventional activist – a regular citizen engaged in voluntary associations and collective decision making – seems to be replaced by the *ephemeral participator* or *episodic democratic monitor*.

Partly in response to the rise of individualized collective action in recent years many governments and political institutions have been championing a more active civil society to counter this perceived participatory pathology. As Warleigh (2001: 620) notes, civil society has been embraced by both "right and left" either to "defeat 'big government'" or to bring citizens closer to decision-making processes. Famously Putnam (2000) emphasized the importance of the internal aspects of associational life for the proper functioning of democracies and societal integration. Civil society associations are seen as contributing to democracy on several fronts: fostering a more participatory democracy;

Tocquevillean *schools of democracy* that generate pro-democratic values, social integration and social capital;[3] as *policy-making partners* (e.g. agenda setting, design, monitoring, evaluation); *representative vehicles*; *countervailing forces* (i.e. to big business and professional interests); or as *surrogates* for those who lack the necessary political resources (e.g. children, human rights, poverty, debt relief, animals).

While the benefits of an active citizenry and dense networks of civil associations appear great, citizens increasingly leave the "playing field" to professional associations and opt for individualized modes of collective action. Several issues are at the core of this development. Chequebook participation is widely accepted by many citizens and groups (Verba *et al.*, 1995; Pattie *et al.*, 2004). In their survey of charitable organizations based in Washington DC Barasko and Schaffer (2008: 202) found that "the contemporary interest groups sector is focussed more on attracting 'checkbook members' than on fostering participation within their organization". In their study of national level advocacy groups active in Washington DC, Minkoff *et al.* (2008: 543) argued that, "Two organizational forms – national 'associations without members' and nonmembership organizations – tend to dominate the imagery of the national advocacy sector." Many citizens do not see membership of groups as a means of being active in politics. They perceive professionally supplied passive involvement as a "benefit" and would find groups that sought to impose the "cost" of active participation as less attractive (see Warleigh 2001 and Maloney in this volume).[4] Much (modern) political participation is of an individualistic nature (e.g. donating money, signing a petition, but especially boycotting and buycotting products or ethical shopping) rather than a collective form (attending meetings, rallies or demonstrations) (see Pattie *et al.*, 2004; Micheletti, 2003; van Deth, 2010). Citizens appear to follow two paths to avoid direct and active political involvement. First, they are content to *contract out the participation function* (Maloney, 1999) to the policy influencing professionals via donations and/or regular financial contributions. Accordingly, these organizations should not be seen as mass political bodies, but as engaged in "supplier/customer" relationships – groups "sell" protest and *ersatz* political involvement (Jordan and Maloney, 1997). Second, citizens are increasingly inclined to *rely on forms of individualized collective action* and shun – almost by definition – involvement in institutionalized organizational life. As Micheletti (2003: 34) remarks:

> political problems need not solely be dealt with in the political system, by established political actors and channels, and through mobilizing for action on the basis of established political identities, ideologies, and organizational settings. Rather, the market, the home, and other seemingly private or non-political arenas are also appropriate venues for general responsibility-taking.

The two strategies strengthen each other and result in a growing distance between civil and political associations on the one hand and citizens on the other. The participatory hallmark of the modern era is a mix of low cost "contracted out" *and* DIY (Do It Yourself) political involvement – citizens make relatively modest financial contributions to contract out campaigning and lobbying on issues of concern to "the professionals" and simultaneously engage in low cost individualistic participation via boycotting and buycotting products or ethical shopping.

There is, however, a paradox at the heart of chequebook participation – it delivers both more participation and simultaneously a democratic deficit. Many groups have mobilized the chequebooks and bank accounts (via automated payments) of supporters who are prepared to fund their campaign and advocacy activities. However, many scholars would see chequebook involvement as shallow and weak because for most citizens their involvement remains passive and devoid of much by way of (internal) democratic content: i.e. supporters play no role in the election of group leaders or the selection of organizational tactics or policies. In additional to this, the professionalized recruitment strategies tend to accentuate political inequality. Much chequebook participation is not spontaneous, but reflects targeted activation (Schier, 2000) strategies of groups "supplying participation". Groups target individuals with specific socio-demographic profiles and lifestyles because they have a greater chance of converting their predisposition into membership. Brady *et al.* (1999) identified *rational prospecting* as the first stage of their explanation of citizen political recruitment. Who is being asked to join is crucial. Groups target those most likely to join and such skewed recruitment practices inevitably deliver skewed participation.

Many organizations also see limiting "supporter" involvement largely to financial contributions as the most efficient way to mobilize. From a democratic perspective there are tensions between finding the best way to produce the most effective results and dealing with a bona fide – active and democratically imbued – membership (input versus output legitimacy). Many groups have very little sense of this dilemma believing that they are following a pragmatic path in contemporary politics. Professionalization and political passivity can be seen as driven by four main (and several subsidiary) factors:

1. *Shared interests.* Many professionalized groups have found that most citizens are content to be financial supporters as opposed to active members and that offering such limited involvement is an efficient way to mobilize. Supporters are persuaded to join through sophisticated recruitment techniques and are only likely to remain supporters (customers) if the demands on them remain financially small. Professional groups appear to share Fiorina's (1999: 415f.) view that "contrary to the suggestions of pundits and philosophers, there is nothing wrong with those who do not participate, there is something unusual about those who do".
2. *Mobilisation of bias.* Groups try to attract citizens (potentially or actually) engaged in individual and collective action. In this way they target the socially and politically most interested (and financially most viable) parts of the population. In short, professionalized groups round up the usual suspects.

3 *"The rise of the unelected"* (Vibert, 2007). The nature of the policy-making process means that groups are also partly driven to professionalization by the requirements of public agencies. Many groups have recognized that in day-to-day politics influencing policy outcomes relies more on expertise and technical knowledge, rather than the mobilization of large numbers of concerned citizens (Crenson and Ginsberg, 2002). Thus, there are several implications of these developments. First, as Saurugger (2007: 397–8) notes, interest groups and social movements "increasingly professionalized to represent the interests of their constituency in an efficient way". Second, professionalization and the highly technical nature of the political discourses around many issues effectively exclude much citizen participation. As Brulle (2010: 83) notes, this development "reinforces existing relationships of power and institutional dynamics. These factors lead to a weakening of efforts to increase political mobilization." Third, the nature and target of lobbying and advocacy campaigns have altered. As Green and Smith (2003: 335) note:

> There is a natural tendency to gravitate toward tactics that command the attention of others, particularly donors. Campaigns crave attention and credibility: expensive, large-scale, professionally crafted communication is a way to demonstrate one's seriousness of purpose. This consideration tends to tilt campaigns away from the sorts of grassroots tactics that foster personal contact with voters.

Fourth, Barasko and Schaffer (2008: 188) highlight the key normative issue:

> As interest groups play an ever-greater role in the policymaking process, it "becomes an increasingly important question whether the organizations replacing former state functions are truly *membership-based* and participatory (Walker & McCarthy, 2005, p. 3; see also conclusions in Schattschneider, 1935)".

As a consequence, important aspects of the democratic polity are fundamentally changed by this "rise of the unelected" (Vibert, 2007).

4 *Members as distraction.* Following from point (3) it is expertise and specialist knowledge that is required to influence policy outcomes and this cannot be bought cheaply. Groups look to major institutional sources for patronage to support their campaigning and lobbying activities. For example, Greenwood (2007: 343) noted the EU Commission spends some €1 billion on funding almost the entire (300) citizen interest group universe and some organizations get up to 80–90 per cent of their funding from the Commission. If institutional sources are prepared to fund organizations to operational levels of 80–90 per cent then members can be seen as a luxury, or a "nonlucrative distraction" (Skocpol, 2003: 134). Why commit significant organizational resources to the identification and attraction of members

when institutional patronage provides the resources required to engage in professional lobbying? In addition to this, being a membership based group increases organizational costs: servicing a membership is more costly than being a donor or supporter based group where organizations make regular appeals for funds, but don't have to expend any effort on elections or involving members in deciding policies and strategies.

Research questions and outline of the volume

The main aim of this volume is to bring together theoretical insights and empirical evidence that contributes to our understanding of the contemporary trends of professionalization and the rise of individualized modes of participation in democratic decision-making processes. Although these developments are not mutually exclusive each is characterized by its own causes, contexts and conditions. The volume consists of two main parts that focus on these two core developments separately. Single contributions to each part deal with different aspects of professionalization and the rise of individualized modes of participation. The implications from the combined developments for democracy are discussed in the concluding chapter.

In the first part of the volume, six chapters deal with various aspects of professionalization and democratic politics. In the first contribution Matthias Freise presents the experiences of German civil society organizations entering public–private partnerships (PPPs) with local authorities. In Germany, PPPs are normally discussed in the context of an increasing involvement of the market sector in public service provision, in particular at the local level (for instance water treatment, waste management or public construction projects). In recent years, however, PPPs also operate in the relations between state and civil society organizations in the broad field of welfare provision. This development challenges the traditional German welfare arrangements based on the principles of neo-corporatism and subsidiarity. It also has a strong influence on the relationship between state and civil society organizations and exerts pressure on the latter to professionalize their activities. Freise argues that the involvement of civil society actors in complex legal and financial arrangements strongly influences the day-to-day business of civil society organizations and illustrates this process by focusing on a case study that examines the relationship between municipal authorities and several self-help groups.

A very different case study of political engagement and professional politics is analysed by Nicolas Maisetti in his discussion of "entrepreneurial participation" in the successful nomination of Marseille as the *European Capital of Culture 2013*. The day after the announcement, the regional press stressed that this success was a "victory of the team player method" because political, economic and cultural actors from 130 districts united in support of a common project. However, this chapter shows how the primacy of economic over political actors was constructed in this bid. It explains changes in local public action and urban governance resulting from the transfer of responsibility-taking from the political to the economic arena institutionalized around the managerial environment.

Local politics are also at the centre of Christopher Rootes' chapter on the environmental movement in England. Remarkably, the centralization of political structures in England has encouraged the development of a nationally centralized environmental movement whose constituents have neither resources nor much inclination to give support to local environmental campaigners. The networking of individual local protests is accordingly difficult, particularly in the absence of any clear national policy that might act as a focus for mobilization. The advent of climate change as the dominant environmental issue has provided valuable new ammunition and facilitated effective networking for some local campaigners. Rootes raises the possibility that national environmental NGOs frustrated by their increasing marginality in national policy making may take a new interest in protest mobilizations at the local level.

Moving from the local to the national level in the first three chapters, Sabine Saurugger looks at the changing structures in the EU and presents a number of lessons from the social movement and party politics literature. Her contribution assesses political participation through "organized civil society". It has been argued that this has led to the increased democratization of the national and international sphere. The chapter starts from the assumption that this discourse has an effect on "civil society actors" and goes on to analyse institutionalization, bureaucratization and professionalization of organized civil society.

Scholars such as Hay and Stoker (2009) bemoan the rise of these large-scale professionalized organizations arguing that these groups provide "ephemeral, thin sporadic" and potentially "ill-informed" engagement. In his contribution to this volume William A. Maloney discusses the democratic "contribution" of professionalized public interest groups. Are these groups part of the alleged democratic pathology? Do professionalized groups drive out members? The chapter points to three main factors that contribute to an explanation of the limited involvement opportunities offered by many professionalized public interest groups: (i) group push and supporter pull effects, (ii) patronage and (iii) the professionalization of the policy-making process – each has affected involvement opportunities and the nature of the linkage offered by these groups. The chapter concludes with a discussion of some potentially democratically redeeming features of professionalized public interest group representation.

In the final contribution to the first part of the volume Grant Jordan provides a detailed examination of supply-side participation – i.e. how groups induce citizens to join, how groups construct individual preferences and the mechanics of professionalized recruitment (targeting segmentation and income generation). Alongside charting this important development Jordan also addresses debates surrounding Mancur Olson's seminal work – *The Logic of Collective Action*. Jordan notes that Olson offered one of the most influential contributions to social science discussions of participation. However, while Olson predicted the under-mobilization of collective organizations (particularly in altruistic groups), group organizers ignored his pessimism and have enjoyed some success. Political science while celebrating the power of Olson's Rational Choice contrarian analysis simply ignored his arguments by assuming that participation is a natural phenomenon – i.e. powered by normative preferences. Jordan rescues participation from the pessimism of Olson, but does so by stressing mobilization powered by groups rather than spontaneous individual action.

After focusing on professionalization and the developments of organized group activities in various contexts, the second part of the volume deals with changing democratic engagement of citizens in democratic societies. In the first of six contributions to this part Jan W. van Deth analyses the relationships between new modes of participation and so-called norms of citizenship. New forms of participation such as boycotting products or ethical shopping appear to be individualistic in a way not seen before. Internet technologies make these modes of participation very attractive and conventional organizations even more obsolete. Citizens seem to be content to contract out participation in policy-making processes to policy-influencing professionals and chequebook participation is widely accepted by many citizens and groups. The rise of individualized modes of participation and the professionalization of groups strengthen each other and the combined effects could have important consequences for democratic citizenship. Van Deth documents an increase in individualized political participation and shows that citizens using new modes of participation are not strongly motivated by an enthusiasm for organized forms of participation or by a relatively strong ethical/moral focus on global issues.

Engagement does not only depend on individual resources and motivations, but also on the political and social contexts and conditions. By providing citizens with minimal standards of living, welfare states could provide a remedy for unequal participation. In her analyses of welfare states' impact on social and political engagement Isabelle Stadelmann-Steffen evaluates the relationship between public welfare provision and individual civic engagement. Distinctively from previous studies that centre on the question of whether welfare state policy "crowds-in" or "crowds-out" civic activities she focuses on the equality problem of civic engagement. It is assumed that welfare state policy does not uniformly affect voluntary activities of various social groups and therefore impacts on the social stratification of civic engagement. Focusing on social and political volunteering the analysis provides support for this hypothesis. Moreover, extensive welfare policy reduces the negative effect of low affluence on social and political volunteering. Accordingly, welfare states have the potential to equalize individual civic participation.

The relevance of contextual factors explaining cross-national differences in political participation is also clearly underlined by Eline A. de Rooij's general finding that advanced democracies are characterized by relatively high levels of non-electoral participation. Usually, this finding is attributed to higher levels of resources, in particular educational attainment levels, combined with an increased psychological engagement with politics among citizens. Little attention, however, is paid to the changing context of mobilization. De Rooij suggests an alternative theory in which the higher levels of non-electoral participation are accounted for by a relative overrepresentation of the number of "peripheral participants" vis-à-vis "core participants". Her evidence shows that "peripheral participants" – who participate in few political acts, requiring little initiative or time – are indeed substantially less psychologically engaged with politics than "core participants". Living in a politicized context or in a context in which opportunities to be mobilized readily present themselves – such as in cities rather than in more remote areas, as well as in contexts where a variety of interests groups and social movements are active – increases the likelihood of participation.

Tom W.G. van der Meer examines the ideological and political composition of professionalized forms of political participation. In particular he assesses the extent to which professional organizations are able to act as surrogates not simply for those who *can't* adequately engage in direct political action, but also for those who do not *want* to spend the time or effort to do so. Can indirect political action via professionalized organizations counterbalance the overrepresentation of leftwing citizens prevalent in more direct forms of political action? Or is there a similar, smaller or even opposite bias in the ideological and political composition of professionalized forms of political participation compared to more direct forms of political action? To what extent are direct (personal) and indirect (professionalized) participation unequal across ideological and policy dimensions? Van der Meer explores the extent to which the relationship between ideological positions with direct (personal) and indirect (professionalized) participation can be explained by citizens' policy preferences as well as the extent to which the various mechanisms behind participatory inequality differ with regard to direct and indirect participation.

Studying changes and developments in youth participation is crucial to provide a more complete democratic audit. Young people are most likely to be affected by societal and political developments and to support newer (individualized) modes of participation. The final two contributions to this part of the volume focus on youth engagement from different perspectives. In an analysis of the development of political orientations among Belgian adolescents Marc Hooghe and Ellen Quintelier assess some empirical claims about individualized political participation. First, they investigate whether these new modes of participation attract a new group of the population, or whether the same active group simply adds new elements to its participation repertoire. Second, they assess whether those who are participating in individualized collective action are truly on the brink of social change. This kind of innovation would probably be present in specific groups of the population before spreading out to the population as a whole. Third, Hooghe and Quintelier address the criticism that individualized participation is just an instantaneous and ephemeral phenomenon, not leading to any durable social ties.

The second contribution on youth engagement focuses on the effect of government projects designed to strengthen youth participation in Australia. In her contribution Ariadne Vromen analyses youth participation mechanisms that have been introduced by the Australian government and service providers explicitly aimed at young people and their participation in political decision-making processes. By looking at top-down strategies she presents new data on how high level policy makers within government and the community sector perceive youth participation and the impact of these programmes. Vromen's contribution focuses on consultation type mechanisms used both by government and by community sector organizations to include young people in decision making. The chapter is based on a large-scale research project on diversity and youth participation commissioned in 2006.

In the concluding chapter we draw some general conclusions on the professionalization of groups and the rise of individualized political participation in democratic political systems. We highlight the main findings from the contributors and assess to what extent these developments are linked. The findings presented below do not support the naive idea that professionalization and the rise of individualized political participation are straightforward developments that can be easily documented in very different situations. It is clear that the parallel spread of professionalization and individualization provides evident challenges and opportunities for democratic systems.

Notes

1 Martens (2009: 230) defines professionalization as "the process whereby problems are dealt with according to subject-specific knowledge and aims at maintaining quality standards and quality work".
2 Many advanced democracies experienced an explosion in the number of organizations in the 1960–2000 period. The *Directory of British Associations* records 7,755 organizations; the US *Encyclopaedia of Associations* numbers Washington DC based organizations at *circa* 23,000 (Jordan and Maloney, 2007); and the EU Commission claims that there are 2,600 lobby groups active in Brussels.
3 We are well aware that there is a dark side to social capital and other "democratic pathologies" associated with groups (see van Deth and Zmerli, 2010).
4 Of course, for some, active involvement is a benefit of membership.

Part I
Professionalization and democratic politics

2 How to domesticate civil society by public–private partnerships
Evidence from German local health policy

Matthias Freise

Introduction

In many European countries governments are currently searching for new ways to involve citizens and civil society organizations (CSOs) in the co-production of public financed welfare services and to reform the existing welfare mix (for an overview see Pestoff and Brandsen 2008). This particularly holds true for Germany where the cooperation of public authorities and civil society actors has a long tradition based on the central state principles of subsidiarity and neo-corporatism (Zimmer *et al.* 2009). For decades the state acted here as a "friendly financer" giving preference to societal embedded CSOs when it came to the implementation of social services like the operation of hospitals, kindergartens, nursing homes and many other social enterprises and person based services in the core fields of the welfare state (Evers 2005). Particularly the 1960s, 1970s and 1980s were shaped by the development of dense cooperation between the various levels of the state and CSOs which have established powerful umbrella organizations, the so-called free welfare associations. At those times, governance instruments like tendering procedures of social services, policy evaluation or lump-sum systems in the health sector were almost unknown. The role of the state was reduced to a generous supporter of CSOs which more or less independently developed their services relatively free of efficiency restrictions and public nannyism. This holds true both for highly professionalized non-profit organizations like hospitals and for voluntary CSOs and patient self-help groups (Zimmer *et al.* 2004).

However, the terms of cooperation between public authorities and CSOs came in recent years under pressure for a number of reasons (Pestoff 2010): first, the semi-permanent austerity in public finances, accentuated by the recent global crises led finance ministers to search for more efficient ways of funding welfare service provision. Second, concepts of privatization and marketization are a result of a neo-liberal zeitgeist that postulates an increased involvement of competition in the production of services of general interest. Third, the ramified new public management debate concentrates attention on the question of how the modern welfare state could become more efficient. Finally, the market deregulation of the European Union stimulated the rearrangement of existing modes of cooperation between state and CSOs. As a result of these developments municipal governments in Germany increasingly questioned the traditional position of CSOs in the welfare mix and began experimenting with privatization approaches and the involvement of profit oriented actors. However, at the same time municipalities are also interested in putting the cooperation with civil society service providers on a new basis by implementing forms of co-production of welfare services (Osborne 2008).

A key term in this debate is public–private partnerships (PPPs). Normally discussed in the context of an increasing involvement of the market sector in public services, PPPs refer in particular to local level infrastructure and service provision, for instance, water treatment, waste management or public construction projects (Flinders 2005). Nevertheless, in recent years, PPPs also occur in the relations between state and CSOs in the broad field of welfare provision. These PPPs redistribute tasks and responsibilities between state and civil society and demand a professionalization of CSOs and their acceptance of the new terms of cooperation (Sack 2009a). This presented a challenge to "amateurish" CSOs at the local level that are mostly run by volunteers using established modes of cooperation. At the same time local authorities faced the challenge of enhancing the efficiency and effectiveness of their cooperation with CSOs without jeopardizing the voluntary character of CSOs (Brandsen 2008). In summary, municipalities have to find a way of gently *domesticating* their civil society partners by involving them in policy and programme development. But how can this get achieved and what do these new modes of co-production mean for voluntary CSOs?

The case study presented in this chapter shows how the German city of Münster rearranged its cooperation with local patient support associations and voluntary self-help groups through the introduction of a jointly maintained municipal health drop-in centre. After introducing the case study, the chapter then demonstrates the impact of the PPP on the local health policy and discusses the consequences of the PPPs for the involved CSOs, volunteers and the local health authority. Finally, the chapter reflects on the lessons that can be learned from the Münster case.

The self-help scene in Germany: introducing the case

Patient support associations and voluntary self-help groups are textbook examples of rather "amateurish" voluntary based CSOs. Mostly established in the 1980s and 1990s, self-help groups have gained significant momentum in the local health policy field in Germany. Although the municipalities are not obliged to cooperate with them by law, currently, almost every German city has a vibrant fabric of many self-help groups covering a multitude of medical diseases and social ills (Möller-Bock 2007). Typically these organizations fulfil a number of functions for their members. First, they offer consultancy services, advice and mutual support for patients and their relatives. Specific cures, communication with social assistance offices, health insurance companies, hospitals and care services are core issues. In addition the organizations bring together concerned individuals and contribute to communication and self-help on a peer basis providing expertise and support for members. Furthermore, patient support associations and voluntary self-help groups act as political interest groups on the local level and on higher provincial and federal levels through their membership in subject-specific umbrella organizations and the so-called Free Welfare Associations. Most of the patient support associations and voluntary self-help groups discussed in this chapter are organized under the umbrella organization Parity (*Paritätischer Wohlfahrtsverband*) – one of the six large Free Welfare Associations in Germany (Boeßenecker 2005).

Typically, these organizations are generously directly and indirectly supported by the public authorities, through grants, rent-free offices in public properties, provision of continuing education or other benefits. At the same time, they are acknowledged as independent corporate actors involved in public welfare provision. This means that they are fully responsible for their own internal organizational procedures, enjoying independence from government interference while a large part of their budgets is provided by public subsidies. However, in recent years, many municipalities have begun to question the privileged position of self-help groups in the budgets, although the valuable contribution of these organizations to the health care system is not denied.

This also holds true for the city of Münster. With 270,000 inhabitants Münster currently hosts over 300 self-help groups registered at the local Parity, which runs a coordination centre for self-help groups on behalf of the local authorities. The very high density of self-help groups in Münster is linked to the fact that the city is the home of one of the largest German university hospitals. Hence, a number of self-help groups specialize on rather less well-known diseases like sleep apnoea or chronic porphyria.

Nevertheless, almost every German city has numerous self-help groups and usually cooperates with them by financing services and premises on the basis of a neo-corporatist approach (Müller-Bock 2007). This means that for many years the cities had budget items for self-help groups from which the CSOs usually got subsidies without a contract that details the organizations' contributions. In addition the cities contributed rent-free facilities in public buildings and other gratifications. The exploratory case study at hand will show how the city of Münster has converted this modus of cooperation with the self-help groups into a PPP.

The membership of the self-help groups ranges from very few in the highly specialized organizations up to several hundred in the "big seven" (dementia, diabetes, cancer, apoplexies, paralysis, drug abuse and depression). According to the coordinator of the Münster self-help groups, approximately 70 per cent of the groups in the city work on an exclusively voluntary basis. The members of these groups organize themselves and develop their services. In contrast, a little less than one-third of the self-help groups – normally the bigger ones – also employ staff, offering professional consultancy/advisory services. Usually, these employees work part-time or on a fee basis and provide information to those suffering from the respective disease. Nevertheless, these organizations are highly dependent on the volunteering efforts of their members – mutual exchange and support of concerned peers are central ideas of the self-help movement.

Both kinds of self-help groups – exclusively voluntary and partly professional – traditionally are supported by the cities by a number of benefits. The most important one is the allocation of municipal premises, but also grants for participation in skill enhancements, the production of brochures and other information material, attendance at health fairs and partly funding wages of freelancers. Other important contributors to the budget of the self-help groups are the public health insurance funds in Germany, in some case the churches and (however, rather seldom at the local level) the pharmaceutical industry. The local coordinator of the self-help groups in Münster illustrates that most of the organizations in Münster receive between 80 and 90 per cent of their annual budgets from public subsidies and just a small part from membership fees. He also estimates that this is a typical budget structure of self-help groups elsewhere in Germany.

Below we focus on the activities of the local municipality as it reforms the established modes of cooperation with CSOs and we assess the impact of PPPs on these relationships. We conducted 23 qualitative interviews in spring 2009 with civil servants in the municipal health department, local politicians and representatives of the involved self-help groups. We interviewed chairs and ordinary members of voluntary organizations. The interviews aimed to investigate the self-evaluation of the partners and their appraisal of how the implementation of the PPPs changed the mode of cooperation between municipality and self-help groups. In addition, available documents like web pages, flyers and other grey literature have been analysed.

Rearranging a local self-help scene

The Healthy House

In the late 1990s the local self-help scene and other local health services in Münster were very fragmented. The various premises of the self-help groups, public services of the local health authority and public and private health insurances were shared in a variety of locales throughout the municipal area. Thus, the ruling Social Democratic and Green Party coalition decided to rearrange local health services by establishing one central "drop-in centre". In the context of the new public management debate at that time the politicians discussed a number of ideas. First and foremost, a central drop-in centre for various local health services was seen as a way of enhancing citizen involvement because it simplified the bureaucratic structure and increased the visibility of a broad spectrum of public and private activities. Furthermore, the governing coalition aimed to take greater control of the local budget and sell the municipal buildings that were used for these services. Finally, the politicians wanted to rearrange the cooperative procedures with the civil society groups, particularly self-help groups by involving these organizations directly in public service provision, instead of simply supporting their activities. To attain this goal the municipality needed an attractive incentive. The *Healthy House* established in 1998 in the city centre proved to be an effective incentive. The building co-locates many municipal health services under one roof and provides rent-free professional facilities for CSOs active in the field of local health policy.

The project was financed by the health department and two private foundations. These foundations had financially supported health care in Münster since the sixteenth and seventeenth centuries. After the death of the founders the administration was transferred to the jurisdiction of a specific board of the city council which made it possible to raise the construction costs of almost €5 million from the earnings of the foundations. The two foundations also contribute €250,000 per annum towards maintenance expenses (in particular janitorial services and energy costs). In return the municipal health authority entered a contractual agreement for at least 25 years to delegate (and pay) an executive director and other civil servants to undertake the activities and promote the advancement of the Healthy House in cooperation with other municipal departments and voluntary self-help groups. The building with its 1,200 m^2 of work space is state-of-the-art. It is wheelchair accessible, accommodates a number of modern conference facilities and includes space for permanent exhibitions on several health topics. With this high quality building the local health department easily convinced seven self-help groups to move in and involved them in its joint operation. In addition to the rent-free facilities the city offered grants for the payment of freelancers, promotion material and further education for the members of the self-help groups. In return the invited self-help groups were contractually obliged to cooperate with the local health authority in the operation of the facility and to participate in the corporate identity of the Healthy House. This involved taking over new responsibilities like guaranteeing joint business hours, professional consultation services and the participation in joint events of the Healthy House. This obligation had significant impact on the organizational life of the self-help groups which were based on mutual support and now had to add various services to the scope of their activities.

According to the typology developed by Sack (2009b), the Healthy House can be classified as mixture of an organizational and a self-committing PPP. The object of the partnership is the joint operation of a service centre on a contractual basis in which the partners commit themselves to close cooperation. Today the partners involved are with the municipal health authority, two private foundations administered by the city of Münster, ten voluntary self-help groups (dealing with dementia, diabetes, various forms of cancer, cardiovascular diseases, apoplexies, paralysis, drug abuse, depression and disabled children) and some other municipal departments.[1] Furthermore, offices of the local adult education centre, the local volunteer service centre and the committee of retired citizens were relocated to the Healthy House.

The partners established a highly professionalized service, consultancy and information centre that was widely accepted in the local political and civic communities. Therefore, they established a governance mode which does not have much in common with the modus operandi in the years prior to the establishment of the Healthy House. While in the 1990s cooperation was marked by a rather hierarchical governance mode in which the health authority decided on the applications for self-help groups autonomously, now cooperation can be characterized as being close to an open-door policy of cooperation between partners who meet monthly to negotiate and agree the joint services of the Healthy House.

In its external communications Healthy House acts as a cooperative independent actor, and not as a branch of the city. The partners have agreed on a joint cooperative design with their own logo, a joint website and joint brochures of activities. They also agreed on core business hours, joint events (for instance fairs for men suffering from diseases) and advanced training for the volunteers and freelancers. This comprehensive form of cooperation places great demands on self-help groups that are based on voluntary work, but also on the municipal health authority which needed to restructure its cooperation modes with civil society actors. In the following sections the effects of this partnership on the organizational life of the CSOs and the governance of local health policy is analysed (by drawing on qualitative interviews).

How to domesticate civil society through PPPs

The domestication of CSOs can be understood in its literal Latin sense: the self-help groups have been invited by the municipality to share their rooms ("domus") with the local health authority in the same building. In return, they had to accept participating in the services and activities of the health authority. Politicians and civil servants of the local health authority saw this as a very successful allocation of human resources from civil society. By signing a contract on the rights and duties of the self-help groups the organizations had to accept a much higher degree of commitment.

At the same time the partnership demanded a process of professionalization within the organizations. For instance, the chairmen of the voluntary organizations that were responsible for the organizational life within their groups became members of the governing body of the Healthy House which decided on the joint activities and the technical organization of the various services offered jointly by the partners. At the same time the voluntary organizations had to transfer some of the consultancy services from volunteers to freelancers which could guarantee the contractual commitments. Furthermore, the civil society groups had to ensure that their members involved in the joint service provision in the Healthy House met the quality standards they agreed on with their partners. As the executive officer of the facility pointed out, the city animated the self-help groups teaching their members how to conduct professional counselling interviews on the phone or in face-to-face settings. Finally, the members of the self-help groups have been educated to participate in the public relations of the Healthy House. The contract between the municipality and the self-help groups requires all partners to cooperate in the consultancy of the "customers" by guaranteeing permanent staffing at the reception in the entrance of the building and the telephone switchboard.

In this context "customers" is a remarkable label in the contract since self-help groups usually talk about "members" or "concerned persons". Also for the health authority "customers" was a new term. The partners confirmed they used "citizens" before. In other words, the launching of the partnership transformed the partners from "amateurish" civil society participants to service providers with a customer base.

For the health authority of the city of Münster the PPPs are beneficial for several reasons. Foremost, it received a first-class building from the funds of two private foundations with a relatively small co-payment (the obligation to delegate officers who are getting paid by the city in any event). In times of limited local budgets, frequently, such forms of cooperation are the only possibility to achieve innovations of this type. In practice, the municipality was also able to achieve substantial savings, since it could disinvest several public properties in which the self-help groups were located prior to the construction of the Healthy House. By centralizing resources, the municipality was able to reduce the amount of physical space required for certain facilities (e.g. conference and seminar rooms as well as exhibition space). The executive manager interviewed considers the Healthy House a much more efficient way of cooperating with self-help groups compared with the modes prior to its establishment.

However, the Healthy House means much more than just improved efficiency in public administration. It is also an example of the realization of new public management strategies that have been broadly discussed in German local politics since the early 1990s (Lorig 2008). The municipality was able to establish a central contact point for its citizens for all questions related to health topics. The executive manager explained that previously five different offices in different buildings were responsible for health information and advisory services and "we sent clients often on an odyssey".

Therefore it was necessary to rearrange the local health governance by increasing the involvement of voluntary self-help organizations in professional service provision. The manager explains:

> From the perspective of the health authority the services of the self-help groups were for sure in need of improvement. For instance, they had no reliable office hours, and there was no guaranteed quality assurance. So it was clear that we had to put a curb on our partners without alienating them.... However, our new facilities were an interesting return.

On the other side, the new mode of health governance had to adapt to dealing with civil servants as well as self-help groups. In the new governance arrangement the municipality is much more dependent on the services of the self-help groups. The partners meet monthly to negotiate the programme of the Healthy House and the modalities of its management. Thereby, a form of network governance was established in which the overall governance mode is deliberation. The obligatory participation in this deliberation process is a precondition for all CSOs involved in the partnership.

Typical contents of the monthly meetings are the corporate design of the Healthy House, strategies for public relations, joint lecture series and other joint activities. For instance, every partner involved is responsible for the organization of one high publicity event to keep the Healthy House in the continuous attention of the media. However, the practical implementation of this governance is not always easy, because it assumes a professionalized approach of civil society partners. Since the self-help groups are largely based on voluntary work it is difficult to commit them to binding agreements, e.g. on office hours or deadlines for the submission of texts for information brochures. Although the executive manager theoretically has great power (since he can contract out the rental agreement with the self-help groups when contractual agreements are not assured) he is dependent on the willingness of the self-help groups to cooperate to maintain the services. That is why the partnership is based on a deliberation system characterized by a naming and shaming strategy of the executive manager:

> It is very effective to laud the activities of one partner in the monthly board meetings and to criticise the shortfalls of others.... From my perspective all partners try their very best to contribute to the services of the Healthy House.

He also came to the conclusion that all self-help groups in the facility professionalized in recent years and sought donations for ensuring the office hours by freelancers. Currently, every self-help group dedicates much greater resources towards the costs of wages than was required ten years ago. Altogether, the representatives of the municipality are very satisfied with the development of the Healthy House and describes it as a good example for the implementation of citizen oriented health policy, characterized by synergetic effect caused by the cooperation of professional and voluntary partners. He describes the PPP as a win–win situation for all partners involved. Nevertheless, he is aware that the cooperation is not always easy for the civil society partners. That is why the municipality is enhancing education and training for volunteers. For instance, the Healthy House offers fundraising courses for voluntary self-help groups to reduce the dependence on public subsidies in the longer term.

What does professionalization mean for self-help groups?

The members of several self-help groups interviewed predominantly appreciated the positive benefits of the PPPs and stressed the advantages for their organizations. In the first place they are happy about the new infrastructure. A long-time freelancer of a self-help group states: "The old building was a ramshackle hut, the new one is almost luxurious and perfect for our purposes."

Furthermore, all members of self-help groups interviewed appreciate the cooperation modes within the partnership. In particular they stressed that the health authority is much more stakeholder oriented than before the Healthy House was established. In the old system self-help groups submitted applications for projects and expected to be funded from the city budget. For many years the public subsidies were more or less a safe bet, but in the late 1990s cost-cutting measures were applied, so that the self-help groups were happy to move into the Healthy House. Today, the self-help groups feel directly involved in voluntary health policies of the municipality. They appreciate that they are able to develop services like the telephone information and advice service or joint information meetings in close cooperation with the executive manager of the Healthy House. This has significantly broadened the spectrum of activities of the self-help groups who started in the partnership as organizations with a clearly defined target group (namely, citizens suffering from a specific disease and/or their relatives). Inside the partnership they took over other tasks, for instance the organization of events like health fairs, public relations for the Healthy House or the participation in the monthly steering group meetings. These additional tasks are seen as an extra burden for the self-help groups and they agree that only larger groups who are able to employ freelancers or part-time employees, can become full members of such a partnership. Smaller groups tend to get over-stretched.

All self-help groups appreciate that they are also able to cooperate with other organizations co-located in the building. The siting of similar businesses/organizations next door to each other promotes inter-organizational learning. Furthermore, the self-help groups confirm that they were able to draw synergetic effects from the partnership. For instance, staff of self-help groups no longer need to coordinate the use of the seminar rooms. This is done centrally by a delegated civil servant of the health authority. They can also cooperate with other self-help groups in further education programmes for volunteers and freelancers. Members of the cancer self-help groups greatly appreciate this.

All members of self-help groups interviewed were convinced that their work today is more efficient and effective than under the "old" health governance in Münster. The Healthy House is built on a highly visible location close to the city centre and it is easy to find. A member of a self-help group points out: "We are permanently in the focus of publicity. Without any doubt, the Healthy House is an improvement of the service orientation of local health policy in Münster." Furthermore, those self-help groups that are not permanently represented with their own offices profit from the facilities of the Healthy House since they can use conference rooms for the group's meetings and can use the Parity coordination service. Hence, the network of self-help groups in Münster became much denser in recent years. It is also agreed by all that fundraising has become much easier since they have a promotional base which can be used for advertising.

Although the self-help groups investigated in this research are very happy with the PPPs, they all are aware that the state has to some extent incorporated them into public service provision. This implies a professionalization of all partners involved. All self-help groups with their own offices in the Healthy House permanently train volunteers as well as their freelancers offering services. This puts pressure on organizations. However, they perceive this pressure differently. For the largest group (cancer self-help), the partnership was never a problem:

> We always had many Volunteers and the Healthy House even offers an incentive to volunteer, since it has such great working conditions. A much bigger problem is the office hours. Who wants to get up at seven in the morning [laughing]?

Nevertheless, the cancer self-help group has to invest organizational capacities in the education of its members which have to get diverted from the original activities of the organization. Previously, volunteers organized meetings and mutual help for patients affected by cancer; some of these volunteers now work in a specific group established for putting together the timetable for the volunteers working at the reception in the Healthy House.

For other organizations the partnership is much more problematic. The representative of the self-help groups of physically disabled children and their relatives explain that it is sometimes very difficult to guarantee the services they have agreed on in the monthly steering group meeting. Thus, there have been discussions inside the organization about leaving the Healthy House and reducing the level of services: "It is a difficult balancing act. On the one hand we want to offer professional services and a customer focus. But on the other hand, we are a voluntary organization and not service providers." This is why some members of the self-help groups complain about the negative effects on mutual elements in the organizational life. The associational culture of the organization has been slightly changed and not everybody appreciates this.

This case study is also a good example of the changing opportunities for CSOs to participate in the co-production of service provision by getting involved in a partnership with the local authorities. This has also influenced the organizational life of groups. Before the partnership the day-to-day life of the self-help groups was predominantly self-centred. Affected patients became members benefiting from the support offered by the groups. The only contact with the municipal authorities was the annual application procedure for public grants which was more or less the exclusive business of the treasurer. The rest of the membership participated in the activities of the organization. Now, the organizations are for the first time involved in the co-production of public services and they have to decide on political and administrative questions, for example, setting the priorities of the Healthy House concerning the joint programme. At interview the partners confirmed that the involvement in the co-production of public services gave the debate inside the organization a much more political component and has changed the culture of discussion. Previously it was very consensus oriented; today it is task oriented in partnership with the municipality. The core question is the extent to which CSOs should provide public services and how the organization's representative in the board of the Healthy House should cooperate.

All of those interviewed confirmed that the city of Münster is a fair partner that is interested in cooperation based on trust. The health authority exercises its influence inside the partnership. Nevertheless, all self-help groups are aware that they are still dependent on the state as the partner who "calls the shots". In the light of the benefits all partners accept this. In any event, they all know that the city of Münster used the Healthy House as a cost-cutting measure and they have not matched their budget for voluntary health services in recent years. That is why some members of self-help groups are afraid that the city wants to withdraw from its commitments in this policy field.

Conclusions

The Münster case is not representative of the general German situation because other municipalities cannot rely on such experienced and well-established local foundations. On the contrary, more than one-third of German municipalities are currently facing significant budget deficits and have to reduce their voluntary grants. These are services the municipalities are not obliged to provide by federal or provincial law. Grants for self-help groups and health education are typical examples of those voluntary grants (Robert 2004). Consequently, many municipalities have withdrawn or reduced public money from this part of the local voluntary sector and also the relatively wealthy city of Münster had to reduce its budget because of the current international financial crises (2008/09).

This case clearly illustrates how a German city has tried to rearrange its cooperation with local civil society groups in the co-production of municipal services in the field of local health policies by involving them directly in consultancy services and the operation of a central drop-in centre. This approach is typical for the implementation of the new public management model that is broadly discussed in Germany (Lorig 2008). One aspect of this discussion is how citizens could get brought into the production of public services and the case at hand shows that PPPs between municipalities and CSOs might serve as an example for best practice when additional resources are available to realize such a project.[2] The Münster case provides evidence that those partnerships have significant effects on the organizational life of the involved partners, the modes of governance and the opportunities for citizens to participate in local politics.

For the self-help groups the partnership in the Healthy House meant foremost a much higher degree of commitment. They are now contractually obliged to contribute to the professional service provision of the drop-in centre. Therefore, members had to get trained and additional freelancers had to be recruited. Through the partnership the CSOs overcame their private self-reference and now play a fuller role in a public service provision. As a result the organizational expenses of the voluntary organizations increased. People suffering from a specific disease who formerly participated in the self-help group now also contribute to services that are not directly connected to the original business of the voluntary organization. Some self-help groups have problems with this and the question remains whether such a partnership project can overburden civil society partners.

The municipality was able to domesticate the self-help groups through co-location and by including them in the strategic development of the Healthy House. In return for access to professional facilities and additional public grants the self-help groups partly gave up their autonomy and are now contractually bounded partners of the municipality with clear defined tasks and responsibilities. From a governance perspective this has changed the mode of cooperation from a hierarchical approach to network governance: the local health authority is still steering the network but today it is much more dependent on the adjustment and deliberation with its civil society partners that are directly involved in the strategic development of the Healthy House. Hence, the question of how this new form of cooperation is influencing the democratic legitimacy of local politics is arising. What does it mean for local democracy and political accountability when the municipality is selecting its partners from civil society for co-production of public services?

Clearly the cooperation of local authorities and CSOs has to be advantageous for all partners (Oppen and Sack 2008). However, the factors for a stable and successful partnership between local authorities and CSOs are still not that clear. Current research has collected a number of best- and worst-case practices (for an overview see Flinders 2005). The Münster case may be close to a best-case scenario but further research on PPPs and their preconditions is still necessary. Obviously, partnerships on the local level are attractive to civil society because they strengthen grassroots organizations as political players and equip these groups with an understanding of the changes in state delivery practices that are required if they are to address citizen needs (Mitlin 2008: 357). Nevertheless, in particular, self-help groups have to avoid a complete domestication by the state. Their field of activity is shaped by mutual support and solicitousness and this is not always compatible with professional service provision. That is why civil society organization sometimes will have to resist the temptations of the co-production of public services.

Notes

1 See the website of the Healthy House, online, available at: www.muenster.de/stadt/gesundheitshaus/.
2 For instance the government of North-Rhine Westphalia presents the Healthy House as a role model for further partnerships. See online, available at: www.landtag.nrw.de/portal/WWW/GB_I/I.1/EK/EKALT/13_EK2/Gesundheitshaus_Muenster.jsp.

3 Entrepreneurial participation in international local politics

The case of Marseilles, European Capital of Culture for 2013

Nicolas Maisetti

Introduction

On 16 September 2008, an international selection panel recommended the European capital of culture 2013 be awarded to Marseilles.[1] 'A successful balance between cultural quality, political commitment and economic support ensured victory for the Marseilles-Provence project' (Ministry of Culture and Communication 2008).

The previous day at the Musée d'Orsay, Paris, the delegates of the finalist cities – Bordeaux, Toulouse, Lyon and Marseilles – had taken the last oral exam. Jacques Pfister, President of the Marseilles-Provence Chamber of Commerce and Industry (MPCCI) and Chair of the Marseilles-Provence 2013 Association, and Bernard Latarjet, managing director of the bid, sat before the board of examiners. They were flanked by the city mayor of Marseilles, Jean-Claude Gaudin, the President of the Conseil général, Jean-Noël Guérini and the President of the Provence Alpes-Côtes d'Azur region, Michel Vauzelle. Employers at the front, politicians behind, the presentation contrasted with the defeated Bordeaux delegation led by Mayor Alain Juppé.

The Marseilles approach clearly shows the subordination of politics to the technical and economic domains. However, it also reveals the will to express unity within the political sphere.

The day after the announcement, the regional press and local actors argued that 'Marseilles 2013 is the victory of the team player method'. Pfister said 'the success of a tremendous momentum for Marseilles-Provence territory. Political, economic as well as cultural actors from 130 districts have managed to come together in support of a common militant project' (MPCCI 2008e). During the press conferences, the three main local politicians congratulated each other for their unity. According to Guérini (2008), 'Together, beyond the political divisions, we have risen to the challenge. Together, we will make culture win in the Bouches-du-Rhône and in Marseilles'. Gaudin (2008) declared, 'Team spirit has prevailed. We have had the support of 80 local authorities each with extraordinary resources. We all came together and we won'. Lastly, Vauzelle (2008) summed up:

> Today's victory is the result of an exemplary partnership initiative between various local authorities of which the Region is very proud. We have shown

> a good image of politics and of our region by proving our ability to work together – politicians from all sides, cultural and economic actors – on a major project in terms of our development and our influence.

Without wishing to deny the impact of such a display of unity the purpose of this chapter is to show how the primacy of economic over political actors was crucial to the success of the bid. I intend to establish a link between business mobilization in local public action and urban governance. To do so, I will try to demonstrate that the bid was designed in line with the (business) entrepreneurial attempts to construct a new political territory. This strategy resulted from the transfer of responsibility-taking from the political to the economic arena, institutionalized around the managerial environment provided by the Chamber of Commerce.

According to a regional daily, a meeting between the political triumvirate was organized by Bernard Latarjet, immediately before the official final presentation.

> The goal? Brief them so they can speak with one voice ... The first obvious fact is that political unity worked to the full. The worst thing possible would have been for the institutions, necessarily bound by the project, to move forward without a united front.

This remark about the subordination of elected officials to local business should be interpreted with caution. Nevertheless, these issues allow us to reconsider the dynamics of business' collective mobilization in the light of the three following questions: the internationalization of urban functions, the use of cultural policies in the promotion of a territory and the transformation of local public action through the analysis frame provided by urban governance.

The Chamber of Commerce is a professionalized organization that aims to represent and defend the interests of economic actors on a metropolitan scale. The non-political establishments' participation in the drafting, implementation and monitoring of international oriented public action resulted from business leaders' wish to use the corporate world's repertoire of collective action to promote their own interests in the local development field and to project their own representations of a territory they wish to embody – i.e. a truly international metropolitan city. Furthermore, this collective mobilization aims to counter institutional fragmentation and side-step political battles. Finally, this chapter will examine the oligarchic features of the group that are predicated on and bolstered by professionalized expertise. Such expertise was preferenced over the involvement of large numbers of cultural actors.

The entrepréneurial mobilization relies on resources provided by the political decision-marking arena. The fact that the economic elite has driven this public action had an impact on the composition and capacity for action by local government. In this particular case, the Marseilles European capital of culture bid was defined and constructed by organized business interests and there was effectively no challenge from above (politicians bordered on 'consensus') or below (citizens and cultural non-profit organizations were largely excluded).

This study of the role of Marseilles business and the Chamber of Commerce within the bid is based on an analysis of the trajectory of Mécènes du Sud, as well as the Top 20 Club ambition project. The material supporting the arguments is derived from semi-open interviews with local representatives, business leaders, members of the Chamber of Commerce, members of the association Marseilles-Provence 2013 and members of local cultural organizations.[2] The interviews were designed to analyse the sociology of public action in two directions: first, re-enacting processes of collective action in their social context, and, second, understanding practices and representations that support and drive these proceses (Pinson and Sala Pala 2007).

An analysis of the regional media, as well as an examination of grey literature (application forms, minutes of meetings, institutional brochures) have been used to check the interview information. The theoretical corpus comprises academic works about metropolis dynamics in Marseilles (Donzel 2001), the internationalization of urban spaces (Savitch and Kantor 2002), the organization of business interests and collective action (Offerlé 2009) and changes in urban governance (Le Galès 1995; Stoker 1998).

In order to analyse the entrepreneurial dynamics of collective territorial mobilization, we will see, first, the role assigned by local elite to culture and to cultural policies to raise the scale of the territory and to replace the metropolis in the territorial competition. Then the trajectory of the bid from Mécènes du Sud to the institutionalization within the Chamber of Commerce is assessed. Finally, we examine the effects of entrepreneurial framing and professionalized interest groups' involvement over local public action and local democracy.

Culture and the promotion of a less-integrated metropolitan territory

According to the bid promoters, the European capital of culture label should accelerate the metropolis and international projection of the Marseilles territory. Cultural policy should reinforce territorial identity and improve Marseilles' ability to (re-)attract foreign investment that fled this declining industrial city. Culture is used as an asset for the metropolitan strategy to renew the frame and the rules of the game of local policies and politics.

Marseilles, a declining city? From objective criteria to militant expertise

The alleged decline of Marseilles' economy refers largely to the failed harbour rejuvenation project. The intensified competition on the oleaginous market after the Second World War and decolonization forced a reorganization of production structures and trade strategies. The colonial mourning and the effect of the economic crisis of the 1970s also partly explain the economic slack in Marseilles (employment, population, tourism, notoriety). Marseilles was no longer a Marshallian system: interdependencies between industrial production, harbour trade activities and the city were no longer a reality (Donzel 2005).

In 2003, DATAR – the French inter-ministerial agency for urban planning and regional attractivity – published a ranking of European cities (Rozenblat and Cicille 2003) in which Marseilles was ranked twenty-third. The criteria referred to access and communication, economy, showcase, cultural and academic strength. Marseilles totalled the same number of points as Florence and Hamburg, ahead of Naples, Bordeaux and Liverpool, but behind Lyon and Milan.

Expert and academic statements about the limited metropolitan integration of Marseilles' urban region drew similar conclusions. The Marseilles Metropolitan Area think tank published two studies about this issue (Viard 1994; Langevin and Chouraqui 2000). Those papers, written by researchers, experts and corporate managers are a continuation of Marcel Roncayolo's seminal works about the 'disagglomeration' of Marseilles' urban area (Roncayolo 1990). They stressed the lack of shared thought about planning issues, economic, social and cultural development at the metropolitan level. They aimed to promote the construction of an economically functional territory. The ambitions of the regional epistemic community – bridging the gap between institutional fragmentations and economic integration – are contrasted with political blockages. The metropolitan supporters advocated for territorial integration that would bypass institutional, economic, social and political mechanisms. The diagnosis was that political rivalry, particularly in the field of inter-municipal cooperation was to blame for metropolitan weakness (Olive and Oppenheim 2001). Indeed, metropolitan cohabitation made the situation worse: the UMP mayor of the inner city had to deal with a socialist-ruled *Région* and *Département* since 1998 and urban community since 2008.

Culture as a lever to speed up the metropolization process: changes in cultural policy and cultural politics

Marseilles' urban regional identity and centrality remain to be reconstructed through the restructuring of harbour activities and investments in new technologies. The trajectory of the bid follows a marketing objective of territory promotion. The aim is to improve the dynamism of the local economy and to change the local profile through culture in order to attract foreign capital, firms and tourists. Emmanuel Négrier (2005) showed how cultural policies could be associated with metropolitan economic outcomes:

> The cultural issue has turned out, in discursive way, to be one of the possible means to embody a new territorial reality: culture as a means to give credit to the existence of a new institution and new territory, ferment for political identification, bearer of image and of capacity for action.

The entrepreneurial logic of the cultural sector can be observed by questioning the idea that territories would make cultural policies change. Is metropolitan construction modifying the terms of public action? According to Pierre Muller

(2007), public action is not built from a territory, but public actions produce a particular territory. Arguments about the territorialization of public action are assessed in the case of Marseilles-Provence 2013.

The bid would have projected territory both in metropolitan and in transnational spaces. Local economic elite gathered around the MPCCI to become a creative force. They built the Marseilles-Provence 2013 case to promote a territory beyond the level of the district. European Capital of Culture status would create a favourable environment for the international projection of the city and to support a potential leadership in the Mediterranean basin. The functions of cultural radiation are used for their lever effect to fulfil economic tasks, which directly create value (investment, infrastructure, finance, research, attractiveness). However, the constraints of the fragmented system of actors limited the impact of the managerial strategy. A go-between situation occurred and prevented the bid from fully escaping from Marseilles' political actors and mechanisms, despite the metropolitan extra-political agenda.

Economic elite efforts to bypass the blockade resulted in studies to define a 'common strategic identity', such as the 'Strategic Charter for territory communication' (MPCCI 2007b). This was supported by an agency for economic development labelled the Provence-Promotion and it was created by the *Conseil général* and the Chamber of Commerce. It reflects the distribution of roles between public authorities and economic elite and the entrepreneurial dynamics of the collective mobilization attempted to generate 'mechanisms of institutionalisation of urban actors systems' (Pinson 2009).

The bid promoters relied on study programmes, largely based on á comparison with Lille's European Capital of Culture bid in 2004. Meetings were organized with staff members of the Chamber of Commerce of the Grand Lille. As Pfister's principal private secretary testifies:

> Our reference is Lille. In Lille, it was the economic community, which had launched the idea of European capital of culture after the unsuccessful bid for the 2004 Olympic Games. We used this as a pattern and we developed this mobilization of the economic community, this federation of energies to be part of the bid.
> (interview with an MPCCI member)

Marseilles is commonly viewed as a city of consumption, production and diffusion of literary, pictorial, musical, cinematic and theatrical creation (Guillet and Galli 1996). The cultural radiation is a major urban referent for the dynamism of urban spaces involved in the global competition (Alliès *et al.* 1994). It is a metropolitan tag which recounts the movement of ideas and identities. In Marseilles, common sense refers to a so-called cultural web, which would be thick and strongly productive. In fact, it is very heterogeneous composed by a mass of tiny organizations dependent on municipal subsidies. Consequently, it is ill adapted to a managerial-led project and considered as 'bloodless' by business leaders because it lacked national visibility.

Despite the processes of decentralization that transferred numerous local policies to the urban community level, culture has remained a municipal competency (Négrier 1999). Local cultural policies have traditionally supported vote-catching strategies (Mattina 2004a). Local officials have disseminated subsidies to numerous small cultural organizations. However, the prospect of Capital of Culture status could potentially disturb the equilibrium. The regulation of grants could no longer pass through interpersonal relations, driven by political interests and submitted to opacity, owing to European Commission strict control over financing operations. This change led to the marginalization of local politicians.

The trajectory of the bid: from business patronage to entrepreneurial institutionalization

In order to juxtapose institutional perspectives with observations about actors' careers, we try to focus on 'the strength of weak ties' which unites the economic elite and structures their relations with outside groups, such as those in the political and cultural spheres. Business leaders took advantage of a change in the MPCCI leadership – an opening to external actors – as well as the reworking of strategies in territorial marketing.

The founders of Mécènes du Sud, corporate patronage and reshaping of the economic landscape

In the middle of the 1990s, Christian Carassou-Maillan was head of the executive board of Vacances Bleues, a hotel chain targeting seniors. In order to improve its attractiveness, he decided to invest in contemporary art because 'through art, the firm profile can be reshaped' (interview with Christian Carassou-Maillan).

In 2003, Carassou-Maillan, Patrick Ricard (Pernod-Ricard CEO), Emmanuel Barthélémy (new business leader of the Société Marseillaise de Crédit (SMC)), Corinne Brennet (Courtage de France CEO), Richard Caillat (President of High Co), Laurent Carenzo (Head of communication of Olympique de Marseille) and Éric Chaveau (Pébéo CEO) created a non-profit organization called *Mécènes du Sud*, which aims to promote territory from culture.

These firms represent Marseilles' economic landscape in an exemplary manner and illustrate its deep restructuring. High Co and Courtage de France are recent firms, founded in the 1990s in the sectors of big box stores marketing for the former, and corporate insurance and events for the latter. The rest of the founding group are at the core of a long economic history of the region, endowed with a prestigious past, but trying to transform the contemporary image of the territory. Besides, some of the leaders came from interrupted (SMC) or continuing (Ricard, Pébéo) family dynasties.

Ricard is associated with the Pastis label. In 1975, the firm increased its international profile via a partnership with the Swiss group Pernod. SMC is a bank founded in 1865 by Marseilles and Parisian bankers and manufacturers. It was historically linked with the regional economy, especially in the 1920s, when the president of the firm was the leader of both Saint Louis refinery and a shipping company. SMC intervened then as a business bank involved in urban renewal (dock reframing, street construction). Nationalized in the 1980s and privatized in the 1990s, SMC soon became debt-ridden to the tune of F70 million. Pébéo, a manufacturer of tints and accessories for fine arts, leisure and teaching, is a family business founded in 1919, which became a global firm. The current CEO, grandson of the company founder, is looking towards international markets. More than half of the sales come from American, Spanish, British, Italian, Danish and, more recently, Chinese subsidiaries. Finally, Olympique de Marseille (OM) is more than the city's football team. The Vélodrome stadium is a proxy space that conveys Marseilles' identity and carries out 'functions of affiliation to the city and social unification' (Donzel 1998).

At the end of the 1990s, these companies were looking to revitalize for a variety of reasons: financial difficulties (SMC, OM), new market penetration (High Co, Courtage de France, Pébéo) and product positioning issues (Vacance Bleues, Pernod-Ricard). This new path was not limited to strategic reorientation of activities, but included collective corporate patronage within the framework of Mécènes du Sud. Territorial commitment justified the collective approach since the companies were trying to reach a new strategic place in the global marketplace.

These leaders knew each other before the bid. Different stratums of socialization arenas shaped the morphology of sociability networks: firms' consular institution, culture and artistic fields, and social proximity. According to a business leader, meetings were organized:

> at the Chamber of Commerce, but also at the companies. Pulman Palm Beach is our partner and welcomed us during our meetings. We meet in culturally charged places. It is varied. On the other hand, we, founders, have become friends and we see each other very often. We dine at each other's place. It is very nice.
> (interview with an MPCCI member)

The former journalist, video producer and administrator of a documentary festival, Laurent Carenzo, was appointed head of communication for OM in 2002 before becoming chief of staff for MPCCI's president. His biographical trajectory exemplifies the nature and dynamic of the cultural project. The accumulated relational capital acquired throughout his career allowed ties between groups. Business leaders are set in social networks and find common interests in cultural activities. The weak intensity of bridging ties between corporate managers and the local artistic sphere could help explain the bid structuring. 'The weak links, as bridges between groups, disperse information between different social circles' (Forsé 2008). Mark Granovetter (1973, 1983) pointed out that weak links between two social groups are more efficient than strong links inside one particular group. Interactions among members led to the expression of both operational and institutional content. This organizational formulation is the starting point for collective mobilization.

Mécènes du Sud is a non-profit organization, founded in June 2003 with the statutory vocation to support contemporary creation in Marseilles. The organization was created in a favourable legislative context. Indeed, at that time, the French Parliament adopted a patronage act, which provided tax benefits to promote public generosity towards cultural, social, environmental and general interest causes.

The organizational misson statement set several strategic axes for action:

- The will to contribute, other than economic success, to the radiation of home base;
- The certainty that corporate environment can also be a major cultural actor in the city;
- The strong belief that contemporary creation feeds collective imagination and society, and that the firms do not move forward without innovation;
- The desire to give Marseilles the position it deserves in the orchestra of cultural European and Mediterranean capitals.

(Mécènes du Sud 2008)

The seven founders have since opened the organization to other partners and today there are 25 member companies. Patronage activities are chosen by an artistic committee that finances cultural projects.

The entrepreneurial institutionalization: MPCCI and Pfister agenda

The starting point of the institutionalization of interests was the arrival of a new leading team driven by Jacques Pfister at the head of the MPCCI in November 2004. The Marseilles-Provence Chamber of Commerce is historically not only a place for economic elite integration and socialization, but also a privileged location for local power. Pierre-Paul Zalio (1999) studied the trajectories of merchant and industrial families in the twentieth century. A series of portraits suggests the existence of a specific dynamic for local capitalism. The generational careers of business leaders and families who ruled the economic scene between 1880 and 1950 showed the weight of harbour activities. The entrepreneurial culture (corporate managers as much as family chiefs; wholesalers and speculators rather than industrials or innovators) explains the dynamics of the economic and the social results of the local capitalism.

At the beginning of the twentieth century, the era of strong growth was marked by an increasing volume of local production for exports. Deprived of inherited social and economic capital, the newcomers opened up small size businesses and developed outlet strategies. Economic growth and social mobility are closely linked to rising opportunities.

Zalio's analysis establishes connections between local economic dynamics and the social division of space. As for economic power relations with local government, we notice a lack of interactions. Economic elite were not involved in the formal political decision-making process (Zalio 2004).

When Pfister was elected at the Chamber, he was head of Orangina-Schweppes, a group born from the merger of two Pernod-Ricard subsidiaries. His programme for action was listed on the 'Top 20 ambition', i.e. making progress in the 'European championship of metropolis' (MPCCI 2008a). It was based on DATAR ranking and stated that Marseilles metropolis was behind in the European competition: 'Marseilles is ranked 23rd out of the 180 European largest cities! The DATAR report is tough. But, it is a thought-worthy report. It represents the opportunity to look straight at our assets and hindrances' (MPCCI 2005). Pfister's programme intended to break off the archipelization dynamics of the metropolitan area in the context of the crisis of the city as 'collective actor' (Bagnasco and Le Galès 1997).

The 'Top 20 Ambition Club': business collective mobilization

A window of opportunity was opening to promote a larger-scale ambition by the following factors: political fragmentation; economic, expert and academic objectification of the decline in the territorial situation; the arrival of a new leadership at the MPCCI; and the Mécènes du Sud project as an available resource.

In 2005, the MPCCI published a brochure to present the 'Top 20 report' (MPCCI 2005). It was based on the city's decline diagnosis and the weakness of the metropolitan integration 'impaired by divisions', which created conditions for a 'brain drain'. The cultural issue was not the most prominent. The article, entitled 'Culture, a strategic weapon to stand out from the crowd', was published at the end of the report and underlined the division of labour between Aix-the cultural and Marseilles-the industrial. However, it referred to a 'new ambition' at Marseilles' disposal:

> A task force has been formed to study the feasibility of a major project or international cultural event ... Enclosed was an application form for the title of 'European capital of culture' for 2013 and the 10 million euro bonus granted to the winner.
>
> (MPCCI 2005)

The lexical proximity between the study stage of 'feasibility' and 'application' can be explained by the precedence of Mécènes du Sud activities. The non-profit organization provided resources to create the Top 20 Ambition Club and a 'task force' was designated to mobilize the business environment. Built as a 'professionalized interest group' (Beyers *et al.* 2008a), the Club is expected to engage in the positive effects of the cultural criteria (urban tourism, exhibition, international congress, museum) that could improve the city rank and speed up the accomplishment of the metropolitan area. The benefits for all actors would be higher than the mutual costs for economic actors and partly externalized 'costs' for political actors.

Urban governance and business collective mobilization

Political involvement and turbulences

A breaking point occurred in 2004, when the Marseilles city hall expressed its will to get directly involved in the European capital of culture project. Having failed to host the America's Cup, representatives and officials underlined international cultural awards (2002 Eurocities trophy), thus justifying their desire to take part in internationally oriented projects. In 2001, the Cultural Affairs Department of the City Hall prepared a paper draft called 'Marseilles 2002–2012 – culture at the heart of the debate' (Marseilles City Hall 2001).

This 'Cultural Policy Master Plan' did not refer to the prospect of European Capital of Culture, but collected existing policies, infrastructures and announced further investments. According to municipal civil servants and elected representatives, this draft is the basis of the bid. This was definitely not the view of the Chamber. The bid involved struggles between local elites and business, political and cultural actors. All claim sponsorship of the project. This rhetoric is far from public discourses about a united front.

The Top 20 members considered the political involvement as negative interference. A Club coordinator stated:

> We found that the way things were taking shape was quite disturbing ... There were rivalries among Marseilles officials; it was old style policy. So, at that moment, we decided to get in touch with Bernard Latarjet to restructure the whole project.
>
> (interview with an MPCCI member)

The link was clearly established between political commitments and the 'dismarseillization' corollary of depoliticization. The Chamber got in touch with people external to the local context to bypass the usual political decision-process arenas. According to entrepreneurs, the aim was to avoid political pollution, engendered by local rivalries and to construct a stable extra-political system of actors.

Bernard Latarjet was a member of Lang's Cabinet at the Ministry of Culture and Mitterrand's Cabinet at the Presidency of the Republic in the 1980s. Business and cultural actors recognized that if Latarjet was not from Marseilles, it was an asset since he could help depoliticize the issue: 'we were too inclined to look at the issues politically, not enough technically'. Following the narratives of the bid promoters, the arrival of Latarjet appears to be crucial. The first visit of Latarjet in Marseilles took place in December 2006, during the opening of an exhibition called 'Culture Acts', which aimed to bring economic and cultural backgrounds closer:

> I got his phone number and I called him. I said 'we are organising this, are you available?' He said 'yes, I am, I am coming over now. I like your idea to integrate the business actors in it'. So, he perfectly understood, from the

beginning, that he could benefit from economic involvement. Oddly enough, his first official event as the bid director was at the Chamber.

(interview with an MPCCI member)

By contrast, the tale sounds quite different from other perspectives, including the one that comes from Latarjet's associates. According to them, the mayor got in touch with Latarjet with a clear set of political objectives. The idea was to entrust a leftwing man with the cultural project to neutralize attacks from political opposition and from cultural actors:

> Latarjet received a call from Gaudin. Of course, everybody claims to be the founding father. It was Gaudin who called him. After that, everybody came along. The Chamber could not have had the idea since the idea to entrust the Presidency of the 2013 association with the Chamber intervened six months after Latarjet's arrival. During these six months, he did not even realize the Chamber existed.
> (interview with a Marseilles-Provence 2013 member)

When Latarjet was asked to take control of the non-profit organization, the city of culture bid had become the priority of the Chamber and city hall. The European label would fit with extrovert ambitions in the context of territorial competition (MPCCI 2008b). The promoters found a consensus around the will to show that Marseilles could be considered equal to Barcelona, Milan, Liverpool or Hamburg. Both strategic and marketing targets are shared by local authorities:

> The ambition is about international radiation. It is not incoherent to take this ambition in consideration and express it through a label. If we had refocused and re-concentrated on Marseilles while the whole object was to get this city out of itself, it would take the cake!
> (interview with a local representative)

Furthermore, cultural reclassification in the local agenda seems to be have been hastened by political involvement. Hence, one cannot conclude that political actors were not involved in collective business mobilization. The economic promoters made use of political resources to convey and support their priorities. It was not about bypassing politicization, but about taking advantage of resources in order to achieve specific technical and strategic objectives. In this sense, local authorities contracted out the participation function to entrepreneurial expertise.

The important point for the bid coordinators was to keep politicians away from the institutional and operational project implementation. The Chamber 'succeeded in persuading Gaudin not to run the association. It had to be the Chamber; the President of the Chamber, hence business. I told him that he would thus avoid potential blows and also get the results' (interview with an MPCCI member).

Marseilles-Provence 2013 governance

The composition of Marseilles-Provence 2013 executives shows the domination of metropolitan entrepreneurs. The President of Marseilles-Provence 2013 Board is the President of the Chamber and the managing director is Bernard Latarjet. Pfister had succeeded in becoming a consensus figure for political and economic actors. Finally, the Marseilles-Provence 2013 area and governance managed to defuse and freeze political ambitions:

> It means that if, tomorrow, by elections, choices, municipal or regional majority changes, all those political hazards; well, Marseilles-Provence 2013 exists. The organization is not headed by a politician, it has its own lifetime and its own function led by an artistic manager, who is not under the control either of the city or of the region, who is here to manage the programme and complete the bid successfully.
>
> (interview with a local representative)

Indeed, the Marseilles-Provence legal status defines an equal representation of members in the decision-making process (one member, one voice). According to a member of the Chamber, 'it provides a clear balance and prevents any of the members to claim a first place'. The egalitarian feature of this governance model does not reflect the bid process. If the strategic driving of the bid is not in Marseilles' official hands, expected gains for the city centre are incommensurable in contrast with peripheral local authorities.

The role of the Top 20 Ambition Club is to provide a marketing package and to consolidate a lobby group. In this respect, the Club members have organized trips to support the bid as well as to exert influence over European decision makers. Business leaders visited Dublin and Liverpool, former winners of the Cultural Capital label in 1991 and 2008. Two business trips took place to meet European Commissioners in Brussels and Members of Parliament. Eventually, on 3 September 2008, a business delegation met the members of the selection panel during their visit to the finalist cities (Marseilles-Provence 2013 Association 2008b; Marseille City Hall 2008a).

The control of business elites over the bid definition, as well as the metropolitan and internationalized perspective had profound effects on the bid content. The artistic contribution of the business was the 'Thousand Talents' project. It appeared in the application form under the title 'Euromediterranean Workshop' defined as 'a major European project of intercultural dialogue and mobility for artists' (Marseille-Provence 2013 Association 2008a).

The business trips not only aimed to gather information about European Commission expectations or at transferring so called best practices, but also allowed some reshaping of the project and rebalancing between European and Mediterranean focuses. Business roadshows were also conceived as part of the territorial promotion stratgey to 'make obvious to Europe the support of the business environment to this bid' (MPCCI 2008c).

Within European decision-making arenas, the bid promoter narratives exemplify the business world mistrust of local politics competition: 'we brought our regional Members of European Parliament together to help them take the topic in their hand and we realized it was an unfinished job' (interview with an MPCCI member). The elected representative is viewed as subordinate compared to entrepreneurs, but politicians are not excluded from the process. The technical training provided to officials is a prerequisite for success; they have the skills to successfully address public opinion, the media and European decision makers (MPCCI 2008d).

Lessons on local government: a new configuration of actors and scale change, but what about legitimacy?

Business-organized mobilization proved to be successful because the European Capital of Culture was awarded to Marseilles-Provence for 2013. This achievement raises issues about local government changes. The effectiveness of the entrepreneurial dynamics of the collective action should not hide the effects on democratic practices. Business-organized mobilization has unquestionably been the midpoint in the decision-making process. In other words, local public action was planned outside political arenas. One can question a potential loss of political control resulting from negative externalities engendered by the (business) entrepreneurial dynamic. As we have seen, social and political actors have not been swept away from public action production. Urban governance does not make the government or the social context disappear (Pinson 2006). Indeed, mobilization from business interests and their methods coexisted with traditional forms of mobilization (Balme *et al.* 1999).

Marginalization of cultural actors

It is somewhat paradoxical to note the marginalization of cultural actors in a culturally defined project. The designation of the city and the expected economic effects provide the opportunity to organize cultural events. Nonetheless, cultural organizations were not a driving force for Marseilles-Provence 2013. The Chamber worked out its own criteria to build the bid in terms of scale, content and future prospects. According to a cultural organization, 'even if Marseilles 2013 is in mind, it is still very vague'. When bid promoters are asked who were the cultural actors centrally involved in the project they usually give the following explanation:

> On the cultural field, I could not say. Everybody was more or less part of it. I did not see anyone who played a more important role than anyone else. I have seen many who are worried that 2013 might not bring what they expect, which is a reality.
> (interview with a local civil servant, Department of Culture)

Indeed, some of them are worried about the lack of cooperation between Marseilles-Provence 2013 and cultural organizations. Besides, the hiatus between the local focus of numerous local cultural organizations and international focus promoted by the Chamber has not been resolved.

The cultural organizations involved in the bid are limited to those able to complete complex subsidy forms. Cultural actors were reluctant to be part of a general policy that exceeded the cultural dimension. They were unenthusiastic about using culture to promote urban regeneration or in the territorial competition. 'La Fête est finie' ('the party is over') initiatives born in the wake of Lille European Capital of Culture in 2004 are also relevant in the Marseilles case – most notably protests against the economic focus. However, some of the cultural non-profit associations have tried to act as 'rocks of sand' to bring endogenous components into the bid. The cultural field is divided between those who refused any involvement and those who chose to join the fray to interfere with the managerial path: 'We were involved to say "let's do a critical work". Let's be independent. We will bring other insights, not to do pure denunciations, but to see in prospect the issues of gentrification, for instance' (interview with the director of a local radio). Nevertheless, cultural actors felt torn between their traditional practices and the business mechanics of the project. This contradiction has been summed up by the metaphor of 'the angel versus evil on each shoulder'. It triggered exit strategies led by cultural actors and could explain their marginalization.

The first provisory lesson about local government drawn from this study is the risk of the lack of social anchorage – i.e. the lack of legitimacy of public policies produced by the business impulse. Events organized by local cultural organizations will probably not match the original formulation. Thus, protests have recently emerged about specific projects. For instance, a 'Comité d'intérêt de quartier' lodged an appeal to cancel the building permit to the Museum of European and Mediterranean Civilizations. This action slowed down the work's progress and could delay the opening until after 2013.

Politics as resources and constraints

The relative discretion of the political circle and the lack of weak ties, which would relate it to the technical circle, are noteworthy. The strategy is summed up by a member of the Chamber as follows:

> Pfister has been very sensitive to allow the bid to become a real cultural project, which would not take political turmoil in consideration. It had to be extremely technical. And Latarjet was very clever, because he never hurt anyone. He gained the confidence of the panel.
> (interview with an MPCCI member)

The scale change, the methods used and the defensive interests induced by the bid widen the gap with local political habits. The political economy of culture in Marseilles is usually organized around the financing of specific clients. They are small-sized organizations with no international profile. Previous research about the 'Marseilles political worlds' has highlighted the extent of clientelism, fiefism, political inheritance and leadership that regulate political behaviours (Mattina 2004a). In the case of the Marseille-Provence bid, the initial orientation has impacted the distribution of the resources among local actors. While business actors led the decision-making process, the local authorities were lagging far behind: 'People who work at the culture department of the city hall had the feeling that Latajet was above them. He became a kind of super-ministry for territorial culture. Some of them were upset about this disappropriation' (interview with a Marseilles-Provence 2013 member). While the local bureaucracy was considered as a 'partner' it was not heavily involved in public policy framing.

Politics back in town: the Euromediterranean issue

The designation of the city in September 2008 brought politics back to town. Politicians are trying to benefit from a project that marginalized them. Consensual effects produced by the entrepreneurial trajectory of the bid could have faded away: 'governance is exactly balanced since we are in a sort of consensus. This city does not like this situation anymore, but, for the moment, they cannot change it' (interview with an MPCCI member).

In June 2008, the deputy mayor of Marseilles, Renaud Muselier, was ousted from the urban community presidency by his own political faction. Four months later, the mayor appointed him head of a special delegation to 'prepare the city to become European capital of culture' (Marseille City Hall 2008b). Muselier is now responsible for coordinating elected representatives around the 2013 horizon. In March 2009, his first attempt was to propose the creation of a one-stop service that would monopolize the provision for label granting and project financing. This initiative sparked immediate reactions from political rivals, MPCCI, as well as the Marseilles-Provence 2013 board. The latter organized an extraordinary governing board to reassert:

> its independancy and its autonomy in the respect of the rights of each partner. It is the Association, and only the Association, which provides the building projects of the cultural programme. It is the Association, and only the Association, which selects cultural projects and labels them.
> (Marseilles-Provence 2013 Resolution, 6 April 2009)

This blistering communiqué will not help Muselier get higher visibility for non-profit organization actors and business leaders. The relative retreat of politics and the progressive and unsuccessful comeback can be explained by the specific temporality of the European label. The city was designated five years before the beginning of any major events. According to a local official, it is:

> then that we will see who is in position, politically. There will be a stronger appropriation but it will be more justified and more legitimate if it is

regarded a success then … It is a political calculation too. People say 'lets keep a low profile' and when it really becomes something, I am not sure the low profile attitude will continue.

(interview with a local representative)

Besides, in October 2008, the French President of the Republic appointed Muselier responsible for a cultural council of the Union for Mediterranean (UfM). According to the decree of appointment, this authority's objective is to 'arouse public and private initiatives about the development of cultural dimension of the French Mediterranean policy, including the UfM and mobilize all Mediterranean living forces at the service of Marseilles-Provence 2013 European capital of culture project'.

National and local politicians pursue diplomatic goals when they invest the European Capital of Culture label. The label is not only a way towards prosperity through territory promotion, but also a means to tick the cultural box of the Euromediterranean partnership. The internationalization of urban functions opens a space for local diplomatic positioning. In Marseilles, speeches and postures about decentralized diplomacy have revolved around a vague but unifying notion: Marseilles as 'Mediterranean capital' (Sanmarco 2000). It appeared through the polarization of international institutions (World Bank, European Commission and Parliament, UNIDO, Plan Bleu), national agencies (UbiFrance, IRD), world-sized firms (CMA-CGM) or regional headquarters (Monster, Expedia, Compass Group).

The Euromediterranean focus of the bid also helps explain both the federative local political support and success in national and European areas. In the local scene, the Euromediterranean grammary is shared by political actors beyond the vagueness of the concept and despite the contradictory interests (Visier 2005). Far from being natural, historical or geographical based, the Euromediterranean referent is seen by political actors as a way to gain electoral support from migrant communities, especially from North African countries. The Marseilles-Provence 2013 bid employed Euromediterranean narrative as strategic focus to promote local and national political agreement around the project. According to a Marseilles-Provence 2013 executive, the bid was a 'geopolitical' one.

In 2008, during the French presidency campaign, the candidate Sarkozy proposed to relaunch the Euromediterranean Partnership. Two months after his election, he organized a summit with the EU members and the heads of states of Mediterranean countries to launch the UfM. Consequently, the Euromediterranean core of the bid echoed the diplomatic priority of the French President. This political background is brought forward by the bid promoters to explain the final choice of Marseilles-Provence 2013 project: 'after the Elysee Summit, we understood the idea was working. We hold course on Euromediterranean feature' (interview with a Marseilles-Provence 2013 member).

Collective mobilization and territory building

The scale change in cultural territorial policies is noteworthy. The European Commission grants the label to a city. However, in the opinion of business promoters, the strict local scale is not relevant to change the image of the city, attract investors and create resources. The scale of international projection and exposition is the metropolitan one. According to an executive of Euroméditerranée:

> We are not in a purely French thought any more. We cannot build the economic development of a city like Marseilles anymore without thinking about a projection in an international perspective. We are not here to build the south of France, but we are in Euromediterranean dynamic.
> (interview with a *Euroméditerranée* member)

In other words, the bid was invested by business actors to create a new territory based on a metropolitan scale (Marseille-Provence) as well as a transnational focus (Mediterranean Basin). International projection of local policies was speeding up with the business-organized mobilization. It has encouraged a wider geographical exposure on the political agenda. The scale change could eventually allow business interests to escape from local political contingencies. The evolution of the metropolis process is not due to a hypothetical political consensus or to popular wishes, but to technical incentives. Metropolis dynamics and internationalization of territorial public policies are changing the content and the targets of public action as well as international local politics. The need is less to gain citizen support, but more to win world market shares and to contact international institutions and foreign groups.

The provisional budget is close to €100 million, compared with less than €80 million for Lille 2004. From now on, a more operational phase is expected from Marseilles-Provence, despite the likely delay due to the current economic crisis. The sacred union over an unachieved metropolitan territory, two départements, 130 communes and 2,300,000 inhabitants will probably face a severe test. Will the model of 'collective governance' (MPCCI 2008e), led by the economic sector, resist the current political push? Can the European Capital of Culture label reshape a fragmented territory in the wake of *Euroméditerranée* urban operation? Can Marseilles' urban governance get used to a long-term marginalization of politics, which would limit the citizens' place in the decision-making process? Will the redeployment of the metropolis in the European ranking lead to a renewal of social fabric, deeply torn by social polarization?

Conclusion

The case of the Marseilles-Provence European Capital of Culture for 2013 bid illustrates a specific shape of collective action building. The contribution of private arenas in urban policy is neither isolated nor new as far as public policy opening process towards public–private partnership is concerned (Lorrain and Stoker 1997). However, the entrepreneurial collective action suggests a particular trend towards local spaces since it leads to new territory invention as well as new public policy styles.

Concerning the issue of professionalized and individualized collective mobilization, the hypothesis advanced is that the original allocation of resources and interests in favour of market actors led to the political endorsement of changing habits in public policy design and implementation. Consequently, new representations of territory are likely to emerge.

In a broad sense Marseilles' corporate managers belong to 'civil society' (Saurugger 2006) since it gathers groups of actors that don't draw their legitimacy from elections. Involved in the institutional framework provided by the Chamber of Commerce, they are part of the European Capital of Culture bid decision-making process. Their contribution can be interpreted as a response to the supposed weakness of local public actors in terms of legitimacy as well as capacity for actions (Andrew and Goldsmith 1998). As such, local business leader mobilization can be first seen as private participation in local democracy. Second, they are becoming major actors in articulation dynamics of political frames within the local economic system. These dominant partners of decision-making process put business 'economic' and 'social' capital (Putnam 1995) and know-how to good use in public action.

Accordingly, they are taking up the vacant position left by actors and practices that formerly regulated political configurations – in the Marseilles case, the exchange involved municipal authorities and organized clients, such as migrant communities or inhabitant unions, called Neighboured interest Comity (Mattina 2004b). Local business managers no longer act as family heads who establish links with associate rivals sharing the old industrial-harbour system. They are organized within extra-political spaces as consolidated professionalized associations that promote their own perceptions of territory.

This situation lacks social anchorage. On the one hand, elected staff are reduced to actors among others. On the other hand, it excludes traditional addressees from collective action. In this particular case, the European Capital of Culture label is not only a local cultural policy aiming to subsidize programmes or cultural events, it is also designed to attract tourists (both cultural and business), investors (both public and private), as well as informal rating agencies. These factors affect changes in the image of a city. Such criteria are increasingly crucial in the context of inter-territorial competition (Scott 1998).

Market actors' incentives have upgraded territorial internationalization targets over endogenous local development. The trend supports the previous proposition and results in loss of democratic substance. A localized political analysis has considered exogenous conditions, which have contributed to the driving out of citizens from decision-making processes.

The last result drawn for the inquiry foresees both policy and political change and contributes to two major evolutions. On the one hand, local systems have been moved from a status of scale of public action to that of multi-positioned actors who keep interacting with supra-local levels. On the other hand, the entrepreneurial dynamics claim for metropolitan widening of legitimate frame for collective action. In other words, the democratic City (Polis) is no longer the centre of command for the City, which produces richness (Urbs). New models of interaction between Polis and Urbs are intensifying tensions between prevailing groups – those who master the market, and European know-how as well as globalized ways of thinking – and the respect of collective choices coming from election. From this point of view, the increasing entry cost in the decision-making process induced by professionalized collective action includes some negative effects adding to the democratic deficit. Breaches in the bounds between elected authorities and citizen have been accompanied by 'the weakness of strong links', which unify economic actors and local representatives.

Notes

1 Official designation by the Council of the European Union occurred in May 2009 (Council of the European Union 2009).
2 The survey is made up of 14 interviews with the following individuals: two company CEOs, members of the Club Ambition Top 20; the Administrative Manager of the Club; the Principal Private Secretary of the CCCIMP President; the former Deputy Mayor, delegated to Cultural Affairs; assistants for a local politician; the Administrative Manager for the Cultural Affairs Department at the Marseilles City Hall; the Administrative Manager for the *Mission Marseille 2013* at the *Secrétariat général* of the Marseilles City Hall; the director of a local radio; one of the administrators of a local cultural project; a cultural non-profit organization employee; a Marseilles-Provence 2013 manager for patronage (former *Euroméditerranée* manager for economic development); the former Marseilles-Provence 2013 art director; a Marseilles-Provence 2013 manager for international relations. Only seven are directly quoted in this chapter to illustrate the practices and representations (both individual and institutional ones) as well as to recount the narrative of the bid.

4 New issues, new forms of action?
Climate change and environmental activism in Britain[1]

Christopher Rootes[2]

Introduction

There is considerable debate about the extent to which the forms of political participation have changed with the advent of the Internet and other new communications technologies, but not all changes in the pattern of political participation can be attributed to changes in technology. Changes in the social economic and political contexts also impact upon the forms of political participation. So too do changes in the issue-specific contexts of forms of action.

My concern here is with the forms of action associated with the environmental movement. For almost two decades, the story most often told about the environmental movement is that of its institutionalization. Certainly, many environmental NGOs (ENGOs) have become substantial organizations, relatively well funded and increasingly formally bureaucratic. No longer relying principally upon enthusiastic volunteers, they are increasingly staffed by professionals who have more in common with professionals in other kinds of NGOs in the voluntary sector than with grassroots activists. Given their need for a steady flow of funds in order to pay their staff and in order to sustain their activities, they rely less and less upon the casual donations of supporters and more and more upon the regular donations of their most committed supporters and, increasingly, upon legacies as their oldest supporters die off. Now characterized by professionalized action and professional fundraising, ENGOs have even been described as 'protest businesses' (Jordan and Maloney 1997).

If many ENGOs have become institutionalized internally, the institutionalization of environmentalism also has another, external face (van der Heijden 1997). As environmental organizations have risen to prominence, and as they have achieved a degree of organizational stability, so increasingly they have been drawn into relationships with more powerful actors in government or corporate sectors. In many respects this external institutionalization is simply a reflection of and counterpart to their internal institutionalization. As environmental organizations become professionalized, so they become more plausible partners for governments and/or corporations. This clearly impacts upon their styles of action. Their resources and their professionalism facilitate effective lobbying and negotiation outside the public gaze, but are less clearly relevant to the kind of grassroots mobilization of the mass public that is stereotypically associated with social movement activity. Moreover, to the extent that they have developed fruitful relationships with more powerful actors, environmental organizations may, in the interests of maintaining those relationships, be constrained to avoid forms of action that might possibly embarrass their interlocutors and so might compromise ENGOs' access to them. The overall effect has been to encourage ENGOs to work within the frameworks of such partnerships rather than attempt to mobilize the wider public, except in so far as that might be necessary to raise financial resources.

Where ENGOs have enjoyed ready access to policy makers and decision makers at national and regional levels, so long as these relatively institutionalized channels of access exist, and as long as policy and decision makers appear responsive, the strategy of professionalization and seeking institutionalized access appears to be rewarding. But what happens if policy and decision makers become unresponsive, or if the action that governments and powerful corporations are prepared to take appears to be inadequate to the scale of the problems identified? If ENGOs become despondent about their prospects of making progress by semi-institutionalized means, might they then resort to mobilizing the public instead?

Writers such as van der Heijden (1997) have worried that institutionalized ENGOs have lost the capacity to mobilize the public, and that this will, ultimately, erode their capacity to exert political influence, since it is its capacity to disrupt business as usual that is the ultimate source of the veto power of a social movement.

In what follows, I shall consider the case of the environmental movement in Britain as it attempts to address what environmentalists have identified as the biggest environmental problem of our time: climate change. For two decades, ENGOs have identified global warming and climate change as problems requiring urgent attention, but they have repeatedly been disappointed by the policies and, especially, by the actions of the powerful in response to those problems. What do ENGOs do when lobbying and polite representations have failed to realize their goals? And, since the environmental movement is more than simply the collectivity of environmental NGOs, what do its footsoldiers do if the increasingly institutionalized actions of ENGOs have failed to produce adequate results?

The British environmental movement in context

Long established and organizationally diverse, ENGOs in Britain are well supported: almost one adult in five claims to be a member of one or more environmental organizations, and the aggregated number of their members or financial supporters exceeds five million (Rootes 2007, 2009a).

The British environmental movement has always been a complex, hybrid phenomenon. Contrary to what has sometimes been assumed, the earliest ENGOs were not mostly focused upon the preservation of nature for its own sake but were principally formed to preserve access to recreational space for an increasingly urbanized population. The Commons Preservation Society (1865), established to ensure the protection of London's commons, consolidated more local efforts to preserve ancient footpaths. It was preceded by local groups dedicated to the preservation of customary rights of way, a movement that culminated in 1935 in the establishment of the Ramblers Association to promote the right to roam across the open countryside (www.ramblers.org.uk/aboutus/history, accessed 25 August 2010). The National Trust (1895) also sought to preserve unspoiled landscapes, gardens and historic buildings for the quiet enjoyment of people whose daily lives were made hectic by industrialization and urbanization. Although the iconic Royal Society for the Protection of Birds (RSPB) (1889) was indeed a purely preservationist organization, purely nature conservationist organizations were, until after the Second World War, the exception rather than the rule. Even the Council for the Preservation of Rural England (CPRE) (1926) was an initiative of architects and planners concerned mainly to promote rational land-use planning to inhibit the aesthetic blight of ribbon development along country roads, and to seek the establishment of national parks to preserve unspoiled landscapes for human enjoyment. There is, then, nothing novel about ENGOs that address the human dimensions of environmental change.

Although all of these early ENGOs were, at least in origin, campaigning organizations, most campaigned principally at elite level by lobbying the powerful, and it was only after the Second World War that environmental organizations sought to become mass membership organizations. Rarely, however, did they aim to encourage mass involvement in their activities, let alone their governance; more usually they were content to tap their supporters' pockets. Thus when the World Wildlife Fund (WWF) launched in 1961, it made an unprecedented appeal in the pages of a mass-market newspaper, but it did so only in order to raise funds for scientific research, and not with the aim of mobilizing the public. Even the upstarts of the 1970s – Friends of the Earth (FoE) and Greenpeace – did not set out to be mass mobilizing organizations.

Institutionalization

Environmental NGOs in Britain are relatively highly institutionalized, formal organizations. Necessarily hierarchical and, to some degree, bureaucratic because of their size, they generally employ professional staff rather than relying mainly upon enthusiastic amateurs and volunteers. Yet, although they are relatively well resourced by comparison with their counterparts in some other countries, their resources are severely limited by comparison with those of their interlocutors in government or the corporate sector. Nevertheless, they have enjoyed relatively easy access to policy makers, and the relative openness of the British administrative system has, compounded by their increasing professionalization and their limited resources, encouraged ENGOs to focus upon policy and policy making rather than mass mobilization.

Although the campaigning organizations FoE and Greenpeace grew spectacularly in the 1980s, more recent growth has been concentrated in nature protection organizations (notably the National Trust, RSPB, the Wildlife Trusts and the Woodland Trust) (Rootes 2007) (see Table 4.1). Those organizations more concerned with practical conservation, provision of services and management of reserves, and less with public campaigning and, especially, the mobilization of the mass public, have grown most and are increasingly well resourced. By contrast, among the dozen largest environmental organizations, it is the campaigning organizations that have grown least since 1990 and have fewest resources. Neither FoE nor Greenpeace ranks among the top ten ENGOs in terms of income, staff numbers or grant income from private foundations and trusts (Cracknell and Godwin 2007; Cracknell *et al.* 2009). FoE and Greenpeace together have a combined annual income smaller than that of the Woodland Trust alone; older conservation organizations are much wealthier and employ many more staff (see Table 4.2).

Because their resources at national level are relatively limited, even campaigning ENGOs have only limited capacity to contribute to local campaigns (Saunders 2007). Limited resources inform and compound a strategic preference for investing resources in national campaigns whose agendas national ENGOs can control rather than in local campaigns in which the interests of local campaigners may differ from the priorities of national NGOs. Greenpeace has been especially clear-eyed about this, occasionally intervening in local environmental disputes in ways that are helpful to local campaigners, but always as autonomous Greenpeace actions that spectacularly highlight the general issues consonant with Greenpeace's national campaign priorities rather than the particular issues of special concern to locals. Greenpeace makes no pretence of being a grassroots membership organization; where it does have local groups, they are support groups, charged with raising funds for the national organization and awareness of Greenpeace's national campaigns and the Greenpeace brand, but prohibited

Table 4.1 Membership of selected environmental NGOs (1971 to 2006; thousands)

	1971	*1981*	*1991*	*2001*	*2006*
National Trust (NT)	278	1,046	2,152	2,729	3,480
Royal Society for the Protection of Birds (RSPB)	98	441	852	1,020	1,062
Wildlife Trusts[1]	64	142	233	382	657
World Wide Fund for Nature (WWF)	12	60	227	287	330
Woodland Trust[2]	–	20	63	100	160
Campaign to Protect Rural England (CPRE)[3]	21	29	45	59	60
Friends of the Earth (FoE)	1	18	111	95	102
Greenpeace	–	30	312	224	221

Sources: adapted from Haezewindt (2003) and supplemented with information supplied by the organizations themselves or drawn from their websites.

Notes
1 Includes the Royal Society for Nature Conservation/Royal Society for Wildlife Trusts.
2 Figure for 1981 from Evans (1997: 197);
3 Council for the Preservation of Rural England 1926–1969; Council for the Protection of Rural England 1969–2003.

Table 4.2 Leading British ENGOs (2005)

	Year founded in UK	Members/donor supporters (thousands)	Income/budget (£ million)	Staff size	Local groups	Manage property or reserve	Focus
RSPB	1889	1,042	63	1,500	175[1]	Yes (190)	Birds and their habitat; nature reserves
National Trust	1895	3,400	315	>4,000	>60[2]	Yes	Landscapes, historic buildings
Wildlife Trusts*	1912	588	107	<1,500	47	Yes (>2,200)	Wildlife and habitat, nature reserves
CPRE	1926	60	3	50	200	No	Countryside, land-use planning
Wildfowl and Wetland Trust	1946	139	14	275	–	Yes	Birds and wetlands
British Trust for Conservation Volunteers (BTCV)	1959	0.365[3]	23	588	No[4]	No[5]	Community conservation projects
WWF-UK	1961	330	39	290	200[6]	Not in UK	Conservation, sustainable development overseas
FoE (England, Wales and Northern Ireland)	1971	102	9[7]	159	200	No	Environmental protection, social justice
Woodland Trust	1972	147	21	223	No	Yes	Woodland (preservation and new planting)

Greenpeace UK	1977	n/a	11[9]	100	102	No	Environmental protection (especially marine), nuclear
Sustrans	1977	n/a			163	No	Walking, cycling
Wildlife and Countryside Link**	1980	35 organizations including all above (except BTCV and Sustrans)	22			No	

Sources: annual reports, websites and information supplied by organizations themselves.

Notes

* Royal Society of Wildlife Trusts, plus 47 autonomous local/regional Wildlife Trusts.
** Umbrella organization linking autonomous member organizations.
Staff numbers include part-time staff, where separately declared as such, as 0.5 of full-time:
1 plus 110 youth groups;
2 plus >40 property-based groups of 'friends' or 'volunteers';
3 BTCV has only 365 'members' with voting rights, but according to its website 'supports 140,000 volunteers';
4 BTCV 'supports 2,225 local community groups' but these are not BTCV groups as such;
5 BTCV assists with management of various projects but does not manage property or reserves of its own;
6 estimated for 2002;
7 includes £3.8 million for FoE Trust;
8 includes 8,000 'active supporters' who assist in delivery of Greenpeace campaigns;
9 figure for 2004; includes £1.9 million for Greenpeace Environmental Trust.

from using the Greenpeace name in autonomous local campaigns. There is a separate 'active supporters' network whose members are offered training and are sometimes recruited for Greenpeace protest actions, but most supporters of Greenpeace are not involved in campaigns.

Sometimes, however, a weak local presence exists despite rather than because of the strategy of the national organization. Thus for more than two decades its network of some 200 local groups has been central to the identity of FoE, but those groups vary greatly in size and levels of activity and their membership is in aggregate only about 10 per cent that of the national FoE organization; most members of FoE nationally are not members of a local group and most are never actively involved in an FoE campaign. FoE's network of local groups gives it better connections to grassroots environmental politics, but it also raises expectations that FoE, unlike Greenpeace, should be involved in local campaigns. Limited resources mean that the national FoE organization is often unable to meet such expectations, and where local FoE activists are involved in local campaigns, it is often either as individuals or collectively under banners specific to the local campaign in question. Although this means that the FoE flag may not be flown very conspicuously in local campaigns, it does enable FoE to escape the dilemma that arises where, as often happens, the concerns raised by local campaigners are not consistent with the campaign priorities or even the science based concerns of the national organization's officers.

Although a relatively centralized political system combined with relative administrative openness has encouraged national ENGOs with limited resources to focus upon national level policy *making*, the institutionalization of ENGOs in Britain has not been accompanied by a monotonic decline of environmental protest. Indeed, during the decade from 1988 – the period that marked the consolidation of institutionalized environmentalism – environmental protest became not only more frequent but relatively more confrontational (Rootes 2003a). But that was not because institutionalized ENGOs suddenly abandoned the boardroom for the streets. In four-fifths of the environmental protests reported in the *Guardian* during that decade, no established ENGO was reported to have been involved. The involvement of the ENGOs most frequently mentioned in reports of environmental protest – Greenpeace and FoE – was, apart from the peak of protest in 1995, relatively stable throughout the decade and did not vary as much as the overall incidence of protest from year to year. The only other institutionalized NGOs mentioned in connection with protests – WWF and the RSPB – were each reportedly involved in barely more than 1 per cent of all the reported protests during the decade, and almost invariably in entirely conventional forms of action. Only Greenpeace was reportedly associated more often with non-conventional forms of action such as demonstrations or confrontation than with relatively conventional forms (Rootes 2003a: 39–41). The great majority of the more than 120 national environmental NGOs were never mentioned in reports of environmental protest during that turbulent decade.

Overall, then, the modal repertoire of institutionalized environmentalism in England was conventional even during the peak decade of environmental protest.

That is not, however, to say that there were no links between uninstitutionalized environmental protesters and ENGOs; Greenpeace, WWF and especially FoE all gave advice and support to environmental protesters at various points (Rootes 2009a, 2009b). But the surge of environmental protest during that decade occurred largely independently of institutionalized NGOs.

The institutionalization of ENGOs did not entail their withdrawal from protest simply because most had never resorted to protest even during their early development. Greenpeace and, to a lesser extent, FoE were the exceptions in an environmental movement that had mostly pursued its various goals by informational activities, lobbying and practical action focused on conservation and/or environmental remediation. The eruption of environmental protest in the 1990s was not so much a recapitulation of an earlier period of mass mobilization as an entirely novel development.

Climate change

In their review of philanthropic funding of environmental conservation, Cracknell *et al.* (2009) identified climate change as a conspicuous blind spot for environmental philanthropy in the UK, even by comparison with the USA. Whilst British ENGOs cannot be accused of being blind to the seriousness of climate change, it is only recently that it has become a leading campaigning priority.

FoE began campaigning on climate change in the late 1980s, initially in response to the nuclear energy industry invoking the issue to justify its own expansion. In 1987, however, FoE commissioned a report on the state of scientific knowledge about climate change, and its publication as *The Heat Trap* in 1988, coinciding with a severe drought, contributed to rising concern with climate change legitimated by Prime Minister Thatcher's speeches later that year (Lamb 1996: 160–2). Greenpeace also played a part, sponsoring *Global Warming: The Greenpeace Report*, published by Oxford University Press in 1990. In general, however, climate change was not in this period a key campaign priority for ENGOs that appear not so much to have introduced the issue of climate change as to have ridden a wave generated by concerned scientists and to which UK government agencies were already responding (Price, 2011). For the most part, even FoE and Greenpeace left campaigning on climate change to the umbrella organization, Climate Action Network, of which both were members.

Although British ENGOs were active in lobbying government and in international summitry on climate change following the Rio Earth Summit (1992) and in the lead-up to the negotiation of the Kyoto Protocol, the major effect of their experience at Rio appears to have been to engage them in the United Nations Conference on Environment and Development (UNCED) process with heightened sensitivity to less-industrialized states' concerns to develop economically in the interests of the well-being of their citizens (Rawcliffe 1998: chapter 8). Thus, in the name of 'sustainable development', a concern with global social justice competed with the interest in environmental sustainability (Rootes 2006), and climate change, though it never disappeared from ENGOs' agendas, was relatively eclipsed as a focus of campaigning. FoE did add a climate change section to its website in 1997 and in 1998 highlighted the impacts of transport upon the atmosphere, but insofar as action was advocated, it was in terms of individual responsibility rather than demonstrative action; a search of the activist newsletter *Schnews* yielded no reports of public protest on climate change before 2000 (Price 2011).

Only after the 2000 UN climate conference (COP6) in The Hague did climate change achieve pre-eminence on the domestic public agendas of British ENGOs. In pre-conference negotiations, the US declared that it would only accept an agreement that included nuclear power in the Kyoto Protocol's Clean Development Mechanism (CDM), by which industrialized countries might receive greenhouse gas emissions credits for selling 'clean', low carbon technologies to developing nations. This prompted long-standing anti-nuclear campaigning NGOs, including Greenpeace and FoE, to protest vigorously at COP6, both against the nuclear option and in favour of an effective emissions reduction regime (www.nirs.org/climate/cop6/cop6home.htm, accessed 25 August 2010). Although they succeeded in changing the US position and in having nuclear energy removed from the CDM, COP6 collapsed without agreement when certain EU states would not agree to concessions designed to keep the US in the Kyoto process.

COP6 marked a turning point. Thereafter, at the international level, the NGOs that had been so effective at COP6 took a closer interest in UN climate negotiations. The fallout in Britain was an increased focus of environmental activism upon climate change.

Rising Tide, which describes itself as 'a grassroots network of independent groups and individuals committed to taking action and building a movement against climate change', was formed out of the ad hoc coalition brought together to mount protests at COP6. Drawing on the activist milieu associated with Earth First!, it has an uncompromisingly anti-capitalist stance but, although it quickly gained namesakes in the US and Australia, its progress in England was modest.[3]

In another response to the failure of COP6, in 2001 the Campaign against Climate Change (CCC) began organizing demonstrations demanding action on climate change. Its profile was raised considerably when its December 2005 marches as part of the International Day of Climate Protest attracted an estimated 10,000 people in London and 400 in Edinburgh. Its collaboration with the Stop Climate Chaos (SCC) coalition in 2006 mobilized much larger numbers and marked a high point of its mobilization efforts.

SCC, which embraces major aid, trade and development as well as environmental NGOs, was launched in October 2005.[4] Its architects hoped to raise the political profile of climate change in the way that Make Poverty History, culminating in a march of almost 250,000 people in Edinburgh on the occasion of the G8 meeting at Gleneagles, had done for fair trade, more and better aid and the reduction of poverty in the global South. SCC's I-Count campaign, which induced almost 200,000 people to pledge to reduce their carbon emissions, culminated on a sunny Saturday in November 2006 in a rally in London's

Trafalgar Square at the confluence of marches organized by CCC and the student group, People and Planet, that attracted perhaps as many as 30,000 people, including a contingent of 1,500 from such strangers to demonstrations as the RSPB. However, whilst there is no doubting the conviction of aid, trade and development NGOs that climate change is a key issue in the struggle against global injustice, the participants in the November 2006 march and rally were, by a wide margin, more closely affiliated with environmental than with aid, trade and development NGOs (Saunders 2008). Moreover, although the CCC/I-Count march and rally was hailed as the biggest environmental demonstration ever seen in Britain, it was tiny by comparison with the Make Poverty History march in Edinburgh on 5 July 2005, the pro-hunting Countryside marches of 2002 and 2004 in London, and the march against the imminent Iraq war in February 2003.

After November 2006, SCC was plagued by differences among the coalition partners, some of whom feared that continued action under the banner of SCC would compromise their brand identities, and for a time SCC disappeared from public view. Subsequent marches and rallies organized by CCC as part of international days of action attracted smaller numbers, and only in December 2009, as part of the build-up to the Copenhagen COP15 summit, did SCC and CCC together attract more than 40,000 people into the streets of London.

New forms of action: climate camp

The new form of action associated with climate change that has perhaps made greatest impact, both upon policy in the UK and by its example internationally, is the Camp for Climate Action (climatecamp.org.uk). Although its roots may be traced to the Earth First! summer gatherings, the more immediate inspiration for its development was the campsite set up at Stirling as a base for activists planning to demonstrate on the occasion of the G8 meeting at Gleneagles in Scotland in July 2005.

A mixture of information exchange, education, training, practical example, prefigurative utopia and protest, the climate camps have been designed not only to facilitate direct action against climate change, 'but also to be an exemplar of sustainable living and a site for alternative education' (Saunders and Price 2009: 117). The first, in 2006 at Drax, the largest coal-burning power station in Europe, was followed in 2007 by a second at Heathrow airport and in 2008 by a third at Kingsnorth, the site of an existing coal-fired power station and a proposed new one. Although the numbers of participants were not large – perhaps 600 in 2006, over 2,000 in 2007 and 2008 – they attracted massive and continuing media attention to the issues upon which they focused – the contributions of coal burning and aviation to carbon emissions – and they highlighted contradictions between the government's rhetorical commitment to action on climate change and its failure to develop policy to mitigate the largest and fastest rising contributors to climate change.

The climate camps have been notable for their openness and tolerance of difference. Many who participated in the discussions at the camps did not participate in the associated protests, and only a minority were involved in direct action. Visitors to the campsites were welcomed, and efforts were made to reach out to the neighbouring communities. The climate camps' model of non-sectarian activism attracted public interest and sympathy, especially after the Kingsnorth camp was subjected to what even Her Majesty's Inspectorate of Constabulary (2009) subsequently recognized to have been inept and oppressive policing. In an attempt to make it more readily accessible to a larger population, the summer 2009 climate camp used Greenwich Park at Blackheath as a base for activist forays into the city of London; policing was unobtrusive, and so the outreach activities of the campers were less obstructed.

Although the climate camps probably deserve most credit for highlighting the burning of fossil fuels to generate electricity and the contribution of aviation to climate change, they were conspicuously assisted by characteristically spectacular protests at power stations, airports and even on the roof of the Houses of Parliament staged by Greenpeace and the campaign group, Plane Stupid. Thus the distinctively new forms of action were conjoined with those of the pre-eminent professionalized protest organization of the previous two decades.

The impact of the rise of climate change agenda on local campaigns

The rise of climate change as the master frame of environmental movement activity had considerable impacts at local level. Campaigns – such as those against airports and waste infrastructure – that had remained frustratingly local and had been difficult to network acquired new salience, and local contention could more easily be represented as part of a global movement. This was true even of anti-roads protests from 2004.

Roads

Although anti-roads protests had achieved iconic status in the mid-1990s, they did so because they became focal points of resistance to an unpopular government. Anti-roads protests arose in reaction against particular road-building projects, were linked by their shared relationship to the Conservative government's 'Roads for Prosperity' programme and gained momentum from that government's obdurate commitment to a policy that was increasingly unpopular even with its own supporters. They were also legacies of the campaign against the Thatcher government's attempts to reform local taxation by replacing property based taxes with a poll tax. The success of that campaign – the most widespread wave of civil disobedience in Britain in the twentieth century – provided inspiration to direct action against roads projects, and encouraged activists to believe that they could win (Rootes 2003b). However, with the Conservative government's abandonment of the road-building programme, and with the election in 1997 of a Labour government that appeared determined not to provoke large-scale environmental protest, environmental activism declined and the focus of the environmental movement shifted to lobbying a broadly sympathetic government.

As the Labour government prioritized public transport rather than road building, the anti-roads movement became an increasingly distant memory, and only when in 2004 the government's 'Future of Transport' White Paper envisaged the resumption of large-scale road and motorway construction did transport campaigners and veterans of the 1990s protests come together to form a new anti-roads campaign network, Road Block (www.roadblock.org.uk, accessed 29 December 2008). Road Block, formed to assist local anti-roads groups to campaign through the planning system, is not a direct action organization, but a separate organization, Road Alert, linked to the Earth First! eco-action network, supports peaceful direct action against road building. However, although anti-roads protests revived and sometimes involved protest camps and other forms of direct action similar to those of the 1990s (Plows 2006), they were neither as numerous nor as well supported as those of the mid-1990s and they attracted little national media attention.

Road Block assisted local anti-roads campaigners to see their local struggles in the context of larger strategic issues such as climate change and energy policy (www.roadblock.org.uk, accessed 29 December 2008), and in 2007 became part of the Campaign for Better Transport (the former Transport 2000), marking a new stage in the reframing of the roads issue into broader policy concerns. The original concerns of anti-roads campaigners with the loss of landscape, wildlife and tranquility were thus incorporated within the newly dominant master frame of climate change. As environmental conflicts had since the mid-1990s moved out of the backyard and on to the global stage, the reframing of roads protests in terms of climate change was perhaps a necessary defensive strategy as much as a reflection of activists' widening horizons.

Waste

Waste and waste disposal facilities have long been objects of concern for local environmental campaigners. Poorly managed sites earned landfill a deserved reputation as a bad neighbour, and proposals for new landfill sites stimulated objections from local residents wherever they were proposed. Objectors were, however, often dismissed as NIMBYs who would have remained oblivious to landfill if it had been sited on somebody else's doorstep, and it was notoriously difficult to develop even the most rudimentary networks of campaigners; at best, CPRE played a linking role in some rural areas. Increasing concerns about climate change, and about the emissions of methane, a more potent greenhouse gas than carbon dioxide, gave campaigners against landfill a new weapon, and during the 1990s policy shifted decisively against landfill. The search was on for more climate-friendly means of waste disposal (Rootes 2009b).

Advocates of waste incineration seized upon increasing concern with climate change to promote the virtues of 'energy from waste' as a green alternative to generating electricity by the combustion of fossil fuels, and for more than a decade anti-incinerator campaigners struggled to develop or maintain an effective national network (ibid.). Then, however, research commissioned by FoE from an independent consultancy (Hogg 2006) concluded that burning waste to generate electricity usually emits at least as much carbon dioxide as does the burning of fossil fuels, and this has enabled anti-incinerator campaigners to more credibly propose alternatives such as recycling and anaerobic digestion as more climate-friendly alternatives. Against this background, and with FoE playing a critical role in securing the coordination and third-party funding (from a philanthropic foundation), a national network of anti-incinerator campaign groups, UK-WIN, was established in 2008 (Rootes 2009b). Climate change has thus provided a universalizing discursive frame that has facilitated the networking of hitherto isolated local anti-incinerator (and anti-landfill) campaigns.

Airports

Campaigns against the expansion of airports in Britain have a long history, but they have typically been campaigns mounted by and on behalf of those people who would be directly affected by increased noise, air pollution and the degradation of their immediate environment. Although some of these campaigns were protracted, they were mostly conducted in relative isolation or even sometimes, as in the London region, in competition with one another. Even in the case of Heathrow, which, as Britain's busiest airport, has greatest national salience, the resistance to successive stages of expansion – mostly recently the construction of a fifth terminal and proposals for a third runway – was based primarily in the communities adjoining the airport or under its flightpaths.

Before 2000, there was no unambiguous national policy concerning airport development, and so there was no clear national target against which local campaigners could combine. To lay the ground for such national policy, protracted consultation preceded the aviation White Paper, 'Future of Air Transport' (2000–2003), which provoked pre-emptive campaigns against the expansion of Heathrow and Stansted airports and in 2000 stimulated the formation of an umbrella organization, AirportWatch, to campaign for a demand management approach to aviation. AirportWatch members and supporters included most of the leading national environmental NGOs, and by 2008 it networked more than 30 local groups campaigning against the expansion of more than 20 airports. However, although AirportWatch reached out to involve MPs and women's groups, among others, it was largely failing in its ambition to build a broader coalition to persuade the government to change its policies until the crescendo of concern about climate change transformed airports policy from a transport issue and a series of local battles into a key site of contention over the fundamentals of environmental strategy.

The crystallizing moment in this process came when in August 2007 the second Camp for Climate Action was held adjacent to Heathrow airport. The week-long Camp, designed to highlight the increasing contribution of aircraft emissions to climate change, attracted much media attention, and succeeded in making links with, and highlighting the plight of, people living in the communities that would be obliterated should the proposed third runway be built.

Since 2007, there has been a significant and perhaps decisive shift in the policy environment that has transformed the battlefield for anti-airport campaigners and that has materially enhanced their prospects of success. Although the pro-airport lobby continues to assert the indispensability of expanded airports to the national economy, the argument has gained traction that an expansion of aviation is inconsistent with the declared aim, now given legislative force in the Climate Change Act 2008, of dramatically reducing the UK's emissions of carbon dioxide and other greenhouse gases. Thus it is the national emergence of the global issue of climate change as the master frame of environmental contention rather than any local efforts of anti-airports campaigners that has made airport expansion into a compelling national issue.[5]

Climate action at local level: innovation and change

The Campaign against Climate Change (CCC) website has, since 2008, listed some 30 local CCC groups; in August 2010, it listed 31 Climate Action groups in England, three in Scotland and a longer list of contacts of other allied individuals and groups (www.campaigncc.org/local.shtml, accessed 22 August 2010). Few of these local groups appear to have established a strong local presence, and they overlap with and are supplemented by a wide variety of other local green and environmental NGO groups.[6]

The Transition Towns network (www.transitionnetwork.org/initiatives, accessed 25 August 2010) has a more impressive local presence, with some 169 'official' local groups in the UK (and another 153 elsewhere, and a further 219 'muller' groups that are not yet official Transition initiatives but are 'mulling it over').[7] With the aims of educating and persuading people about the twin threats of climate change and peak oil, developing greater resilience in communities in the face of those threats, and ultimately developing 'energy descent action plans' to realize less energy-intensive ways of living, it has grown rapidly since its birth in Totnes, Devon in 2006. Practice varies from group to group, but the Transition network is primarily oriented towards practical local action rather than national policy change (Bailey *et al.* 2010). It is not a protest movement, and its links with the wider environmental movement are those of shared concern and overlapping individual affiliations rather than common collective action. Nevertheless, some local Transition groups are very active and unabashed about political entanglements, and several advertised their presence among the participants in the December 2009 climate march in London.

Also focused upon encouraging practical action to mitigate climate change, but more political in the sense that it also demands government action and 'a universal and equitable framework' for greenhouse gas emissions reduction, is the network of Carbon Rationing Action Groups (CRAGs). Working at community level, CRAGs is a network of local grassroots groups dedicated to reducing their own carbon footprints and those of their communities by setting its members carbon allowances that reduce year-on-year. It aims to make people aware of their personal carbon footprints and of means of reducing them, to argue for the adoption of similar schemes at national and international levels, and to build solidarity among the growing community of carbon conscious people and share practical knowledge and experience.

Inspired by the first national climate march, the first CRAG was established in the West Midlands in December 2005, and in August 2010 the CRAGs website listed 21 active CRAGs in the UK, 11 in process of formation and six that had become dormant. Each CRAG is an autonomous entity able to adopt its own rules. The CRAG 'network' has no central office, no staff, no funding, no constitution and no links with any political party or commercial organization. It makes no press releases but CRAGs use the website 'to cooperate and coordinate, share help and information, and provide an umbrella for new groups looking to follow the CRAG model' (www.carbonrationing.org.uk, accessed 25 August 2010).

Another promoter of community based action on climate change is the Climate Outreach and Information Network (COIN), a charity formed in 2004 to directly engage the public about climate change (www.coinet.org.uk, accessed 25 August 2010). Based in Oxford, it has facilitated the formation of Climate Action Groups (CAGs) in Reading, Sheffield and the London borough of Camden.

A more professionalized approach to local action on climate change is promoted by the Greening Campaign, which seeks to 'green the country community by community'. Supported by local authorities and the South East of England Development Agency amongst others, the Greening Campaign aims to make fighting climate change visible in communities by linking individuals, groups, councils, schools and government in a joint programme of exemplary practical action. Householders are encouraged to take a branded information card, listing ways to save energy at home and at work, and to give an undertaking to put into action a set number of these ideas and display the card in a front window. The success of this first stage of the campaign is then evaluated by a combination of public surveys and card counts. From the information thus collected, the emissions reduction achieved by the community can be estimated and reported.

By 2010, Greening Campaign forums had been established in London and 14 mostly southern English counties. Started in Hampshire in 2007, the campaign claims over 180 active local groups, with the 112 local 'subforums' listed on its website concentrated in Hampshire, nearby West Sussex and Nottinghamshire (www.greening-campaign.co.uk, accessed 25 August 2010).

The rise of climate change as the pre-eminent environmental issue has, then, both changed the prospects of existing local campaigns by making them easier to network and by integrating them into the new dominant discourse of the environmental movement, and it has stimulated the development of new groups. What is striking, however, is that these new groups are for the most part oriented towards practical action rather than contentious politics; these are not so much new forms of political participation as community based alternatives to political action. This pattern is, in part, mirrored at national level.

New issue, old politics?

The predicament of ENGOs that attempt to mobilize the public on climate change is illustrated by the experience of FoE's Big Ask campaign (www.foe.co.uk/campaigns/climate/news/big_ask_history_15798.html, accessed 8 January 2009). Launched in May 2005 (and later endorsed by SCC), the campaign was in support of a Bill, drafted in outline by FoE and sent to Parliament by a cross-party group of MPs, which required government to ensure reductions in emissions of carbon dioxide of 3 per cent year-on-year, thereby entailing an 80 per cent cut by 2050.

By the end of 2005, over 300 of the 646 MPs had signed the Early Day Motion (EDM 178) requesting the government to adopt the Climate Change Bill and, by October 2006, this had grown to 412. In November 2006, the government announced that a Climate Change Bill would be included in its legislative programme for the coming parliamentary year, and, in March 2007, published a draft Bill envisaging a 60 per cent reduction in emissions by 2050. In response to sustained lobbying, this Bill was strengthened by the inclusion of annual emissions reductions targets and five-year carbon budgets, and by the raising of the target for carbon emissions reductions from 60 per cent to 80 per cent by 2050. At the last moment, in response to pressure from the public and MPs, the government widened the scope of the Bill to include emissions from aviation and shipping.

In November 2008, the Climate Change Act came into force, making the UK the first nation to adopt legally binding targets for reductions in carbon emissions. The outcome was a triumph for FoE's campaign: the Act as passed included all three of its major demands. FoE estimates that nearly 200,000 people contacted their MPs – by letter, electronically or in person – as part of the campaign, many as part of local group actions. Yet although the campaign was lauded as an outstanding demonstration of people power, it is in no way to diminish its importance to observe that the speed with which MPs signed up to the Bill, and the lack of serious resistance on the part of the government, suggests that FoE was pushing at a door that was already at least half open. When the campaign was launched, three-quarters of the British public agreed that government should take more action on climate change, all three major political parties had already identified climate change as the biggest threat facing Britain and all advocated ambitious targets for cutting carbon dioxide emissions. FoE's complaint was that, in spite of such proclamations, substantial progress on reducing carbon emissions remained elusive. Thus the major achievement of the Big Ask campaign was not to put climate change on the political agenda, for it was already there, but to maintain the pressure and to accelerate the momentum towards binding emissions reduction targets, and, crucially, to give such targets the force of law. The campaign thus appears to have been a striking example of orchestrated conventional lobbying, by persuading MPs to put pressure on government to take effective action in pursuit of its own declared policy ambitions. Neither in its tactics nor in its aims did it much resemble the great social movement mobilizations of the past.

Ironically, just as the Climate Change Act was passed, the Director of Green Alliance, Stephen Hale, was putting the finishing touches to a pamphlet lamenting the failure of ENGOs' efforts to address climate change and implicitly highlighting the shortcomings of the Big Ask.

> Politicians ... frequently call publicly and privately for more political space for action, and 'a Make Poverty History' on climate change. But the Make Poverty History model is not the right one for climate change. That campaign, though it involved phenomenally large numbers of people, was short-lived and wholly focused on advocacy ...
>
> Climate change requires sustained political mobilization, to secure the lasting action we need. It is also a much more diffuse and socially embedded problem than international development. A commitment to action on climate change may mean changing your choice of transport, holidays, shopping and the way you run your home too. We will need both a much higher degree of political mobilization and a greater degree of personal action in order to succeed.
>
> (Hale 2008: 17)

But climate change is not only a 'diffuse and socially embedded problem'; it is for the most part a slow motion catastrophe that provides few conveniently manageable targets about which public mobilization might readily be achieved.[8] Moreover, for ENGOs, climate change may be crucially important, but it is not the only game in town, and if politicians and the public have generally accepted the significance of climate change, they have been much less ready to appreciate the significance of biodiversity or of persistent ground level air pollution.

For all these reasons, public mobilizations may be most readily achievable around what may be represented as the particular, local tokens of the universal problem, whether they are campaigns against roads, airports or waste infrastructure.

The concern with climate change has made energy infrastructure issues more central in Britain than at any time since the abandonment of the nuclear power programme in the early 1980s. Climate change has, in particular, made the burning of coal to generate electricity unprecedentedly problematic. Greenpeace has mounted spectacular if brief occupations of several coal-fired power stations, and the Camps for Climate Change Action have targeted existing and proposed new coal-fired power stations. A rash of applications for new or extended opencast coalmines has been locally contentious and has encountered opposition, sometimes successful, from CPRE. Thus coal based energy schemes have become increasingly contested. The Labour government clearly registered this discontent and the inconsistencies between its carbon reduction strategy and any new investment in coal without associated carbon capture and storage (CCS); in the absence of proven CCS technology, it postponed any decision on new coal-fired power stations, and this moratorium has been continued by its successor.

If climate change has given urgency and success to new campaigns against old energy technologies, the increasingly desperate search for alternatives has exposed new divisions within the environmental movement. In the interests of energy security as well as mitigating climate change, the government has in principle approved a new generation of privately financed nuclear power stations, but this has been strongly opposed by the Sustainable Development Commission as well as ENGOs such as Greenpeace and FoE on the grounds that nuclear will be an expensive distraction from investment in energy efficiency and renewables. However, in the absence of firm proposals for particular sites there has been nothing substantial for anti-nuclear critics to mobilize against. Moreover, the environmental movement appears split over the issue, a number of prominent environmentalists taking the view that the fight against climate change is now so urgent that nuclear power, as a low carbon source of electricity, is preferable to continued burning of fossil fuels. Because it is expected that new nuclear facilities will be sited adjacent to the existing power stations they would replace, little resistance is expected from local communities long used to living with the nuclear industry and dependent upon it for employment.

ENGOs have for many years seen massively increased investment in renewable energy technologies as a principal weapon in the war against climate change. However, although the exploitation of Britain's abundant wind resources is strongly advocated by FoE, there has been opposition from many regional branches of the CPRE, some wildlife groups and numerous local campaign groups to many proposed windfarms, usually because of concern about their impact on the landscape and on bird life, and sometimes about their impacts on the health and well-being of their neighbours. Exploitation of tidal power by the construction of a barrage across the Bristol Channel was strongly opposed by bird protection organizations as well as those who feared its impact on the landscape, and was ultimately rejected by government on environmental grounds.

In sum, although the threat of catastrophic climate change has given unprecedented prominence to environmental issues, it has brought as many problems as advantages to environmental movement activists.

Climate change provides local environmental campaigners with a new master frame that provides effective bridging not merely between the local and the national but between the local and the global (Rootes 2005, 2006), but climate change itself has not so far sustained widespread local campaigns in Britain, and even the national campaign has involved only limited direct mobilization of the public in any but politically conventional ways. Because climate change is a universal issue, and because it is difficult convincingly to attribute particular local impacts wholly or mainly to climate change, it presents few promising targets for protest action. As a result, local action on climate change more often takes the form of support action for the campaigns of national ENGOs, lobbying and persuasion to get local councils and businesses to adopt climate-friendly policies, or practical energy-saving projects. The call in December 2008 by the then Secretary of State for Energy and Climate Change, Ed Miliband, for a national popular mobilization on climate change comparable with that of Make Poverty History failed to elicit any positive response.

ENGOs, protest and participation

The emergence of climate change as a master frame for the environmental movement has raised new dilemmas for environmental NGOs. Government and opposition politicians in Britain have overwhelmingly accepted the seriousness of the issue, and this has limited the scope for ENGOs to mobilize around it.

The sustained rise in the numbers of members and/or supporters of environmental organizations has been seen as an indicator of and a vehicle for the development of a participatory civil society that might compensate for the decline in membership of political parties and fluctuating turnout in elections. Yet few environmental organizations offer their members much opportunity for participation in their internal decision making or even their actions. In recent years several ENGOs have given up even the pretence of being membership organizations and instead now count not their 'members' but their 'supporting donors' or 'financial supporters'. Such professionalized organizations are less concerned with mobilizing their supporters than with tapping their financial resources. If this has long been true of 'service providing' nature conservation organizations, it is increasingly true of campaigning or 'advocacy' organizations as well.

Greenpeace established the model of the professionalized protest organization, a formally organized and tightly controlled operation in which an international board licensed national or regional branches that in turn licensed local groups of supporters who are obliged to provide financial support for the parent organization but have no autonomy to conduct local campaigns using the Greenpeace name. Its high profile direct actions are undertaken by trained protesters rather than amateur enthusiasts and rely for their impact not upon the mobilization of large numbers but the mediated impact of the spectacular actions of a few. Greenpeace was long viewed as an anomaly within the environmental movement, but its model is increasingly respected as ENGOs are exercised about the efficacy and efficiency of their actions.

The twin drivers of these concerns are the increasingly alarming evidence of environmental degradation and the looming threat of runaway climate change on the one hand, and the limited and often precarious resources of ENGOs on the other. Mobilizing large numbers of people for well-organized public protest is a major logistical feat that requires the investment of large amounts of scarce resources, and so it is not surprising that many ENGOs calculate that greater impact may be achieved at less cost either by lobbying or directly negotiating with governments or corporations or, in the case of Greenpeace and its imitators, by staging small but spectacular actions designed to have effects via the media attention they attract. The trend to professionalism reflects the difficulties that resource-constrained ENGOs face in combining policy input/lobbying with grassroots organizing; especially when opportunities for the former appear relatively abundant, it is no surprise that few should devote resources to the latter.

The few that do attempt to mobilize the public do so for essentially ideological reasons. Thus FoE continues to nurture local groups, to extend them great autonomy in campaigning and to overrepresent them in its governing structure, not out of any consideration of campaigning efficacy but because grassroots action has become central to FoE's identity. At national as at international and local levels, FoE pays some price in terms of efficiency (Doherty 2006) but the pay-off is in the form of its legitimacy, internally and within the wider movement, and its unusual ability to mount or lead campaigns that entail at least some public involvement (as, for example, with its 'Big Ask' campaign).

Nevertheless, FoE is not unlike other British ENGOs in that it has never relied heavily upon mass demonstrations. When there are large-scale environmental demonstrations such as those organized by the Campaign against Climate Change, FoE members are conspicuously present with their flags, banners and placards, and they sometimes act as marshals, but they, like those of the Green Party, tend to 'show the flag' at such events rather than devoting any high proportion of their resources to organizing them. Perhaps because opportunities for access to mainstream administrative and political circles have only rarely and briefly been closed to environmental groups, they have developed habits of participation/lobbying rather than of protest wholly external to the political system.

The problem is not, however, simply that the professionalization of ENGOs entails the demobilization of environmental protest. Indeed, as I observed above, the professionalization and institutionalization of environmental movement organizations that occurred during the late 1980s and early 1990s was not accompanied by a monotonic decline in the numbers of reported environmental protest events, although there did appear to be a decline in the numbers of participants in environmental protests (Rootes 2003a).[9]

Prospect: towards convergence?

How should ENGOs conduct themselves at a time when environmental issues have moved to an unprecedentedly central position on the political agenda? There are ironies in the present situation. Opportunities of access to lobby and potentially to influence policy formation have seldom been greater, but, especially when viewed from the perspective of the enormity of the environmental challenges confronting us, the yield in terms of policy output and effective government action has so far been disappointing. Democratically elected governments worry that effective action on climate change will incur costs for which the public is unprepared, which led Labour government ministers to urge ENGOs to mobilize the public to demand the policies that governments know they must implement. Yet governments baulk at providing ENGOs with the resources necessary to undertake any such mass mobilization.

Moreover, as climate change and energy policy have moved to positions of prominence, so they have drawn into the policy process all kinds of highly organized and well-resourced pressure groups and vested interests with which ENGOs are ill resourced to compete. To the extent that governments and corporations are frustrated by the inability or unwillingness of ENGOs to respond to their demands for input quickly or at all, they are likely to divert their attentions to those interests that are sufficiently well resourced to respond in the manner and on the timescale that governments and corporations expect. ENGOs may, as a result, find themselves increasingly marginalized and may come to ask themselves whether continued dialogue with governments makes best use of their limited resources, especially when governments and corporations profess their good intentions but seem insufficiently willing to take the action necessary to reduce carbon emissions quickly, drastically and permanently.

There are indications that frustrations with governments are leading some ENGOs to choose outsider strategies that leave them free to ask the more radical questions that governments are unwilling to consider. Thus FoE, no doubt partly influenced by its partners in FoE International, increasingly focused upon climate change as an issue of social justice, and upon the elephant in the room – capitalism. That focus bridges the gap between FoE and more radical environmental groupings such as Rising Tide, the climate camps and 'disorganizations'/ informal networks such as Earth First! and that raises the possibility of an increase in grassroots direct action networked nationally and internationally by major ENGOs.

As the December 2009 London march demonstrated, even traditionally non-activist conservation NGOs such as the Wildlife Trusts as well as the RSPB have been drawn into mass demonstrations demanding action on climate change; banners and placards proclaimed the presence of members or representatives of a broad spectrum of groups, from Buglife to the Woodland Trust, many of which had never previously been seen at a street demonstration. Despite attracting over 40,000 participants, that colourful and noisy demonstration, however, was scarcely a highly contentious protest: the organizers even hired a security company to provide marshals, consigning the police to the role of onlookers who were at no point required to intervene. Especially in light of the scant media attention received by this, the largest environmental demonstration ever seen in Britain, it appears to have been more a ritual to reaffirm the solidarity of the participants than an effective political intervention.

Nor are the rise of the Transition Towns movement and the resurrection or mere persistence of civic amenity societies[10] unambiguous indicators of a revival of political participation from below. Local groups are notoriously unstable and dependent upon the energies and commitment of very small groups of people, often of a single individual. Greenpeace local support groups and FoE local groups come and go, and local amenity societies emerge, briefly flourish as they mobilize against particular intrusions upon the community, and gradually wither as the particular threat fades. Although the rapid spread of the Transitions movement demonstrates that the idea of relocalization has traction at a time of economic and energy insecurity, Transition Towns groups, once established, often struggle to make an impact and are driven by the variety of interests of the people they attract.

The emergence and re-emergence of such groups is testimony to the persistence of an aspiration to community participation, but their travails testify to the difficulty of achieving or sustaining it. The habit of active participation has withered through neglect. Homes have become more comfortable, traditional public spaces such as the pub are in steep decline and people are ever more busily engaged in privatized and individualized pursuits. The result is that although people may be contacted quickly and efficiently by means of electronic social networking media, even when they are moved to participate, they often lack the social and organizational skills to sustain community organization. Very often the social benefits of participation are set off against the organizational requirements of decision making and the carrying out of agreed tasks.

Where there are no moral sanctions for non-performance, every collective achievement is a minor miracle, but usually one too rarely performed for it to have much exemplary value. People, we are told, 'want to be told what to do' rather than themselves participate in deliberation, but they then do not feel themselves bound by any collective decision. Perhaps we should, with Benjamin Barber (1971), ask why we should *all* be condemned to wear the crown of thorns when we can elect others to do it for us. If that sounds like a backhanded justification for representative politics, it is not one that need leave NGOs out in the cold. Arguably, NGOs are more accountable than political representatives elected for a term of years because the supporters of the former, unlike those of the latter, can turn off the tap or increase the flow of funds and support at any time. The problem, of course, is that climate change is a problem of such magnitude that addressing it will require not sporadic surges of public concern but sustained commitment over decades to mitigate a problem that is, for the moment, largely invisible, and whose worst consequences are temporally and/or geographically remote.

Campaigning against climate change entails campaigning *for* carbon reductions and for legislative and executive action to enforce emissions reductions. There is, however, nothing especially unusual about popular mobilizations that demand legislative, executive or judicial action. Social movements typically have both positive and negative moments. Even anti-war movements, which are summoned into existence to protest against the conduct of particular wars, are also movements for peace and for an ordering of society in which conflict is subdued by realization of our common humanity. What is perhaps distinctive about the forms of action associated in Britain with the mitigation of climate change is the relatively restricted opportunities the issue has provided for protest compared with those it has opened for positive campaigning and practical action. It is a moot point whether even the recent modest and sporadic public mobilization can be maintained or even whether, at a time of continuing economic insecurity when the priority of government is to achieve a sustained contraction of the state, local grassroots initiatives will continue to develop.

Notes

1 Many of the developments discussed here have taken place mainly or, in some cases, exclusively, in England. In particular, some ENGOs are exclusive to one or sometimes two of England, Scotland and Wales, but many of the larger processes have not respected political boundaries, and since there is not space here to detail all the distinctions, the term 'Britain' is used throughout.

2 I am grateful to Stephan Price for commenting on an earlier draft. Some passages of this chapter are elaborated in Rootes (2012).
3 In 2009 its website listed 14 local groups but of these only those in London, Bristol, Norwich and Reading appeared to be even moderately active (http://risingtide.org.uk/, accessed 3 January 2009); in mid-2010 the number had shrunk to 12 in England and one in Scotland (http://risingtide.org.uk/, accessed 22 August 2010) and the listed Reading group appeared no longer to be active (personal communication, S. Hendry, 18 August 2010).
4 At its launch, it counted 17 members, including the main aid and development charities – Oxfam, Christian Aid, CAFOD and Tearfund – as well as the ENGOs, Friends of the Earth, Greenpeace, Network for Social Change, Oxfam, People and Planet, the Royal Society for the Protection of Birds, the World Wildlife Fund, the Wildlife Trusts, the student organization People and Planet and the Women's Institute.
5 The Brown Labour government in 2009 decided to approve the construction of a third runway at Heathrow, but the Conservatives and Liberal Democrats made it a key issue in their campaigns in marginal seats in west London, and soon after forming a government following the election of 6 May 2010, they announced the abandonment of Heathrow's third runway and a freeze on airport expansion in the greater London area.
6 In the 2008 national climate march, organized by CCC without the SCC umbrella, more than 50 groups participated with identifying banners or placards (observations by G. Swain and C. Rootes).
7 The criteria for acceptance as a Transition Initiative are quite relaxed, and it is not clear how well embedded all such initiatives are in the member communities. While some, including Totnes, Glastonbury and Leicester, appear well organized and have made significant inputs into local planning processes, others appear to operate as small local social networks, and some 'official' Transition initiatives are little more than information networks. In July 2008, Somerset County Council voted to become the UK's first Transition local authority, but in some other cases relations with local government remain tentative at best, especially where local government gives highest priority to economic development.
8 Cf. the obstacles to convincing grant-givers of the value of funding action on climate change (Cracknell et al. 2009: 15–16).
9 Although we do not have systematic data for the years since 1998, it is probable that both the number of nationally reported protest events and the numbers of people actively participating in environmental protests declined thereafter, at least until the rise of climate protests from 2006. Yet if the years 1992–96 appear extraordinary for the numbers of environmental protests, they do not appear to have been quite so remarkable for the numbers of people involved in environmental protest: most of the reported protests in that decade were small, and it is likely that most that went unreported were smaller still. The environmental direct action of the 1990s directly involved no more than a few thousand activists in aggregate. Although there was undoubtedly a larger number of camp followers and sympathizers, these became progressively harder to distinguish from apolitical participants in the party scene and rave culture (Rootes 2003a, 2003b).
10 The Civic Society, which networked amenity societies in England, was declared insolvent and dissolved in 2009, but a new organization, Civic Voice, was swiftly formed.

5 The professionalization of the EU's civil society
A conceptual framework

Sabine Saurugger[1]

Introduction

Numerous studies conducted on non-state actors in the European Union have led to an in-depth and detailed understanding of day-to-day politics and policy processes taking place in Brussels (for an overview see Beyers *et al.* 2008b). The recent accent in political and academic work on the EU's legitimacy deficit has led to new puzzles for research in this area. This development mirrors a turn in comparative political studies more generally where one of the main questions is whether the involvement of non-state actors improves the democratic character of a political system or hinders its development.

From the point of view of European institutions, linking 'civil society organizations' to EU decision-making procedures is an attempt to bring citizens closer to the Union.[2] Since 'civil society organizations' claim an associative non-profit status they are almost automatically identified with the development of a 'European public space'. As Zimmer and Freise (2008: 39) point out, EU documents advance two main arguments in favor of civil society participation. The first argument is closely linked to output legitimacy, in short, efficiency in policy making. The second argument focuses on input legitimacy as civil society organizations offer the opportunity to mobilize the public and foster citizen engagement. Yet, taking ideals as the sole factor underlying this process runs the risk of overlooking other imperatives driving the participation of the 'European civil society' in the decision-making processes. Empirically as well as theoretically both arguments are questionable because they fail to address the key question of whom civil society organizations actually represent.

Accordingly we should question the automatic link that is drawn between civil society representation and democracy. The better informed and organized a group, the greater its chances of access to the European institutions. Expertise and perceived efficiency are central access goods for civil society. However, this may lead to an expertise–representation gap (March and Olsen 1998). Better structured and organized groups may be able to offer the necessary expertise, but members may feel less represented. In other words, there is a permanent tension between the efficiency of civil society organizations as effective representative vehicles and the socializing role of civil society organizations, providing organizational infrastructure for civic engagement and civic activity (Zimmer and Freise 2008: 26).

However, we still lack a systematic conceptualization of these phenomena, most notably the professionalization of the organized civil society.[3] The aim of this chapter is to analyze the literature that addresses these questions – approaches on party politics, social movements, associations and interest groups, as well as research on social capital – to draw lessons for the study of the transformation of civil society organizations' structures in the EU. The chapter aims to systematically isolate the main factors explaining the professionalization of non-state actors. Conceptual clarification is required before we can meaningfully address this question empirically. The aim is to develop a map that provides coherence to the empirical inquiry into civil society organizations' internal structures and roles.

This chapter will analyze a number of road maps developed in different subfields of collective action research. While the social capital literature argues that civil society socializes citizens and leads them to participate more effectively in decision making processes, the empirical evidence from the party politics and social movement literatures point in different directions. Although distinct, these literatures combined share a common thread – i.e. the institutionalization and professionalization of civil society is ongoing. This phenomenon seems to begin in democratic systems in tandem with mass participation. The European Union is no exception in this respect.[4]

Below we discuss the main arguments in the social capital, party politics, social movement and interest group literatures with regard to the institutionalization and professionalization of groups. The chapter presents an attempt to bridge these literatures discussing the most significant and relevant components for the research agenda on professionalized 'organized civil society' and links them to a conceptual framework that aims to facilitate future empirical investigation.

Three conceptual approaches

The professionalization of collective action in politics is neither a new phenomenon nor a new research area. From the moment a truly political activity appeared, scholars started to be interested in political staff as a research object and to look for political explanations. The work in political parties at the beginning of the twentieth century can be considered to be the starting point to systematically study the professionalization of political representation. The social movement literature used the professionalization term in the 1980s, insisting that this transformation could help social movements represent their claims in a more forceful way, become full-fledged members of political systems and move from outsiders to insiders. This idea was further developed in research on associations and interest groups, contributing to opening up the black box of groups and attempting to link internal logics of membership to external logics of influence. Finally, while the initial argument in social capital research was based on the Tocquevillian idea that organized groups would allow for socialization of citizens, recent studies have shown empirically the limits of this assumption (Warren 2001).

We begin with a discussion of the expected benefits of civil society for the creation of a politicized and value based citizenship – this assumption is not very far from the official discourse of EU institutions on civil society as remedy to the alleged legitimacy deficit. We then present the basic assumptions from the party politics literature on the nearly teleological movement found in every organization toward professionalization. Finally, we discuss the social movement and interest group literatures contradicting the hopes raised in the social capital work for citizen participation and socialization beyond elections.

Social capital and a professionalized civil society

Social capital approaches, as heterogeneous as they may be, agree that the existence of social capital, that is individual and/or collective capacities in a social space, are fostered through participation in groups and associations. With the exception of Bourdieu, whose social capital approach is linked to capacities of individuals, the analysis of social capital insists on the importance of associational involvement and the participatory behavior of citizens (Putnam 2000). In this sense, social capital approaches are Tocquevillian: associations are both 'schools for democracy' and collective goods producers. In the EU context, this hypothesis is intuitively appealing, leading to the argument that individuals participating in internal structures of groups become socialized and develop trust and identification with EU and European institutions. Associations, in this view, help generate social capital. The internal and external functions of associational membership facilitate political socialization and democratic efficiency or output legitimacy. However, as Hooghe (2008: 569–70) underlines:

> The finding of a positive relation between associational membership and political efficiency since then has been repeated quite routinely, however, without any firm conclusions on the matter of causality.... Why would associations have more powerful effects than, for example schools, families, friends or work environments?

Three main arguments can be formulated against the social capital hypothesis in contemporary and EU politics. The first counter-hypothesis refers to staff domination of groups. Groups in the EU are staff dominated and 'make little or no effort to educate their supporters about the need for engagement with EU decision makers' (Maloney and van Deth 2008: 7; also Warleigh 2001; Saurugger 2006). Here it seems that precisely the professionalization and bureaucratization of the groups diminishes their capacity for social capital production. In addition to this limitation, there is a second idea referring to self-selection of members or participants: only those who are already deeply convinced of the necessity to meet and cooperate in group structures in order to make their voice heard will join (Hooghe 2008). Finally, many groups have mutated into protest business-type organizations that aim to influence policy making without the active assistance of their members beyond mobilizing their checkbooks (Maloney 2008: 313). In a survey, Jordan and Maloney found that over 70 percent of the members of the British section of both Friends of the Earth and Amnesty International said that the opportunities for active involvement was not 'important' or 'played no role whatsoever' in their decision to join (Jordan and Maloney 1997).

Although EU policy makers aim to bring citizens closer to decision-making processes via Europe-wide participatory democracy based on associations, this appears to meet with very limited interest from the concerned actors – i.e. associations and citizens. Interestingly, the social capital building idea present in the official EU discourses is not far from the neofunctionalist dream arguing that loyalties will be partly transferred from the national to the European level. Formulated differently, the problem with the idea of groups as generators of social capital is the groups' inherent tendency to professionalization.

Party politics and the professional structuring of political spaces

As noted above, the phenomenon of the professionalization of representation has a long history. According to Weber (1963: 109–10), the appearance of 'a new sort of professional politicians' is correlative of the development of the modern state. The monarchy finally managed to expropriate the aristocracy of these means of domination and to assure itself the monopoly of legitimate physical violence. The centralization by the monarchy of the means of political domination as attributes of state power is linked to the disappearance of a type of organization in which all the managerial functions of society were simultaneously exercised by the same individuals. Their replacement leads to the bureaucratic state in which the functions are specialized and exercised by employees. Cut off from the means of management and engaged in a more and more specialized activity, politicians are increasingly obliged to make a living out of their activities, to live not only 'for' politics but also 'on' politics and to become professional politicians. The appearance of professionals as politicians also implies the appearance of competition for the conquest and the exercise of political power.

Less concerned with the state as such, Ostrogorski ([1912] 1993) focused more specifically on leaders of local party machines. According to Ostrogorski, professionalization leads to a distinction between professionals and laypeople and the development of new attitudes, beliefs, references and career interest.[5] Michels ([1914] 1959) presents similar arguments. Work division had created specialization insofar as political actors had to develop specific competencies (social and communications skills). Laypeople in comparison are considered incompetent which legitimates in return the competence of political actors. Every party is destined to transform and to pass from an initial phase in which the organization is entirely dedicated to the realization of its cause, to a later phase in which the growth of the party's size, its bureaucratization, the apathy of its supporters after their participatory enthusiasm and the leaders interest in preserving their own power, thus transform the party into an organization in which the real end is organizational survival.

Comparisons between firms and political parties can be drawn. Parties also attempt to 'brand' their products in the same way as companies try to monopolize the clientele and dominate the market. The political principles, doctrines and programmes are the brand names that allow the professional politician to distance herself from competition, to establish and manipulate a clientele and to secure a dominant position in the competitive fight for political power (Schumpeter 1942). This is linked to the principle of political representation: the incapacity of the masses to manage their own interests makes the existence of professionals necessary. However, in the context of this it is crucial to question the relationship between the represented and the representatives. Does the professionalization of civil society organizations deliver more efficient policy making?

Both Panebianco (1988) and Katz and Mair (1995) see in the transformation of parties neither the end of democracy nor the failure of political parties. However, Panebianco and Katz and Mair draw different conclusions. While Panebianco's work is deeply rooted in a sociological institutionalist or sociology of organizations approach, offering precise distinctions that can be used in research on the professionalization of civil society, Katz and Mair concentrate more on the influence of the political environment and the internal and external party structures in their theoretical model of the cartel-party.

From an organizational sociology perspective, organizations in general, and parties in particular, require a division of labor for coordination between different offices and specialization in relations with the external environment (Panebianco 1988). Insisting that parties are organizations that tend both to adapt and to transform their environment in accordance with their own needs, Panebianco's analysis helps us understand the contemporary situation that confronts civil society organizations in the European realm. Civil society organizations are both transforming their organizational structures and participating in the creation of structures that trigger transformation.

Similarly, according to Panebianco's (1988: 18–30) distinction, civil society organizations would be caught between a 'system of solidarity' and a 'system of interest', leading in the first case to the category of 'believers' and in the second to 'careerists'. Believers are activists whose participation depends primarily on collective incentives of identity. Careerists' participation depends primarily on selective, material or status oriented incentives. This differentiation should be seen as a continuum not as opposite poles. Organizational maturity – i.e. party institutionalization – sees participation decline, leading to the passage from a social movement type of participation (referring to a system of solidarity) to a professional type of participation.

While the distinction between careerists and believers can be heuristically useful if understood as a continuum, this dichotomy, however, does not allow for the development of a more nuanced understanding of the professionalization process of organizations. More precisely, it is possible that 'careerists' and 'believers' are roles that the same individual may play at different times.

Another distinction is offered by differentiating between the notions of bureaucratization and professionalization. The distinction between professionals and bureaucrats appears to be clear-cut. While they both require specialized knowledge, the professionals' training takes generally longer than that of bureaucrats. The control systems to which both professionals and bureaucrats are submitted are different: while the bureaucrats' control system is hierarchy, the professionals' is peer review (Abbott 1988). Heuristically, however, the concept of roles has greater explanatory power. According to Panebianco party personnel play different roles. To structure this nuanced approach, he offers a sevenfold classification: managers (or political entrepreneurs), notables, representative bureaucrats, executive bureaucrats, staff professionals, hidden professionals, semi-professionals.

However, the central question is whether it is useful to look for clues in the party politics literature when analyzing the transformation of 'civil society organizations'. The main difference between civil society organization and political parties is the latter's main *raison d'être* is competing for political office.[6] Interest groups or 'civil society organizations' represent interests (advocacy) or operate on the ground (service providers) and do not engage in electoral campaigns in pursuit of political office.

Still, the lesson drawing exercise can be useful if one concedes that both collective actors share the common goal to be representatives of citizens, one through elections, the other through membership. Hence, taking stock of developments in party politics helps us to conceptualize the transformation of organized civil society.

Social movements and interest groups

A number of studies on 'new social movements', associations and interest groups have addressed similar questions as those tackled in the party politics literature. Meyer and Tarrow (1998) underline in their study on social movements that professionalization and institutionalization may be changing the major vehicle of contentious claims – the social movements – into an instrument within the realm of conventional politics. Here, references to classical social movement literature offer a certain amount of guidance in professionalization studies of the EU's civil society organizations (ibid.; Imig and Tarrow 2001).

Zald and McCarthy ([1987] 1994b: 375) define professionalized associations – or non-state actors more generally – as entities characterized by (a) a leadership that devotes full time to the association with a large proportion of resources originating outside the constituency the group claims to represent, (b) a very small or non-existent membership base or chapter membership where membership implies little more than allowing the use of one's name upon membership rolls, (c) an attempt to represent or to speak in the name of a potential constituency and (d) attempts to influence policy toward that same constituency.

The actors stop putting forward utopian visions as demands or calling for comprehensive reforms in the ways political decisions are made: i.e. bringing 'participatory democracy', 'power to the people' or 'grassroots democracy'. These professionalized social movements are less interested in changing the rules of institutional politics than in exercising greater influence within it – they wish to represent their interests.

This phenomenon, however, leads to a reorganization of organizational structures. Increasingly, core activists may see organizational involvement as a potential or actual career option. Activists may move from movement to movement for both political action and employment. Professionalization in this context is also about drawing boundaries between accredited persons and others (Moore 1996).

The social movement literature also looks at the political consequences of professionalization. Although the fuzzy boundaries between professional activists and their constituencies may support the ethos of democracy, they may also undermine the prospects of sustained and effective mobilization (see March and Olsen 1998). Ironically, a movement organization concerned with affecting democratic reforms in the polity may be most effective by abandoning certain democratic and amateurish political practices (see also Zald and McCarthy [1987] 1994a).

Different studies on the professionalization of social movements show that this process must be understood as a larger phenomenon than solely the bureaucratization of the group. Linked to the formula of the network, professionalization may also mean the establishment of different networks at different times. They have greater discretionary resources, enjoy easier access to the media and have cheaper and faster geographic mobility and cultural interaction. These features seemed to have made permanent, centralized and bureaucratic organizations less important than they once were in attempts to advance effective challenges to elites or authorities (Kriesi and Koopmans 1995).

These network structures are managed by professionals; a long experience in organizing events, demonstrations or connections to the media are required in order to gain access to the highest positions. In the 1990s, the social movement literature transferred their interest from informal movements on to well-structured and transnational non-state actors, commonly called NGOs. In this context studies on humanitarian aid (Siméant and Dauvin 2002; Siméant 2005) argue that the growing competition between NGOs encourages them to turn global in order to adapt and expand their abilities to obtain financial and human resources. In the European Union realm, the internationalization of NGOs began in the 1980s and was hastened by the founding of the European Commission Humanitarian Office (ECHO) as well as the transfer of important financial means from the World Bank and the International Monetary Fund toward humanitarian NGOs. This led to a situation where the competition for obtaining these funds increased, which led to a rather sudden rationalization of the sector. This rationalization entailed the professionalization of NGOs and the adaptation of the internationalized agency model perceived as capable of acting on a large scale (Siméant 2005: 855).

Similarly, studies on associations question the transformation of internal organizational structures.[7] Skocpol's (2003) study starts from the assumption that Americans have long been pre-eminent organizers and joiners of voluntary associations that shape and supplement the activities of government. Late twentieth century Americans have however ceased to be such avid joiners (Putnam 2000). In her research, Skocpol shows that today, nationally ambitious civic entrepreneurs do not recruit activists and members in every state and across many towns and cities, but turn to private foundations for funding and then recruit an expert staff of researchers and lobbyists. She also shows the influence of the political and administrative environment on the transformation of group structure. Ever since the Ford Foundation began its patronage programme in the late 1950s, foundation grants have been a crucial source of funding for US public interest associations, encouraging their professionalization and allowing many of them to reduce their reliance on membership dues. However, not only the emergence of private funding structures has changed the internal functioning of groups and associations. Changes in the structures and activities of the federal government have encouraged the professionalization of associations. Thus, the openness of the federal courts to class action suits encouraged the formation of public law firms and stimulated many other advocacy groups to add lawyers to their staff.

Skocpol's work shows that the times of learning through associational participation seem to be over and millions of Americans are no longer cycled through official responsibilities where they were taught how to run meetings, handle money, keep records and participate in group discussions. However, this account of public life never applied to the European Union. The main EU idea was, and still is, to involve groups – public as well as private – in decision-making processes, initially to improve the efficiency of decision making, and then from the beginning of the 1990s to address the question of the legitimacy deficit.

At the EU level, the hypothesis that European associations model their behavior around the techniques of interest representation that are fostered by European officials seems to have gained large acceptance (Marks and McAdam 1996). Thus, associations lobby institutions instead of engaging in more contentious behavior, or at least they must use these action repertoires in order to gain influence. They organize conferences and carry out expert studies for the Commission, while country based groups engage in more contentious forms of politics (Guiraudon 2001).

By studying NGOs in the development policy domain at the EU level, Warleigh (2001: 623) found that the secretariats of these organizations dominated the agenda setting processes. They made 'little or no efforts to educate their supporters about the need for engagement with EU decision makers'. This is a contradiction of social capital claims and more particularly the fact that the participation of the 'civil society organizations' would lead to an increase of democratic legitimacy of the decision-making processes (Castiglione *et al.* 2008: part II). The social capital expectation is that groups should be open with transparent decision-making processes and have an accountable and responsive leadership in order to promote democracy itself. In the British context, Maloney (2007: 80), notes that 'the most interesting aspect about many public interest groups is not that they are oligarchic in nature, but that there are not even symbolic concessions to a democratic structure'. Maloney (2007; Jordan and Maloney 1997, 2007) has underlined the fact that the professionalization of representations leads to biased participation. As has Skocpol (2003) in the American case, Maloney and Jordan have shown for Great Britain that professionalized and bureaucratized interest groups staffed by communications experts, lawyers and lobbyists are increasingly supported by sophisticated fundraising departments and management structures. Grassroots members in public interest groups, or the so-called 'civil society organizations' have become checkbook participants. The number of members has also increased dramatically over the last 20 years, and it is these numbers which are used by professional groups in their argumentation about participation. These numbers are used to compare the number of members of political parties and those of large 'civil society organization', leading to the idea of the decline of the party and the creation of alternative modes of participation.

Maloney (2007: 77) rightly states that while democratic deficit scholars judge participation by the degree of personal involvement, much group participation is chosen because it is undemanding in terms of personal effort.

Empirically, illustrations of these hypotheses can be found in a number of case studies on European associations. The recruitment logic of associations at the European level seems to correspond more to career logic than to an activist one. The example of the European Women's Lobby shows after the gradual retreat of the founding mothers the emergence of a frontier between elected representatives and staff members. This frontier is the outcome of the establishment of a meritocratic recruitment procedure. Associational 'civil servants' seem to emerge (Cavaille 2004: 13).

In the field of trade unions, this institutional professionalization is at the origin of important critiques regarding the 'high level unionism' or the 'elite and expert unionism' (Gobin 1997). The European trade unionists are considered to be the new elite, integrated in the universe of European high ranking civil servants and other professionals. Here we observe a competition between different modes of trade unionism that puts into question the legitimate basis of unionism. Thus, interest groups and 'civil society organizations' create in the EU political spaces as 'political sites of contestation, in which actors are strategically constructing bounded fields of social power in their own right, at the same time as building successful remunerative careers in these emergent professions' (Favell 2007: 127). In a random analysis of eight CVs of current and former members of the EU's Civil Society Contact Group board members and coordinators, Kohler-Koch *et al.* (2008: 21) found that only three CVs from eight showed grassroots level experience, five from eight CVs give evidence of EU non-state actors careers and two of eight show experiences within the European Commission and the European Parliament.

It is however important to note that the career logic does not systematically replace the activist logic in the organized civil society structures at the EU level. In a number of groups – farmers, the European Women's Lobby and trade unions – activists still represent the majority amongst the elected representatives. It is in the secretariats that we see a professionalization of the association, where individuals move from association to association in order to pursue their career path. This phenomenon seems, however, to be growing in importance. At the international level, Martens (2005, 2006) has convincingly argued that the professionalization of human rights NGOs has led to their increasing significance in international relations. Others, such as Siméant (2005) or Saurugger (2006) hint at a legitimacy problem: if they have become more influential, they simultaneously appear to lose part of the representative character they claimed to possess in order to gain a legitimate place in transnational governance structures.

Finally, the subject of professionalization is also touched upon by a number of publications centered on business interests in globalized politics and the European Union. The many similarities between public and private interest organizations make the analogies between public and private interest groups, business interest and NGOs tempting, as these private organizations have a number of points in common at the international level (Streeck and Schmitter 1999; Ronit and Schneider 2000; Lahusen 2004; Streeck et al. 2006). This research centers implicitly or explicitly on Schmitter and Streeck's (1990) 'two logics' concept that theorizes the intermediary position of interest associations between membership and influence environments. The profound social change triggered in past decades by economic and political internationalization raises the question of how interest associations cope with an increasingly complex environment, in terms of membership and political decision-making institutions. Greenwood (2002) more precisely questioned the degree of governability of EU associations appreciating the influences exerted by the institutional environment in which they act. He concludes that associations need to have autonomy from members in order to bring value to them. Those that are too closely controlled by their members become a mouthpiece for their short-term demands, while those who have acquired some autonomy from their members' demands have the flexibility to participate in policy making with EU institutions. In general, these studies concentrate rather on the institutional environments and less on the individual backgrounds of the individuals representing the members' interest.

Thus, one could argue that the fundamental question in studies of the role of the organized civil society should be who participates. For this reason, it is central to understand who represents the actors included in the civil society definition given by the European institutions. The concept of professionalization, more than that of bureaucratization or institutionalization, allows for the two dimensional analysis Steffek et al. (2007) call for. On the one hand, an analysis of the political interactions between the center of the political system and the organized civil society, and, on the other, the interaction between the citizens or demos and civil society organizations.

From what precedes, it is possible to conceptualize professionalization at the intra-organizational level as the proper coordination of the various professionals in order to guarantee the overall performance of a given agency.[8] This includes management of the various departments, the coordination between the strategic arena and the implementing arena (Dijkzeul and Gordenker 2003), resource allocation etc., to guarantee optimal service and product delivery. Increasing professionalization also refers to the transformation of power relations between elected members and grassroots activists and the secretariat, and increasing external – public as well as private – funding.

Bridging the assumptions

These three conceptual approaches allow for an opening up of the European 'civil society organizations' black box. Thus far, the chapter has shown to what extent classical and contemporary sociological research on parties, social movements, associations as well as business interest groups, put the accent on two parameters. First, the organizational structure and, second, the sociographical structure of groups – to understand the tension between democratic polity and decision-making processes.

The central hypothesis is that the more efficient groups are at representing their interests in a constructive, precise and coherent manner, the more influence they exert. These activities, however, require major expertise on the group's and movement's side which contributes to modeling the style of militancy and leads to greater internal professionalization. Thus the organizational structures of civil society have reformed to match better the perceived access structure of the European political system. Organized civil society – organized as groups or social movements – has a tendency to become increasingly professionalized to represent the interests of their constituency in an efficient way (Saurugger 2007).

Organizational structure

The majority of approaches discussed above help to conceptualize the day-to-day working of European civil society actors. It is central to understand to what degree these organizational structures are staffed with professionals and/or activists. From preliminary and small-scale research projects, it seems that there are fewer staff coming from the grassroots level than being employed after training in law or communication.[9]

In order to analyze the organizational structure of groups, two parameters have to be taken into account: on the one hand an endogenous parameter (a) the power relations between elected members or grassroots activists and the secretariat, and on the other an exogenous one (b) the influence of the institutional environment, in particular the funding of 'civil society organizations'.

Power relations between elected members or grassroots activists and the secretariat

At the organizational level, professionalization leads to an internal adaptation problem. On the one hand, this may lead to a potential conflict between the headquarters (strategic level) and the field within the organization. On the other, professionalization entails a potential conflict among the professionals and the militants/membership leading to the professionalization paradox. This means that in order to be efficient and successful in the market going hand in hand with the ambition to participate and influence the political decision-making process may lead to an increase in the distance between the members and the professionals within the organization. The process of professionalization implies a 'conversion process' where, as in the transformation process of political parties, professionals and bureaucrats increasingly occupy the secretariat of civil society organizations. Grassroots members are either represented through a checkbook activism (Maloney and Jordan 1997) or through elected assemblies. However, even elected assemblies cannot react rapidly to demands of expertise necessary to participate in day-to-day decision-making processes at the European level. The assumption in this context is that the operational organization structure active both in advocacy and lobbying activities as well as in fields activities is increasingly staffed with professionals in Panbianco's sense (executive bureaucracies, in opposition to representative bureaucracies) (Panebianco 1988: 224).

Influence of funding/patronage

The EU has provided significant levels of funding to many civil society organizations. A recent study shows, more generally, that the Commission's funding decisions reflect its goals of supporting supranational EU 'civil society organizations': in particular EU integration groups, European youth, education and intercultural exchange groups as well as citizenship, democracy promotion and education groups. The findings also show, however, that when it comes to societal cohesion, the Commission's funding practices are not in line with its rhetoric. Rather than equal funding across members states, or extra support for the organized civil society in the new member states, it is the oldest and wealthiest members that are receiving the largest numbers of grants and the largest amounts of funding (Mahoney and Beckstrand 2008).

Sanchez-Salgado (2007) has analyzed the influence of European funding on a number of NGOs' accounting structures. Here the question is to what extent external funding structures, in particular those of the European Commission transform the internal structures and make them more professionalized. With regard to NGOs, the European Commission, in particular after the 1999 stepdown of the Santer Commission due to internal fraud, required specific managerial and organizational abilities of groups it was funding. Thus funded groups had to adapt rapidly based on functional requirements. These transformations are, however, value loaded. New instruments carry new normative contents, as Lascoumes and Le Galès (2007) have shown, and lead to the recruitment of new professionals into the organizational structure. An in-depth research must allow for appreciating the percentage of these newly recruited professionals compared to former staff. What precisely does this transformation mean for the link between the representatives and the constituency?

Sociographical analysis of social actors

The analysis of career patterns reflects another aspect of the professionalization of 'civil society organizations' in the European Union and illustrate another aspect of funding. Organizations that rely heavily on public funds may not require grassroots membership. Zald and McCarthy ([1987] 1994a) establish a significant correlation between institutional and financial support for social movement organizations and the emergence of life careers in movements. As a result of the massive growth in funding it has become possible for a larger number of professionals to earn a respectable income committing themselves full-time to activities related to social movements. Outside financial support means that a membership in the classic sense is almost dispensable as it allows a leadership to replace volunteer manpower drawn from the base of paid staff members chosen upon criteria of skills and experience. The authors show that in the US case associational professionals have been able to pursue successfully such careers for some time, moving in and out of governmental agencies, private agencies, community organizations, foundations and universities. However, they argue that these new professionals in social movement organizations are distinguished from their colleagues in the traditional professions such as public relations directors, membership and development specialists, lawyers and engineers by their rejection of traditional institutional roles, careers and reward structures. They define their opportunities less in terms of the use of professional skills and more in terms of social change objectives. While both in the US and the European Union, professional competence rather than broad citizen action seems to characterize these organizations, the heavy use of the media as a lever for social change prominent in the US is absent in the EU given its poorly developed public space.

Thus, generating information about gender, age, geographical or national origin, and social origin as well as the educational attainment levels and types (of specialist) qualifications would allow us to study the European interest representation as a marketplace. Variables such as the type of employment and patterns of recruitment can be decisive. Do volunteers or activists and delegated personnel identify more or less with the group than permanent full-time staff who have chosen the workplace as a career move (Kohler-Koch et al. 2008)? How are these professionals trained? What specific Masters programmes in European politics, economics and law exist in order to see whether special training programmes are provided for future lobbyists and interest representatives?

However, it is important to exercise some caution. It might be extremely difficult to establish a clear-cut distinction between activists and professionals. The possibility exists that activists are also professionals. It seems thus necessary, to think more of a continuum on which these distinctions are based, than a final distinction of roles.

Conclusion

The chapter aimed to develop a conceptual framework that allows for the analysis of the internal adaptation processes that 'organized civil society' undergoes in order to participate in the decision-making process. Based on analytical tools developed by the party, social movement and interest group scholars, two central elements were identified which facilitate an understanding of the degree and extent of organizational adaptation: first, the organizational structure of 'civil society organizations', and, second, the sociographical characteristics of the individual actors involved in these organizations. With regard to the organizational structure two factors are of particular importance: one endogenous, the power relations between the secretariat and the members, the other exogenous, the role of patronage in the transformation of structures. The sociographical analysis aims to question training structures in which 'organized civil society' representatives were enrolled, as well as studying the different career paths of these actors. Collecting more of this data should allow us to provide a fuller answer to questions related to the emergence and nature of the representation elite at the EU level – i.e. the level of homogeneity.

The reason for developing a conceptual framework is based on the observation that the main argument in favor of 'organized civil society' participation in the EU is linked to the idea that the more the 'organized civil society' contributes to decision making, the more democratic decision making would be and the more politically socialized the European space would become. This topic is worthy of study because a fundamental question is: who does 'organized civil society' actually represent and how does it do so? In order to answer this question it is very useful to return to the general political science and sociological literature discussed above. Political parties and social movements have undergone changes in their internal organizational structures as well as in their relationship with their multiple environments, leading to increased professionalization of their internal organizational structures as well as of actors' characteristics. It seems central to anchor research on the professionalization of the European civil society organizations in this literature which will allow for developing comparisons and avoid that research on EU governance processes remains an $n=1$ research design.

Given that the 'organized European civil society' is increasingly seen as a crucial element in the enhancement of the EU's democratic credentials, we need to provide some insights precisely into if and how 'civil society' can help reduce this democratic deficit. While this has been done with regard to the study of participatory structures created by European institutions, and the question on what forms of participatory structures should be established, less work has been done relating to the question of who participates and who represents this civil society in civil society organizations (see also William Maloney's chapter in this volume).[10]

In this sense, and normatively speaking, the professionalization processes, as complex as they may be, may be nothing more than a step further into the 'normalization' of new forms of democratic governance.

Notes

1 I would like to thank Jens Steffek, Kristina Hahn, Meike Rodekamp, Martina Piewitt, Yannis Papadopoulos, Patrick Bernhagen, Jan van Deth, William Maloney and the participants of the ECPR joint Session Panel in April 2009 for perceptive comments on earlier versions of this chapter.
2 Without engaging in a large-scale debate about definitions (see, amongst a increasingly large number, Cohen and Arato 1992), I define 'organized civil society' in the EU context narrowly as collective actors representing interests on behalf of their constituency both in the public sphere and toward political actors. (inside and outside lobbying). This definition is very similar to that of interest groups, a similarity which is not entirely coincidental (Saurugger 2010).
3 Professionalization is understood in its largest sense here and does not refer exclusively to the existence of occupational groups controlling expert knowledge, in this case the capacity to represent a constituency's interests (Abbott 1988).
4 Which seems to confirm the necessity of normalization of EU studies (Rosamond 2007).
5 His proposal to replace parties by ad hoc movements is a rather early normative demand of what some of the most radical associative democracy philosophers request today.
6 Although Panebianco questions this because this differentiation does not explain why parties frequently adopt positions which have proven counterproductive to their goal to win elections – such as the French Communist Party being in permanent opposition without any chance of building a greater consensus (Panebianco 1988: 6).
7 It is again important to note how thin the dividing line is between what scholars define as 'social movements', 'associations' and 'interest groups'.
8 See Eberwein and Saurugger (2009).
9 This seems particularly visible in studies focusing on the transformation process of central and eastern European countries. In this context the organizational as well as thematic structures of civil society actors were created in conformity with the program priorities of large international donors such as USAID, the Open Society Fund or German Party Foundations (Stone 1996; Pevehouse 2005).
10 See CONNEX, online, available at: www.mzes.uni-mannheim.de/projekte/connex/ as well as CINEFOGO, online, available at: www.cinefogo.org/.

6 The democratic contribution of professionalized representation[1]

William A. Maloney

Introduction

European democracies appear to be suffering from a democratic squeeze. Voter turnout, partisan consistency, partisan identification, party membership, and trust in politicians and government – all crucial to a healthy functioning democracy – are declining (see Mair 2006). Hay (2007), Hay and Stoker (2009), and Stoker (2006a and 2006b) see great peril for (UK) democracy:

> it is difficult to get away from the idea that a general and widespread disengagement from and disenchantment with formal politics does not sit comfortably with the long-term health of democracy. Indeed a pessimistic reading of the degree of disenchantment from formal politics is that it will in the end undermine support for democracy and democratic decision-making.
>
> (Stoker 2006b: 182–3)

Of course, not everyone shares such a pessimistic perspective. Hibbing and Theiss-Morse (2002: 1–2, 3) boldly argue that:

> The last thing people want is to be more involved in political decision making: They do not want to make political decisions themselves; they do not want to provide much input to those who are assigned to make these decisions; and they would rather not know all the details of the decision-making process ... Evidence of the people's desire to avoid politics is widespread, but most observers still find it difficult to take this evidence at face value ... when people say they do not like politics and do not want to participate in politics, they are simply ignored. Elite observers claim to know what people really want – and that is to be involved, richly and consistently, in the political arena. If people are not involved, these observers automatically deem the system in dire need of repair.

The key issue for Hibbing and Theiss-Morse is that in democracies citizens can participate if they want, and that if they choose not to *get involved*, then so be it.

However, Hay and Stoker (2009: 227) maintain that government and the political elite have failed to recognize the profoundity of the contemporary democratic malaise: 'Political parties, single issue campaign organizations and the media all play a vital part in politics. Put simply, *they too are part of the problem; they need also to be seen as part of the solution*' (emphasis added). In line with this perspective, participation through interest groups is seen both as developmentally beneficial for citizens and as a functional policy-making necessity. Interest groups should act as effective representative vehicles that secure policy outcomes that better fit citizens' preferences. They should also act as Tocquevillian (1969)/Putnam (2000) schools of democracy that produce better democrats via in-group pro-democratic and pro-civic experiences. To meet these expectations, groups must reconcile two seemingly conflicting organizational principles. On the one hand, they have to be well structured and efficient: *i.e. professionalized*. On the other, they have to maintain claims to representative and democratic legitimacy. In short, a multitude of engaged and vibrant groups is not a desirable luxury, but a democratic necessity.

Recent years however, have witnessed the rise of supporter based, memberless groups – *Protest Business* (Jordan and Maloney 1997) (and more individualized participation: e.g. *political consumerism*,[2] see Pattie *et al.* 2004; Stolle *et al.* 2005). Many of these groups are organized according to hierarchical business principles aimed at maximizing the efficiency of operations. As Shaiko (1991: 124) wryly noted, 'The era of the flannel-shirted, "Flower Power" antiestablishmentarianism has virtually vanished ... public interest organizations are hiring economists, Ivy League lawyers, management consultants, direct mail specialists, and communication directors'. The ideal-typical professionalized interest group can be characterized as an entity: (1) with a full-time paid staff that generates income, from supporters dues and donations, through the sale of goods and services, and through institutional patronage (governments and private and charitable foundations); (2) where supporters have few, if any, internal democratic rights; (3) in which campaigns, strategies, tactics, and policies are centrally formulated and supporters have no direct means of influence – *exit* being the only option; (4) where campaigning is carried out by staff rather than supporters; (5) where supporters are largely unknown to each other and lack face-to-face contact; (6) that actively shapes perceptions of problems and offers passive checkbook (Hayes 1986) participation; and (7) which pursues a technocratic and scientific approach to organizational maintenance and influencing policy outcomes (Jordan and Maloney 1997, 2007).

It is clear that most members/supporters of large-scale professionalized interest groups have limited political involvement and many groups have sought to influence policy outcomes largely without the active assistance of members – beyond mobilizing their direct-debit/automated payments. Two major participation studies – Verba *et al.* (1995) (US) and Pattie *et al.* (2004: 77–8, 98–9) (UK) – found that chequebook participation was the most popular form of political involvement and the UK study found that most political participation in Britain was of an individualistic (e.g. donating money, signing a petition, boycotting products, or ethical shopping) rather than collective form (attending meetings, rallies, or demonstrations).

Hay and Stoker (2009: 230–1) lament the rise of professionalized organizations claiming that they deliver 'ephemeral, thin sporadic' and potentially 'ill-informed' engagement:

> the advocacy of special interests through lobbying and the challenge and dissent presented through various forms of protest, offer vital links in the democratic chain between governors and governed. But they all are failing to engage citizens-at-large in politics.
>
> (231)

As noted above, within the literature there is some tension between the need for more open and democratic groups on the hand and professionalization on the other: i.e. professionalization appears to drive out members and reduces openness, transparency, and internal democracy. Accordingly, this chapter assesses the democratic 'contribution' of professionalized public interest groups. Are these groups part of the alleged democratic pathology? Can profesionalized groups offer any democractic enhancements? Accordingly, in the remainder of this chapter we discuss three main factors that help explain low levels of participation in many professionalized public interest groups. First, there are *group push* and *supporter pull* effects, second, *patronage*, and, third, *the increasing professionalization of the policy-making process*. The chapter concludes with a discussion of some democratically enhancing features of professionalized public interest group representation.

Accounting for low levels of participation

Group push/supporter pull

The democratic potential of groups to enhance citizen participation is less effective than might be assumed for two main reasons. First, groups believe that attempting to influence policy outcomes can be conducted more efficiently without the active involvement of *political amateurs* – i.e. supporters and members. As Rootes (2009a: 210–11) highlights, the founders of groups like Greenpeace and Friends of the Earth never envisaged their organizations as being responsive, accountable democratic entities vis-à-vis their supporter base. These bodies were viewed as 'uninhibited campaigning' beasts engaged in protest activities conducted by 'committed activists' – campaign effectiveness was privileged over democratic involvement. Second, many groups have found that simply asking citizens to donate money and not requiring them to engage in any additional higher-cost participatory activities is crucial to generating large-scale support. Members don't want to be actively involved; they simply want to financially (and passively) support professionalized activism (see below for more details).

There are several group *push-type* factors that lead many large-scale professionalized public interest groups to offer limited involvement. Lansley (1996: 222–3) identified the following several factors. First, *size* creates logistical problems. It is impracticable (and impossible) to involve large numbers of members in a group's work. By necessity, groups are drawn to staff-run/dominated structures. Second, *the degree or complexity* or the depth of professionalization. The division of labour in large-scale groups will be predicated on specialization. Third, Lansley says, Michels' (1915) 'iron law' also operates in these groups. As they have evolved into large organizations ('who says organization, says oligarchy') *differentiation* and *specialization* have seen some players recognized as carrying out key tasks and duties and gaining power and control. Fourth, the *organizational structure* – i.e. the degree of centralization or decentralization – is important. Groups that have a regional structure comprising local branches and chapters offer greater opportunities for, and in some cases have a greater need of, member involvement. Fifth, the *ideological commitment* of members is relevant. If members actively seek out groups or join because of a strong commitment to the cause then there may be greater pressure on the leadership to either pay close attention to their concerns or to offer internal democracy. If the ideological commitment of members is weak, or if the group has used sophisticated marketing techniques to recruit members, then members may make little demands on the organization and their ideological attachment will be weaker. The latter is the case in the professionalized interest group sector. As Barakso and Schaffner (2008: 187) note, 'When members face few barriers to exiting a group, democratic procedures are of little value, and the group is more likely to be oligarchic.' They (2008: 192) further argue that groups can of course increase the barriers to exit, for example by offering *voice*. If groups institute 'some sort of membership voice' partly as a selective incentive, it may have some pay-off in terms of membership retention. Sixth, legal restrictions or organizational constitutions may limit the degree of membership involvement.

The UK trends are also evident at the EU level. Sudbery (2003: 90) found that with scarce resources groups prioritized 'effective results' over raising awareness. A senior representative of the European Environment Bureau (EEB) told Sudbury that 'While ideally it would be good to get people involved ... my role is not to encourage the most participatory governance, but to ensure the best results for the environment.'[3] Warleigh (2001: 623) found that NGOs in the development policy area active at the EU level were 'wanting' in terms of their internal democratic procedures and decision making was heavily centralized and elite driven. Staff made 'little or no effort to educate their supporters about the need for engagement with EU decision-makers'. Warleigh also highlighted that supporter *pull-type* factors were operating, 'Moreover – and perhaps more worryingly – I found no evidence that supporters are unhappy with this passive role, displaying at best little interest in the EU as a focus of campaigning or locus of political authority' (623). Even members of the European Commission Governance team were candid about the tension between efficiency and citizen participation. 'We simply do not have the resources to deal with all civil society organisations ... Perhaps the most effective way to link with the citizen ... is by more effective results ... The issue about bringing in the citizen is for speeches, for the rhetoric' (quoted in Sudbery 2003: 91–2).

Turning to supporter *pull-type* factors we see that many large-scale groups have found that chequebook involvement is an efficient way to generate support because many citizens find such limited involvement appealing. Members/supporters are content to embrace a politically marginal role and contract out their participation to groups and many do not see membership of groups as a means of being *active in politics*. Indeed, quite the reverse. Survey evidence confirms that members share this view. In our own surveys in the early 1990s of Amnesty International (British Section) and Friends of the Earth (FoE), very few members saw their membership as a means of being 'active in political issues' and approximately 70 per cent of FoE and Amnesty members said it was largely or wholly irrelevant in their decision to join (Jordan and Maloney 1997). These findings were echoed by the group leaders in research we conduced *circa* ten years later with campaign group leaders in the UK. A Royal Society for the Protection of Birds representative stated that 'we're sort of acting as a de facto for an individual ... if they could do it themselves they would but because they can't, they trust us to get on with it' (ibid.: 162). For many supporters 'inactivity' is a 'benefit' and they would consider leaving organizations that sought to impose the 'cost' of active participation. A representative of the Campaign to Protect Rural England stated that the organization would lose support if it pressed its members to be more active,

> because they're people who want to give money and they don't want to do anymore than that ... So the whole task [of recruiting people] has to be geared around saying 'oh don't worry, we're not expecting you to come to meetings and things, we just want your support'.
>
> (ibid.: 158–9)

Accordingly, it is important to stress that participation rights are not being denied to frustrated members. It is 'thin' chequebook participation that is sought. In summary, there is some reinforcement in group push and supporter pull factors – moving towards limited involvement.

Patronage

> *Without the influence of patrons of political action, the flourishing system of interest groups in the United States would be much smaller and would include very few groups seeking to obtain broad collective or public goods. If all sources of patronage suddenly disappeared, the interest-group system would immediately shrink.*
>
> (Walker 1991: 101, emphasis added)

Many public interest groups are heavily reliant on patronage for their financial survival.[4] Walker (1991: 49) argued that one of the most important reasons for the rapid expansion of the citizen groups sector in the US was the growth of patronage.[5] While Bosso (1995: 106) notes in the public interest group field, *It's Money that Matters*.[6] Professionalized interest representation is not cheap. Groups now draw on technical, scientific, and legal expertise in promoting their causes, and with regard to organizational maintenance large-scale public interest groups use the latest communication and fundraising technologies and employ professional marketing and managerial expertise.

As Mahoney and Beckstrand (2008: 4) highlight, government supports groups for two main reasons: *legitimacy*, 'public policy outcomes are more legitimate if it appears there was balanced input into the process' and *civic vibrancy*, 'a vibrant civil society is important in its own right, as it can help build a common identity for a polity, solve problems and produce new ideas'. Greenwood (2007) highlighted that the EU Commission spends approximately €1 billion on funding groups – and almost the entire citizen interest group universe mobilized at the EU level receives some funding. A survey of 248 conservation and environmental organizations in 1989 in the US found that membership dues accounted for only 32 per cent of total revenue, while foundation grants, corporate gifts, federal grants and contracts, and state grants and contracts accounted for 24 per cent; a further 19 per cent of revenue came from individual contributions (Bosso 1995: 107). In their survey of campaign groups in the UK, Jordan and Maloney (2007) found that many groups received patronage from institutional sources and that it was a highly important income stream. Table 6.1 shows that approximately one-third of the groups surveyed received patronage from charities, corporate sponsors, and government. When we look at *the most important* income source individual subscriptions are crucial for just over one-third of groups. However, if we sum the (patronage) percentages from charities, corporate sponsors, and government we see that 23.5 per cent of groups state that these patrons are the most important income source.

While many of these funding efforts are laudable – e.g. trying to provide a more level playing field between citizen organizations and business groups – there are potential downsides. For example, Cigler and Nownes (1995: 79) argued that there is evidence that patronage affects the composition of the public interest sector by diverting funds to professional rather than activist

Table 6.1 UK campaign groups' income source and most important source

	Individual subscriptions (%)	Contributions from charities (%)	Contributions from corporate sponsors (%)	Government grants/awards (%)
UK campaign groups' income sources, n=239 (99%)	83.3	33.1	30.5	31.0
UK campaign groups' most important income source, n=196 (81%)	37.2	7.7	4.6	11.2

Source: constructed from Jordan and Maloney's (2007) data.

organizations. External funding may also affect the representative basis of organizations. Groups that are heavily reliant on patronage may not require a grassroots membership and may, as Euchner (1996: 47) argues may contribute to cutting off leaders 'from their constituency'.

Some EU groups are close to being almost entirely solvent on the basis of patronage receiving 80–90 per cent of their operating budgets from EU institutions. The EEB received an annual average of €831,008 in the five years between 2003 and 2007 (a total of €4,155,040) (Mahoney and Beckstrand 2008: 25). Hadden (2009: 5) notes that the EU Commission has 'offered vast resources to those active on climate change' and that private foundations have also been very generous patrons of environmental NGOs. Hadden (ibid.) concludes, 'For civil society actors working on climate change, the issue is that they have *too much* money these days, and often have to find novel ways to spend it' (original emphasis). If institutional sources are prepared to fund organizations to operational levels of 80–90 per cent then members become a luxury because groups can exert influence without them. As Skocpol (2003: 134) acerbically puts it, 'Members are a nonlucrative distraction.'

There are other possible negative externalities associated with patronage. It may divert or alter the aims, objectives, and strategies, or dampen the disapproving tones from groups heavily reliant on institutional funds for organizational survival. They may become more reformist, more ready to work within the mainstream of the political system, rather than pursuing a more challenging and contentious path and may have a 'stronger orientation' to their patrons than those who do not receive such funds (Mahoney and Beckstrand 2008). Lowery (2007: 16) argues that membership organizations with a weak financial basis may specifically tailor their issue selection to 'better reflect the preferences of a few deep pocketed patrons rather than issues preferred by mass members or organizational leaders'. Groups are also keen to be seen as responsible and useful policy-making participants. A Greenpeace EU staff member told Hadden (2009: 12) that:

> We are anxious about overusing protest strategies because we don't want people to think that we are just environmental Nazis who like hanging themselves from things. We want to be seen as reasonable and professional people who understand what is politically possible.

Mahoney and Beckstrand (2008: 5–6) argue that groups' advocacy power may be diminished because groups may fear punishment, 'closer monitoring and more rigorous regulation'. Sanchez-Salgado (2009: 3) maintains that the EU provides funds to engender a specific type of behaviour. Groups should engage in *inside lobbying* and adhere to what she labels the *Brussels consensus* avoiding

> confrontation and try to establish long-term a relationship based on mutual trust with MEPs and European civil servants. These groups seldom engage in activities of protest in Brussels or beyond, even if according to some sources, the 'radical flank' is considered as a successful strategy.

There is of course a counter-argument to the reformist and non-confrontational impact of institutional patronage. One could argue that it is exactly because these groups are supported, they can afford to be critical and organize opposition. For example, Poppelaars (2009: 11–12) stated that 'the maintenance of Dutch interest groups is often ascribed to the willingness of the government to provide subsidies, *even to perceived adversaries*' (emphasis added). While Hadden (2009: 12) noted that the while the non-contentious climate change coalition of environmental organizations has:

> policy positions ... very close to those of DG environment. For some people, this raises questions about how influential the coalition can be. Members of the coalition insist that they have to take positions that are 'politically possible' in order to be taken seriously by decision-makers. As one CAN-E (Climate Action Network Europe) staff member put it, 'when people criticize us for being too close to DG Environment, I tell them that we're not close to them, they're close to us'.

The professionalization of the policy-making process

The increasing professionalization of the policy-making process itself has reduced the need for an active membership. Crenson and Ginsberg (2002: 147) argue that the 'new politics' is open 'to all those who have ideas and expertise rather than to those who assert interest and preferences'. Those admission requirements exclude the great mass of ordinary citizens. Similarly, Chaskin (2003) – who focused on attempts at fostering neighbourhood democracy – highlighted the importance of expertise and argued that this was partly driven by the professionalization of public agencies. Finally, Saurugger (2007: 397–8) notes that, 'Organized civil soc;.iy – organized as groups or social movements – has a tendency to become increasingly professionalized to represent the interests of their constituency in an efficient way'.[7]

From the group perspective the best way to produce effective results clearly has a significant impact on the nature of the 'demands' it makes of its membership. Tensions are felt by groups and policy makers between democratic efficiency and more participatory modus operandi. Poppelaars (2009: 3) in her study of the bureaucratic arena as a policy-making venue quotes a Dutch health care sector bureaucrat, 'The existence of so many highly professionally organized interest groups simplifies the job as they are useful in reaching the proper people and offering new insight.' Professionalization of interest group representation can also lead to the sharing, as opposed to a collision, of world views. Hadden (2009: 16–17) argues that the groups of NGOs working on climate change policy at the EU level have similar 'educational backgrounds in European affairs, have completed a stage at one of the European institutions, and/or have pervious work experience at one of the other environmental NGOs in Brussels'.

Groups appear to have responded to the changing policy-making context and affecting outcomes appears to require less membership muscle and more policy expertise and professionalism. As Bosso (2003: 410) cynically notes: 'what use are "members" when lawyers, scientists, and policy experts are far more valuable in day-to-day policy debates ... members ... are little more than organizational wallpaper, a collective backdrop for professional advocacy'.

Can professionalized groups enhance participation?

Organisations that seek to represent should be able to demonstrate whom they represent and how they represent them.

(Grant 2003: 307–8, emphasis added)

The story so far has presented a somewhat bleak picture with regard to the democratic contribution of professionalized public interest groups. While few professionalized groups are paragons of participatory democracy characterized by a fully empowered membership these entities may not be completely devoid of participatory or democratically enhancing potential. The key question remains: are there specific features of professionalized groups that could be seen as enhancing democratic participation? Do groups that lack formal internal democratic procedures use certain mechanisms that can be seen as democratically responsive? Do chequebook groups have the potential to offer, or the practice of offering, at least limited opportunities for supporter/member involvement?

Grant (2003: 301) argues that most interest groups lack effective internal democratic procedures and even if they have an elected leadership he maintains that the processes often lack transparency and consultation with members can be limited to questionnaires or Internet polls. However, membership is voluntary and members can choose to leave any organization in which they become disenchanted. The *exit* option can be seen as a significant threat and maintains a responsive link between leaders and followers. Hirschman (1970: 21), writing about organizations generally, noted:

> the exit option is widely held to be uniquely powerful: by inflicting revenue losses on delinquent management, exit is expected to induce that 'wonderful concentration of the mind' akin to the one Samuel Johnson attributed to the prospect of being hanged.

Of course some may view this *democratic form* as superficial. Day (1999: 220) maintains that while groups may include policy questionnaires in their targeting mailings to individuals, 'these often are gimmicks to attract members and to stimulate enough interest for respondents to write out their checks'. There may be more substance than Day suggests. For example, Warleigh (2001: 631) reported that the NGO Stonewall regularly surveyed members on their opinions about specific issues. He argued that the surveys 'were used to fine-tune campaigns (but not to choose their subject or objectives)'. Jordan and Maloney's (2007) data showed that 44 per cent of campaign groups in the UK have direct contact with their members, 21 per cent use focus groups, and 45 per cent conduct membership surveys to gauge members' views. The market research used by groups means that their policy direction is steered to some extent by supporter/member attitudes. Strolovitch (2006: 906) interviewed the executive director of an Asian-American association who stated that, 'We don't want to turn off or upset our community ... What's the point of having an advocacy organization if your turning them off?'[8] More worryingly, Strolovitch noted that this association 'avoids addressing violence against women because, she (the executive director) argued, it is "not a topic that is openly discussed in our community"' (ibid.). 'Democratic orientated outcomes' need not be civic or progressive outcomes. These organizations operate on a minimalist democratic basis, treading carefully to avoid members taking the *exit* decision – particularly where they have no *voice*.

Thus policies can be drawn in ways that show some sensitivity to the views of members. Through the use of market research techniques supporter attitudes may feed into policy direction. Many protest business organizations are involved in a fierce competition to attract and retain supporters/members.[9] Loyalty is particularly important to these groups because there is high membership turnover: significant proportions of 'their' support operate on a revolving-door basis. These groups make membership easy and *easy entry may mean easy exit* (Jordan and Maloney 1997). As Euchner (1996: 124) notes, 'members' need to 'be recruited over and over again'. This competition could be presented as ensuring responsiveness and effective representation *of* supporters' interests. If the leadership gets too far out of step with supporters, there may be no followers left to lead. The perspective adopted here echoes Salisbury's (1992) view that interest groups are distinctive because members or supporters can potentially exercise control of leaders through 'exit'. Many groups take great care to try and prevent supporters/members from taking the exit decision.

On balance most (large-scale) organizational members' contributions are financial. However, it is too simplistic to suggest that groups want *only* passive cash-cow members, rather than activists. More accurately it should be seen that groups are prepared to accept membership on that basis, and may welcome more active involvement. This does not lead to the creation of democratically accountable and fully responsive organizations. Barakso and Schaffner's (2008: 202) survey of Washington DC based interest groups found that they tended towards hierarchy with the organizational elite holding 'overwhelming power in most organizations' and members having very limited opportunities to influence decisions.[10]

From the organizational perspective internal democracy may not matter. As Day (1999: 217) argues 'gathering member input actually may detract from an organization's ability to compete with other groups to attain its goals'. Rose (2009: 8) argues that many civil society organizations deliver nominal representation of citizens and that the actual memberships are a small fraction of the numbers of European citizens they claim to represent: 'The shortfall between actual members and those for whom they claim to speak is usually large.' While this can be presented as a representative/democratic *Achilles heel* we should bear in mind that groups can act as *surrogates* for those who cannot effectively represent themselves. Groups may raise the decibel levels of some voices that find it hard to get heard. Or even give voice to those that lack it. Groups can act on behalf of a public that lack the necessary knowledge and expertise. Much group participation seeks to advance many causes that benefit constituencies beyond the direct sectional interests of their supporters (e.g. children or animal welfare). Imig (1994) talks of 'advocacy by proxy' to describe how individuals are mobilized to act on behalf of client groups (e.g. Make Poverty History).

Many (large-scale) supporter based organizations also have local chapters and branches that activate a small percentage of supporters. In such numerically large organizations this can amount to a respectable numbers of citizens. In the UK organizations such as Friends of the Earth, Amnesty International, Greenpeace, the Campaign to Protect Rural England, and the Royal Society for the Protection of Birds, have networks of local branches and chapters.[11] In 2009 the Royal Society for the Protection of Birds had over one million members, of which some 12,500 were volunteers. Jordan and Maloney's (2007) survey of campaign groups in the UK found that 52.7 per cent (n=224) of groups had local groups. Groups also provide advice to supporters on how to be *effective* or *persuasive* if they wish to get active.

Conclusion

The continuing professionalization of the public interest group sector has witnessed the further development of large-scale supporter based memberless organizations that offer limited opportunities for citizen involvement and an increasingly technocratic approach to influencing policy outcomes. These trends have been accentuated by several factors – e.g. groups supplying limited participation opportunities and supporters seeking chequebook participation; the growth of the importance of institutional funding – patronage – that reduces the reliance on individual memberships; and the professionalization of the policy-making process itself.

The shallow invovlement offered by many groups may not be universally welcomed – and participatory enthusiasts may see great problems with such minimalism. However, it can be presented as an efficient market (see Jordan and Maloney 1997, 2007; van Deth 2009). Both parties get what they need. Shallow involvement does not mean that groups are completely deviod of democratic content. Groups do seek to lead *supporters* – as opposed to being fully democratically responsive to an active and vibrant *membership* – and seek out chequebook supporters to make regular donations. Citizens seeking a more participatory role may find opportunities within the branch/chapter structure of many organizations. Chequebook participation may be limited, but it is purposive i.e. 'it reflects some degree of unhappiness with the way things are' (Salisbury 1992: 216). It is purposively directed at funding advocacy, campaigning, and protest, even if it is not about directly joining in the 'fun'.

Many large-scale public interest groups are in the business of lobbying for 'their' causes and supporters remain important providing resources and legitimacy. As Bosso notes (in Putnam 2000: 159) these organizations 'are playing roles that one expects of mature organizations with a political context that forces groups to grow and professionalize or die'. Thus should we expect large-scale public interest groups to be major contributors to participatory democracy? Probably not. These organizations involve large numbers of citizens in 'low cost' participation and generally citizens chose this type of participation because it is undemanding. Nevertheless, groups activate support by individuals for collective ends – overcoming some of the Olsonian (Olson 1971) hurdles – and democracy benefits because these bodies can educate citizens and provide policy expertise that can challenge business groups and government.

Notes

1 This chapter is based on and extends several of the arguments in Maloney (2009).
2 Micheletti *et al.* (2003) define political consumerism as '*consumer choice of producers and products based on political or ethical considerations, or both*' (original emphasis) (in Stolle *et al.* 2005: 246).
3 Jordan and Maloney (2007: 153) also found that while volunteering and mobilizing members are important activities in terms of the democratic contribution of groups (especially in the social capital building perspective), they were not seen by organizational leaders as being of *greatest importance* to their groups. However, promoting volunteering had far more support from large professionalized organizations than medium or small groups. This result resonates with previous findings on voluntary welfare organizations in Britain and Germany. Large groups – who are likely to employ larger numbers of staff – appeared to be more efficient at engendering volunteering than medium- or small-size organizations. Thus, it appears that professionalism does not necessarily 'drive out volunteerism' and that smaller organizations – where the likelihood of greater face-to-face interaction valorized under the Tocquevillian/Putnam model – are not necessarily the vanguard of volunteering (Maloney and Roßteutscher 2005).
4 Not only is patronage important/crucial for group maintenance, it is also very important in the early stages of group formation. According to Nownes and Neeley (1996: 124) patronage allows many public interest groups to 'overcome the "free-rider" problem as much as by-pass it'. They argue that both Walker (1991) and Hansen (1985) see mobilization as more dependent on patronage than members: 'The key to understanding which organizations form, then, is understanding which groups get subsidized and when' (Hansen 1985: 94).
5 Walker (1991: 33) pointed out that the Federal Government in the US (like governments in most democracies) is an important sponsor of many interest groups. However, while the national government

> is unlikely to be the sole sponsor of a group ... its overall impact on the group system, through tax incentives, contracts, and grants, is enormous ... Government support is an important source of patronage for groups in the United States, as elsewhere.

6 Patronage is also critical to political parties. Webb (1994: 112) argued that, 'It is perhaps not too great an exaggeration to say that, at least for Labour and the Conservatives, individual members are simply not crucial to the parties, in either an electoral or in a financial sense.'

7 While Grande (2002: 130) makes the point that professionalized representation in the EU could be 'justified for reasons of system effectiveness, but the democratic quality of their activities is dubious from the perspective of both representative and participatory models of democracy' (quoted in Saurugger 2008: 1279).
8 Strolovitch (2006: 905) found that many of the advocacy groups representing marginalized citizens that she interviewed stated that they were more active on issues they perceived to be important to members and that they would address an issue if they began 'getting lots of phone calls'.
9 In the interest group marketplace in order to be successful groups attempt to occupy a particular niche position in distinction to their competitors. In many instances this market niche leads the organization to seek a narrow membership. The more 'exclusive' membership may be attracted to the group because it is *purer* than some large-scale organization that may have to make internal (and external) compromises to aggregate interests, or maintain an advantageous position in the policy-making process.
10 Barakso and Schaffner (2008: 202) found that older associations were significantly more democratic than newly formed groups, a finding that supports critiques of the contemporary interest group sector as more focused 'on attracting "checkbook members" than on fostering participation within their organizations'.
11 A caveat regarding local chapters and branches is that even where these exist and a small percentage of members are active (e.g. Friends of the Earth or Greenpeace) some local groups are merely affiliated to the national group via the brand logo; there is no mechanism for local group members to become involved in national policy formulation. In groups such as Amnesty International (British Section) there are greater opportunities for membership input into policy decisions.

7 Professionalized supply-side mobilization

Are financial contributors 'meaningful participants'?

Grant Jordan

The annual report (2008/9) of the National Trust (NT) in the UK claimed 3.6 million members. The comparable report for the Royal Society for the Protection of Birds (RSPB) recorded a membership of 1,060,273, including 175,053 juniors. Both organizations encourage 'local and voluntary activity', but most members do not take up the opportunity for an active relationship. Personal engagement is not the typical sort of membership experience in most prominent large-scale UK organizations.

As numerically impressive as the RSPB/NT membership levels are that it is not the sort of group participation that elicits enthusiastic academic approval. The 'desirable' mode is in social movements or informal organizations reflecting 'democratization from below' in a mixture of deliberation and demonstration. The widespread contemporary discussion about the expansion of democracy to 'post representative democracy' (e.g. Rossi and della Porta 2009: 182) does not focus on RSPB/NT-type memberships or the processes and practices covered in this chapter. However such 'thin' participation is arguably overwhelmingly dominant as a mode of activity – though lacking positive normative associations. The argument here (based on Jordan and Maloney 1997) is that the activity stimulated by the group (supply-side) encourages a form of participation that is essentially financial (sustaining professionalized roles by organizational staff), and passive in terms of individualized action. Does this minimal version of participation (still) contribute to an active civil society? Is this 'meaningful participation' in the language of Fisher (2006: 7)? 'Thin' participation perhaps offers little in terms of Tocqueville's famous 'schools of democracy'. While the language of 'membership' is often used to those 'active' in these organizations *regular financial contributor or supporter* is usually a more accurate, if clumsy, label.

This chapter underlines the supply-side factor in securing support:[1] groups have become heavily professionalized in proactively developing levels of support and in securing other sources of funding that reduce the need for individual contributions.[2] And the modern group's attempts to influence political outcomes also often relies on expertise and evidence rather than voice and protest, so in the search for political influence the role of the individual member is often diminished. These professionalized public interest groups are particularly important to the participation debate because it is such cases that yield the large numbers that appear so impressive in discussions about the decline of party and replacement by group activities. But the large numbers relate to the 'slightest' forms of participation – i.e. financial contributions. (Such scepticism can be extended to query other so-called participatory activities such as consumer activity, see van Deth in this volume.)

The increased academic interest in groups reflects the assumption that 'membership' implies 'participation'. However, as signalled earlier, the normatively attractive pattern of participation may not be delivered by modern group membership. Sanders (1997: 347) points out, 'When democratic theorists suggest remodelling our politics, it is in the direction of making them more deliberative.' The deliberative 'turn' built on the participatory turn and perceives active involvement as a requirement of a good citizen.[3] Warren (1996: 241) notes the belief that participation is developmental: that if individuals were more broadly empowered, especially in the institutions that most directly affect their everyday lives, their experiences would have transformative effects. The argument, as summarized by Warren, runs on to the effect that individuals would become more public spirited, more tolerant, more knowledgeable, more attentive to the interests of others and more probing of their own interests...[4] The argument here is that involvement of the sort available in most large-scale, mail order, chequebook groups (Hayes 1986) delivers next to nothing of these sorts of democratic benefits.

Organizational modernization and professionalization

The new conventional wisdom of groups in contemporary politics is that they no longer need amateurish activists to achieve their goals, but professional paid staff with specialist training and expertise in fundraising, recruitment, political communication, campaigning etc. For example, Evans (2009: 149) describes the voluntary effort around welfare in the UK as 'the professionalization of poverty': 'The professionalization of all of these groups occurred in a number of different areas including lobbying activity ... utilisation of the media ... as well as in fundraising'. While Martens (2009) argued that NGOs such as Amnesty International have secured policy influence in international contexts not by mass mobilization but professionalization.[5] (See also Bosso 2003; Fisher 2006; Jordan and Maloney 1997, 2007; Negrine 2008; Skocpol 2003 and Maloney's and Saurugger's contributions to this volume).

Putnam cites the AARP (American Association of Retired Persons) which has experienced a dramatic increase in numbers from 400,000 card carrying members in 1960 to 33 million in the mid 1990s (40 million claimed in a press release on Ledbetter Act 28 January 2009). He concedes the expansion of group numbers, but contrasts this with the decline of participation in a meaningful sense by individuals. Putnam (2000: 51) notes that the 'new association' is almost entirely 'a denizen of the professional Washington hothouse ... not member-centred, locally based associations' with no opportunities for the face-to-face interaction necessary for social capital creation.

Skocpol (2003: 134) summarizes these recent trends in the US (in terms which match UK observations):

> All in all, the very model of what counts as effective organization in US politics and civic life has changed very sharply. No longer do most leaders and citizens think of building, or working through, state and nationwide federations that link face-to-face groups into state and national networks. If a new cause arises, entrepreneurs think of opening a national office, raising funds through direct mail and hiring pollsters and media consultants.

Skocpol also noted a 'shift from membership to management in American civic life'. Those new recruiting strategies and practices of major contemporary groups are unlikely to conform to the traditional interest-group model where members have policy-making influence and are provided with inter-personal educative opportunities.

This sort of observation means that modern group activity may be quite distinct from the traditional assumption that mobilization reflected a desire to contribute to securing collective action by the public. Instead this approach sees financial support as a response by individuals to group solicitation. Accordingly, Jordan et al. (1994b) adopted 'a *marketing perspective* ... group action in attracting the individual into membership/support is a better approximation to real decisions than the public choice approach which assumes mental gymnastics on the part of the individual'. Jordan and Maloney (1997: 145) concluded that much of such activity was part of the funding of protest rather than a means for much individual participation.

While this new conventional wisdom has been (re)discovered repeatedly, the literature is still probably biased (in different senses) towards the normatively attractive 'real', 'thick' participation rather than work that accepts the protest business reality and improves understanding of it. But the pointers to the supply-side are plentiful.

Richardson contended that citizens could be seen as consumers rather than makers of participation. He argued (1995: 135) that *credit-card participation* could be a form of '*surrogate activism* in which individuals support a particular cause – often single issue – but leave the formulation and delivery of the campaign to organizational professionals or to the few genuine activists within the organization' (emphasis added). He also contended that 'credit card membership' should be valued democratically (ibid.). He argued that a contribution reassured the donor that someone else is taking action. The job could be left to the professionals. Tasks are 'contracted out' by the members to the staff.

Supply-side approach: group-induced participation

Focusing on participation continually runs into the problem of possibly generalizing from the exceptional. If, say, thousands are involved, the impression may be given that that groups have solved the Olsonian collective action problem, but these thousands may be from a potential constituency of millions. And it is perhaps difficult for organizers – embedded in optimist networks of perhaps thousands of like-minded supporters – to regard their project as other than on track and reflecting 'normal' behaviour; whatever the actual mobilization rate looks like. In fact even at such levels significant participation still represents exceptional, even deviant, behaviour. Likewise surveys of members who have joined organizations perhaps are not proving it is normal to participate, but explaining why atypical individuals are mobilized – as Olson (1965) had predicted (see Jordan and Maloney 2006 for a full discussion). For participatory-inclined observers of groups the assumption is that the presence of participants shows the feasibility of recruitment and the task is simply to have more of the same. The contrary argument is that those responsive to the factors that produce active participation may be fundamentally different from the subpopulation that is inactive.

On the one hand political science has an Olsonian rational choice dimension that sees non-participation – particularly for citizen groups – as predictable (without the provision of selective incentives). On the other hand there is a normative element that uncritically assumes that participation is both desirable – and non-problematic. The conflicting ideas that participation is natural – for some people – or is unlikely, is a central cleavage in the academic literature. Whereas Olson saw participation as the consequence of an economically rational calculation,[6] others see it as reflecting human instincts and preferences. Pinker (2002: 305) writes, 'Every student of political science is taught that political ideologies are based on theories of human nature. Why must they be based on theories that are three hundred years out of date?' Certainly the implicit battle within political science between 'rational non-participation' and 'participation as irresistible human nature' is rarely informed by psychology. The interface between politics and psychology is still underdeveloped. The temptation for organizers of citizen groups seeking collective goods through individual action is to see their large numbers as the start of an expanding tide; but in the perspective pursued in this chapter the numbers mobilized may represent the finite minority in the public with certain non-selfish tendencies (not requiring selective incentives as an inducement to act) rather than a signal of future growth potential.

Olson's account of the problems of campaigning group mobilization is unconvincing and participation is not as unlikely as he suggested. Instead this chapter stresses a different position (for a substantial but not complete part of the story) – that participation is neither automatic as was assumed before Olson (Sentimental Normative Optimism) nor the result of individual based Rational Olsonian Calculation, but it is generated by group activity (supply-side). The broad argument of the third (supply-side) perspective, as considered in more detail below, is that professionalized communication by groups *alters the levels of support and the level of engagement.*

The supply-side perspective agrees with Olson that mobilization is not 'automatic', but offers a different process of engagement. Johnson (1995: 28) argues, 'Rather, to understand the groups that exist, one must understand that there are organizers and recruiting strategies whose efforts must somehow interact with the attitudinal basis of support in the community.' The stress on (de facto) marketing here attempts to explain the large increases in membership for some public interest groups. Groups seek to shape public perceptions of issues, and of themselves, in a process akin to a commercial brand war. 'Brands' are successful and enjoy premium pricing because they are trusted.

Moreover, in this vein, most of the mobilized public are not frustrated by the provision of passive roles in groups, but *prefer* to participate indirectly and financially rather than personally and actively (see van Deth 2009). In such a perspective, the 'contribution' of the citizen to democracy in the modern world is increasingly likely to be financial rather than personal. Olson's rational choice arguments outline a constraint on participation: mobilization *is* a problem, it is not necessarily spontaneous. But the supply-side view is that this is solved in non-Olsonian ways. As mentioned, the large numbers often cited as demonstrating extensive participation actually represent low percentage mobilization of *'thin' participators*, activated by groups (Schier 2000).

Arguably then, the actions labelled participatory in terms of direct action may have more of the qualities of moral panic than considered response (Cohen 1973). Participation should not be seen in flattering terms simply because of approval about the ends pursued. Action based on low information, external direction and opinion volatility is no less democratically suspect if in pursuit of liberal ends than illiberal. The 'manufacture of consent' is not tied to particular viewpoints. What kind of distinction can be made between 'Plane Stupid' environmental protest and the self-interested 'British Jobs for British Workers'?

The argument that many public interest groups have (particularly since the 1960s) successfully mobilized a *viable* proportion of citizens into support/membership has two important consequences. First, groups have been very successful at turning citizens' latent predisposition towards 'their' causes into supportership/membership. Second, while groups may have relatively 'limited supporterships/memberships' because they recruit only a small proportion of the potential membership pool to their causes, given that the potential membership pool is relatively large, in some cases numbering hundreds of thousands, if not millions, the small percentage actually mobilized can be significant in absolute numbers – i.e. tens of thousands to hundreds of thousands. The group may mobilize only a fraction of its potential pool of support, but a level that provides sufficient financial support and the appearance of representativeness.

The supply-side idea is that the professionalized representation of groups is often funded by a 'membership' that is itself created and mobilized by group-employed professional marketeers, recruiters and fundraisers. Members do not look for groups to join, but groups look for potential members to mobilize. Research about group activities (Jordan and Maloney 1997; Putnam 2000; Skocpol 2003) has found agreement – at least in Anglo-American settings – that the conventional (or sentimental) idea that members of the public are Trumanian self-starters seeking to secure collective goods that they have identified has been overtaken by a consensus that group action has transformed the scale of 'participation'. While of course there is 'authentic', traditional activity for some group members/supporters, it is not the dominant mode for the large-scale groups.

Importantly Berry (1999: 368) in commenting on citizen group growth is not reporting an irresistible bottom-up, individual-lead expansion, but group initiatives: 'Groups on both the right and the left have proved extraordinarily adept at identifying constituencies who are willing to open up their wallets to support them.' While Nagel (1987: 53; quoted in Rosenstone and Hansen 1993) claims, 'a moment's reflection shows that the people initiate little of what we normally call participation ... Acts of participation are stimulated by elites – if not by the government, then by parties, interest groups, agitators, and organizers'. This type of induced-participation is key in understanding the bulk of large group support.

Many groups 'chase' and generate such support. This perspective extends an interpretation of *interest groups as artefacts* (Jordan *et al.* 1994b). Groups take the initiative not only proactively recruiting sympathizers – but importantly make the prior step of influencing public opinion to align it with the views the group seeks to represent. In line with Converse (1964), the assumption that the public's views derive from individual's attachment to abstract ideological principles is rejected. Instead there is a shift from a vending machine image that sees participation emerging in predictable fashion from the existence of shared public attitudes, to stress the importance of group action in framing issues in a way that crystallizes beliefs that can then be aggregated.

Shaping opinions: group construction of individual preferences

In the supply-side perspective support/beliefs are seen as actively *created* rather than emerging autonomously to create membership passively received by groups. As long ago as 1986, Knoke was concluding, 'One thriving topic attracting much empirical and theoretical effort in recent years is the role of association involvement in stimulating individuals' external political activities' (8). As well as appealing to public values, groups may be instrumental in constructing value predispositions (i.e. 'priming'). In essence groups seek to market themselves as the authoritative voice in 'framing' public attitudes.

From the social construction perspective, the transformation of social problems into public concern is not automatic: predisposition is shaped. Media attention, and the connection to pre-existing mass concerns, is crucial. Hannigan (1995: 61) describes how sponsors of competing framings of an environmental problem measure their success primarily 'by gauging how well their preferred meanings and interpretations are doing in various media arena'. This contest for attention influences the nature of group activity. Issues regarded as novel are deemed more 'newsworthy' than those familiar to the public (Macnaghten and Urry 1998: 59; Hannigan 1995). And generally human interest stories also tend to receive disproportionate media attention. Commentators have noted a preference among the media for environmental stories that can be presented simplistically in Hollywood blockbuster style – good versus evil (Szerszynski 1991: 14; Lowe and Morrison 1984: 79).

So news and information for potential supporters is not 'fact' but is inevitably tailored by groups to suit their argument. Dearing and Rogers (1996: 2–3) argue that many social issues never translate into items on the political agenda without 'assistance'. Groups know that contested issues increase newsworthiness, and so the framing of a problem is often to polarize. Dearing and Rogers (1996) note that, 'Problems require exposure – coverage in the mass media – before they can be considered "public" issues', and that the visual power of a story can secure greater prominence in the news process than might otherwise be the case. Groups therefore deliberately offer events that can be presented as news. The 'needs' of the media lead to the staging of 'pseudo events' including protests, direct action and demonstration (Szerszynski 1991: 15, 254).

For many potential group supporters the primary source of information available is from the group itself. The public estimation of the value of participation is likely to be influenced by the version of reality that groups present. For example, when environmental groups highlight the serious problems caused by the destruction of the rainforest and/or the creation of a hole in the ozone layer, these may be both real and serious issues, but the public (and politician) acceptance rests on skilfully presented one-sided summaries of technical debates. The acceptance of this science looks more like the communication of rumour than evidence based policy making. This is not to suggest there is no crisis of global warming, but it is to argue that the public recognition of the 'crisis' is something they accept from sources they respect and not individual conclusions about competing scientific agendas.

Thus the concern about global warming fits in with pre-existing suspicions of modern technology.[7] Science is selectively trawled for evidence to reinforce assumptions. Is the evidence that ice is disappearing at the poles unidirectional? Has temperature been rising in the twenty-first century? Who says? The tendency is that any evidence contrary to prior hunches is dismissed as wrong (i.e. 'evidence' not evidence); as invention by the oil industry or prejudiced campaign groups. For both sides of the debate the question is: how are inconvenient particular studies rated as trivial exceptions rather than the cases that transform the debate?

Groups where crucial political issues are relevant to an industrial sector, professional association or trade union membership may be more suitable for Olsonian analysis than involvement with more altruistically based organizations. In the first type of organization the individual is likely to value the collective benefits, but may be tempted to free-ride to secure them if this is possible. Free-riding a professional association might lead to an individual congratulating him- or herself for his/her economic shrewdness, but would this be repeated with regard to membership of a public interest group? For example, if one worried about a problem such as humanitarian issues in Gaza, would one be self-congratulatory if one could free-ride and let others contribute? The mental calculus is simply different in different settings. This may be part of the resolution of the paradox of participation that Olson presented.

Insofar as 'concern' is the result of group 'shaping', it is a minor extension to say that activity too can be group determined. Membership (at least for some groups, some of the time) is not solely the result of somehow overcoming Olsonian calculation and free-riding, it is also about the social construction of an interest and the construction of a wish to join. Logically it is possible to free-ride a constructed interest, but the nature of some incentives makes free-riding inherently unlikely.

Beyond shaping preferences, groups seek to convert 'shaped preferences' into financial support. Two very broad styles of supply-side stimulation can be sketched. The first is the use of contact by mail or otherwise to pre-identified audiences. The second – discussed subsequently – is face-to-face recruitment. However, before groups can begin their recruitment campaign, they need to identify a viable and mobilizable target group.

Proactive targeting

The tools of mobilization have altered dramatically in recent decades (media technology, direct mail and the Internet) making it much easier to contact potential members (customers). Such technological advancement may have squeezed out small-scale, localist groups with potentially 'higher quality' participatory potential – replaced by large-scale professionalized protest businesses.

Increasingly groups have grown in number and support by direct mail and face-to-face recruiting (see below), rather than social networks or self-starting. Mundo (1992: 18) tellingly used the term 'mail order groups' to identify the direct mail recruiting strategies by large-scale high profile organizations. He noted, 'There are no meetings, virtually no decision-making procedures, and certainly no local or regional divisions within the group.'

A central component of direct mail recruitment is that groups 'recruit' from among specific targeted subsets of the population. Initially they identify predisposed individuals (with the necessary disposable income) most likely to join – for example, buying lists of 'warm names', i.e. individuals whose lifestyle, other supporterships/memberships or purchasing habits that might be predisposed to the relevant cause.[8] The increasing sophistication of finding new recruits is demonstrated by groups purchasing access to the results of web searches to advertise among the interested. Thus in May 2010 typing in a Google search for 'nuclear energy' prompts an advertisement to SONE – Supporters of Nuclear Energy – (with SONE application form link) and SONE briefing notes. Typing in 'trade unions' has sponsored links to the large UK union UNITE. Entering 'fox hunting' gives a link to the Countryside Alliance. 'Animal welfare' as a query links to WWF. 'Deaf' connects to a sponsored link to the National Deaf Children's Society.

Clearly, the competition for support is tough and groups are always seeking out new and innovative ways to find potential members. Once groups have identified the target population then they begin their recruitment campaign in earnest.

While direct mail has been a main staple of group recruitment, it is being supplemented (and in some cases replaced) by on-street recruitment ('face-to-face' – F2F in the jargon) with, in recent years, an increasing shift to 'door-to-door' (D2D in jargon). Thus the 2008/09 RSPB annual report noted:

> In 2008–9, we enjoyed our biggest year for membership recruitment since 1997's 'Million member' campaign, with a total of 130,000 new members recruited. Our marketing teams throughout the UK now place much greater emphasis on face-to-face recruitment (reducing direct mail and magazine inserts as a consequence) and it seems to be working. And all this was achieved for less money than last year.

The RSPB claimed 63 per cent of the 130,000 new members came courtesy of the newer, more personalized, on-street technique.

Jordan and Maloney (2007) analysed free-riding of group support in terms of Olson's dictum that rational individuals would 'leave it to George' rather than contribute themselves. In fact the direct mail industry discovered that it was not George who contributed disproportionately, it was a type of woman – labelled 'Dorothys' in the trade. The *Financial Times* (4 December 2009) noted that 'postal campaigns were delivering a preponderance of so called "Dorothy Donors" – women over 50 whose fondness for catalogue shopping meant they were overrepresented on the direct mail lists that charities used to target potential donors'. On-street recruitment was seen as a way of focusing on a wider and younger demographic to counter the Dorothy bias.

The origin of contracted on-street political recruiting appears to be in the US in the 1970s (but its entry to the UK is usually traced to Greenpeace in 1997 via Austria). For the US, Fisher (2006: 1) quotes a former encyclopaedia salesman – Marc Anderson – who had combined his door-to-door skills with his volunteer political canvassing experience to set up (initially) *Citizens for a Better Environment* and then the *Hudson Bay Company of Illinois* (a sort of advisory tool for other groups). Anderson said, 'If you can sell books to people door to door, you can certainly use the same discipline to talk politics and issues.' This may be business skills applied to 'good ends', but some commentators find this business dimension dissonant.

Fisher describes the activities of the People's Project that conducted a support soliciting service for Greenpeace, Sierra Club, etc. She (2006: 12–13) studied canvassers employed by the People's Project who 'stood on sidewalks recruiting and renewing memberships for progressive national organizations … Although they appear to be working for different organizations, they are, in fact, working for one organization that runs canvasses for many national and state groups.'

Fisher says the goal was to develop a funding mechanism for environmental groups and describes how 'in contrast to canvassers who go door to door collecting predominantly cash and checks, street canvassers ask people to become long-term supporters by providing a credit card number that can be charged monthly' (2006: 13). In a long distance from what was termed earlier Sentimental

Normative Optimism, she (2006: 54) says that involvement in the organization was limited to donating money and filling out postcards on the street or at the door: 'Such membership devoid of any real action or involvement at the local level has become the foundation of progressive grassroots politics in the United States today.'

If the first version of supply-side marketing is direct mail, (ideally) personalized to pre-identified subpopulations (market niches), the past decade has seen on-street recruitment[9] that is actually less sophisticated in terms of identifying potential contributors. Members of the public are approached (usually) by staff of outsourced professional companies on behalf of charities and groups. (Often the impression is given that these recruiters are actually volunteers of the end beneficiary group.) This is in fact an incentive based activity. The recruitment organizations are rewarded financially for attracting supporters, and given the cost of the recruitment activity itself such donors are only 'profitable' if they let their commitment run for several years. As described by Andrew Barton, head of relationship marketing at Oxfam, in the mid 1990s a number of larger charities had begun to promote regular giving rather than one-off donations.

> You had a whole period in the 1990s where the combination of direct mail, telesales and TV advertising was working really well ... But then you started seeing response rates and return on investment start to drop, and there was a decision that we needed to add some extra channels to the way we recruited supporters.
>
> (*Financial Times*, 4 December 2009)

The new approach was to 'contract out' the recruitment to on-street organizations.

This is a relatively neglected area – avoided perhaps by political science as too close to marketing – but it is central to mass recruiting and – depending on definition – participation. Whereas direct mail targeted the audience (segmentation), the on-street recruiters have a more blanket approach, but they are at least subconsciously selective in their contacts. Young people may relate better to other young people. Accordingly in the past decade large volumes of support have been generated for British charities and campaigning bodies as the result of solicitation by street recruiters (as well as direct mail) rather than a decision by a potential member to actively seek out the organization.

Membership, donations and fundraising

Dialogue Direct Fundraising UK (now in liquidation),[10] said on its website that:

> We work in partnership with charities and not-for-profit organizations. This method of fundraising starts with the idea that charities and NGOs need to build a valuable long-term relationship with their supporters and that committed support is best gained initially by directly engaging individuals in a

personal face-to-face dialogue. We pioneered this method of fundraising in Europe in partnership with Greenpeace in the mid-1990s.

Though this technique is motivated by fundraising rather than membership creation, the main point is this is not aimed at one-off 'charity tin' sort of contributions, but to have a financial connection over time.

The average donor gives for five years. These operations secure direct debits (automated payments) initially avoided restrictions on soliciting for cash donations on the street (this has now been overtaken by legislation that brings F2F into line with cash collections) – but in any case an ongoing direct debit is much more valuable to a group than a one-off payment. The recruiting company may get six months or even the full first year income as their fee, thus retention beyond the first year is crucial. By 2009 the cancellation rate was increasing to 57 per cent.[11] Cancelling may trigger refunds from the recruiting company. The Public Fundraising Regulatory Association (PFRA) (*Charity Times News*, 16 June 2003) cited a Henley Management Centre study estimating the average lifetime value of each new donor as £350.

The PFRA – with over 130 charities[12] in membership describes its focus as being on direct contact with donors through face-to-face methods. In 2007–08 charities found 230,000 donors with a further 280,000 donors picked up through the even newer approach of door-to-door fundraising. (This development may be a response to some high street resistance.) The aim is to generate pledges through direct debit or banker's order (automated payments).[13] According to the *Guardian* (24 November 2008) 25 per cent of Shelter's income came from face-to-face recruitment in 2006: 75 per cent of Greenpeace's new subscriptions in 2000–03 came via this method.

Face-to-face fundraising is not only financially efficient, it changes the demographics of giving – being particularly effective in motivating the young (but older donors may be longer lasting and hence more valuable.). In the *Financial Times* (4 December 2009) the PFRA, was quoted saying that its members generate 520,000 pledges a year by on-street recruitment – whose first 12 months of direct debit payments are potentially worth £54 million. Shelter, was said to have used street fundraising since 1998, estimating that about half its regular donors, worth £6 million a year, were recruited by 'chuggers'. The PFRA was also cited as claiming that, across the charitable sector, 1.3 million people – just under one-fifth of all direct debit donors – came by this route.

An article in the *Observer* (9 March 2003) described how,

> You may have seen the sort on your local High Street. Strategically stationed to ensure attempts at evasion are fruitless, they are usually young, bright-faced and impeccably polite. They wear bibs. They carry clipboards. They smile a lot. Many describe them as the most annoying people in Britain.

Based on her own experience the author said:

> We were taught how to approach the public: ask people if they have a minute for the cause, introduce yourself, tell them the problems facing the charity, the proposed solutions and then be upfront in asking for money ... It's not an easy job: although it may be for a good cause, chuggers are trained to be as tough as any other salesperson vying to relieve shoppers of their hard-earned cash.

An underlying normative issue relates to the gap between democratic rhetoric and membership mobilization for money by paid representatives with rehearsed scripts. Fisher (2006) describes the efforts by the groups to get canvassers 'to get the greeting right'. She described how recruits had to get the 'script' right and also use good body language, 'Greeting people [with] smiles.'

Those who see such links between givers and organizations as a disappointing variant of participation will be further concerned that the motivation for compliance may have little to do with wanting to assist the cause, but in wanting to end the asking ... Bob Fennis (quoted in the *Financial Times*, 4 December 2009) said:

> It is a bit counter-intuitive. When you think about charitable behaviour, the first thing that comes to mind is that it is very deliberate and inspired by ideals you have about a just world. But that is not necessarily the case. [Agreeing to sign up] is essentially a behavioural strategy that people in these encounters employ to swiftly end an interaction that is otherwise taxing to them.

The latest development in the area is the on-street securing of contact details that the group can follow up (prospecting). An example from 2008 was described as follows:[14]

> Cancer Research UK Street Prospecting Campaign
> Over a 26-day period in March and April 2007 17,913 prospects were recruited with a target of converting 15 per cent of these to donors.
>
> Cancer Research has not used traditional face-to-face in its fundraising mix before and this attracted a younger type of donor to the charity.
>
> The 15 per cent conversion to regular giving was achieved on the telephone with an average gift of £69 – slightly below target. Collection of phone numbers was 81 per cent against a target of 70 per cent. The campaign showed how conversion to regular giving can be three times sector averages for cold calling, just because prospects have been engaged with first.

The success of direct mail and F2F may have stalled – instituting a search for alternatives such as doorstep contact or on-street 'prospecting' leading to follow-up contact, but spontaneous mobilization is simply too limited for successful modern organizations to depend upon.

Conclusion

Overall the relationship between individuals and organizations described above are at best described as indirect participation by sofa supporters[15] pursuing audience (Manin 1997) or spectator democracy (van Deth 1997). Putnam (2000: 40) describes the modern citizen as watching a 'slick professional game' rather than playing or even watching an amateur or a semi-pro match. He argued (2000: 160) that

> It is not that direct-mail organizations are morally evil or politically ineffective. It may be more efficient technically for us to hire other people to act for us politically. However, such organizations provide neither connectedness among members nor direct engagement in civic give-and-take, and they certainly do not represent "participatory democracy".

A core theme of this chapter is that it is important not to homogenize discussions of all types of participation: consumer purchasing action or chequebook activity may have little in common with democratic contributions involving 'thick' personal participation by individuals in pursuit of collective political ends. Moreover, in all types of participation, the extent to which activity is generated by groups – establishing concerns and facilitating actions – is important. If activity is a matter of individuals responding to group mobilization, then the democratic 'story' may not be as assumed by participatory enthusiasts.

Low effort, cash-cow support is commonplace. Fisher (2006: 71) found group leaders recognized that a significant proportion of their members only wanted to contribute money. She quotes John Passacantando of Greenpeace, 'Some people just say ... I don't want to come out on an action ... *I'm funding you to do this* ... there are people who want to be activists and there are people who just want to give money' (emphasis added). Thus the core 'democrat-ness' in this area lies in the choice of which group to finance or join, rather than policy influence within groups. Additionally, this interpretation of group mobilization explains how viable organizations can be based on low public response rates to groups and low activity in groups. This is because it suits both the group and the (under) mobilized (see Maloney in this volume, and van Deth 2009).

Proactive direct mail and face-to-face tools are viewed as 'suspect' by those who value group based participation. There is the widespread concern that chequebook membership is too impersonal. Hayes (1986: 137) suggests large organizations in particular are concerned with national concerns, lack local level organization and therefore there are few, if any, real opportunities for member interaction. Thus the sort of group led mobilization conflicts with the direction of change sought by some enthusiasts for participation. Conover *et al.* (2002: 60) note:

> Philosophers accord deliberation a special place in democratic theory. And they envision citizens who accord deliberation a special place in their lives. But in fact, the citizens of modern liberal states have neither a special time nor a special place for the practice of democratic discussion.

110 G. Jordan

Much of the expectation placed on the interest group system in terms of delivering for democracy is by those who want decision making to be bottom-up, active and deliberative (and maybe have given up on parties as such vehicles) but this chapter suggests that the big numbers of participation do not promote the valued activity. Groups do involve large numbers, but their role is perhaps a shadow of that sought by participatory enthusiasts. However, if such minimal engagement is worth terming participation, it is important not to conflate big numbers of small efforts with the much smaller numbers engaged in stronger participation.

Underlying this discussion is 'a different picture in our heads' of the nature of participation generating organizations. These modern organizations are not 'mass' in Duverger's sense where the 'base' has control over leaders and policy making. (When mass groups are now discussed it often simply implies a large number organization rather than a statement about accountability.) In broadest terms the largest scale modern type structures are elite dominated, with professionalized lobbying and depending on spectator supporters with walk-on organizational roles – perhaps occasionally mobilized to 'protest' with preprinted placards shoved in their hands, or more likely predrafted emails to forward. If participation is defined much more ambitiously, it would be a much less common phenomenon.

Notes

1 This perspective is covered in more detail in Jordan and Maloney (2009).
2 Many groups develop market organization-like characteristics and draw on de facto instruction manuals that provide blueprints for running groups as business organizations (e.g. Dees *et al.* 2001: 199).
3 The time commitment implicit in the deliberation argument is large. Oscar Wilde's alleged answer to why he was not a socialist was, 'I prefer to keep my evenings free.' Deliberation is time hungry...
4 See Jordan (2007) for more detail of the suspicion of deliberation as a democratic tool in large-scale polyarchy.
5 Martens (2009: 229) defines professionalization as

> the process whereby problems are dealt with according to subject-specific knowledge and aims at maintaining quality standards and quality work (Rucht *et al.* 1997: 55). As a consequence, it has effects on the maintenance, strategies and tactics of movement organization (Staggenborg 1997: 421).

6 Jordan *et al.* (1994a: 530) noted 'Political scientists do not expect that cinema customers should be paid for investing their time in watching a movie.'
7 There does seem more strength in appeals based on 'bad news' than positive stories. This reflects the general idea of 'negativity bias' (Baumeister *et al.* 2001).
8 Frequently a subpopulation is selected because it resembles the existing membership. Thus a self-reinforcing process of segmented mobilization sees groups recruiting on the basis of their existing membership profiles. This practice reproduces the past and 'clones' existing support.
9 Those engaged in this activity are also described as 'chuggers' (charity muggers).
10 Ceased trading in October 2009. (It was itself successor to a version that had folded in 2007; *Financial Times*, 4 December 2009.)
11 See online, available at: www.fundraising.co.uk/news/2008/07/07/first-facetoface-attrition-survey-reports-results. Research by PRFA in 2008 established that the

conventional wisdom of leaving donors alone in case they reconsidered their support was wrong. More communication rather than less was the way to maintain support and prevent attrition.
12 Clients included Oxfam, Greenpeace, Friends of the Earth, Anti-Slavery International, RSPCA, WWF-UK, Shelter, League Against Cruel Sports etc.
13 The move to door-to-door appears to be related to worries that on street recruitment was seen as invasive and 'hurt the brand'.
14 See online, available at: www.fundraising.co.uk/blog/2008/05/02/best-use-facetoface.
15 On the same wavelength Fisher (2006: 8) refers to 'armchair activists'.

Part II
Changing democratic engagement

8 New modes of participation and norms of citizenship

Jan W. van Deth[1]

Participation is organization?

Almost by definition, politics – as the art or science of government or governing – is a collective and social phenomenon. Politics deals with the processes by which groups of people make decisions; not with purely private, non-public or individual matters. For that reason, *political participation is organization*: joining a party, attending a demonstration or signing a petition is done by at least a few people sharing the same interests or aims. Besides, political decision making in mass democracies involves a virtually endless list of parties, interest groups, movements, associations, committees, pressure groups and the like. Recently, the neo-Tocquevillean revival expanded the set of politically relevant groups by emphasizing the importance of engagement in all kinds of voluntary associations for a vibrant democracy. Arthur Bentley's century-old claim that: "When the groups are adequately stated, everything is stated" might be a bit too strong, but still captures much of the essence of the collective and social character of political life correctly.

Although individualistic modes of participation are long-standing (e.g. casting a vote, donating money, signing a petition), these modes require some kind of organization: you can't support a political cause if there are no political organizations to vote for, or support (financially or with time). This is a rapidly changing situation. New forms of participation such as boycotting or buycotting products or ethical shopping appear to be individualistic in a way not seen before. Refusing to buy specific products or brands in order to withhold support for, say, the destruction of rainforests does not require any organization or collective action. To be effective, a large number of people should behave in a similar way – but they can all act individually and separately. Of course, there needs to be some form of political entrepreneurship or organization that raises consciousness. Internet technologies have the potential to significantly enhance these modes of participation and make conventional organizations appear outdated. Accordingly, the organizational costs of participation have been lowered and all kind of concerns and aims are mobilized that may not have been articulated before, or at least would have found it even difficult. As a consequence, almost everybody can be politically active at any moment in time. Shirky (2008) summarized this development neatly in the title of his book *Here Comes Everybody: The Power of Organizing without Organizations*.

The mounting reluctance of citizens to base the expression of their demands and concerns on organized modes of participation has been reinforced by the growth of professionalized associations and groups and their heavy reliance on patronage and acceptance of the role of agents in a principal–agent relationship. Citizens seem to be content to contract out participation in policy-making processes to professionals and pay for this service (Jordan and Maloney 2007: 158–63; Saurugger 2007: 397–8). Chequebook participation and "outsourcing activism" (Fisher 2006) is widely accepted by many citizens and groups. In this division of labour, both citizens and associations can efficiently focus on their own goals. As a result, however, organizations and associational involvement has become less important for citizens and increasingly dispensable for political participation. Although organizations are necessary for decision-making processes, they are not conceived as mass political bodies for the direct involvement of citizens. In fact, contacts between organizations and citizens are increasingly characterized as supplier-customer relationships.

The two developments mentioned – a rise of individualized modes of participation and the professionalization of groups – strengthen each other and the combined effects could have important consequences for democratic citizenship. Citizenship includes engagement in public and political affairs, responsibility, solidarity, equal opportunities and individual rights. The very recognition of these requirements transforms people living in communities into citizens of a democratic polity. In his seminal work Marshall (1950) depicted citizenship as a status granted to individuals who meet specific requirements, changing people from subjects of political processes into participants and doers. Citizenship defines both rights and duties: i.e. citizens have entitlements within their communities/countries as well as obligations towards state institutions (Marshall and Bottomore 1950: 41–3, 45–6). If organizational activity is no longer a requirement for political participation, then engagement in public affairs loses its prominent position in the list of requirements for democratic citizenship. Consequently, some authors note the rise of a new concept of citizenship which is "marked by a radical individualism and extreme libertarianism" and is labelled "The S.U.V. model of citizenship: floating bubbles, buffer zones, and the rise of the 'purely atomic' individual" (Mitchell 2005: 77).

In this chapter the presumed increase in the prominence of new individualized modes of participation (especially boycotting) and its relevance for democratic citizenship are analysed. The first question to be addressed is the extent of individualized political participation and its impact on other modes of participation. Second, citizens using new modes of participation are supposed to be motivated by a lack of enthusiasm for organized forms of participation as well as relatively strong ethical/moral considerations and a focus on global issues. Reliance on Internet technologies is presumed to be another feature of these citizens. Consequently the entry barriers may be reduced and the traditional inequality in political participation may also fall. The empirical validity of these claims will be assessed here by analysing cross-national survey data (especially the European Social Surveys) for a number of established democracies.

Developments in political participation

A continuous expansion?

Political participation can be loosely defined as citizens' voluntary activities aimed at influencing political decisions. While this is a parsimonious definition a virtually endless list of definitions of political participation have been outlined.[2] The main reason for this lack of consent is obvious: politics is a highly diffuse and contested concept. Besides, citizens basically have the opportunity to engage in any kind of activity they consider appropriate to influence political decisions that is not explicitly illegal.[3] Introducing new forms of political participation, then, is straightforward and a continuous expansion of the repertoire seems obvious.

In all established democracies the modes of participation have been expanding rapidly since the 1950s and 1960s. This development reflects the growing relevance of government and politics for citizens in modern societies, the rise of skills and competences among citizens, as well as continuing the blurring of the distinction between political and non-political spheres. In the seminal voting studies of the 1940s and 1950s political participation was mainly restricted to casting a vote and campaign activities. By the early 1960s it was broadly understood as activities concerned with campaigning by politicians and parties, and contacts between citizens and public officials. These forms of activities became known as "conventional" modes of participation. In the late 1960s and early 1970s the modes of political participation were further expanded. First, due to the growing relevance of community groups and direct contacts between citizens, public officials and politicians, and, second, societal developments challenged the idea that political participation only consisted of broadly accepted forms or "conventional" modes. Protest and rejection joined the domain of participation (Barnes *et al*. 1979) and were labelled "unconventional" because they were not in line with social norms in the early 1970s. In the 1990s the disappearing borderline between political and non-political spheres and the revival of neo-Tocquevillean and communitarian approaches ushered in an expansion of political participation to include "civil" activities such as volunteering and social engagement (Putnam *et al*. 1993; Putnam 2000; Norris 2002). The most recent expansion has been characterized by the spread of individualized, ethically/ morally based acts of participation such as "political consumption" (cf. Micheletti 2003; Micheletti and Stolle 2007) or, more generally, "ethical consumer practices" (cf. Harrison *et al*. 2005) are recognized. The continuous expansion of the repertoire of political participation has grown from voting and campaigning in the 1940s to almost every conceivable form of activity imaginable now (van Deth 2001, 2010 or Zukin *et al.* 2006: chapter 3).

Empirically the expansion of the repertoire of political participation is predicated on cross-sectional studies advocating for the relevance of some specific (usually "unconventional" or "new") mode of participation. For instance, the authors of the Political Action study (Barnes et al. 1979) convincingly argued that protest activities belong to the repertoire of political participation, but they could not document an *expansion* or a *shift* in it since previous studies were simply restricted to conventional modes. Although there are numerous cross-national studies conclusions about long-term developments are not easy to validate empirically.[4] This is mainly due to the fact that, almost by definition, newer modes of participation have not been included in older studies. More frustratingly, however, is the apparent lack of willingness to include instruments in similar ways in different studies. Question wording, response scales or the number of items used differ considerably between various studies and make comparison difficult.[5] Furthermore, more recent studies use a 12 month time horizon for engagement in relevant activities. Scrutinizing the questionnaires of the Political Action study (PA), World Value Surveys (WVS), European Social Surveys (ESS) and the Citizenship, Involvement, Democracy study (CID)[6] results in only four modes of participation that have been used in each study in more or less similar ways:

- voted in the last (national) elections[7]
- signed a petition
- took part in a (lawful) demonstration
- boycotted certain products.

While this very short list falls quite some way short of covering the almost unlimited repertoire of political participation, it clearly includes the most important modes of participation. If the barriers to political participation have disappeared and people increasingly tend to prefer individualized modes of participation, then we can expect a continuous rise in the use of especially boycotting. Beside, the total share of people being politically active is likely to increase, since the addition of newer forms of participation to the action repertoire will increasingly mobilize parts of the populations that have not been active before.

Figure 8.1 shows the use of boycotting products for political reasons as a major form of individualized political participation for the seven European countries included in the first wave of the PA study in the period between 1974 and 2008. The graph corroborates the expectation of a rise of individualized modes of political participation in the last 35 years. Whereas less than 5 per cent of citizens had boycotted a product in the early 1970s this rises in each country until the late 1990s.[8] Contrary to expectations, however, the percentages of people using boycotts does not increase continuously but remains more or less at the same level (Finland), increases (Germany) or goes down (all other countries) in more recent studies. Although country-specific differences are considerable, in general boycotting products for political reasons increased popularity and reached a plateau between 1999 and 2002.

The distributions of voting, signing a petition, demonstrating and boycotting for the seven countries between 1974 and 2008 are summarized in Table 8.1

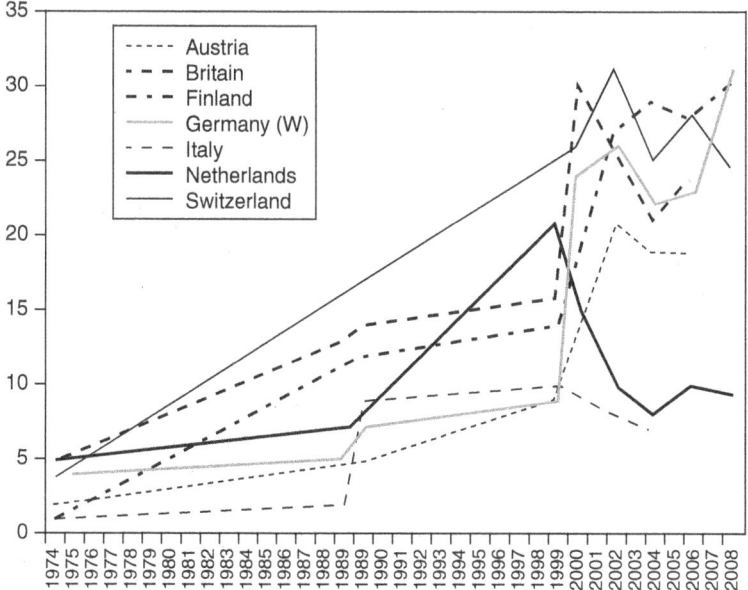

Figure 8.1 Use of individualized modes of political participation (boycotting) in Austria, Britain, Finland, West Germany, Italy, Netherlands and Switzerland, 1974 to 2008 (sources: datasets used: PA-1 (1974), EB-31 (1989), WVS (1989 and 1999), CID (2000), ESS (2002, 2004, 2006, 2008)).

Notes
Percentages "have done" of the total number of respondents; weighted with design weights, PA not weighted.

(first parts of the table for each country). These figures partly support the expectation. Firstly, the rise of boycotting for political reasons is mirrored in the figures for demonstrations. The percentages of people demonstrating in the early years are higher than those for the more recent period, and the last decade seems to show a stabilisation or slight reduction in the use of this form of participation. These results corroborate the idea that organized, collective modes of participation have become less attractive. As a mixed type of participation signing petitions developed differently in several countries, with a clear increase in Finland, Britain and Italy; a stabilization in Germany and the Netherlands; and a decrease in Austria and Switzerland. Finally, voting is declining in all countries. The more recent ESS studies show considerable fluctuations in participation rates in a short period of time. The general picture, then, suggests the growing importance of individualized modes of participation such as boycotting, which seems to have peaked around the turn of the century.[9]

In order to trace the developments among the different modes of participation several indicators have been computed (second parts for each country in Table 8.1). Looking at the percentages of citizens using at least one of the four modes

Table 8.1 Forms of participation in Austria, Britain, Finland, West Germany, Italy, Netherlands, and Switzerland, 1974 to 2008

		PA-1	EB31	WVS 2, 4		CID	ESS 1, 2, 3, 4			
		1974	1989	1989	1999	2000	2002	2004	2006	2008
Austria	Vote[a]	87	–	71	71	–	81	65	76	–
	Petition	34	–	45	56	–	27	24	21	–
	Demonstration	6	–	10	16	–	10	7	4	–
	Boycott	2	–	5	9	–	21	19	19	–
	At least one[b]	90	–	82	86	–	87	75	82	–
	None[c]	10	–	18	14	–	13	25	18	–
	Consistency[d]	0.31	–	0.38	0.42	–	0.42	0.37	0.39	–
	Coherence[e]	0.03	–	0.07	0.05	–	0.03	0.05	0.04	–
Britain	Vote[a]	72	78	82	69	74	67	62	67	64
	Petition	22	68	75	78	41	40	35	41	38
	Demonstration	6	11	13	13	4	4	4	4	4
	Boycott	5	13	14	16	30	26	21	24	24
	At least one[b]	78	93	94	91	85	80	76	78	77
	None[c]	22	7	6	9	15	20	24	22	23
	Consistency[d]	0.33	0.37	0.45	0.44	0.41	0.44	0.41	0.46	0.44
	Coherence[e]	0.07	0.07	0.08	0.08	0.08	0.10	0.07	0.12	0.13
Finland	Vote[a]	76	–	68	77	–	72	73	75	73
	Petition	19	–	34	47	–	24	26	32	32
	Demonstration	6	–	12	14	–	2	2	2	3
	Boycott	1	–	12	14	–	27	29	28	30
	At least one[b]	81	–	78	86	–	82	83	86	85
	None[c]	19	–	22	14	–	18	17	14	15
	Consistency[d]	0.26	–	0.45	0.53	–	0.27	0.28	0.27	0.49
	Coherence[e]	0.05	–	0.08	0.11	–	0.02	0.04	0.04	0.05
Germany (West)	Vote[a]	88	78	83	72	79	78	72	73	76
	Petition	31	28	57	48	31	30	32	27	31
	Demonstration	9	7	25	25	9	11	9	7	8
	Boycott	4	5	7	9	24	26	22	23	31
	At least one[b]	92	83	92	85	85	85	81	81	84
	None[c]	8	17	8	15	15	15	19	19	16
	Consistency[d]	0.35	0.38	0.46	0.46	0.49	0.44	0.44	0.43	0.40
	Coherence[e]	–0.00	0.10	0.06	0.05	0.10	0.07	0.08	0.07	0.04
Italy	Vote[a]	76	57	62	61	–	84	79	–	–
	Petition	10	38	42	52	–	17	13	–	–
	Demonstration	17	18	32	33	–	11	12	–	–
	Boycott	1	2	9	10	–	8	7	–	–
	At least one[b]	83	72	79	82	–	88	83	–	–
	None[c]	17	28	21	18	–	12	17	–	–
	Consistency[d]	0.13	0.43	0.50	0.47	–	0.44	0.43	–	–
	Coherence[e]	–0.01	0.13	0.08	0.07	–	0.03	0.04	–	–

Table 8.1 Continued

		PA-1	EB31	WVS 2, 4		CID	ESS 1, 2, 3, 4			
		1974	1989	1989	1999	2000	2002	2004	2006	2008
Netherlands	Vote[a]	75	79	87	90	76	81	77	77	80
	Petition	21	49	49	59	35	22	23	20	24
	Demonstration	7	13	24	31	5	3	4	3	3
	Boycott	5	7	8	21	16	10	8	10	9
	At least one[b]	80	89	93	95	85	86	81	81	84
	None[c]	20	11	7	5	15	14	19	19	16
	Consistency[d]	0.38	0.37	0.55	0.56	0.31	0.31	0.36	0.35	0.49
	Coherence[e]	0.06	0.08	0.06	0.07	0.02	−0.02	0.06	0.05	0.02
Switzerland	Vote[a]	58	–	55	–	56	54	55	51	53
	Petition	44	–	61	–	36	39	38	35	38
	Demonstration	8	–	15	–	7	8	9	7	8
	Boycott	4	–	–	–	26	31	25	28	25
	At least one[b]	74	–	78	–	73	73	73	69	69
	None[c]	26	–	22	–	27	27	27	31	31
	Consistency[d]	0.38	–	0.44	–	0.40	0.44	0.45	0.47	0.50
	Coherence[e]	0.08	–	0.17	–	0.11	0.11	0.10	0.13	0.09

Notes
Percentages "have done" of the total number of respondents; weighted for design effects, PA not weighted.
a For the WVS: percentages of respondents mentioning a party on the question "Which party would you vote for?"
b Percentage of respondents having used at least one of the four modes of participation.
c Percentage of respondents having used none of the four modes of participation.
d Association between modes of participation (Cronbach's Alpha for the four items).
e Relationship between voting and the three other modes of participation (average beta coefficient controlled for age, sex and education).

of participation (first row) or not a single one (second row) it is clear there is no general increase. In most countries, participation in general seems to be steady or to go down slightly, with the clear exception of Austria and West Germany where the willingness to participate was higher in the early 1970s than revealed by more recent studies. In spite of the evident growth in the percentages of citizens using boycotting for political purposes in the last decades, the total number of participants does not seem to increase continuously. This result suggests that newer modes of participation are integrated into existing forms and are not used as vehicles to recruit new parts of citizenries. This interpretation can be further tested by computing indicators for consistency and coherence among the various modes of participation (third and fourth rows). Consistency is indicated by the average inter-correlations (Cronbach's Alpha) for the set of four items in each country. As Table 8.1 indicates these items are positively related, but their interrelationships are not very strong. In general, the coefficients tend to increase, which suggests that the four modes increasingly can be seen as specimen of a common latent construct. In other words, boycotting is increasingly integrated in the concept of political participation. Finally, the average correlation between voting and the three other modes is used as a measure of the coherence of political participation in each country. With a few very minor exceptions, these coefficients are all positive. In spite of the relatively low levels obtained for this indicator, an increasing trend is evident in many countries. This finding highlights the fact that individualized modes of participation have not only become more popular – they are increasingly part of the political action repertoire of citizens and should not be viewed as a specific special type of behaviour.

These conclusions are bolstered when we use a larger set of similar items available in the PA and ESS studies. Table 8.2 shows that between 1974 and 2002 only the use of boycotts for political reasons has increased strongly and significantly.[10] Furthermore, all other indicators in the bottom part of the table underline the idea of stabilization or even a modest decline in political participation at the aggregate level since the turn of the century. Although the relatively high coefficients for consistency might be inflated by the larger number of items available, they certainly support the idea that the eight modes of participation – including boycotting – do not exclude each other. In a similar way, the positive coefficients for coherence support this conclusion. Although the three sets of countries consist of very different countries, no compositional effects are evident. Apparently, the development of participation is more or less similar in all European countries in the period considered.

New modes of what?

The lack of continuous growth of individualized political participation in the last decade and the stabilization at a relatively high level requires further examination. The consistency and coherence indicators presented in the previous subsection suggest that strong crowding-out effects between boycotting and other forms of political participation are unlikely. Yet these newer forms are not simple extensions of the political action repertoire of citizens. How, then, is boycotting related to other modes of political participation, especially to explicit organized and collective forms such as working in a party or in some other organization?

With the recent expansion of the action repertoire the nature of political behaviour changed. Older forms of participation are specific types of behaviour designed to "influence political decisions": casting a vote, joining a demonstration or supporting a candidate are all examples of such activities. As such, refusals to buy, say, a specific brand of coffee or athletic shoes are not forms of political participation, but non-political types of behaviour that could be used for political aims. In this way, the expansion of the political participation repertoire to include individualized forms differs clearly from previous expansions. Whereas, for instance, the addition of protest forms of participation to the action repertoire in the 1960s and 1970s implied an extension with specific types of political behaviour (demonstrating, painting slogans, collecting signatures etc.). The newest forms are characterized by the use of non-political modes of

Table 8.2 Forms of participation in Europe, 1974 to 2008

	All countries available in each study					Same countries in all five studies[a]					Same countries in all four studies[b]			
	PA-1	ESS 1, 2, 3, 4				PA-1	ESS 1, 2, 3, 4				ESS 1, 2, 3, 4			
	1974	2002	2004	2006	2008	1974	2002	2004	2006	2008	2002	2004	2006	2008
Voted last election	77	73	71	69	72	78	74	69	71	72	72	70	70	72
Contacted politician	28	15	12	12	11	27	15	13	14	17	15	13	13	14
Worked in political party	15	4	4	4	3	15	4	3	4	3	4	4	4	3
Worked in another organization	–	14	12	11	10	–	16	16	17	19	15	15	15	15
Worn badge/sticker	–	8	8	6	5	–	7	6	6	6	8	7	8	7
Signed a petition	26	26	21	20	17	28	33	32	32	33	28	27	27	27
Demonstrated	9	9	10	7	7	7	8	7	6	6	9	10	8	8
Boycotted products	3	17	14	13	13	4	24	20	22	25	19	18	18	20
At least one[e]	86	83	81	77	79	86	85	81	82	83	82	81	81	81
None[d]	14	17	19	23	21	14	15	19	18	17	18	19	19	19
Consistency[e]	0.51	0.62	0.62	0.61	0.62	0.53	0.58	0.58	0.59	0.58	0.62	0.62	0.62	0.62
Coherence[f]	0.07	0.05	0.05	0.05	0.05	0.06	0.06	0.06	0.07	0.07	0.06	0.06	0.06	0.06
N (weighted)	10,869	37,793	47,799	49,207	58,456	6,588	14,093	14,285	14,438	14,567	29,736	30,250	30,710	31,116

Notes

Percentages "have done" of the total number of respondents; ESS weighted with design weights and weights for country size; PA not weighted.

a Same countries in all five studies: Britain, Finland, Germany (West), Netherlands, Switzerland.
b Same countries in each of the four ESS studies: Belgium, Switzerland, Germany, Denmark, Spain, Finland, France, United Kingdom, Netherlands, Norway, Poland, Portugal, Sweden, Slovenia.
c Percentage of respondents having used at least one of the modes of participation.
d Percentage of respondents having used none of the modes of participation.
e Association between modes of participation (Cronbach's Alpha for the sets of items).
f Relationship between voting and other modes of participation (average beta coefficient controlled for age, sex and education).

behaviour (product boycotts etc.) for political purposes. The distinction between boycotting a product because you don't like its taste or shape on the one hand, and boycotting it for political reasons on the other, can *only be based on the expression of these aims by the person involved*.[11] Especially Micheletti (2003: 14) advanced a strong argument for "political consumerism" as a newer form of individualized collective action.

> political consumerism is politics when people knowingly target market actors to express their opinions on justice, fairness, or noneconomic issues that concern personal and family well-being. When they shop in this fashion they are using their consumer choice as an ethical or political assessment of favorable and unfavorable business and government practice.

Apparently neither the activity as such, or the target is crucial to the political consumerism label. New individualized modes of participation should be "ethically" based and considered as an "expression of opinions".[12] As Shirky (2008) and many others remind us, instead of conventional (mobilizing) organizations it is the opportunities provided by modern Internet technologies that are crucial for mobilization via these new modes of participation.

As a radically different type of participation boycotting products for political reasons does not have to be related systematically to other modes of political participation. Although the figures for coherence and consistency presented above are not very strong, they do suggest that boycotting belongs to the political action repertoire of citizens. As novel as boycotting may be it is systematically related to other political activities. In order to explore this interpretation more closely we examine the correlations between boycotting and other modes of participation. Instead of exploring bivariate coefficients separately the relationships between boycotting and other modes of participation, we investigate the latent structure. Table 8.3 shows the results of these explorations (PCA) for eight modes of participation available in all four waves of the ESS. If boycotting is a mode of political participation it should be grouped among other modes of political participation on some latent dimension which can then be interpreted as "political participation".[13] Starting with boycotting the number of political items included in the analyses is increased step-wise until a one-dimensional solution is no longer appropriate (eigenvalue of a second component evidently larger than 1.0). After several attempts a similar single dimension appeared in both sets of countries in each of the four waves including six of the eight modes of participation available. The parameters for the fit of this single dimension all suggest that it can be seen as an appropriate summary of the six items in each study. The position of boycotting on this dimension is ambivalent. On the one hand, boycotting fits into the structure and is clearly positively correlated with such political activities as working in a party or attending a demonstration. Boycotting, therefore, is an ordinary part of the *political* action repertoire as defined by the six items. On the other hand, we see that boycotting products for political reasons is a very weak member of the set of participation items: the communalities for boycotting

Table 8.3 Explorative structure of political participation in Europe, 2002 to 2008

	All countries available				Same countries in all four studies[a]			
	ESS 1	ESS 2	ESS 3	ESS 4	ESS 1	ESS 2	ESS 3	ESS 4
	2002	2004	2006	2008	2002	2004	2006	2008
Worked in political party or action group	0.30	0.32	0.31	0.29	0.30	0.32	0.28	0.26
Worked in another organization	0.35	0.40	0.37	0.38	0.34	0.38	0.36	0.36
Worn badge/sticker	0.44	0.44	0.43	0.42	0.43	0.41	0.43	0.41
Signed a petition	0.43	0.42	0.43	0.45	0.41	0.41	0.43	0.42
Demonstrated	0.42	0.38	0.39	0.38	0.43	0.37	0.40	0.36
Boycotted products	0.27	0.27	0.26	0.32	0.26	0.27	0.25	0.30
Variance explained (%)	37	37	37	37	36	36	36	35
KMO-Test	0.75	0.75	0.75	0.76	0.75	0.76	0.75	0.74
Cronbach's Alpha	0.64	0.65	0.64	0.65	0.62	0.62	0.62	0.61
N (weighted)	37,793	47,799	49,207	58,456	29,736	30,250	30,710	31,116

Notes
Excluded items: "vote in last election" and "contacted a politician".
Principal component analyses; communalities of single dimensional solutions; weighted with design weights and weights for country size.
a Same countries in all four studies: Belgium, Switzerland, Germany, Denmark, Spain, Finland, France, Hungary, United Kingdom, Netherlands, Norway, Poland, Portugal, Sweden, Slovenia.

are among the lowest in each analysis.[14] Boycotting belongs to the political action repertoire, but it clearly is one of the weakest among the set of items defining political participation.

Structural analyses as summarized in Table 8.3 corroborate the conceptualization of individualized forms of participation as modes of political participation. They do not establish a unique type of behaviour unrelated to activities such as working in a party, signing a petition or attending a demonstration. The spread of newer modes of participation implies an *extension* of the political action repertoire of citizens and not the rise of radically different or alternative modes of participation (cf. de Rijke *et al.* 2008: 142–3). Mainly due to this extension the general level of political participation has been stabilized at a relatively high level in Europe in the last few years.

Citizenship

Although the various modes of participation belong together different parts of the populations might select different modes of participation for a variety of reasons. As noted above, several authors maintain that there has been a shift from collective, organized modes of participation towards individualized, "ethically" based forms. These two statements are not mutually exclusive: newer, individualized forms of participation can be part of the political action repertoire and – at the same time – be used by people who dislike organizations and are motivated mainly by normative considerations. Do people supporting specific norms about the role of citizens in democratic societies use new modes of participation more frequently than those less supportive of such norms? If individualized forms of participation are meant to express and emphasize moral/ethical considerations, are people using these newer modes characterized by relatively high levels of support for democratic norms of citizenship?

Determinants of individualized and collective forms of participation

In order to explore the impact of ethical/moral considerations empirically, a typology of participants using only individualized and organized modes of participation is constructed (i.e. boycotting and buycotting).[15] While other modes of participation might have individual features, boycotting and buycotting do not require some kind of organizational or collective coordination. To be effective, it certainly helps that a large number of people behave in a similar way – but they can all act individually and separately and no top-down coordination is required. With the items "worked in a party or action group" and "worked in another organization or association" two unambiguous organizational modes of participation are available. With these two sets of two variables four types of participants can be identified (see Table 8.4).

The first type consists of people who do not discriminate between available modes of participation and are involved in both individualized and organized forms. They are labelled *activists*. Next, we have *individualists* who specialize in

Norms of citizenship 127

Table 8.4 A typology of individualized and organized modes of participation

	Individualized modes of participation:	
	used boycotting or buycotting	not used
Organized modes of participation:		
active in party or association	Activists	Collectivists
not active	Individualists	Others

individualized modes of participation and do not use organized forms. *Individualists* are characterized by the combination of involvement in individualized modes of participation and abstention from organized forms. Similarly, we distinguish *collectivists* as those citizens who are engaged in organizations but do not use individualized modes of participation. The remaining citizens are simply called *others*; they are not involved in either individualized or organized modes of participation analysed here, but they may of course, be involved in some other mode of participation. Table 8.5 shows the distributions of these four types of participants in each of the four waves of the ESS. These figures, once again, underline that individualized modes of participation are very popular in Europe, but that a continuous increase cannot be observed.[16]

The difference between *individualists* and *collectivists* is expected to be closely related to a distinction in the normative orientations they support. Information about norms of citizenship seems to be particularly relevant for understanding changes and differences in participation. Norms of citizenship shape citizens' behaviour in specific ways (cf. Theiss-Morse 1993: 370; Verba *et al.* 1995: 105–21). Since *individualists* are likely to base their actions on ethical/moral considerations they are expected to show relatively high levels of support for various norms of citizenship as compared to *collectivists*.

Although discussions about the various meanings of citizenship are centuries old, there is a paucity of empirical research on the normative aspects of citizenship.[17] In the first wave of the ESS a question on the personal image of a "good citizen" is used which captures various aspects of these normative considerations:

To be a good citizen, how important would you say it is for a person to…:

- support people who are worse off than themselves?
- to vote in elections?
- always obey laws and regulations?
- form their own opinion, independently of others?
- be active in voluntary organizations?
- be active in politics?

Respondents expressed their opinion for each item on an 11-point scale ranging from "extremely unimportant" to "extremely important". On the basis of a similar set of items in the CID study Denters *et al.* concluded that: "in each of

Table 8.5 Types of participation in Europe, 2002 to 2008

	All countries available in each wave					Same countries available in all waves[b]				
	Types					Types				
	Activist	Individualist	Collectivist	Others	N	Activist	Individualist	Collectivist	Others	N
2002[a]	8	21	7	64	37,793	9	24	8	60	30,656
2002	5	12	10	73	37,793	6	13	11	70	30,656
2004	5	10	9	77	47,799	6	13	10	71	31,250
2006	4	9	9	78	49,207	6	13	11	71	31,738
2008	4	10	8	79	52,747	6	14	10	70	31,116

Notes
Percentages of each type of the total number of respondents, weighted with design weights and weights for country size.
a In 2002 also buycotting products is available and included in the four item typology as a mode of individualized political participation.
b Countries included: Belgium, Switzerland, Germany, Denmark, Spain, Finland, France, United Kingdom, Hungary, Netherlands, Norway, Poland, Portugal, Sweden, Slovenia.

our countries the majority of citizens internalized a fully-integrated concept of citizenship" (2007: 106). Yet support for the various norms appears to differ widely (cf. Roßteutscher 2004; Denters and van der Kolk 2008; van Deth 2009). Whereas autonomy, law-abidingness, solidarity and voting are considered to be very important by (large) majorities of citizens in each country, engagement in voluntary associations and political activities lack broad support. Apparently, casting a vote is widely seen as an important aspect of a "good citizen", but further engagement is considered to be much less relevant. In fact, for many people a "good citizen" is someone who visits the ballot box – not someone who is engaged in public and political affairs beyond voting.[18] People are consistently reluctant to place much value on both social and political participation as core aspects of being a "good citizen" (cf. Theiss-Morse and Hibbing 2005: 242–5). Obviously, the "ideal citizen is not the enlightened political participant cognizant of the common good but the effective one" (Gross 1997: 233).

Are differences in support for these norms of citizenship relevant for participation, or, more specifically, does strong support for these norms increase the likelihood of using individualized modes of participation? In order to answer this question major antecedents of belonging to one of the four types of participants are outlined in the (logistic) regression analyses (see Table 8.6).[19] The first two blocks consist of factors that are considered to be relevant for the use of individualized modes of participation: various norms of citizenship and use of the electronic means of communication.[20] In addition major antecedents of political participation are added: social participation (following the neo-Tocquevillean interpretations that engagement in voluntary associations facilitates political engagement), political orientations (ideology, political interest, efficacy and discontent all have an impact on the willingness to participate), socio-demographic features (traditionally age, sex and education are relevant for participation) and finally dummies for the contextual effects of country-specific factors (participation depends at least partly on the opportunities, institutions and events available in some country).

The results of the regression analyses corroborate a number of expectations. Individualized modes of participation are preferred by people who strongly support the norms to vote in elections and to form their own opinions. On the other hand, support for law abidingness and organizational and political engagement does not increase the chances of engaging in individualized modes of participation. It is of little surprise that people strongly supporting the idea that organizational engagement is an important aspect of a "good citizen" are highly likely to be active in political organizations (the *collectivists*). The coefficients for the prospect of becoming an *individualist* exhibit relatively weak effects (all about 1.0). Concentrating on individualized political actions is not very likely if one strongly supports norms of citizenship – favourable for that type of activity is a combination of support for independence and a rejection of law abidingness and social and political engagement. In other words, support for being a "good citizen" does not increase one's chances of engaging in new individualized modes of participation.[21] However, in line with the expectations, the Internet has

Table 8.6 Antecedents of types of participants, 2002

	Types							
	Activist		Individualist		Collectivist		Others	
	Exp b	R^2	Exp b	R^2	Exp b	R^2	Exp b	R^2
Norms of citizenship:		0.01		0.01		0.01		0.01
• solidarity with people	1.02		1.00		0.94***		1.00	
• vote in elections	1.04***		1.04***		1.00		0.95***	
• form own opinions	1.02		1.09***		1.01		0.93***	
• obey laws and regulations	0.92***		0.96***		1.04**		1.08***	
• be active in organizations	1.10***		0.98**		1.14***		0.95***	
• be active in politics	1.03*		0.97***		0.99		1.01	
Use of the Internet:	1.09***	0.00	1.05***	0.00	1.01	0.00	0.92***	0.01
Social participation:[a]	1.47***	0.10	0.97*	0.00	1.27***	0.02	0.70***	0.05
Political orientations:		0.02		0.01		0.00		0.03
• left–right placement	0.93***		0.97***		1.04***		1.06***	
• political efficacy	1.10***		1.03*		1.05**		0.92***	
• political interest	1.60***		1.24***		1.28***		0.63***	
• satisfaction with democracy	0.97***		0.99*		1.00		1.03***	
Socio-demographic features:		0.00		0.03		0.01		0.02
• age	1.00		1.03***		1.00		0.98***	
• age (square)	1.00		1.00***		1.00		1.00***	
• sex (male)	0.86***		0.60***		1.73***		1.38***	
• education	1.04***		1.07***		0.98**		0.93***	

Country dummies:[b]				
	0.03	0.06	0.03	0.06
Austria	0.55***	0.44***	1.70***	2.29***
Belgium	1.29*	0.38***	2.71***	1.42***
Britain	0.62***	0.84*	0.64**	1.55**
Czech Republic	1.38*	0.46***	3.08***	1.10
Denmark	0.62***	0.82*	0.88	1.71***
Finland	2.26***	0.72***	2.82***	0.62***
France	1.29*	0.55***	1.78***	1.15
Germany	0.87	0.68***	1.22	1.43***
Greece	0.57***	0.22***	1.56**	2.80***
Hungary	0.33***	0.44***	0.63*	4.54***
Ireland	0.64***	0.34***	1.38**	2.28***
Israel	0.32***	0.18***	0.97	3.79***
Italy	0.39***	0.55***	1.41*	4.19***
Luxembourg	0.62**	0.31***	0.97	2.15***
Netherlands	0.54***	0.47***	2.06***	2.94***
Norway	1.05	0.20***	2.11***	1.50***
Poland	0.44***	0.15***	1.49**	3.35***
Portugal	0.39***	0.24***	1.16	4.80***
Slovenia	0.18***	0.20***	0.83	5.38***
Spain	0.93	1.07	3.82***	1.82***
Sweden	1.29*		1.07	0.78**
Nagelkerke R^2	0.26	0.16	0.12	0.35
N (weighted)	34,327			

Notes

Binary logistic regression; Nagelkerke R^2, weighted with design weights.

Significance: * $p<0.05$; ** $p<0.01$; *** $p<0.001$; R^2: variance explained by subsets of variables after controlling for all other variables.

[a] Number of voluntary associations being a member of.

[b] Reference category: Switzerland.

a positive impact on the selection of these modes of participation. Although a relatively high level of Internet access is conducive for all four participative types, the impact is much clearer for *activists* and *individualists* than *collectivists*.

Since the focus here is on explanatory factors for new modes of participation the results for the remaining blocks of variables are not considered in detail. The prospect of being an *individualist* increases with the level of subjective political interest (although the effect is stronger for the other types). Since both the coefficients for age and its square are significant and larger than one, the chances of being an *individualist* also increase with age, but are lower for the youngest and oldest cohorts. Younger people do not find individualized modes of participation very attractive, being young increases the likelihood of passivity. The results for sex are more straightforward. While males are highly likely to belong to the *collectivists* group, or to the less active type, females are more likely to use individualized modes of participation. This reversal of the conventional gender bias in political participation has been noted by many researchers (cf. Stolle et al. 2005: 263; van Deth 2010).[22] The effect of education demonstrates another difference between the backgrounds of people preferring individualized as opposed to collective modes of participation. A relatively high level of education increases the chances of becoming an *individualist* but appears unconducive for selecting collective modes of participation (cf. van Deth 2010). Finally, we see that country-specific effects are especially relevant for this category of participants.[23] Sweden is the only country that does not show significant differences with Switzerland (reference category). More importantly, however, is the fact that the likelihood of becoming an *individualist* depends strongly on specific country features, underlining the strong context dependency of using individualized modes of participation. This last result is surprising since the objects and goals of these actions are usually depicted as aspects of globalization – or at least address causes that are not restricted to the politics of a particular nation state. Apparently, boycotting and buycotting are not expressions of "Ethical Globalization" (Clark 2001: 17–18).

The fit of the models presented in Table 8.6 is not very impressive, but reaches acceptable levels especially for respondents who are either not very active (*others*) or use both individual and collective modes of participation (*activists*). However, comparing *individualist* with *collectivists* we see that a large part of the variance is explained by country-specific factors. Various expectations about the impact of major antecedents are confirmed. Internet usage, social participation, sex and education all affect the choice between individual and collective modes of participation. However, it is clear that newer, individualized modes of participation are not strongly determined by support for norms of citizenship. Apparently, the likelihood of becoming an *individualist* does not depend on whether one supports such norms. The highly significant but low coefficients for the support for traditional citizenship norms – law abidingness, social activities, political engagement – indicate that these ethical/moral considerations are not particularly relevant for the use of newer modes of participation.

Characteristics of participants

The democratic consequences of shifts in participation do not rely solely on the major antecedents of new modes of participation, but also on specific individual characteristics. If different groups select different modes of participation their impact on political decisions and the character of their contributions might be different too. The key question is: does the spread of individualized modes of participation contribute to more equality in participation and representation?

Usually, the problem of unequal participation and representation is approached by comparing the opportunities different groups have to participate (cf. Teorell et al. 2007). Since the main concern here is with characteristics of people using individualized modes of participation, that procedure is not followed. Instead, the perspective is reversed and we focus on the characteristics of different types of participants.[24] Table 8.7 shows the main characteristics of the

Table 8.7 Main characteristics of participants in Europe, 2002

	Types				Average
	Activist	Individualist	Collectivist	Others	
Norms of citizenship:[a]					
• form own opinions	+0.23	+0.23	+0.18	−0.13	8.20
• obey laws and regulations	−0.19	−0.06	+0.09	+0.04	8.05
• vote in elections	+0.29	+0.16	+0.21	−0.12	7.51
• solidarity with people	+0.15	−0.01	+0.08	−0.02	7.39
• be active in organizations	+0.31	−0.08	+0.43	−0.06	5.45
• be active in politics	+0.33	0.00	+0.23	−0.07	3.95
Use of the Internet:[b]	+0.59	+0.33	+0.18	−0.20	0.39
Social participation:[c]	+01.08	+0.26	+0.59	−0.29	1.15
Political orientations:					
• left–right placement[a]	−0.24	−0.07	+0.05	+0.05	4.92
• political efficacy[d]	+0.39	+0.17	+0.24	−0.14	2.82
• political interest[e]	+0.68	+0.38	+0.38	−0.25	2.37
• satisfaction with democracy[a]	+0.06	+0.06	+0.11	−0.04	5.19
Socio-demographic features:					
• age (mean)	−0.10	−0.07	+0.08	+0.03	45.67
• sex (share of males)	+0.07	−0.11	+0.34	−0.01	0.474
• education[f]	+0.62	+0.37	+0.23	−0.23	11.80

Notes
Differences between group average and total average divided by standard variation per variable; weighted with design weights and weights for country size.
a Based on mean scores on 11-point scales.
b Based on mean scores on a dichotomous scale: 1=use of Internet; 0=no use of Internet.
c Based on mean scores on 13-point additive scale for number of memberships in voluntary associations.
d Based on mean scores on 5-point efficacy scale.
e Based on mean scores on 4-point scale for subjective political interest.
f Based on mean scores for the number of years of full-time education.

four types of participants indicated by the standardized deviation of each specific group from the total average.[25] The first block contains the deviations for the support for various norms of citizenship. Surprisingly, the *individualists* show remarkably low levels of support and do not reach the highest score for any of the norms mentioned. In fact, support for norms of citizenship hardly differs from the support that each norm obtains in general.

Support for norms of citizenship does not only appear to be irrelevant for engagement with individualized modes of participation (see above, "Determinants of individualized and collective forms of participation") – citizens using these modes do not support these norms more than others.[26] On the contrary, while *individualists* exhibit relatively low levels of support, it is the *collectivists* and the *activists* who show clear support for norms of citizenship. Claims that people using individualized modes of participation are characterized by relatively high levels of ethical/moral considerations are evidently not valid for long-established norms of citizenship.[27] Moreover, the depiction of new modes of participation as "responsibility-taking" activities (Micheletti and Stolle 2007; Micheletti and McFarland 2011) appear to be true in a rather remarkable way. *Individualists* take responsibility by stressing the importance of forming one's own opinion, but are reluctant to show solidarity with people worse off or to be engaged in organized social activities. Individualized political action apparently is based on rather self-centred considerations.

Individualists and *collectivists* differ in the use of the Internet and the scope of their social networks in the expected ways. In terms of political orientations, however, the distinctions between these two types are modest at best. Much clearer are the socio-demographic differences: on average, *individualists* are younger and more highly educated than *collectivists* and there are clear sex differences. While men represent a clear majority among *collectivists*, women are overrepresented among users of individualized modes of participation. New modes of participation seem to contribute to greater gender equality in participation. Yet the emancipatory gains obtained by the fact that women use boycotting and buycotting more frequently than men are mixed since these higher rates are – at least partly – based on a rather conventional division of tasks with women still mainly in charge of shopping. With respect to the standardized coefficients in Table 8.7, however, the conclusion is more appropriately stated by referring to the fact that larger deviations are found both for *activists* and *collectivists*. The most active part of the population is most clearly characterized by conventional features of engaged citizens.[28]

Comparing the columns in Table 8.7 it is clear that the *individualists* do not deviate strongly from the population in general. It is the *activists* – and not the *individualists* – who use the Internet frequently, have the largest social networks, are more left-leaning, who exhibit higher levels of political efficacy and interest, and are relatively young and highly educated. For *activists* individualized modes of participation seem to be a simple extension of their participation repertoire. These results are in line with the findings presented above on the relationships between several modes of participation (see above, "New modes of what?").

Individualized modes of participation used in combination with other forms of participation by *activists* are characterized by relatively strong support for norms of citizenship and Internet usage. People using only individualized modes of participation do not strongly support these norms – apparently their norms of citizenship are highly individualized too.

Conclusion

As democracy constantly evolves, so does participation. The continuous expansion of the repertoire of political participation is a feature of a vibrant democracy and the creativity of its citizens. Yet the latest round of expanding the modes of political participation appears distinct from previous developments. New modes of participation are individualized: non-political types of behaviour such as boycotting and buycotting do not require any organization or collective endeavour. These forms are expected to be used by people who are looking for opportunities to express ethical/moral points of view and are likely to (gradually) eschew organized modes of participation. Furthermore, the Internet is presumed to facilitate these newer forms of participation.

The empirical analyses presented in this chapter partly support these claims. First, political participation has indeed expanded in many countries in the last decades. This rise is clearly visible in the use of individualized modes of participation that rose rapidly until the turn of the century. However, the recent plateauing – at a relatively high level – casts doubts on the expectation of a continuous rise in the use of these modes of participation. Second, new modes of participation do not appear to be distinct from other modes: i.e. individualized modes of participation fit systematically into a meaningful structure with other forms of *political* participation. Besides, the antecedents of using newer modes of participation are rather similar to the antecedents of the total population, and people using these modes do not establish a clearly distinct part of the population. Finally, several of the presumed characteristics of people using individualized modes of participation were not confirmed. Country-specific factors appear to be very important for the spread of newer forms of participation, challenging the globalization thesis. *Individualists* do not show a high level of support for norms of citizenship and do not use the Internet unusually often. In fact, people using organized modes of participation appear to deviate more strongly from the total population than *individualists*. In that sense, the rise of individualized modes of participation contributes to a reduction of political inequality documented in every study of political participation.

The rise of individualized modes of participation, then, has mixed consequences for democracy and the further development of democratic citizenship. Although any reduction of inequality in participation should be welcomed, it is clear that people using newer modes of participation do not strengthen support for norms of citizenship. In fact, people using only individualized modes of participation are characterized by relatively low levels of support for these norms. Their idea of "responsibility taking" is evidently self-centred and based on clear support for the norm to form your own opinions and a reluctance to support solidarity and social engagement. Fisher's observation that recent organizational developments have "significantly limited the diversity of entry points into progressive politics from the grassroots level" (2006: 85) is certainly not compensated by the rise in individualized modes of participation since this rise implies a weakening of support for norms of citizenship. Citizens using organized modes of participation or those who combine organized and individualized modes appear to be much more supportive of citizenship norms. *Activists* and *collectivists* differ, more clearly from the general population than *individualists*. Support for norms of citizenship comes with less equality whereas more equality implies less support for citizenship norms.

Politics is still strongly based on organization and many citizens do not discriminate between individualized and collective forms of participation. Those who restrict their activities to individualized modes are not distinct from the general population. Therefore, "the power of organizing without organizations" (Shirky 2008) will change the issues articulated and weaken the position of conventional associations in political decision-making processes since it is the *activists* and *collectivists* who differ more clearly from the total population. The more important development, however, is the weakening of support for norms of citizenship which comes with the spread of individualized modes of participation. In spite of fashionable (post-modern) claims about the evaporation of the borderline between private and public affairs, *individualists* seem to be most clearly characterized by this distinction. They have much more in common with the image of a consumer than a citizen: 'the transformations of citizens into consumers is understood as diminishing the collective ethos and practices of the public domain (embodied in the figure of the citizen) and both privatizes and individualizes them (in the figure of the consumer)' (Clarke *et al.* 2007: 17). How to cope with the combination of individualized participation and a rising accentuation of self-centred norms among participants seems to be an important challenge for the way contemporary democracy functions.

Notes

1 I am grateful to Christian Schnaudt and Sarah Odrakiewicz for their assistance preparing the empirical results presented in this chapter and my collaborators at the Department of Political Science and at the Mannheimer Zentrum für Europäische Sozialforschung (MZES), University of Mannheim for their stimulating comments on an earlier draft.
2 See Verba und Nie (1972), Brady (1999) or van Deth (2001) for overviews of the literature.
3 This open-endedness has been a characteristic of many definitions of participation for a long time: "citizen participation is a categorical term for citizen power. ... it is a means by which [the have-nots] can induce significant social reform which enables them to share in the benefits of the affluent society" (Arnstein 1969: 216).
4 See Inglehart and Catterberg (2002) for an exception.
5 For instance, the World Values Surveys do not ask about voting behaviour and the European Social Survey changed the number of participation items in its first three

Norms of citizenship 137

waves considerably. Examples of the arbitrary design of instruments offer the International Social Survey Programme (ISSP) and the Eurobarometer (EB). For instance EB 62.2 presents a list of 11 participation items at once and invites the respondent to tick the items used. The ISSP module on Citizenship (2004) simply combines boycotting and buycotting. As a result of these practices, the levels of participation measured are unrealistically low or high in each country – making any comparison with the results from other studies meaningless.

6 Detailed information and data for the studies used can be obtained from the following sources – PA, online, available at: http://info1.gesis.org/dbksearch13/SDesc2.asp?no =0765&search=political%20action&search2=&db=E; WVS, online, available at: www. worldvaluessurvey.org/; ESS, online, available at: http://ess.nsd.uib.no/index.jsp?year=- 1&module=download&country=; CID, online, available at: http://info1.gesis.org/dbk-search13/SDesc2.asp?no=4492&search=CID&search2=&db=E; EB, online, available at: http://zacat.gesis.org/webview/index.jsp?object=http://134.95.45.58:80/obj/fStudy/ ZA1750.

7 Astonishingly, not even voting is included in each study. In order not to lose information about the most common mode of participation, for the WVS the question "Which party would you vote for?" had to be used. All respondents mentioning a party are considered as voters here.

8 Changes in question wording clearly speak against this trend. Whereas PA and WVS simply ask for activities, EB-31 mentions as a time horizon for being politically active "the last ten years". Starting with the CID study this time horizon has been lowered to "the last 12 months". These restrictions make a reduction of the level of participation as measured with the unrestricted questions very likely. Yet boycotting has not been strongly affected by this bias: the number of people using this mode of participation is much higher in the newer studies where a very restricted time horizon is applied.

9 The lower levels of participation in the recent studies, however, might be another artefact of the ways participation is measured by introducing time horizons for these activities (see Note 6).

10 The results in Table 8.2 are for several sets of countries – all countries available in each study, the same five countries available in each study from 1974 to 2008, and the same 14 countries available in each study from 2002 to 2008.

11 See van Deth (2010) for a discussion of the consequences of this changing character of the modes of participation by solely relying on expressions of participants.

12 More extreme modes are usually presented as indicators of "the irresistible rise of global anticapitalism" (cf. online, available at: www.weareeverywhere.org/).

13 Notice that the aim of these analyses is not to detect a latent structure for "political participation" but to explore the correlations between boycotting and other modes of participation efficiently.

14 The communalities for boycotting are computed using the square of the loadings as a measure of the variance accounted for by the single dimension constructed.

15 The terms buycotting refers to buying products for political reasons (usually to support some producer or product) as opposed to boycotting which means a refusal to buy certain products. Both activities are specimens of "political consumerism", "ethical shopping" or "ethical consumer practices" (cf. Harrison *et al.* 2005: 3). Much more elaborated variants are known under such labels as "consumer guerrilla" or "hedonism" (cf. online, available at: http://hedonist-international.org/?q=en/taxonomy/term/10).

16 On the basis of British data Pattie *et al.* present similar conclusions and suggest that the "rise of individualistic forms of participation at the expense of collectivist forms" has already resulted in the spread of "atomised citizens" (2004: 275).

17 A detailed analysis of the various concepts of citizenship is presented by Janoski (1998). See van Deth (2007a), Dalton (2008a) and Pammett (2009) for empirical research in this area. A different approach is presented by Hooghe and Dejaeghere (2007).

18 See van Deth (2007a, 2009). Other surveys relying on measures from the CID project arrive at similar conclusions (cf. Pattie *et al.* 2004: 48–50; Dalton 2008b).
19 Unfortunately, only the first wave of the ESS contains all relevant variables. Besides, since the objective here is to detect determinants of each of the four types of participants, multinomial models are not applied.
20 The use of the electronic communications is measured by the question "how often do you use the Internet, the World Wide Web or e-mail – whether at home or at work – for your personal use?" (seven-point scale ranging from "never" to "everyday"). For Germany the additional category "don't know" has been treated as "never". In France the highest score of the two distinct responses for "at home" and "at work" is used as a proxy.
21 Although Dalton does not focus on newer modes of participation, his findings for the US underline that norms of citizenship "encourage electoral participation but do not carry over to other forms of action, and actually discourage participation in protest" (2008b: 88).
22 Notice, however, that these claims are usually based on the fact that women are over-represented among citizens using newer modes of participation whereas the results here indicate that being a woman increases your chances of becoming an *individualist* (see below, under "Characteristics of participants").
23 See for a clear description of cross-national differences in participation and the importance of socio-demographic factors Marien *et al.* (2010).
24 An example can make the differences between these two perspectives clear. If equality of opportunities is the main concern we point out, for instance, to the fact that donating money is higher among highly educated people than among people with low levels of education. If the characteristics of donating money as a type of political participation are relevant we have to show that people donating money are higher educated than people not using that mode of participation.
25 In order to compare the impact of various factors Table 8.7 contains the standardized differences between the average score for a group and the total average for that variable. The original differences between the averages for the four types all are highly significant (F-Test; $p < 0.000$) for each variable.
26 See van Deth (2010) for similar conclusions based on analyses of the CID data.
27 In fact, these characteristics are astonishingly similar to the depiction of a "consumer" from a "neo-liberal" point of view: "The consumer thus embodies the private (rather than the public), the market (rather than the state) and the individual (rather than the collective)" (Clarke *et al.* 2007: 18).
28 This deviation has been noted by many authors and does not necessarily have to be considered as negative for democracy (Jordan and Maloney 2007: 188–92).

9 A remedy for unequal participation?

How welfare states impact on social and political engagement

Isabelle Stadelmann-Steffen

Introduction

An active civil society is often seen as an antidote to declining political participation rates. This perception may be somewhat optimistic as civic participation suffers from the same deficiencies as conventional political engagement and collective decision making. Only a minority of citizens participates and, more importantly, civic engagement is unequally distributed among the citizenry, i.e. individual volunteering tends to increase with rising education attainment and income levels (Brady *et al.* 1995: 285; Friedman 2003: 15; Gaskin *et al.* 1996; Wilson and Musick, 1997; Verba *et al.* 1995).

There are two main reasons why unequal civic participation should be viewed as a 'problem' (Schlozman *et al.* 1999). First, civic engagement can be seen as a means for (equal) protection of interests in public life. Through civic activities – similar to conventional political participation – citizens have the possibility to articulate and aggregate their preferences and influence policy outcomes. Unequal civic engagement implies that a specific social group (usually more advantaged citizens) has their interests more effectively represented. As long as individuals differ in their preferences and interests, civic participation needs therefore to be equal (ibid.: 429f.). Second, participation in voluntary activities is also supposed to develop individual capacities. In this view, civic engagement is educational and those that get engaged become 'more independent, efficacious, and competent, larger in their capacities for thought, greater in their respect for others and their willingness to take responsibility, better able to appraise their own interests and those of the community' (ibid.: 428). Moreover, through civic engagement individuals make social contacts and become part of a network. If less resource rich citizens are underrepresented in civic activities they are likely to profit less from these advantageous effects of civic participation. Unequal civic engagement is likely to increase the political inequality gap between citizens with low and high socio-economic status (SES).

Accordingly, this chapter assesses the extent to which welfare state policy can moderate the (in)equality of social and political civic participation. In so doing, it follows an important strand of research on the relationship between welfare state and civic activities (i.e. Boje and Strandh 2005; Curtis *et al.* 2001; Dahlberg

2005; Kääriäinen and Lehtonen 2006; Künemund and Rein 1999; Ruiter and De Graf 2006; Van Oorschot and Arts 2005). However, these studies, by focusing on the question of whether generous welfare states lead to more or less civic engagement, miss one crucial issue: it is not only the level of civic engagement that matters, but its distribution.

The chapter addresses the welfare state effect on the equality of civic participation. Equality refers to an equal representation of different social groups among those who engage voluntarily. Following Larsen (2007), welfare regimes generate very dissimilar living conditions, mainly at the bottom of society. Two social groups are therefore distinguished: citizens with low levels of income and education attainment and those with relatively high levels.[1]

By asking whether state activities can influence civic engagement and act as a corrective to skewed civic participation, this chapter focuses on an important 'new participatory dimension' in the analysis of individual collective action: first, it assesses the role of the state in enhancing or driving out citizens' participation, and, second, it focuses on the problem of socially unequal civic participation from both a supply and a demand perspective.

The chapter goes beyond existing research in two respects. First, unlike former studies I argue that an overall analysis of civic engagement is not appropriate. More precisely, while public social services may quite heavily influence civic activities in welfare state related areas, i.e. social action, this relationship can be different in other fields (Day and Devlin 1996: 38). In addition to this, different forms of volunteering may offer better or poorer conditions for the participation of those with low SES. This contribution therefore distinguishes between two types of volunteering, namely social and political civic engagement. Second, as the welfare state does not affect the entire population in the same way it is reasonable to believe that the effect welfare state policy has on civic engagement is also not uniform (Scheepers and Te Grotenhuis 2005: 456). Rather its effect varies depending on individual resources, values, and behaviour patterns (Schmid 1984: 281). While wealthiest citizens contribute more to the welfare state (largely through taxation), the least advantaged citizens stand to benefit most from it.[2] Thus it is reasonable to assume that the welfare state context influences various social groups differently with regard to their propensity to civic engagement and affects the social stratification of civic engagement. Group-specific welfare state effects will be hypothesized and modelled (see Elster 1998).

In examining the relationship between the welfare state and individual civic engagement, we are faced with a multilevel phenomenon: individuals are nested within specific welfare state contexts, which are expected to moderate individual behaviour (see Hedström and Swedberg 1996). The study therefore adopts a multilevel approach. Bayesian estimation is applied, which performs better than maximum likelihood when employing logistic multilevel models with a small number of level two units (Browne and Draper 2006). Data from the fourth wave of the World Values Survey (WVS), 1999–2004, form the empirical basis of the contribution, which is complemented by context data for 23 OECD countries.

The focus on the OECD world is justified not only in terms of data availability, but also theoretically. As Walzer (1992) states: It is the 'paradox of the civil society argument' that a democratic civil society seems to require a democratic state, while a strong civil society seems to require a strong and responsive state. The use of a broader country sample including developing countries implies even more complex processes that are not at the centre of this chapter and are therefore excluded.

The remainder of this chapter is organized as follows. In the second section, a short overview on the level and the social stratification of civic engagement among the OECD countries is presented. In the third section the theoretical background on the relationship between the welfare state and civil society is addressed and the hypotheses regarding inequality in civic engagement is outlined. In the fourth section, the methodological approach and the operationalization of the variables are detailed. Finally, the empirical results are presented, and the chapter concludes with a discussion of the most important findings.

The variety of civic engagement: forms and social stratification of volunteering

Civic engagement in this chapter refers to activities outside the household 'in which time is given freely to benefit another person, group, or organization' (Wilson 2000: 15). Obviously, this broad definition includes a collection of somewhat different activities, from political activism to the supervision of sports training. The concept's heterogeneity and its consequences are particularly evident with regard to the relationship between welfare state policy and civic engagement. First, it is not reasonable to assume that welfare state policy equally affects all forms of volunteering. More precisely, extensive welfare policies should substitute civic activities that directly 'compete' with public social policy, while the effect on other types of volunteering in culture, sports, leisure or for political purposes can be very different. While public services may crowd out civic activities in welfare state related areas, the converse could be true in other fields (Day and Devlin 1996: 38). This assumption corresponds to Rothstein's (2001: 217, 229) finding for Sweden whereby voluntary organizations have followed quite different trajectories during the last decades. While some areas of the voluntary sector such as social service, health care or elementary education have weakened, others such as sports, cultural or environmental organizations have grown. Salamon and Sokolowski (2003: 87) illustrate that a differentiation between various areas of volunteering is important in some cases in order to reveal the relationship between the type of welfare state and a country's level of volunteering. Accordingly, we distinguish between two forms of civic engagement, namely *social* and *political* volunteering. While the former is most directly related to public welfare state activities and to the crowding out hypothesis, the latter has been most intensively discussed in terms of social stratification and is most closely related to the (complementary) resource effect of welfare state policy.

Figure 9.1 gives an overview of social and political volunteering rates across the OECD countries.[3] Three observations stand out from this illustration. First, the population share that gets socially or politically engaged varies substantially among the 23 countries. While the United States, Great Britain, Canada and Sweden score high on both forms of volunteering, the share of political and social volunteers is relatively low in Portugal, Hungary and Germany. Second, engagement rates vary among social groups. The comparison of high/medium income individuals (light grey bars) and the low income group (dark grey bars) shows that in some countries civic engagement is very unequally distributed. Mainly in the Anglo-Saxon countries low income individuals are substantially underrepresented, while the high income group shows very high rates of volunteers. In contrast, especially the Scandinavian countries exhibit a somewhat lower level of volunteering, but there is much less difference between social groups. Finally, and related to the aforementioned point, the two figures demonstrate that social volunteering tends to be more equal than political volunteering. This can be seen from the fact that the difference in volunteering rates between low and high income individuals is larger in the political than in the social sphere.

Generally, countries differ not only in respect of the level of social and political volunteering, but also regarding the social stratification of civic engagement. More importantly, the level and equality of volunteering do not systematically correlate: while some countries exhibit high levels of volunteering and a rather equal distribution (e.g. Sweden), others combine high shares of volunteering with a rather unequal participation (e.g. United States, Great Britain). At the same time, at the lower end of the ranking equal (Czech Republic) as well as unequal distributions (Portugal) of civic engagement can be found.

Group-specific welfare state effects and civic engagement: theoretical accounts

To what extent are patterns of volunteering related to different welfare state provisions? Do the welfare state and its redistributive approach have a significant impact on a society's social stratification and levels of civic engagement? I begin our analysis by focusing on two established theoretical approaches regarding the relationship between welfare states and civic engagement.

The first and most prominent view suggests that public social services *crowd out* civic activities in general (Dahlberg 2005: 743ff.). According to this substitution theory, an extensive welfare state reduces the importance of other actors, such as voluntary organizations, and leads to a *crowding out* of civic engagement. Formulated in a more positive way, voluntary action emanates from an unsatisfied demand for collective goods that is not met by the state (Salamon and Sokolowski 2003: 78; Weisbrod 1978). In essence the assumption is that the supply of social services is a zero-sum game, implying that there is 'a certain number of tasks to be done and the only question is who will do them' (Finsveen and van Oorschot 2007: 4). If the state performs these tasks, the engagement of

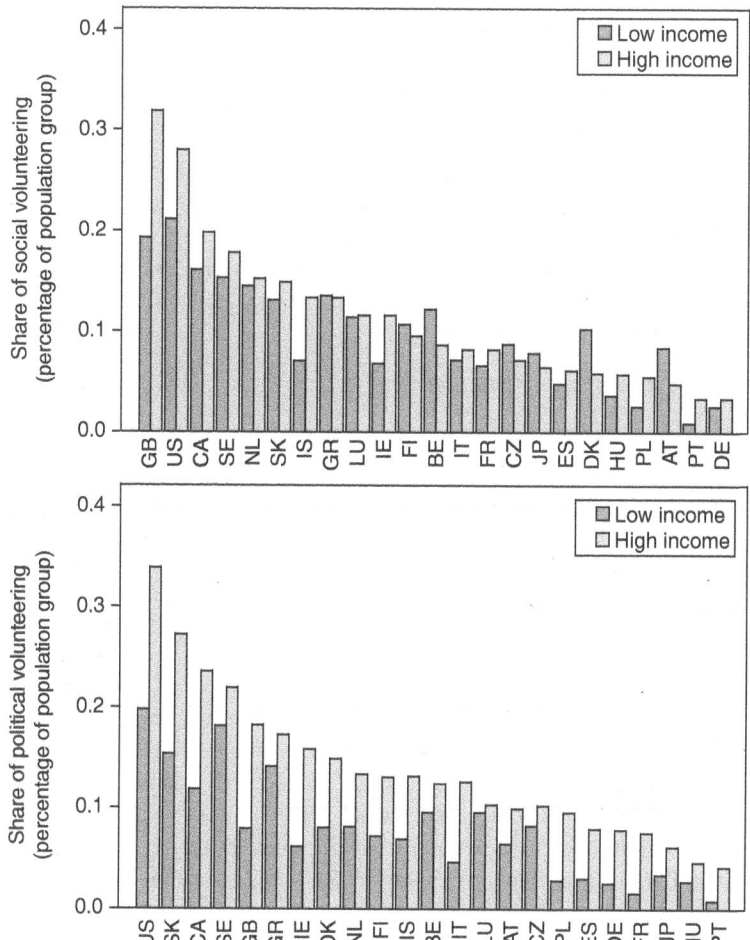

Figure 9.1 Social and political volunteering of low and high income individuals respectively (source: WVS, fourth wave).

Notes
Share of social and political volunteering respectively, in per cent of the relevant population group, own calculation.
AT=Austria, BE=Belgium, CA=Canada, CZ=Czech Republic, DE=Germany, DK=Denmark, ES=Spain, FI=Finland, FR=France, GB=Great Britain, GR=Greece, HU=Hungary, IE=Ireland, IS=Iceland, IT=Italy, JP=Japan, NL=Netherlands, LU=Luxembourg, PL=Poland, PT=Portugal, SK=Slovak Republik, US=United States.

civil society is rendered unnecessary and will consequently lead to a decline in civic engagement.

In contrast to this view, a second approach assumes that there is a complementary relationship between welfare state and private initiative (Dahlberg 2005: 743ff.). Accordingly, the state and civil society do not necessarily perform the same tasks. Extensive welfare provision should therefore not replace civic activities, but rather provide people with the financial resources and security as well as the free time needed to be involved in voluntary activities – also known as the *crowding in* of civic engagement. Furthermore, universal welfare states in particular decrease the perceived cultural distance between the majority and 'the bottom' (Larsen 2007), thereby fostering the willingness to serve others. Along these lines, an extensive welfare state generates the structural and cultural conditions for a flourishing civil society (Hyden 1997: 13ff.; van Oorschot and Arts 2005: 6).[4]

Based on these two approaches, group specific hypotheses for the two types of civic engagement, namely social and political volunteering, can be formulated.

Welfare state effects and social volunteering

Social volunteering is the form of civic engagement which is theoretically most directly related to welfare state policy. These activities are most likely to be substituted by extensive public service provision and with regard to volunteering we are likely to see a tendency towards crowding out (Stadelmann-Steffen 2011). Initially, the crowding out approach is based on the idea that a context of extensive welfare state policy reduces civil society's *responsibility* to engage voluntarily. At the individual level, this generates specific incentives and conditions for social volunteering generally. Volunteering can come at a personal cost. Thus we may find that socially disadvantaged people who lack many of the requisite resources are much less involved in voluntary activities. Their below average engagement is also ascribed not only to their lack of resources but also because these individuals are apparently less sensitized for community action (Friedman 2003: 15; Gaskin *et al.* 1996; Wilson and Musick 1997). In other words, they are less able and willing to pay the individual costs of volunteering. Against a background of generally low propensity to volunteer, crowding out cannot have a substantial impact on individuals with low levels of income and education. This population group exhibits the least advantageous preconditions for voluntary work and generally does not consider social volunteering a duty. Whether it is the state or civil society that bears responsibility for public social services therefore does not significantly influence their social engagement. On the other hand, individual volunteering is more likely with increased education and income (Friedman 2003: 15; Gaskin *et al.* 1996; Wilson and Musick, 1997). Not only do these individuals have the necessary financial and human capital resources, but also they attach higher value to the immaterial gains of volunteering, such as helping others or self-confidence (Brady *et al.* 1995: 285). In an extensive welfare state, wealthier citizens will be the main redistributive target – i.e. proportionally bigger funders of the welfare state programme. Accordingly, they could eschew volunteering for two main reasons. First, somewhat self-interestedly, they could take the view that they do not need to also volunteer in this area because they already contribute significantly. Second, they may simply be crowded out by the extensive provision of the state and see no need to volunteer. Accordingly, it is plausible to hypothesize that more affluent individuals in an extensive welfare state are likely to withdraw from social volunteering.

Unlike the first responsibility based perspective, the second approach is based on complementary theory which focuses on how the *redistributive consequences* of the welfare state have a differential influence on voluntary behaviour. Generally speaking, less affluent citizens who are likely to benefit most from an extensive welfare state – as the primary recipients of social services – exhibit low levels of voluntary engagement (Friedman 2003: 6, 15). It can be hypothesized that an extensive welfare state provides these individuals with basic financial resources and security and possibly some of the free time needed for voluntary engagement (van Oorschot and Arts 2005: 6). Moreover, extensive welfare states reduce the consciousness of belonging to disadvantaged social groups (Larsen 2007), which bolsters the probability of volunteering. A complementary effect of a generous welfare state on civic engagement can therefore be expected for individuals with low levels of income and education. Individuals with a high socio-economic status, by contrast, are quite differently affected by welfare state redistribution. While they are important contributors to the welfare state and arguably benefit relatively less from public social services, regarding the redistribution of resources, a complementary effect therefore cannot be expected for these individuals. Moreover, as these citizens generally have the necessary resources as well as a strong propensity for volunteering (Wilson 2000: 219f.), their voluntary activities can be expected to be fairly independent from extensive welfare state activities.

These two perspectives suggest different effects of welfare state policy on social volunteering of social groups, but eventually both lead to the same conclusion in terms of equality in social engagement. It can be expected that extensive welfare state policy decreases social inequality in civic engagement. In the first case this is due to a negative effect on more affluent individuals, but not the relatively disadvantaged. While the second approach sees welfare state policy as bolstering the social engagement of less affluent citizens but less so of the wealthy.

Welfare state effects and political volunteering

The logics of crowding out and in can also be applied to political volunteering, even though the mechanisms are somewhat different. Against the background of crowding out and following *conflict theory* of political engagement, it can be argued that there is less conflict and a greater consensus about the shape of policy in more extensive welfare states than in more austere ones (Solt 2008: 49). As a consequence, individuals with low and high SES are less motivated to engage politically. This can be seen as a crowding out of political volunteering in that extensive redistributive policies are seen to make political engagement unnecessary. It can, however, be argued that this negative effect will be more pronounced for more affluent individuals because the propensity of citizens with low SES to politically volunteer is generally limited.

In contrast and analogously to the mechanism regarding social volunteering, the *crowding in* logic clearly suggests a positive effect on the political volunteering of less advantaged citizens. Not only can extensive welfare state services provide these individuals with necessary resources to volunteer, as mentioned before, but extensive welfare state policy can also bolster 'political awareness' of these groups and thus encourage political participation (ibid.: 58). In particular, large welfare states will generate a motivation for political civic engagement in order to protect welfare provision. This resource perspective of political participation implies that more affluent citizens lose some of their comparative advantage in an extensive welfare state. Their resources decrease through redistribution, while lower class individuals now have relatively more resources to pay the cost of engagement (ibid.: 50). Therefore we expect to see no crowding in of wealthier citizens.[5]

To sum up, the impact welfare state policy has on the equality in political volunteering is somewhat less straightforward, but an equalizing total effect can still be expected. While in the crowding out situation the negative effect on individuals with high SES should be stronger than for those with low SES. The redistributive consequences of generous welfare state provisions are expected to promote civic engagement of less affluent citizens, but not of their wealthier counterparts.

Data and method

In the remainder of the chapter the hypotheses presented above will be empirically tested. The dependent variables are individual social and political volunteering. For the measurement of the dependent variables the following question from the Word Values Survey was used: 'Please look carefully at the following list of voluntary organizations and activities and say ... for which if any, are you currently doing unpaid voluntary work?'[6] Regarding *social volunteering*, those individuals that indicated voluntary engagement in one of the following areas were assigned the value of one: voluntary work related to social welfare service for elderly, handicapped or deprived people, local community actions on issues like poverty, employment, housing, racial equality or concerned with health. All others were allocated the value zero. It should be noted that other categories of unpaid work can also be socially motivated (e.g. religious unpaid work, youth work or voluntary activities taking place in the area of third world development and human rights). However, these latter activities are not within the scope of national welfare states and/or include forms of unpaid work without any social orientation. They are therefore excluded from the following analyses. For the variable *political volunteering* individuals that indicated a voluntary engagement in labour unions, political parties or groups, local community actions, professional associations and women's groups were assigned the value of one. All others were allocated the value zero.[7]

The main focus of the analysis is, however, not on the dependent variables as such. *Equality in civic engagement* is predicated on the relationship between two individual level concepts – an individual's socio-economic background and individual civic participation. The strength of relationship between those two measures determines how unequally civic engagement is distributed among different social groups. Put differently, the hypotheses of this chapter suggest that welfare state policy can moderate this relationship and eventually influence the degree of inequality in civic engagement (Figure 9.2).

Methodologically, I therefore apply random intercept and random slopes models with cross level interactions (Jones 1997; Steenbergen and Jones 2002).[8] These interactions actually model how the welfare state context moderates the effect social status has on individual civic engagement. As the dependent variable is dichotomous, individual volunteering is transformed to a logit structure. While recent studies reveal that maximum likelihood performs quite badly regarding bias and coverage when employing logistic multilevel models with a small number of level two units, a Bayesian estimation approach is applied, which has been shown to be a better alternative (Browne and Draper 2006).[9]

The central independent variable at the individual level is *individual socio-economic status* in terms of education and income. A high level of education and financial resources is related to a high propensity and probability to volunteer (cf. Salamon and Sokolowski 2003: 77; Wilson 2000). Here we distinguish between a low and a medium/high level of income and education attainment.[10]

For the crucial independent variable at the contextual level, *welfare state effort*, the focus is on the core areas of welfare state policy (cf. Evers 2005: 738). More precisely, for the construction of the variable based on the OECD Social Expenditure Database (SOCX) public social expenditures as a percentage of GDP in the following categories are summarized: old age, incapacity, family and unemployment related expenditures. These elements of welfare state expenditures are most directly related both to civil society's activities and to possible welfare state resource effects.[11] By using expenditure data, I follow Castles (2008: 60) who has recently shown that a disaggregated expenditures approach is very useful for establishing 'not only the variety of what welfare states do, but also the determinants and the outcomes of such interventions'. The proposed GDP-related variable can be seen as a measure for the importance of welfare state policy relative to a country's overall resources. While almost all countries have been influenced by similar trends and challenges to the welfare state in recent years the country-specific conceptions of the welfare state have proven to be very stable over time (and so have country differences in social expenditures).[12]

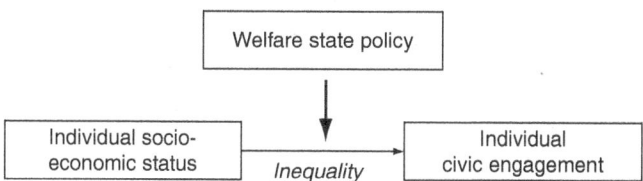

Figure 9.2 Interaction between welfare state policy and individual civic engagement.

In order to explain individual civic engagement further individual characteristics need to be integrated into the analysis (cf. Dekker and Halmann 2003; Gaskin and Smith 1997; Salamon and Sokolowski 2003: 77; Wilson 2000; Wilson and Musick 1997; Verba et al. 1995). First, a high degree of social integration (e.g. through employment) is expected to increase the likelihood of an engagement.[13] Furthermore, socio-demographic factors such as age and gender should influence an individual's civic activities. Finally, religious values are incorporated into the models, which can be linked to an individual's propensity to altruistic behaviour. All individual variables are taken from the fourth wave of the WVS, 1999–2004. At the contextual level and in addition to the central policy variable, a country's logarithmized GDP, 1998/1999, is integrated into the models in order to control for different degrees of economic and social development.[14]

How welfare state expenditures moderate social inequality in civic engagement: empirical findings

In this section, models analysing the influence of the welfare state context on individual social and political volunteering are presented. First, preliminary analyses demonstrate that the respective probability of social and political volunteering substantially differs among the OECD countries. The variance coefficients at the country level are significantly different from zero in both models and this finding continues to hold when individual characteristics are controlled, indicating that country differences in civic engagement are not due to differences in population structures. Basically, the contextual variance of individual volunteering provides support for multilevel analysis and, more specifically, for the modelling of the welfare state context.

The central hypotheses of this contribution can be tested by modelling interaction effects assessing the effect of welfare state policy on the different income and education groups (see Figure 9.2). Table 9.1 presents two models for each area of volunteering; one differentiating between educational groups, the other accounting for different income groups.

Table 9.1 shows that men have a lower probability of social volunteering than women, while the contrary is true regarding political volunteering. Initially both forms of volunteering tend to increase and then to decrease as an individual ages. Employment increases the probability of political engagement. The higher probability of social volunteering of those outside the labour market can be seen against the background of the above average engagement of homemakers in this area. Religious people exhibit a higher propensity to civic engagement in general. Finally, at the contextual level, the degree of economic development in terms of GDP per capita somewhat bolsters civic engagement, but only in one out of four models (Model 2).

In respect of the crucial independent variables – income, education and welfare state effort – the marginal effects cannot be directly seen from the table when modelling interaction terms. While the coefficient for welfare state effort

Table 9.1 Overall context effect of welfare state policy on social and political volunteering

	Social volunteering		Political volunteering	
	Model 1	Model 2	Model 3	Model 4
Fixed effects				
Constant	−1.23 (0.69)	−1.19 (0.80)	−0.74 (0.71)	−1.04 (0.69)
	(−2.37/−0.08)	*(−2.43/0.17)*	*(−1.83/0.48)*	*(−2.19/0.06)*
Sex (male)	−0.25 (0.05)	−0.25 (0.05)	0.16 (0.04)	0.16 (0.04)
	(−0.32/−0.17)	*(−0.32/−0.17)*	*(0.09/0.23)*	*(0.08/0.23)*
Age	0.02 (0.00)	0.02 (0.00)	0.02 (0.00)	0.02 (0.02)
	(0.02/0.02)	*(0.02/0.02)*	*(0.02/0.03)*	*(0.02/0.03)*
Age squared	−0.00 (0.00)	−0.00 (0.00)	−0.00 (0.00)	−0.00 (0.00)
	(−0.00/−0.00)	*(−0.00/−0.00)*	*(−0.00/−0.00)*	*(−0.00/−0.00)*
Not employed	0.10 (0.05)	0.09 (0.05)	−0.33 (0.06)	−0.33 (0.06)
	(0.01/0.19)	*(−0.00/0.18)*	*(−0.42/−0.23)*	*(−0.42/−0.24)*
Religious person	0.37 (0.05)	0.37 (0.05)	0.13 (0.05)	0.13 (0.05)
	(0.29/0.46)	*(0.28/0.47)*	*(0.05/0.22)*	*(0.05/0.21)*
Low education	−0.09 (0.49)[+]	−0.47 (0.05)	−0.90 (0.01)[+]	−0.54 (0.05)
	(−0.90/0.72)	*(−0.55/−0.38)*	*(−1.60/−0.20)*	*(−0.62/−0.45)*
Low income	−0.10 (0.05)	−0.85 (0.28)[+]	−0.26 (0.05)	−0.66 (0.32)
	(−0.18/−0.01)	*(−1.32/−0.39)*	*(−0.35/−0.18)*	*(−1.20/−0.16)*
GDP (logarithmized)	0.69 (0.74)	1.30 (0.80)	−0.02 (0.74)	0.38 (0.72)
	(−0.55/1.88)	*(−0.00/2.58)*	*(−1.24/1.20)*	*(−0.84/1.57)*
Welfare state	−0.04 (0.02)	−0.05 (0.03)	−0.04 (0.02)	−0.04 (0.02)
	(−0.08/−0.00)	*(−0.10/−0.01)*	*(−0.08/−0.01)*	*(−0.07/0.00)*
Welfare state * low education	−0.02 (0.02)	–	0.01 (0.02)	–
	(−0.04/0.01)		*(−0.01/0.04)*	
Welfare state * low income	–	0.03 (0.01)	–	0.01 (0.01)
		(0.01/0.05)		*(−0.01/0.03)*
Random effects				
Contextual level variance	0.35 (0.13)	0.43 (0.16)	0.36 (0.13)	0.38 (0.14)
	(0.19/0.60)	*(0.24/0.73)*	*(0.20/0.61)*	*(0.22/0.64)*
DIC	*14,851*	*14,861*	*15,244*	*15,258*
N	*24,169 (23)*	*24,169 (23)*	*24,169 (23)*	*24,169 (23)*

Notes
Posterior distributions of log odds (standard deviation in brackets); second line (italic), 90% credible interval. All models were calculated in MlwiN using MCMC estimation (800,000 iterations, burn-in 50,000, diffuse [gamma] priors); [+] = variable randomized at the individual level.

stands for the impact of welfare state expenditures for individuals with medium/ high income and education, respectively, the marginal effect for individuals with low SES amounts to the sum of this single coefficient and the interaction coefficient. In Bayesian terms, the joint posterior distribution of the main welfare state effect and the interaction coefficient has to be calculated in order to obtain the welfare state effect for individuals with low levels of income and education.

Table 9.2 therefore displays the marginal effects of the welfare state context (i.e. their posterior distribution) on social and political volunteering, depending

Table 9.2 Group-specific welfare state effects on social and political volunteering

		Mean	SD	5%	95%	Middle/high > low
Marginal effect of welfare state effort on social volunteering dependent on the level of ...						
...education	Low	-0.06	-0.03	-0.11	-0.01	18.9%
	Middle/high	-0.04	0.02	-0.08	-0.00	
...income	Low	-0.02	0.03	-0.07	0.02	99.7%
	Middle/high	-0.05	0.03	-0.10	-0.01	
Marginal effect of welfare state effort on political volunteering dependent on the level of ...						
...education	Low	-0.03	-0.03	-0.08	0.02	79.3%
	Middle/high	-0.04	-0.02	-0.08	-0.01	
...income	Low	-0.02	-0.03	-0.07	0.03	88.7%
	Middle/high	-0.04	-0.02	-0.07	0.00	

Notes
Posterior distributions of marginal log odds. All models were calculated in MlwiN using MCMC estimation (800,000 iterations, burn-in 50,000, diffuse [gamma] priors); all models control for individual variables and a country's wealth (GDP) as shown in Table 9.1. Middle/high > low: proportion of iterations in which the welfare state effect for persons with middle/high social status was stronger (more negative) than for low educated/low income individuals.

Impact of welfare states 151

on an individual's respective levels of education and income. The results demonstrate that public welfare state provisions do not affect all individuals equally. For those with high SES the 90 per cent credible intervals do not include zero, meaning that we can speak of a clearly negative relationship between extensive welfare state policy and the probability of both forms of volunteering. These results lend support to the crowding out argument. In countries that spend a high share of their GDP on welfare policy, the probability of social and political voluntary engagement by those with high SES is substantially lower than in small welfare states. Theoretically this can be interpreted as meaning that in an extensive welfare state this group transfers social responsibility to the state and refrains from social engagement – i.e. it finances the welfare state through taxes and contributions. At the same time, the findings regarding political volunteering imply that these individuals do not shift their engagement from social to political volunteering. The negative relationship between welfare state effort and political civic engagement rather supports conflict theory suggesting that political participation is lower in large welfare states due to a lower level of political conflict.

With regards to individuals with low SES the findings differ. In fact, the marginal welfare state effects are generally not different from zero for these individuals. This result is in line with the expectation that welfare state activities will not substantially deter those individuals that generally exhibit a very low propensity to volunteer. An exception is however social volunteering of the lowest education group which is again characterized by a crowding out tendency.

Moreover, another indicator of the group differences in welfare state effects is the proportion of iterations that produced more negative marginal effects for high SES individuals than for their less advantaged counterparts (last column, Table 9.2). This actually provides us with the probability that welfare state policy decreases inequality in civic engagement. With regard to income, the findings are clear. With a probability of 99.7 per cent and 88.7 per cent generous welfare state policy decreases inequality in social and political volunteering, respectively. Regarding educational differences the results are again less clearcut. While the probability that inequality in political volunteering is diminished due to extensive welfare state services is almost 80 per cent, the opposite seems to be true for social volunteering.

Overall, these findings corroborate the central hypothesis of this chapter – i.e. welfare state policy can reduce social inequality in civic participation. Extensive welfare states tend to decrease the social and political volunteering of those with high SES but not the involvement of their less affluent peers. Accordingly, extensive welfare states can contribute to a reduction of skewed participation. This conclusion is further supported by the fact that welfare state policy substantially moderates the influence of low affluence. A negative effect of low income on social and political volunteering can only be found in small welfare states.[15] Figure 9.3 illustrates this point depicting the marginal effect of low income on the two forms of volunteering for different levels of welfare state effort.

In small welfare states, low income clearly and negatively influences the respective probability of social and political voluntary engagement. However, as

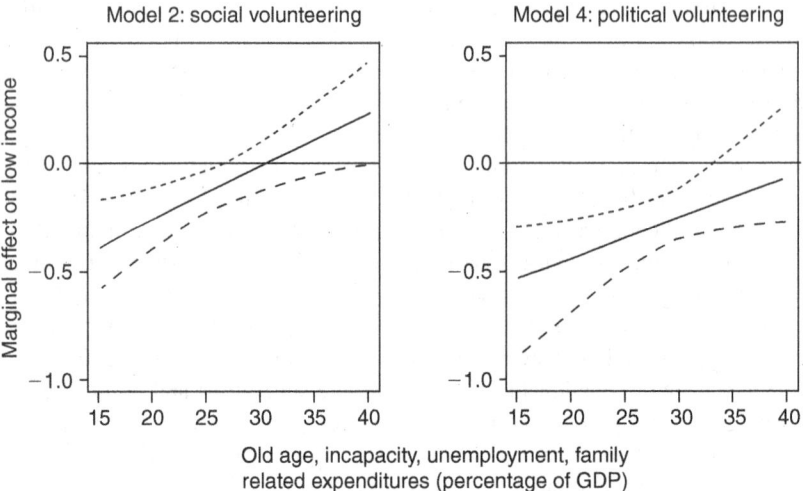

Figure 9.3 Marginal effect of low income on social and political volunteering respectively.

Notes
Posterior (marginal) distributions of the interaction effects (1,000 last iterations from posterior distributions for different values of welfare state expenditures). Solid line, median marginal effect (log odds); dashed line, 90 per cent credible interval; left graph, based on Model 2, Table 9.1; right graph, based on Model 4, Table 9.1.

we move to countries with a more extensive welfare state, the negative effect of low financial resources diminishes and ultimately fails to reach statistical significance. If a country spends more than roughly 26 per cent of GDP on old age, incapacity, family and unemployment benefits low income does not significantly decrease social volunteering. This applies to nearly half of the countries, including Luxembourg and the Scandinavian countries, but also the traditional continental welfare states of France, Austria, Germany and Italy. For political volunteering the negative impact of low education disappears if a country spends more than about 33 per cent of GDP on social policy, which is the case in Luxembourg, Austria, Spain, Poland, Denmark, Sweden, Germany and France. These findings not only reveal varying income effects among OECD countries, but also that we can speak of an indirect positive effect of high welfare state expenditures on civic engagement.

In contrast, the educational effect on civic engagement is not systematically moderated by welfare state effort, but remains highly significant across all countries. Considering this context, it is not surprising that welfare state effects can be found for low income, but not in the presence of low education. Income is the main eligibility criteria for welfare benefits, while the individual level of education is not always a good indicator for welfare state dependency. Against this background, the different findings for education and income can be interpreted

Impact of welfare states 153

to mean that an (indirect) positive welfare state effect is indeed closely linked to a resource effect.

Extensive robustness analyses have been conducted that show that the findings presented are robust vis-à-vis alternative model specifications and measurements. First, alternative operationalizations of social volunteering, including or omitting categories of unpaid work (e.g. local community action, youth work), did not alter the findings. Second, slightly different measurements of welfare state effort, including or omitting particular SOCX-spending categories (e.g. health), lead to the same conclusions. Third, it could be argued that measuring 'social class' by simple dummy variables is too limited. However, a different operationalization, by using three categories (high, middle, low income/education) or even a 'metric' variable distinguishing eight educational levels (variable x025 in the WVS) and ten income deciles (x047), respectively, confirms the findings presented in this chapter. It also shows that the simple one/zero categorization is not only reasonable with respect to the small number of cases at level two, but also captures the essential group differences regarding welfare state effects. Fourth, further models not presented here included a number of other potential contextual controlling variables in various combinations. Indicators measuring ethnic and religious heterogeneity, income inequality, the age structure, the share of Catholics and Protestants, the level of schooling, a dummy for former communist countries, as well as measures for democratic development and stability did not improve the explanatory power of the model, nor did they influence the reported results. Finally, alternative link functions (e.g. complementary log-log, which assumes that a positive outcome is a rare event), as well as extensive outlier analyses, confirmed the presented findings.

Conclusion

Can welfare state policy impact on the social stratification of civic engagement? Against the background of two competing propositions, one of which assumes a fostering effect of public social services on volunteering, the other a crowding out of civil society's activities, the preceding analyses sought to clarify this matter. The focus on social and political volunteering was chosen because the first type of voluntary engagement is theoretically most closely linked both to welfare state activities and to the crowding out hypothesis, while the second one is probably most dependent on a complementary welfare state effect due to the particularly strong social stratification. The findings can be summarized as follows.

First, the effect welfare state policy has on individual volunteering is indeed not uniform across social classes. While social and political volunteering for the middle class is characterized by a crowding out tendency, this is different for individuals from the working class. The latter group typically comprises the main recipients of welfare state services and the resources that welfare state provides them for everyday life may also be conducive to encouraging volunteering. Put differently, the welfare state provides less wealthy individuals with resources, which they can re-invest in volunteering. The finding is of practical and policy relevance and means that welfare states have the potential to level the civic participation playing field.

However, the analyses in this chapter highlight a dilemma. As an extensive welfare state increases equality of civic participation, but rather decreases a country's total share of volunteers, these two aspects of societal integration may not be maximized at the same time. Formulated in a different way, this can be interpreted to mean that civil society can to some extent compensate for extensive welfare state policy. However, the relatively high level of social and political volunteering in small welfare states like Great Britain, Canada or the US goes at the expense of socially unequal civic participation in these areas. These results corroborate the notion that welfare state effort and civic engagement is not a zero sum game (Finsveen and Oorschot 2007: 4). As processes of crowding out and crowding in go hand-in-hand, public welfare services cannot be retrenched and civil society will just 'take over'; rather a stronger role of civil society may be at the expense of an increase in unequal participation.

Lastly, in the context of this volume's main theme, the chapter's findings add another participatory dimension of civil society. While the conventional ways of citizens' participation, like voting or traditional collective action, have lost some appeal, new and less formalized ways of engagement are on the rise. In this vein, an active civil society is often perceived of as a means to compensate declining conventional political participation. This chapter however demonstrates that a strong civil society, in terms of its citizens' civic engagement, does not deliver equal representation of social groups and interests, but rather individuals with high SES are grossly overrepresented in these activities. This inequality in (social and political) engagement becomes even more of an issue due to increased professionalization of civil society and the 'rise of the unelected' (Vibert 2007). Against this background, the potential of welfare states to countersteer social stratification in civic engagement must not be underestimated.

Notes

1 Throughout the chapter the notions 'higher/lower social stratum' and 'higher/lower social group' are used synonymously.
2 This argument is of course not uncontested. Le Grand (1982: 137) for instance argues that 'public expenditure on health care, education, housing and transport systematically favors the better off and thereby contributes to inequality in final income'. I, however, base my argument on the finding that all western welfare states exhibit at least some redistribution, i.e. a reduction in inequality from market income to disposable income (Korpi and Palme 1998). This can be interpreted to mean that even in the smallest welfare states higher income classes contribute more compared to lower social classes.
3 The analysis includes the OECD countries (before 2010) with the exception of Australia, Korea, New Zealand, Norway and Switzerland, as data for these countries is lacking.
4 On the other hand, and from a more sceptical point of view, a declining (welfare) state will also lead to a declining civil society (Friedman 2003: 11).

5 It must, however, be mentioned that for higher class individuals the crowding out dynamic in social volunteering discussed above could be seen as a complementary effect from a broader point of view: if social volunteering is rendered unnecessary due to substantial state activities, these individuals could invest their resources in other areas of civil society – such as politics – due to their high propensity to volunteer.
6 In wave 4 of the WVS, respondents could indicate the following categories of civic engagement: social welfare services for elderly, handicapped or deprived people (a081); religious or church organizations (a082); education, arts, music or cultural activities (a083); labour unions (a084); political parties or groups (a085); local community actions on issues like poverty, employment, housing, racial equality (a086); third world development or human rights (a087); conservation, environment, animal rights groups (a088); professional associations (a089); youth work (scouts, guides, youth clubs, etc.) (a090); sports and recreation (a091); women's groups (a092); peace movements (a093); voluntary organizations concerned with health (a094). The variable names in brackets refer to the pooled data set 1984–2004.
7 The question of which activities are part of what is considered as civic engagement, is actually one of the major disagreements in the literature (Boje and Strandh 2005: 4). In the context of this chapter, the question of the WVS seems to be a sensible way of measuring individual civic engagement. It focuses on the *area* in which voluntary activities take place rather than on organizational aspects, i.e. if it is a formal engagement within an organization or institution, or whether it is rather informal in nature. This corresponds well to the research question of this chapter focusing on the *subject matter of an engagement*. In this vein, it is the type of voluntary work that determines whether an activity belongs to the respective area of social or political volunteering. An example is the category 'women's groups' which is perceived of as political civic engagement. It can be assumed that if this category was chosen, the main issue of the voluntary work are indeed women's interests. In contrast, the respondents would have chosen other categories if their engagement *within* a women's organization concerned mainly cultural, education or charity issues.
8 Given that weighting of the data always involves the danger of adding new bias to the data and as I focus on relationships rather than on the prediction of country specific population shares, I refrain from applying weighting procedures.
9 For an easy interpretation of the Bayesian estimation results I present the mean and the standard deviation of the posterior distribution, which can be interpreted like in a standard regression situation: the mean is the average effect (here: log odds) of an independent variable on the outcome variable and the standard deviation gives a sense of the statistical reliability of this estimate. Moreover, I present the 90 per cent credible intervals, which are the Bayesian analogue to the confidence intervals in a standard regression context.
10 Regarding education the highest completed level of education has been recoded into a dummy variable (x025r): 1=low educational achievements (inadequately completed elementary education, completed (compulsory) elementary education, incomplete secondary school); 0=middle educational achievements (completed secondary school, incomplete and complete university preparation) or high educational achievements (some university level education without degree, university level education with degree). Income is measured by means of the household's income level, whereby the scale of income has been recoded into a dummy variable (047r): 1=low income; 0=middle income or high income.
11 Conversely, health related expenditures – which contain mainly medical goods, while cash benefits related to sickness are recoded under incapacity related benefits (OECD 2007: 15) – as well as the categories housing and active labour market programmes are excluded, since they cover public expenditures which are much less directly connected to individual civic activities.

12 It would nonetheless be desirable to measure these crucial aspects of welfare state policy (also) by means of eligibility criteria and actual benefits; however, such comparable data is not readily available for a large country sample. The benefit generosity index proposed by Scruggs and Allan (2006), for example, only includes 18 OECD countries – which are moreover not identical to the WVS country sample.

13 In contrast, I refrain from integrating an occupational variable, which is often used to measure social class differences. In the context of volunteering, which is precisely an activity outside the labour market, such a restriction would exclude respondents not integrated into the labour market and, hence, an important group of volunteers (e.g. housewives, pensioners, students).

14 Even though GDP is part of the measure of social spending, the GDP variable as such is also integrated into the models for two reasons. First, a correlation analysis demonstrates that the relationship between the level of GDP (logarithmized) and social spending as a percentage of GDP is only weak (Pearson's $r=0.29$). This shows that GDP should still be integrated into the models in order to control for the level of economic and social development. Second, the GDP variable also accounts for a shortcoming of the social spending variable: the welfare state indicator not only depends on public social spending, but also on GDP meaning that high values in this indicator can be driven both by substantial social spending and low GDP. Further information on the operationalization of the variables is provided for by the author upon request.

15 Again the marginal effect of low income is dependent on the level of social spending and – in conventional statistical terms – amounts to the sum of this single coefficient and the interaction coefficient multiplied by the level of social spending (e.g. for Model 2 the mean marginal effect of low income amounts to: $-0.85+0.03*$ welfare state effort).

10 Peripheral participants
The activation of the politically less engaged in advanced democracies

Eline A. de Rooij

Introduction

One of the more interesting puzzles in the academic literature on political participation is that while in many countries educational levels have been on the increase as a result of socio-economic modernization, turnout rates and arguably campaign activities have not (Dalton 2006; Franklin 2004). An individual's level of education is one of the most consistent predictors of participation. However, it seems that neither rising levels of education, nor the increased access to information through the rise of mass media have resulted in higher levels of these more traditional, institutionalized forms of political action.

Scholars such as Inglehart (1997) and Norris (2002) argue that we are witnessing changes in the modes of participation rather than simply stagnation or even a fall. Modern highly educated and informed citizens have become increasingly disillusioned with, and are aware of, the limitations of traditional politics. They are eschewing traditional types of conventional participation (e.g. voting, joining political parties), in favour of a broader political action repertoire that includes extra-institutional, direct forms of political action, such as signing petitions, boycotting, buycotting and demonstrating (commonly labelled unconventional participation). Instead of a less engaged population, individuals in advanced democracies are said to have become more engaged, in specific types of participation that place increasing demands on participants, are more elite-challenging in nature and are acted out in non-traditional political contexts such as the World Wide Web and the market place (Dalton 2006; Norris 2002). By now there is ample evidence showing that protest politics has increased in recent decades in advanced democracies and that rates of petition signing, demonstrating and boycotting are higher in advanced democracies than in relatively newer democracies (Rucht 2007).

This view, however, fails to take into account an important explanatory factor for political participation, namely mobilization. Brady *et al.* (1995: 271) famously summarize the three main answers to the question of why individuals might *not* participate in politics: "because they can't, because they don't want to, or because nobody asked".[1] That is, it is an individual's level of resources, their level of engagement with politics and whether or not they were asked to participate that explain whether or not they participate (Verba *et al.* 1995).

Accordingly, another interpretation is that although advanced democracies might be characterized by high rates of non-electoral forms of participation,[2] this does not necessarily reflect an increased engagement with politics, but rather a change in the modus operandi. This chapter argues that advanced democracies in Europe have experienced an increase in (the activation of) "peripheral participants" – resourceful, but *less* psychologically engaged individuals who only participate when mobilized through increasingly professionalized interest groups and/ or when political issues are particularly salient (e.g. during national elections). This interpretation implies that optimistic views about increased representation should be tempered until we more carefully evaluate the role of interest groups in the process of representation.

Using data from the European Social Survey, we distinguish two distinct patterns according to which peripheral and core participants are likely to become involved and which are based on both the number and type of participatory acts individuals engaged in. The chapter then goes on to explore how countries can be characterized along these two patterns of involvement. Finally, we examine how variations between countries in the prevalence of interest groups and the salience of political issues can explain differences, as well as the extent to which individual resources and levels of political engagement affect the likelihood of adopting a peripheral rather than a core pattern of involvement.

The mobilization of peripheral participants

In recent decades there has been a proliferation of interest groups and social movements in advanced democracies that target citizens for political mobilization, such as political parties, trade unions, voluntary organizations and community groups (Berry and Wilcox 2009; Norris 2002: 37). These so called "mobilizing agencies" (Norris 2002) have become an increasingly institutionalized and important aspect of democracy. According to Kriesi (2008: 149): "the process of representation has become organised, and the collective actors and their agents who have come to control this process have become the key figures in democratic systems". This organization of representation through groups is said to be beneficial to democracy as it offers a more effective representation with a closer connection between public policy and citizens' preferences than representation solely through political parties (Jordan and Maloney 2007: 2).

However, with the increased importance and prevalence of a wide range of mobilizing agencies, these agencies have become more professionalized. This professionalization has led to "business-like groups" that are structured as professional organizations and run by salaried employees who are hired for their managerial and fundraising skills, rather than their ideological commitment or activist's résumé (Jordan and Maloney 2007: 114–16). One area in particular in which this professionalization has made an impact is the mobilization of individuals in support of a group's cause.

Mobilization can be defined as the "process by which candidates, parties, activists, and groups induce other people to participate" (Rosenstone and Hansen

1993: 25) and relies heavily on the use of commercial marketing strategies. It has become more targeted towards specific groups of potential participants and more effective, lowering participation costs for potential participants by "supplying participation" and reducing the amount of time needed to participate. Schier (2000) distinguishes between "mobilization" and "activation". *Mobilization* refers to the old-style, inclusive, communication of partisan messages by political parties through social networks and the media. *Activation* refers to the exclusive and finely targeted modern campaigns conducted not only by political parties but by a broad range of interest groups.

Several authors have gone as far as to suggest that the way in which movements recruit new members or mobilize individuals for their cause might be at least as influential in determining their success as their ideological goals – "the 'whys' or 'reasons' for joining [social movements] arise out of the recruitment process itself" (Snow *et al.* 1980: 799). There is mounting experimental evidence that activation strategies which rely on simple incentives such as enhancing the entertainment value of participation by organizing a social gathering with free refreshments (Addonizio *et al.* 2007), or applying social pressure by threatening to expose one's lack of participation to neighbours or family (Gerber *et al.* 2008), can be highly successful.

Socio-economic development and the associated rising educational levels have led to a larger group of resource-rich potential participants in more advanced democracies. Accordingly, activation strategies can be targeted at a wider group of potential participants, including many who have previously eschewed political participation. Many of those mobilized by professional advocacy groups are stimulated to engage in "low cost" activities such as signing a petition or donating money, and have been shown to be rather satisfied to contract out their participation and/or to be "chequebook participants" (Jordan and Maloney 2007). Verba *et al.* (1971: 46) put it succinctly: "[i]nsofar as one can engage in an activity with relatively little initiative, then it may be that one can participate that way without much psychological involvement – perhaps *in response to the inducements of others*" (emphasis added).

In order to evaluate whether advanced democracies, when compared to less advanced democracies, can indeed be characterized by a relatively higher preponderance of less politically engaged individuals who are activated to participate, we draw a distinction between "peripheral" and "core" participants.

The idea of peripheral and core is taken from Campbell (1960) (see also Campbell *et al.* 1966), who used the terms to distinguish different types of voters to explain the surge and decline in turnout across elections. According to Campbell *core voters* go to polls in low stimulus, low visibility settings, and have high levels of political interest. In contrast, *peripheral voters* only vote in high salience elections and have lower levels of political interest.[3]

Peripheral participants are individuals who have lower levels of political interest, and are less politically engaged than core participants. They are likely to participate in politics in high salience contexts and/or when the cost of participation is substantially reduced by the efforts of mobilizing agencies. If they engage, peripheral participants will engage in low cost activities – e.g. signing petitions (not organizing them!), joining flash demonstrations, wearing a badge or donating money. They are less likely to engage in high cost activities that require greater initiative, such as contacting a politician, or an ongoing time investment, like working for political parties or interest groups.

Core participants exhibit a high level of interest in politics and need relatively little stimulus to engage in political participation. When these individuals engage, they engage in a wide range of political acts – i.e. both high and low cost activities. Whereas peripheral participants become active mainly through activation efforts of others, core participants are more likely to have developed an affinity with politics through their socialization and are more likely to be self-starters (Campbell *et al.* 1966: 42).

In sum, the increasing prevalence of professionalized mobilizing agencies, together with a larger pool of resource-rich individuals who are not highly politically motivated, implies that higher levels of non-electoral political participation can best be accounted for by a higher preponderance of activated peripheral participants vis-à-vis core participants. This assumption directly challenges the idea that individuals have widened their political action repertoire and have actually become more engaged in advanced democracies (Dalton 2006; Norris 2002) – i.e. we are not witnessing a burgeoning in the number or proportion of core participants. Accordingly, we advance that in contexts where mobilizing agencies are highly active and/or prevalent the number of activated peripheral participants vis-à-vis the number of core participants should be higher.

Peripheral and core participants across Europe

In order to empirically test these ideas cross-nationally comparable data for a large number of countries and individuals is needed. We use survey data from the first round of the European Social Survey (ESS),[4] fielded in 2002 and 2003 (Jowell *et al.* 2003),[5] which includes several questions on non-electoral political participation, as well as questions regarding relevant explanatory individual characteristics and voluntary association membership and participation. Moreover, for this round of the ESS important political events that made front-page news around the time of the survey were recorded.[6]

The data include a battery of ten items aimed at measuring non-electoral political participation.[7] Building on definitions formulated by Verba *et al.* (1995: 38–9) and Brady (1999: 737) of political participation will be defined as: voluntary activities by ordinary people directed towards influencing, directly or indirectly, political outcomes at various levels of the political system. As acting is central to the definition, membership in (political) organizations is excluded, as are any (expressions of) political attitudes or orientations.

Central to the way in which core and peripheral participants can be expected to participate is both the degree of initiative or effort required for a political act, as well as the frequency of involvement. Arguments about the changing nature of political participation in advanced democracies have mostly relied on comparisons between conventional and unconventional participation (e.g. Dalton 2006; Kaase 1989; Topf 1995). However, comparing participation rates in this way ignores the fact that some unconventional political activities (e.g. signing a petition or boycotting products) can be seen as relatively low cost. A failure to recognize this might generate partial or even misleading interpretations or insights.

Accordingly, in this chapter political acts are differentiated by the degree of personal initiative or effort required – i.e. between high and low cost involvements. Voting, for instance, requires little initiative because the "occasion for voting is presented to the citizen in the form of regular elections; he does not have to create the occasion" (Verba *et al.* 1978: 53). The ten political acts under consideration are grouped according to four increasing levels of initiative. "Worn or displayed a campaign badge/sticker", "signed a petition", "boycotted certain products" and "deliberately bought certain products for political, ethical or environmental reasons" can be considered political acts that require the lowest level of initiative on behalf of the participant. A participant simply has to sign his or her name when presented with a petition, wear a badge when given one, or make an ethical consumer choice when doing groceries. "Donated money to a political organisation or group" requires slightly more initiative than this first group of acts, as it often involves an additional step, namely writing and mailing a cheque, or going online to transfer money.

A third group of political activities requires substantial effort and initiative, e.g. "worked in a political party or action group", "worked in another organisation or association", "taken part in a lawful public demonstration" and "participated in illegal protest activities" (Shingles 1981; Verba *et al.* 1971). These activities involve organization, being in a certain place in order to participate in the act, as well as demanding a fair amount of time investment.

Finally, following Verba *et al.* (1971: 17) "contacted a politician, government or local government official" is classified as requiring the highest level of initiative, because an individual independently decides who to contact about the specific issue of concern. Moreover, in most cases this is a solo activity – an individual cannot generally rely on the help of others because the good sought is often a "particularized benefit" (ibid.: 15) accruing directly to the participant.

The cost of political participation can also be measured through the number of acts participated in. Individuals who participate in many political acts exhibit a greater degree of effort and investment of time than those who only participate in one political act. Accordingly, core participants, with their higher level of affinity with politics, can be expected to participate on a more frequent basis than peripheral participants, who are more likely to engage sporadically. Based on both the number of acts participated in and the four different levels of cost involved, a typology consisting of two distinct patterns of participation can be distinguished according to which activated peripheral and core participants can be expected to engage. This typology is schematically shown in Figure 10.1.

Core participants should be more likely to engage in four or more non-electoral political acts than peripheral participants, which demonstrates their commitment to be politically active. They should also be more likely to participate in two political acts if those acts include at least one of the acts requiring a

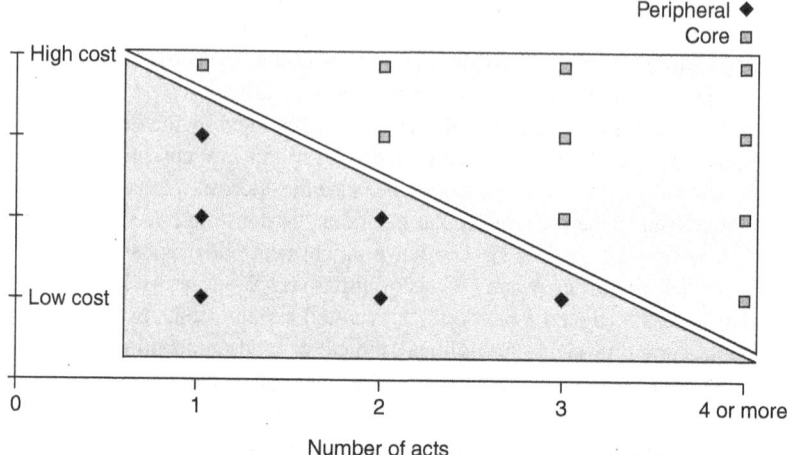

Figure 10.1 Typology of peripheral and core political participants according to the number of political acts participated in, and the cost of the most costly political act participated in.

higher level of initiative and effort than donating money, and in three political acts if those acts include at least donating money or a more costly act. Finally, we can expect core participants to be more likely to contact a politician, as this is the political act requiring the highest level of initiative and most unlikely to be a result of activation. In contrast, peripheral participants should be more likely to participate in only one of the other political acts, as they have only a fleeting interest in participating in politics. They can also be expected to be more likely to have participated in two or three of the least costly acts, as a result of activation by mobilizing agencies. Perpetual non-participants or non-activated participants will not participate at all.

Figure 10.2 shows the distribution of participants according to the two different patterns of participation and of non-participants across the twenty-one countries in the dataset. There are substantial differences across countries between the percentage of people who have not participated in any non-electoral act (Figure 10.2a). In the advanced democratic countries of Northwest Europe – Sweden, Finland, Norway and Denmark – as well as in Switzerland, as much as 70 per cent or more of the adult population has participated in at least one act of non-electoral political participation. In contrast, in the relatively newer democracies of Southern and Eastern Europe less than 50 per cent of the adult population has participated. This finding confirms that levels of non-electoral participation are indeed higher in more advanced democracies, as found by many authors (e.g. Inglehart 1997; Norris 2002).

However, we find a very different pattern when we look at the distribution of the two types of participants only (Figure 10.2b). The difference between the

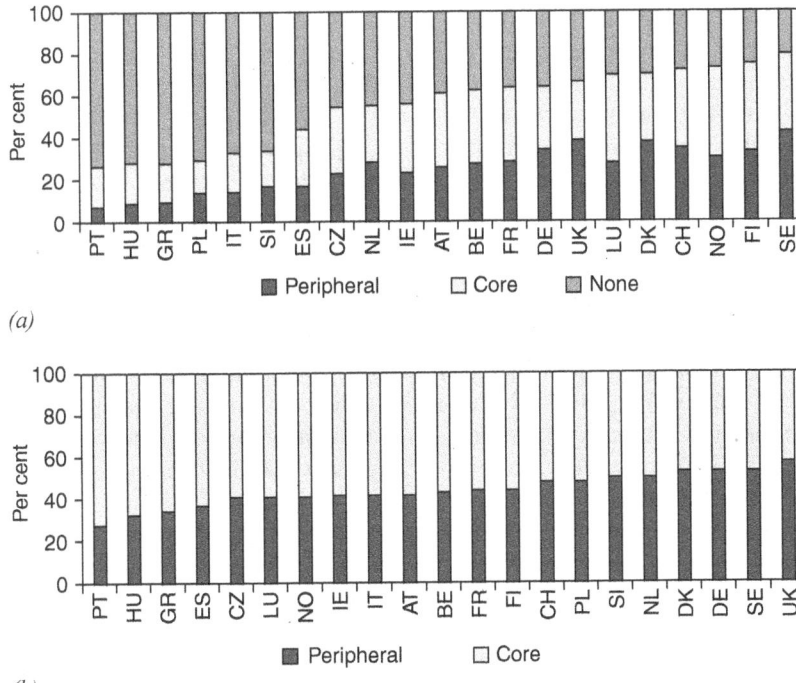

Figure 10.2a and 10.2b Type of participant (by country) (source: ESS1e06).

Note
Weighted by design weight.

country with the smallest (Portugal) and the highest percentage of peripheral participants (United Kingdom) is as much as thirty percentage points. In Portugal, Hungary, Greece, Spain and the Czech Republic, all countries with relatively low participation rates, peripheral participants are substantially outnumbered by core participants: only approximately 40 per cent or less of all participants can be classified as a peripheral participants based on their pattern of participation. This might be an indication that in these countries there is a lack of mobilizing agencies which reduce participation costs to such an extent that they mobilize even less engaged individuals into participation. In contrast, more than half of all participants can be classified as peripheral in Slovenia, the Netherlands, Germany, Denmark, the United Kingdom and Sweden. In this more diverse set of countries there are more individuals participating in only one or two political acts requiring little initiative on their behalf. It is this variation in the number of activated peripheral vis-à-vis core participants that we aim to explain.

Explaining the relative prevalence of peripheral participants

There are a number of circumstances under which mobilizing agencies can be expected to be highly prevalent or particularly active, and under which we should therefore find a relative overrepresentation of peripheral compared to core among those who participate.

A first circumstance is when there is a major political issue on the public agenda or around election times, when participation levels tend to be higher (Rosenstone and Hansen 1993). Moreover, within the literature on voter turnout, it is a common finding that the closeness of the election race increases turnout (e.g. Blais 2006; Franklin 2004). Accordingly, in years in which political issues are relatively more salient due to elections, mobilizing agencies can be expected to be particularly active. Consequently, even the normally less politically engaged, peripheral, participants are likely to be mobilized to participate in non-electoral participation. Similarly, when a major political issue dominates the media, like for instance a country going to war or an economic recession, mobilizing agencies are also likely to be more successful in their attempts to mobilize peripheral participants.

To take into account whether there was a *major political issue* on the agenda in a particular country, a variable was constructed measuring whether in the year preceding the survey there was an election or there was a major political issue high on the public agenda. (As part of the documentation of the ESS, event data was recorded registering front-page news in each of the countries.[8] Any event that triggered mass participation was included in the measure.)[9] Figure 10.3 shows the percentage of all participants that can be classified according to a peripheral rather

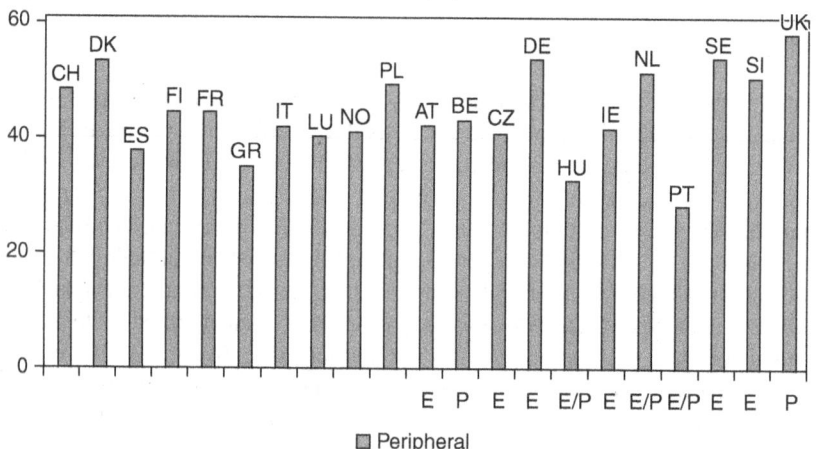

Figure 10.3 Percentage of all participants that are peripheral (by whether there was a national election (E) and/or a major political issue (P) on the agenda in a country) (source: ESS1e06).

Note
Weighted by design weight.

than a core participation pattern for each country and its score on this variable. Although there is substantial variation among countries, in countries that had a major political issue on the agenda in the previous year, the percentage of peripheral participants is on average slightly higher than in countries that did not.

A second circumstance under which mobilizing agencies can be expected to be highly prevalent is in urban settings. In urban contexts the density of mobilizing agencies is likely to be higher. Moreover, political activities such as demonstrations, political conventions and consumer boycotts are easier to organize in urban than in rural contexts due to the higher concentration of potential participants. The fact that there are more opportunities to be mobilized means that participation costs are lower in urban environments, attracting individuals who might not otherwise participate. Not surprisingly, previous studies on political participation have found that urban contexts differ from rural contexts in the extent to which individuals engage in types of political participation, with protest and consumer politics being more prevalent in urban contexts (e.g. Teorell *et al.*, 2007). Citizens in countries characterized by a high degree of urbanization should be easier to mobilize and we are likely to find a relative overrepresentation of activated peripheral compared to core participants.

A second important variable, *urbanization*, is the percentage of the total population of a country that lives in an urban environment (UNDP 2004). Figure 10.4 suggests that a higher degree of urbanization might indeed be related to more (activated) peripheral participants: in four of the countries with a degree of urbanization that exceeds 80 per cent, more than half of the participants can be classified as peripheral.

As a general determinant of the prevalence of mobilizing agencies in a country, we combine several measures of different types of mobilizing agencies

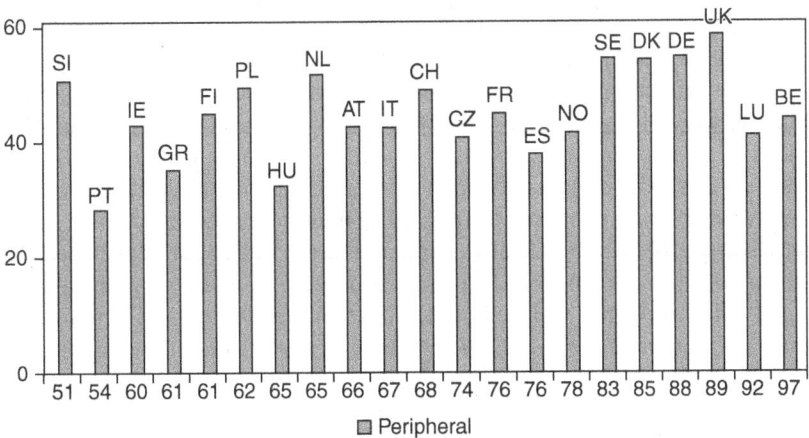

Figure 10.4 Percentage of all participants that are peripheral (by the percentage of urbanization in a country) (source: ESS1e06).

Note
Weighted by design weight.

into one variable called *mobilization*. Three elementary types of mobilizing agencies "that are designed to promote collective interests in order to influence political decision-making and, ultimately, social change" (Rucht 1996: 187) are commonly distinguished (see also Kriesi 2008; Norris 2002): interest groups, political parties and social movements.

Unions are a particularly important interest group due to their prevalence and relatively large size. Therefore, as a first measure the proportion of union membership is included. To measure the prevalence of political parties the proportion of political party membership is used. Measuring the prevalence of social movements in a country is more difficult, especially because many social movements mobilize individuals through informal networks. As a measure of the density of networks we will therefore use the proportion of membership, participation and volunteering in non-political associations in a country.[10] An additional measure, also suggested by Paxton (2002), is the number of International Non-Governmental Organizations (INGOs) and international orientated NGOs per million of the population in a given country (Union of International Associations 2004). While INGOs are a specialized subset of all associations in a country, due to their nature as voluntary associations often aimed at promoting the "common good of humanity" (Paxton 2002: 262), they can be expected to be especially active in mobilizing individuals. By taking the log of this measure less weight is given to the extreme values of Belgium and Luxembourg. As important centres for the European Union's bureaucracy these countries attract a disproportionate number of INGOs of which a substantial portion is unlikely to target the national population for activation.

Using the scores resulting from a factor analysis of these four measures, one variable called *mobilization* was constructed, indicative of the prevalence of a diverse set of mobilizing agencies in a country.[11] The most striking difference in the percentage of peripheral participants between countries is found according to the presence of mobilizing agencies. Countries with fewer mobilizing agencies tend to have substantially fewer activated peripheral participants (Figure 10.5).

Finally, we will also include a variable in the analysis for the level of economic development in 2002, measured as Gross National Income (GNI) per capita in current US dollars (World Bank 2006). As previously discussed, an alternative explanation for higher rates of non-electoral participation in some countries might be that as countries become more economically developed the resources of their population increase, leading to a more psychologically engaged citizenry with a widened political action repertoire, that is, more core participants. Although the degree of economic development and the prevalence of mobilizing agencies are strongly related, we theorized that both should be positively related to the number of peripheral vis-à-vis core participants. Figure 10.6 confirms this expectation. The level of economic development in a country tends to be positively associated with the percentage of peripheral participants. Countries with a GNI of less than $20,000 per capita are among those with the lowest percentage and those with a GNI of more than $25,000 per capita are among those with the highest percentage of activated peripheral participants.

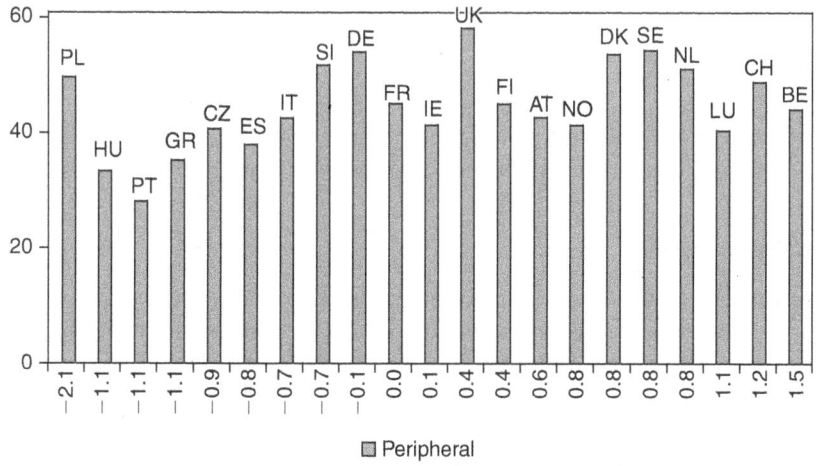

Figure 10.5 Percentage of all participants that are peripheral (by the mobilization score of a country) (source: ESS1e06).

Note
Weighted by design weight.

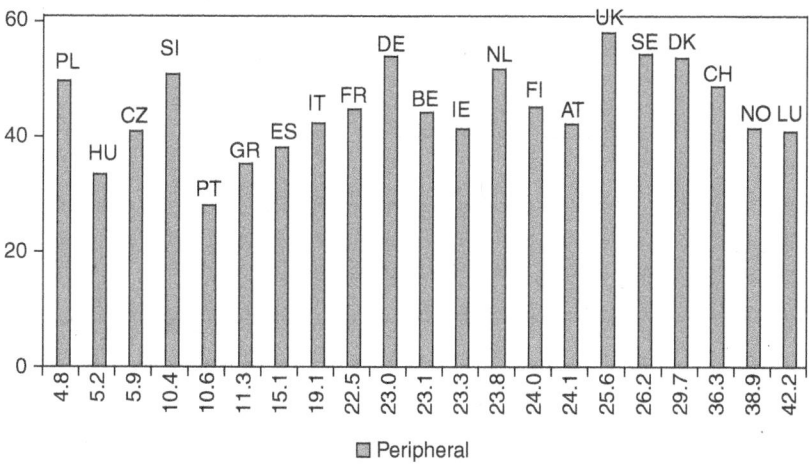

Figure 10.6 Percentage of all participants that are peripheral (by GNI per capita in US$1,000 of a country) (source: ESS1e06).

Note
Weighted by design weight.

Although these figures provide some indicative evidence of the importance of different country characteristics in explaining the prevalence of activated peripheral participants over core participants, a more robust test takes individual attributes into account. A multilevel model allows us to conduct this test and will also enable us to do justice to the two levelled nature of the data by nesting individuals within countries. Moreover, this model is also used to test whether resources and levels of engagement can indeed predict participation patterns.

Multilevel analysis

In order to capture the variance in the number of peripheral participants vis-à-vis core participants across countries, a two level logistic regression model with a random intercept is used. This type of model allows for the fact that individuals within the same country share many (un)observable characteristics and are therefore not independent of each other. Thus, the first level consists of individuals and the second of countries. Being a peripheral, rather than a core participant (the outcome Y_{ij}) consists of an expected value (P_{ij}) and an individual level residual (R_{ij}) with mean zero:

$$Y_{ij} = P_{ij} + R_{ij} \tag{10.1}$$

We can write a model in which we have q country level explanatory variables z_1 to z_q, and r individual level explanatory variables x_1 to x_r as follows:

$$logit(P_{ij}) = \gamma_{00} + \sum_{h=1}^{q} \gamma_{0h} z_{hj} + \sum_{h=1}^{r} \gamma_{h0} x_{hij} + U_{0j} \tag{10.2}$$

in which P_{ij} is the probability of being a peripheral participant, rather than a core participant, and U_{0j} is the random component of the intercept, which is assumed to have a zero mean (Snijders and Bosker 2004).

Although core and peripheral participants have similar levels of resources, peripheral participants are less politically engaged than core participants. Consequently, we should find that resources do not affect the probability of participating according to a peripheral rather than a core pattern of participation – while political engagement does.

The three most important resources for participation are time, money and civic skills (Verba et al. 1995). The level of income and civic skills tend to be higher among those with higher levels of educational attainment and those in higher-end jobs, enabling participation (ibid.). This is the premise of the classic socio-economic status (SES) model of participation (e.g. Campell et al. 1960; Milbrath 1965; Verba et al. 1978). Measures of *education* and occupational *class* are therefore included in the analysis.[12] One's *main* daily *activity* is used as a measure of the amount of time available for participation. In particular those who are unemployed, in education, or retired should have more time available for participation than those in full-time employment. Although core participants are more likely to engage in time-intensive activities, my argument implies that this is due to their commitment and *not* because they actually have more time. In addition, *citizens* are assumed to have more (country-specific) civic skills than non-citizens. They are also likely to have more experience with the political system of their country, and to be more knowledgeable about it and to feel more involved with its politics than individuals who have not (yet) acquired citizenship and the right to vote.

Political engagement is measured through a number of different variables. A high degree of political interest, discussing politics regularly, holding a belief that participation is an important aspect of being a citizen and feeling close to a particular political party – all signal that politics is an important part of an individual's life. Accordingly, we expect to find that individuals with higher levels of these variables are more likely to behave like core rather than peripheral participants. Political efficacy – the belief in one's ability to make a difference in politics – should, as a measure of political engagement (as suggested by Verba *et al.* 1995), also better predict core rather than peripheral participation. Alternatively, if political efficacy rather reflects the evaluation of one's own civic skills, we would expect to find no effect. Finally, the relationship between political trust and different patterns of participation is assessed. However, to the extent to which distrust functions as a motivation to be politically active (e.g. Norris 1999), we would expect that highly engaged core participants are more critical of society's political institutions than the less engaged peripheral participants. Which in turn would make them more likely to participate in high cost activities, as well as in more activities.[13]

In addition to the measures for resources and engagement individual level variables measuring mobilization opportunities are also included. The rationale for doing so is to test whether the national context of mobilization affects the probability of participating as a peripheral rather than a core participant, independent of whether an individual is already part of an organization. Through participation in organizations individuals are said to acquire the civic skills necessary for political participation and are more likely to be asked to participate (Verba *et al.* 1995). However, there is some debate about whether the relationship between organizational membership and political participation is a spurious one, explained by the fact that "joiners" by nature will self-select into both (Theiss-Morse and Hibbing 2005). We include measures for union membership, regular church attendance and membership in non-political voluntary associations that will allow us to get a better handle on the effect of the national context of mobilization. Using the same rationale we also include an individual level measure of locality – i.e. whether an individual lives in an urban or rural setting. However, in this instance the additional effect of the degree of urbanization of a country would indicate that even individuals who live in a rural setting in a highly urbanized country are more likely to participate as peripheral rather than core participants.[14]

Finally, we include variables for gender (*male*) and *age* (in years). Both variables have been shown to be central to explaining political participation. Men are commonly said to participate more in most forms of non-electoral political participation, except consumer politics, due to their higher level of resources and political engagement, as well as the fact that they are socialized with more emphasis on politics (Lane 1959; Teorell et al. 2007; Topf 1995; Verba et al. 1995). Older and/or middle-aged individuals are said to participate more in conventional types of participation due to an accumulation of resources, rising payoffs from participation and an increased integration into the community (Duch 1988; Teorell et al. 2007). Younger individuals are said to participate more in unconventional (rebellious) types of participation because they "enjoy the physical vigor, the freedom from day-to-day responsibilities of career and family, and have the *time* to participate in the pursuit of the energetic kinds of political activity" (Marsh and Kaase 1979: 101). Moreover, younger generations in particular are said to have become (more) disillusioned with politics, turning them to less traditional ways to influence politics (Inglehart 1997; Norris 2002).

The first model in Table 10.1 includes only the individual level variables. Using the results from this model, we can evaluate how resources and engagement affect the likelihood of participating as a peripheral rather than a core participant. Women are more likely to be peripheral as opposed to core participants than men, but there is no difference according to age.[15] Furthermore, although those with a lower level of education are equally likely to be peripheral participants as those with an upper- or post-secondary degree, those with a tertiary degree are less likely to participate as peripheral participants. As for occupational class, blue-collar workers are more likely to participate as peripheral participants than their white-collar counterparts. Moreover, citizens of the country in which they live are equally likely to be peripheral participants as non-citizens.

Looking at individuals' main daily activity, those who have the time and/or flexibility to participate are not less likely to participate as peripheral participants. That is, individuals who are unemployed, in education, retired or doing housework are not significantly less likely than those in full-time employment to be a peripheral rather than core participants.

In sum, the idea that resources do not predict whether an individual is more likely to engage as a peripheral rather than a core participant must be rejected. However, this applies only to resources measured in terms of civic skills and money and not to the amount of time available for participation. Moreover, a lack of resources does not result in a greater likelihood of participating as a peripheral rather than a core participant. We find no effect for those who hold less than an upper- or post-secondary degree, for those who have never held a paid job or who are unemployed, and for citizens.

Individuals who are more interested in politics, who feel close to a political party, who more frequently discuss politics and who place a greater value on political participation as an important aspect of being a citizen, are less likely to participate as peripheral rather than core participants. The same applies to those who feel more politically efficacious. Therefore, the idea that political engagement is an important predictor of not only the number of political acts, but also the type of political involvement cannot be rejected. In addition, it seems that the most politically trusting individuals are more likely to participate as peripheral as opposed to core participants. Thus, in so far as political distrust works as a stimulant for participation, it does so more for high cost and a greater frequency of acts.

With regards to personal opportunities to be mobilized, we find that individuals living in urban areas are more likely to participate as peripheral participants than those in rural areas. Moreover, as can be expected, individuals who regularly attend religious services, who belong to a union and who are active in non-political voluntary associations are less likely to be peripheral participants.

In the next model in Table 10.1 two of the country level variables of interest (major political issue and mobilization) are added to the first model. In Model 3 mobilization is replaced by GNI per capita, the measure of the level of economic development. As mobilization and GNI per capita are highly collinear, that is, they are strongly – and in this case positively – related, including them together in one model would lead to inflated standard errors and potentially to biased estimates of the coefficients.

The degree of urbanization in a country proved not to exert a significant independent effect on the number of peripheral participants vis-à-vis core participants, nor did it affect the estimates for the other variables in the models.[16] As we have seen, the individual indicator for living in an urban environment does positively influence the propensity of being a peripheral rather than a core participant. Thus, once we take an individual's locality into account, there is no additional effect of the degree to which a country is mainly urban rather than rural. This makes sense, as a significant effect of urbanization would indicate that even individuals living in rural environments are more likely to be mobilized in urbanized countries. This is clearly not the case: mobilization efforts resulting in an increase in peripheral participants seem to be restricted to the city. We decided to leave the degree of urbanization out of the final models for the sake of parsimony.

The aim of adding the country level variables is to reduce the variance across countries in the probability of being a peripheral participant, rather than a core participant (the intercept variance). In both models, including the country level variables in the model reduces the country level variation in peripheral vis-à-vis core participants from 0.12 to 0.09 (0.10 in Model 3), a substantial reduction of about one-quarter.

After controlling for the individual level variables, as well as other country level variables, the effect of a major political issue being on the agenda, such as a national election, on the number of peripheral participants is negligible in Model 2. Although its effect is greatly increased by replacing mobilization with GNI per capita in Model 3, it still fails to reach statistical significance. These results indicate that the current political context as reflected in the media and, as we have argued, acted upon by mobilizing agencies contributes little to the explanation for the variation across countries in peripheral vis-à-vis core participants. Other variables, such as the prevalence of mobilizing agencies might be more relevant.

The effect of the prevalence of mobilizing agencies on the number of peripheral participants is positive (and significant with a p-value of 0.053), even after controlling for individuals' membership in associations. This provides evidence

Table 10.1 Two level logistic regression model predicting being a peripheral participant (as opposed to core) with individual characteristics and country characteristics, regression coefficients with robust standard errors in parentheses

	Model 1		Model 2		Model 3	
Male	**−0.20**	**(0.06)**	**−0.20**	**(0.05)**	**−0.20**	**(0.06)**
Age (effect*10)	0.03	(0.02)	0.03	(0.02)	0.03	(0.02)
Education – reference category: upper and post-secondary						
Primary or first stage of basic or less	−0.14	(0.12)	−0.14	(0.12)	−0.14	(0.12)
Lower secondary or secondary stage of basic	0.05	(0.08)	0.05	(0.08)	0.05	(0.08)
Tertiary	**−0.16**	**(0.03)**	**−0.16**	**(0.03)**	**−0.16**	**(0.03)**
Class – reference category: service class						
Routine non-manual worker	**0.13**	**(0.05)**	**0.13**	**(0.05)**	**0.13**	**(0.05)**
Self-employed	0.19	(0.13)	0.20	(0.13)	0.20	(0.13)
Self-employed farmer	*−0.25*	*(0.15)*	*−0.25*	*(0.15)*	*−0.25*	*(0.15)*
Skilled manual worker	**0.22**	**(0.07)**	**0.22**	**(0.07)**	**0.22**	**(0.07)**
Semi-unskilled manual worker	**0.12**	**(0.06)**	**0.12**	**(0.06)**	**0.12**	**(0.06)**
Farm labourer	0.15	(0.16)	0.15	(0.16)	0.15	(0.16)
Never held paid job	−0.05	(0.09)	−0.05	(0.09)	−0.05	(0.09)
Main activity – reference category: in paid work						
Unemployed	0.00	(0.11)	0.01	(0.10)	0.01	(0.11)
In education	0.01	(0.10)	0.01	(0.09)	0.01	(0.10)
Retired	0.08	(0.07)	0.09	(0.07)	0.09	(0.07)
Housework/caretaker	0.10	(0.07)	0.10	(0.07)	0.10	(0.07)
Other	**−0.37**	**(0.17)**	**−0.37**	**(0.17)**	**−0.37**	**(0.17)**
Citizen	0.01	(0.08)	0.03	(0.08)	0.03	(0.08)
Urban	**0.24**	**(0.05)**	**0.24**	**(0.05)**	**0.24**	**(0.05)**
Church attendee	**−0.20**	**(0.05)**	**−0.19**	**(0.05)**	**−0.19**	**(0.05)**

	Model		Model		Model	
Union member	-0.09	(0.05)	-0.09	(0.05)	-0.09	(0.05)
Association member	-0.51	(0.04)	-0.52	(0.04)	-0.52	(0.04)
Political interest	-0.25	(0.04)	-0.25	(0.04)	-0.25	(0.04)
Political trust	0.05	(0.02)	0.05	(0.02)	0.05	(0.02)
Political efficacy	-0.17	(0.02)	-0.17	(0.02)	-0.17	(0.02)
Close to party	-0.20	(0.05)	-0.21	(0.05)	-0.21	(0.05)
Political discussion	-0.06	(0.02)	-0.06	(0.02)	-0.06	(0.02)
Participation norm	-0.19	(0.03)	-0.19	(0.03)	-0.19	(0.03)
Constant	0.05	(0.13)	0.14	(0.12)	0.07	(0.12)
Country level variables						
Major political issue	–	–	0.01	(0.16)	0.14	(0.18)
Urbanization	–	–	–	–	–	–
Mobilization	–	–	*0.18*	*(0.09)*	–	–
GNI per capita	–	–	–	–	0.17	(0.08)
Country level variance	**0.12**	**(0.03)**	**0.09**	**(0.03)**	**0.10**	**(0.03)**
Deviance (df)[a]	22,242.81	(28)	22,235.86	(30)	22,236.30	(30)

Source: ESS1e06.

Notes
a Significance compared to Model 1.
N level 1 = 17,512; N level 2 = 21.
Parameters significant with $p \leq 0.05$ in bold; parameters significant with $p \leq 0.10$ in bold italics.
Scaled design weights are used for Level 1 (as recommended by Rabe-Hesketh and Skrondal (2006); scaling method 2 was used), and level 2 weights are included to adjust for differences in sample size, weighting each country equally.

that the wider context of mobilization is indeed important in encouraging those less politically engaged to participate. This finding is strengthened by the finding that, as we might have expected on the basis of Figure 10.6, the higher the level of GNI per capita in a country, the more, rather than fewer, peripheral participants vis-à-vis core participants.

In sum, in contexts where mobilizing agencies are highly active and/or prevalent the number of active peripheral participants vis-à-vis the number of core participants is indeed higher. We explored three such contexts: the saliency of political events, the urban context and the prevalence of a variety of mobilizing agencies. Both living in a city and in a wider national context where mobilizing agencies are active, increase the likelihood that an individual will politically participate, albeit in a not highly involved way. In addition, although we found no clear significant effect of the saliency of political events, it might be too early to reject the importance of what is on the public agenda altogether.

Conclusion

Studies comparing levels of political participation between established and new(er) advanced democracies seem to indicate no systematic difference in the level of turnout, but a higher level of non-electoral participation in advanced democracies. Authors studying political participation using survey data have concluded that the higher level is due to greater levels of resources, in particular higher educational attainment levels, combined with an increased psychological engagement with politics.

Little attention, however, has been paid to the changing context of mobilization. This chapter has tried to address this gap and suggested an alternative theory, namely that the higher levels of non-electoral participation in advanced democracies can best be accounted for by a relative overrepresentation of the number of activated peripheral participants vis-à-vis core participants. These resourceful, but not necessarily highly engaged, peripheral participants are mobilized into action by numerous professionalized mobilizing agencies.

The evidence presented shows that individuals who are less psychologically engaged with politics are indeed more likely to participate as we would expect peripheral participants to participate; that is, in few political acts, requiring little initiative or effort. Moreover, although the most resource-rich individuals in terms of their civic and financial resources are less likely to participate as peripheral participants, individuals who are the least resource-rich or who have less time available for participation do not differ in their likelihood of participating as peripheral rather than core participants.

Under certain circumstances rates of these peripheral participants are higher compared to core participants. The evidence suggests that living in a context in which mobilization opportunities are greater – such as in cities rather than in more remote areas, as well as in contexts where a variety of interests groups and social movements are active – increases the likelihood that an individual who might not otherwise participate will do so, albeit in a less involved manner.

For now we have to reject the idea that the relative rate of peripheral participants compared to core participants increases in politicized contexts such as during national elections or when countries are experiencing conflict over wars or economic issues. This finding is likely due to a lack of more precise measures of the saliency of political events. Research predicting trends in turnout has long recognized the importance of including measures of the saliency of elections and/or the closeness of an election race (e.g. Franklin 2004) and points to the importance of taking the current political context into account. However, survey research on non-electoral political participation has mostly neglected whether certain political issues were particularly high on the public's agenda during a certain period.

Although there is no doubt that more individuals participate in the more advanced democracies of Europe than in the newer democracies, however, many only participate in acts that require little initiative on their behalf, and rely on the mobilization efforts of others, most notably professionalized interest groups who substantially lower the costs of participation. This raises the question about the quality of political involvement.

In so far as equal political participation ensures the equal consideration of needs and preferences (Verba 2006: 525), many would agree that more participation is better – providing it is not skewed even further towards the politically advantaged. However, individuals who participate mainly as a result of the social incentives that are at play in mobilization efforts (e.g. the use of social pressure) are vulnerable to having their interests represented in a way that does not fit with their actual needs and preferences. As interest groups become increasingly successful as mobilizing agents, the extent to which these groups manage to successfully represent the interests of their constituencies democratically is becoming ever more important.

Notes

1 Another reason, as pointed out by Brady *et al.* (1995: 290, note 1), is that an individual might not be (legally) allowed to participate.
2 By non-electoral political participation we mean all conventional and unconventional acts of political participation except voting.
3 In Campbell's *et al.* (1966: 42–3) own words:

> A large proportion of the turnout in any national election consists of people whose level of political interest is sufficiently high to take them to the polls in all national elections, even those in which the level of political stimulation is relatively weak. These "core voters" are joined in a high stimulus election by additional "peripheral voters," whose level of political interest is lower, but whose motivation to vote has been sufficiently increased by the stimulation of the election situation to carry them to the polls. There remains a sizable fraction of the electorate which does not vote even in a high stimulus election; some of these people are prevented from voting by poor health, failure to meet eligibility requirements, or conflicts of one sort or another. Others do not vote because their level of political interest is so low that no amount of political stimulation will motivate them to vote.

4 The twenty-one European countries included in the first round of the ESS and their respective abbreviations used in the rest of this chapter are: Austria (AT), Belgium (BE), Switzerland (CH), Czech Republic (CZ), Germany (DE), Denmark (DK), Spain (ES), Finland (FI), France (FR), Greece (GR), Hungary (HU), Ireland (IE), Italy (IT), Luxembourg (LU), Netherlands (NL), Norway (NO), Poland (PL), Portugal (PT), Sweden (SE), Slovenia (SI) and United Kingdom (UK). Only individuals of eighteen years or older, and therefore legally of age, are included in the following analyses.
5 The data are archived and distributed by the Norwegian Social Science Data Services (NSD). For more information on how the survey was conducted see online, available at: www.europeansocialsurvey.org.
6 Although data spanning a number of decades would be preferable, the comparability of measures of political participation over time is problematic as one would have to utilize a combination of datasets from different sources, each with their own question wordings. So we will rely on comparing different countries within Europe with different lengths of democracy and levels of socio-economic development.
7 The question was worded as follows: "There are different ways of trying to improve things in [country] or help prevent things from going wrong. During the last 12 months, have you done any of the following?"
8 There was no clear-cut definition of which events should be registered, making cross-national comparisons potentially problematic. However, as the lack of systematic coding most likely resulted in the omission of certain events, finding an effect will only prove more difficult. A separate, systematic content analysis of all relevant media in each country during 2002–3 is beyond the scope of this chapter, and there is no other general database describing events available for Europe.
9 For most countries the preceding calendar year was 2002 (most fieldwork was done towards the end of 2002), except for France (2003). In addition to national elections (IDEA 2010), the following five events were coded as indicative of major political issues: mass protests against the Iraq war in Belgium in January, February and November 2002 and in the UK in September 2002 and early 2003; mass demonstrations in Hungary in August 2002 protesting against the new media-law; the murder of the politician Pim Fortuyn in the Netherlands in May 2002, resulting in peaceful demonstrations and which substantially increased turnout in the following elections; and labour strikes from August until October 2002 in Portugal (Jowell *et al.* 2003). Although the actual number of individuals engaging in protest events reported in the media is likely to be too small to register in the survey, we take the events to be an indicator of high politicization, hypothesizing that they have led to an increase in mobilization in general.
10 These proportions are derived from the ESS data (weighted by design weights). Because we only include membership of unions and political parties, as well as activities in non-political associations, these measures do not overlap with my dependent variable.
11 The analysis produced one factor with loadings between 0.32 and 0.94.
12 As there is no reliable, cross-nationally comparable measure for income available we will only use education and class – both strongly related to income – in the analysis. The measure for *class* is based on the seven-category EGP class schema (Erikson and Goldthorpe 1992).
13 *Political interest* ranges in four categories from "not at all interested" to "very interested". The frequency of discussing politics and current affairs is measured in seven categories: never, less often, once a month, several times a month, once a week, several times a week, every day. *Participation norm* consists of the scores of a factor analysis of three 0–10 scaled items on "[t]o be a good citizen, how important would you say it is for a person to…": "vote in elections", "be active in voluntary organisations", "be active in politics". The analysis produced one factor with loadings between 0.41 and 0.84. *Close to a* political *party* is a dichotomous measure. *Political efficacy*

Peripheral participants 177

consists of the average score on two 0–4 scaled items with a significant correlation of 0.41 ("How often does politics seem so complicated that you can't really understand what is going on?" "How difficult or easy do you find it to make your mind up about political issues?"). Finally, *political trust* consists of the scores of a factor analysis of 0–10 scaled items on trusting each of the following four institutions: parliament, legal system, police, politicians. The analysis produced one factor with loadings between 0.61 and 0.81.

14 All four measures are dichotomous and indicate, respectively, whether someone is or has been a member of a trade union or a similar organization (*union member*), attends religious services at least once a month or more often (*church attendee*), has been a member, participant or volunteer in the last twelve months in either a sports/outdoor activity club, a cultural/hobby activity organization or a social club (*association member*), and lives in a town or small city, the suburbs or outskirts of a big city or a big city (*urban*).

15 Age was also tested for having a curvilinear relationship with the dependent variable, as middle-aged individuals have been found to participate more than older individuals. Growing older is said to be associated with a loss of mobility and/or interest (Teorell *et al.* 2007). The curvilinear effect of age also proved insignificant.

16 Although the degree of urbanization is positively associated with both GNI per capita and with mobilization, the insignificant effect is not the result of collinearity: when urbanization is included as the only country level variable it also fails to reach significance.

11 Surrogates for the underrepresented?

Ideology and participatory inequality in personal and professional political action

Tom W.G. van der Meer

Introduction

Citizens' participation in political life is a central concern in representative democracy. Governmental policy depends on citizen participation aimed at influencing policy outcomes (Verba *et al.* 1978). However, we know that some social groups are more likely to engage in political activities than others and that this participatory inequality means these groups are likely to exert a greater influence on outcomes. Participatory inequality is especially acute along ideological or policy conflict lines: i.e. ideological or political groups are more likely to participate than others and are more likely to be heard by policy makers.[1] Ultimately, this leads to ideologically or politically biased policy.

There is evidence that some direct personal forms of political participation are unequal and there is an ideological dimension (van der Meer *et al.* 2009a). Leftwing citizens participate more than rightwing citizens (although rightwing citizens are more likely to vote during elections). Citizens with an extreme ideological position are more likely to participate than ideological moderates. And citizens who perceive a large ideological gap between their position and the government react by getting engaged directly in political activities.

The literature on participatory inequality focuses mainly on conventional forms of direct, personal political action like voting, contacting officials, campaigning, and signing a petition: "activities by private citizens that are more or less directly aimed at influencing the selection of governmental personnel and/or the actions they take" (Verba and Nie 1972: 2). This approach ignores the supposed shift in the repertoire of political action toward more indirect, professionalized and collective forms (see the introductory chapter to this volume). Both individual citizens and their organizations increasingly tend to contract out the actual act of political participation to professionals (Jordan and Maloney 2007: 158–63; Saurugger 2007: 397–8). Fisher (2006: 67–86) labeled this as "outsourcing activism". When supporters or donators spend money in this way, they influence politics without undertaking direct political action by effectively hiring professionals to lobby, campaign, and petition on their behalf. Scholars refer to the role of individual citizens in this professionalized system of political involvement as "mere card-carrying members" (Putnam 2000: 59) and "checkbook participants" (Skocpol 2003: 292). Indeed, by far the most prevalent mode of involvement in interest and activist associations is passive membership (van der Meer *et al.* 2009b).

The rise of professionalized interest and activist associations has been lamented for creating "ephemeral, thin, sporadic" and "ill-informed" forms of political involvement (Hay *et al.* 2008: 11). However, the picture may not be so bleak. Maloney (2009: 284) suggested that professional organizations can "act as *surrogates* for those who cannot effectively represent themselves – i.e., acting on behalf of a public that lack the necessary knowledge and expertise". Whereas Maloney explicitly focused on organizations as surrogates for those who lack resources, his line of reasoning may be extended. Along similar lines, I theorize in this chapter that professional organizations may act as surrogates not only for those who *can't* adequately engage in direct political action, but also for those who do not *want* to spend time or effort to do so. If so, indirect political action (through professionalized organizations) could counterbalance the overrepresentation of leftwing and extremist citizens that we find in more direct forms of political action. The question then arises whether there is a similar, smaller or even opposite bias in the ideological and political composition of professionalized forms of political participation. To what extent are direct (personal) and indirect (professionalized) participation unequal across ideological and policy dimensions?

Moreover, the distinction between direct and indirect participation may shed light on the mechanisms that explain the participatory inequalities between ideological groups. On the one hand, one might expect leftwing and extremist bias in participation to be related to specific left-leaning policy preferences. In that case, the ideologically leftwing and extremist bias in political participation should be reflected in specific policy issues. On the other hand, leftwing and extremist citizens may be more likely to participate due to their preference for the process of active participation itself. Empirically, very little is known about these two mechanisms. Theoretically, however, the second mechanism – process incentives – cannot explain participation (and participatory inequality) in professionalized organizations, as chequebook members evidently do not seek active participation. Thus, two additional research questions emerge: to what extent can the relationship between ideological position with direct (personal) and indirect (professionalized) participation explained by citizens' policy preferences? To what extent do the mechanisms behind participatory inequality differ with regard to direct and indirect participation?

Given these considerations, this chapter aims to further the debate in two ways. First, it develops a single theoretical and empirical framework that covers both (modes of) indirect and direct political participation. Second, it tests whether participatory inequality along ideological lines is explained by citizens' policy positions. Through these aims, we assess the extent to which professional organizations function as surrogates for the inactive and as a counterbalance to the overrepresentation of leftwing and extreme citizens in direct personal forms of political action.

Ideology, policy preferences, and participation

Ideology and policy preferences

Citizens' ideological perspectives are commonly expressed by political scientists in terms of left and right. On this ideological left–right dimension the left pole is associated with "policies designed to bring about the redistribution of resources from those with more to those with less, and with the promotion of social rights that apply to groups of individuals taken as a whole even at the expense of individual members of those groups" (Laver and Hunt 1992: 12).

The right pole is associated with "the promotion of individual rights, including the right not to have personal resources expropriated for redistribution by the state, even at the expense of social inequality and of poverty among worse off social groups" (ibid.). Much earlier Lipset *et al.* (1954: 1135) proposed a similar definition, in which the left is seen as "advocating social change in the direction of greater equality – political, economic or social", while the right supports "a traditional, more or less hierarchical social order", as opposed to "change towards greater equality".

The left–right dimension is "a common yardstick" (van der Eijk and Niemöller 1983: 229) for scholars, the media, and voters alike. The left–right orientation is an (informational) ideological shortcut for voters who have incomplete information on the implications of different party policies for their own utility-income (Downs 1957). Various policy positions on multiple policy dimensions could be compressed to a unidimensional simplification (Sartori 1976). The left–right scheme encompasses all separate conflict lines "regardless of how many cleavage and/or identification dimensions exist" (Sani and Sartori 1983: 330).

The ideological left–right dimension supposedly encompasses all policy issues: it is an overarching "super issue" in which economic, social, and ethical issues are clustered together (Laver and Budge 1992). It also includes all sorts of policy issues, such as nuclear energy, abortion, law and order, and so on (van der Brug 1997). All positions on these policy issues may therefore be simplified as being leftist or rightist. Leftwing policy positions are related to equality, solidarity, progressiveness, and system change. Rightwing positions are related to individualism, freedom, conservatism, and system maintenance (Fuchs and Klingemann 1990). However, the specific framing of each policy issue in terms of left and right is context dependent.

This study takes a middle ground regarding the use of the left–right dimension and its relation to specific policy issues. On the one hand, it considers the left–right dimension as the overarching ideological scheme in which citizens position themselves (cf. Sani and Sartori 1983). On the other hand, voters' attitudes on specific policy issues do not always need to be consistent with their general ideological position. For example, while some citizens' general ideological tendencies and policy positions may be leftwing, they may simultaneously also hold views that could be considered rightwing (cf. Middendorp

1978; Himmelweit *et al.* 1981). Moreover, this chapter does not require that the specific meaning of the left–right dimension is the same for all citizens, as long as the overarching meaning is unambiguous. Based on the general definitions and the specific framing of policy issues, positions on these issues may be defined as leftwing or rightwing.

How ideological and policy preferences may drive political participation

Direct political participation is unequal along ideological lines across Western countries (van der Meer *et al.* 2009a). First, leftwing citizens are more likely to participate politically. Theoretically, two mechanisms explain this relationship. Leftwing citizens are supposedly stimulated by both *outcome* and *process* incentives. Outcome incentives are motivational triggers for political action – directly or indirectly (through organizations) – aimed at affecting policy outcomes (cf. Whiteley and Seyd 2002; Pattie *et al.* 2004). Ideologically leftwing citizens exhibit more outcome incentives, because they traditionally aim for system change rather than preservation (Fuchs and Klingemann 1990; Kriesi 1993; Martin and van Deth 2007). Process incentives trigger citizens' political engagement directly because they derive satisfaction from the process of participation itself, regardless of the outcome. According to Inglehart (1997: 252) these process incentives tend to primarily drive participation by postmaterialists, a group of citizens that have predominantly left-leaning views and opinions. All in all, both incentives are important explanatory factors that account for the higher participation levels of leftwing citizens vis-à-vis their rightwing counterparts.

Second, extremism of ideological orientation stimulates participation (Putnam 2000: 342; van der Meer *et al.* 2009a). Ideological extremists are motivated by outcome incentives that seek either to defend or to change the status quo: "the likelihood of being involved in a participatory way increases with the degree of [individual citizens'] polarization" (Martin and van Deth 2007: 328).

Hypotheses

The mechanisms through which ideological direction and extremism are related to participation can easily be transposed to more specific policy preferences. Citizens may have preferences on various policy issues, ranging from socioeconomic issues like income inequality, to ethical questions such as euthanasia. Considering the left–right scale as the overarching ideological dimension (Sani and Sartori 1983), each of these policy dimensions has a "left" pole and a "right" pole. Similarly, some citizens have more extreme preferences than others, although the degree of extremism may differ from issue to issue.

The most naïve and uniform theoretical model suggests that the same incentives stimulate various forms of participation along various policy dimensions similarly. The first set of hypotheses therefore reads as follows:

H1a The more leftwing the specific policy positions of citizens, the more likely they are to participate politically (directly and indirectly through associations).

H1b The more extreme the specific policy positions of citizens, the more likely they are to participate politically (directly and indirectly through associations).

Professional organizations counterbalance the participatory inequalities in political life, when they function as a surrogate for citizens who do not have the resources to participate directly themselves (Maloney 2009). Building on this line of thought, they may also function as a surrogate for citizens who do not have the intent of participating directly themselves. In other words, citizens who do not want to participate may support organizations to participate on their behalf. If there is such a surrogate effect, participatory inequality should be higher for direct, personal modes of participation (such as voting, contacting an official, and protesting) than for indirect, professionalized modes (i.e. through civic action groups, and especially through interest associations and activist associations).

There are various reasons why we should expect participatory inequality to be lower in indirect than in direct modes of participation. Participatory inequality is driven by two types of incentives: outcome and process incentives. However, process incentives – the supposed benefits citizens hope to derive from the activity of political participation itself – hardly apply to indirect modes of participation. How can chequebook members derive satisfaction from taking an active part in political activities when it is passivity they seek? Rather, citizens who take part in associational life – even those associations that are not recreational but have societal aims – often do so exactly because it is less politicized (Eliasoph 1998).

Moreover, from an idealistic perspective, associational life should be a relatively egalitarian sphere of modern society, bringing together citizens from various backgrounds (cf. Skocpol 1999; Putnam 2000). Indeed, across the Western world citizens are more likely to be a member of an interest or activist association than to participate directly in any direct mode – with the exception of casting a vote during elections. Thus with indirect participation being more widespread, it is (statistically) less likely to be highly unequal across social groups. Accordingly:

H2 Ideological and policy positions have a stronger (positive) impact on direct personal modes of political participation than on indirect professionalized modes.

Outcome incentives should be crucial to an explanation of participatory inequality, especially in indirect political action. Outcome incentives concern those specific goals – such as decreasing income differences – that citizens seek through political (or civic) participation. If these outcome incentives explain why ideologically leftwing and extreme citizens participate more than ideologically rightwing and moderate citizens, they should be mirrored in the policy preferences. In statistical terms, if outcome incentives explain the ideology effect, this effect should decrease after the inclusion of policy preferences. A decrease implies that policy preferences (outcome incentives) mediate the relationship between ideology and participation. If not, the relationship cannot be explained by outcome incentives, but probably by process incentives.

Moreover, outcome incentives should provide a more powerful explanation of the relationship between ideology and indirect political participation because process incentives cannot quite explain why citizens would become passive members of professional organizations (see H2). The final set of hypotheses, then, reads as follows:

H3a The relationship of citizens' ideological position to political participation is mediated by their policy preferences.

H3b The intermediate effect of citizens' policy preferences is greater for indirect political participation as opposed to direct political participation.

Data and operationalizations

The test of these hypotheses calls for data on a random sample of individual citizens. It requires information on citizens' ideological positions as well as their policy positions on various policy dimensions. A consistent operationalization of these positions would be beneficial. Second, the data should cover information on various ways of direct and indirect political participation. These demands are well met by the Dutch Parliamentary Election Survey (DPES) 2006, which has one of the most extensive questionnaires on voters' own and perceived policy positions.

The DPES was collected in two waves – one before and one after the 2006 elections for the Dutch Lower House (Second Chamber). It was a random sample of the Dutch adult population and the response rate of the first wave was 71.6 percent (2623 respondents), and 60.2 percent in the second (2359 respondents).

This chapter's focus on the Dutch case follows primarily from the demands the hypotheses place on the data. This focus limits the opportunities to generalize to other political systems. Nevertheless, the Dutch case study is useful for the purpose of theory testing and a (less strict) generalization to long-standing, Western democracies. There is no a priori reason to assume that mechanisms in the Netherlands will be different from those in other countries. Rather, a previous, cross-national study on ideology and political participation showed that the Netherlands was not an outlier or an atypical case (van der Meer et al. 2009a). The figures and tables below confirm the findings of that study.

Dependent variables: direct and indirect political action

We distinguish between three types of direct political action and three types of indirect political action. Direct political action covers both conventional and unconventional activities: *voting* (casted a ballot at the parliamentary elections), *contacting* (contacted a politician or government official during the last five years), and *protesting* (taken part in a protest, march, or demonstration during the last five years). Indirect political action encompasses membership of three types of organizations, that are partly distinguished on the basis of their primary interest (Lelieveldt et al. 2007; Maloney and Roßteutscher 2007): *civic action* groups, *interest associations* (that primarily focus on the interest of their constituents, i.e. trade unions, consumers' organizations, and employers' organizations), and *activist associations* (that primarily advocate broader societal interests, i.e. environmental, Third World, humanitarian, and peace organizations).[2] All six measures are dichotomous, as the most important distinction is between those who participate and those who do not. Respondents with missing values on these variables are deleted listwise from the models.

Independent variables: ideological positions

For respondents' ideological positions we distinguish between two aspects. We apply the readily available *left–right self-placement*, an 11-point scale from zero (left) to ten (right). To measure *ideological extremism* we calculated the distance from the midpoint of the scale (assuming that people who position themselves in the middle are the most moderate). The resulting scale ranges from zero (moderate) to five (extreme).

Independent variables: policy positions

The DPES covers respondents' policy positions on eight political topics: euthanasia, income differences, asylum seekers, crime, nuclear plants, foreigners, European unification, and international military missions. These policy positions are measured as dimensions on a bipolar, seven-point scale.

To assess which positions on these dimensions are leftwing and which are rightwing, we follow both theoretical and empirical paths. Theoretically, supporting a reduction of income inequality is a clear-cut leftwing position. However, for the other policy dimensions such a priori theoretical distinctions are far less evident. Rather, they depend on the framing of each issue, which in turn is context dependent. For instance, support for euthanasia may be considered leftwing as it breaks with the traditional hierarchies in society (Lipset et al. 1954), or rightwing as it emphasizes individual (social) rights (Laver and Hunt 1992). Similarly, issues of immigration, integration, and international missions may be framed in terms of inter-ethnic and international solidarity and group rights (leftwing), or in terms of authority, power, and individual rights (rightwing). In short, the framing of specific policy dimensions in terms of left and right is context dependent.

Therefore, to assess which policy positions are predominantly leftwing and which are rightwing amongst the Dutch electorate, we studied the bivariate correlations of citizens' policy positions with their ideological position (see Table 11.1).

As the first column in Table 11.1 shows, in the Netherlands in 2006 being leftwing is positively and significantly associated with support for euthanasia, propagating smaller income differences, admitting more asylum seekers, considering that crime is fought too strictly, opposition to nuclear plant building programs, allowing non-natives to keep their own culture, and not participating in international military missions. Citizens' opinion on European unification is unrelated to their left–right position. However, despite the weak and non-significant correlation, we consider support for further European unification as being left-leaning.

Respondents' positions on these policy dimensions are calculated similarly for their ideological positions. The *left–right self-placement* on each policy dimension is based on the seven-point scale from one (left) to seven (right).

Table 11.1 Left–right position and policy preferences (correlations)

	Left vs right	*Extremism*	*Perceived distance*
Euthanasia *allowed* vs *forbidden*	**0.15 (0.00)**	0.01 (0.78)	**0.36 (0.00)**
Income differences *smaller* vs *bigger*	**0.31 (0.00)**	**0.10 (0.00)**	**0.24 (0.00)**
Asylum seekers *admit more* vs *send back more*	**0.30 (0.00)**	**0.16 (0.00)**	**0.23 (0.00)**
Crime *too strict* vs *more strict*	**0.20 (0.00)**	**0.08 (0.00)**	**0.22 (0.00)**
Nuclear plants *no more* vs *quickly build more*	**0.23 (0.00)**	**0.11 (0.00)**	**0.26 (0.00)**
Foreigners *keep own culture* vs *adjust to Dutch culture*	**0.31 (0.00)**	**0.13 (0.00)**	**0.27 (0.00)**
European unification *should go further* vs *has gone too far*	0.03 (0.14)	**0.13 (0.00)**	**0.28 (0.00)**
International military missions *never* vs *always when asked*	**0.16 (0.00)**	**0.09 (0.00)**	–

Notes
Unstandardized correlation coefficients, standard errors between brackets.
Bold figures are significant at p<0.05, 2-tailed.

Extremism on each policy dimension is calculated as the distance from the mathematic midpoint, ranging from zero (moderate) to three (extreme).

Control variables

A test of the third set of hypotheses – on the mechanisms that may explain the relationship between ideological position and political participation – needs to take possible spurious explanations into account. Therefore, in the multivariate models we control for several characteristics: gender, age (modeled as a non-linear effect), educational attainment levels (on a five-point ordinal scale), net household income, religious denomination (non-religious as the reference group), and ethnic background (distinguishing between native and non-native Dutch by their country of origin).[3] Theoretically it is highly unlikely that these very primary characteristics causally mediate the relationship between ideological position and political participation.

Results: bivariate analyses

Figures 11.1a–f show the degree and direction of participatory inequality (between left and right, and between extreme and moderate) for all eight policy dimensions in the DPES 2006. To ease interpretation of the figures, we dichotomized ideological and policy positions. The horizontal axis displays the factor by which citizens with a leftwing policy position participate more strongly than those with a rightwing policy position. The vertical axis shows the factor by which extremists participate more than moderates. Positive scores show that leftwing citizens and extremists are more likely to participate; negative scores that they are less likely to participate. Hypotheses H1a and H1b imply that most policy dimensions should be found in the first quadrant (top right section) of the figures.

In Figures 11.1a–f both the participatory inequality along policy positions and the participatory inequality along the overarching ideological position is displayed. Note that the scale of the figures' axes differs from figure to figure, although they look similar at first glance. The maximum bias in voting (0.06) is more than 60 times as small as the maximum bias in demonstrating and membership of civic action groups (3.6). The modified scales improve the visualization of the differences between various policy dimensions in each figure. Tests of significance (not displayed) confirm that both direct and indirect political participation differ along policy preferences.

Left vs right

Hypothesis H1a claims that leftwing citizens should be more likely to participate than rightwing citizens. The horizontal axes in Figures 11.1a–f indeed show marked differences between leftwing and rightwing citizens – although the extent of these differences differs along the various modes of political participation.

Figure 11.1 Participatory inequalities along policy lines (left vs right and extreme vs moderate).[a]

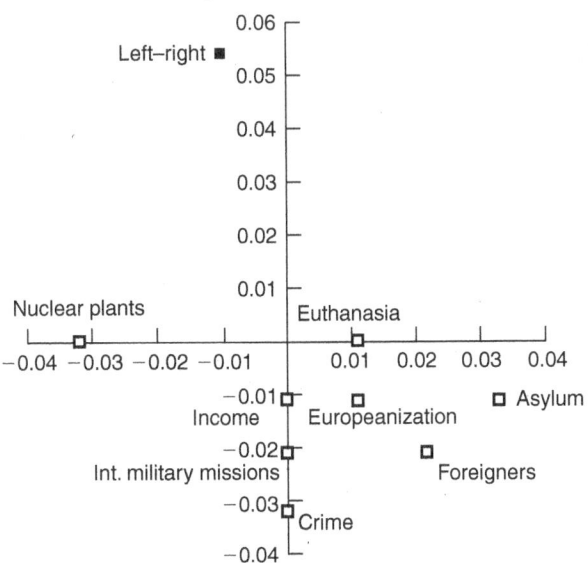

Figure 11.1a Voting.

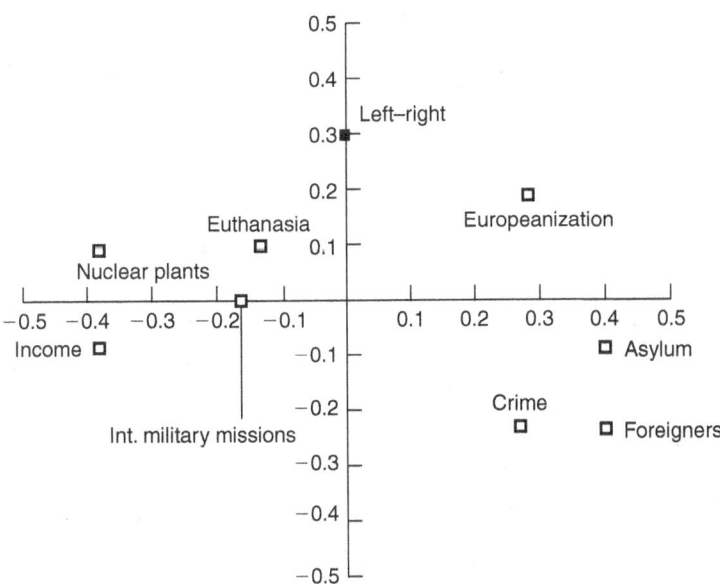

Figure 11.1b Contacting.

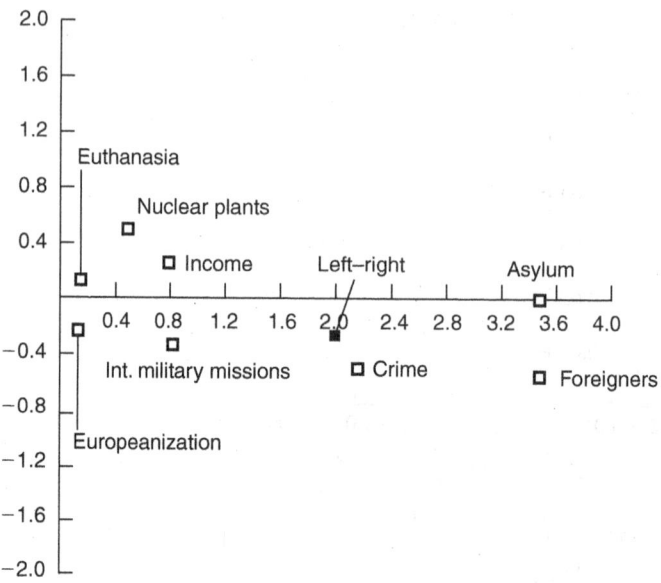

Figure 11.1c Demonstrate.

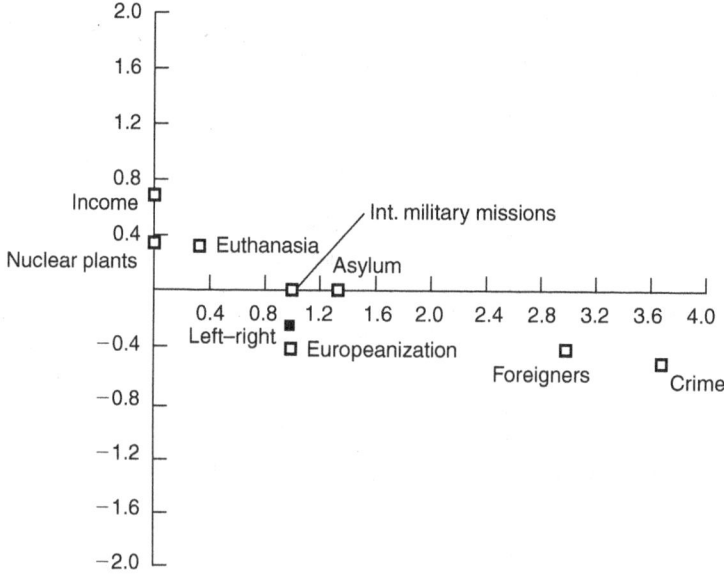

Figure 11.1d Civic action.

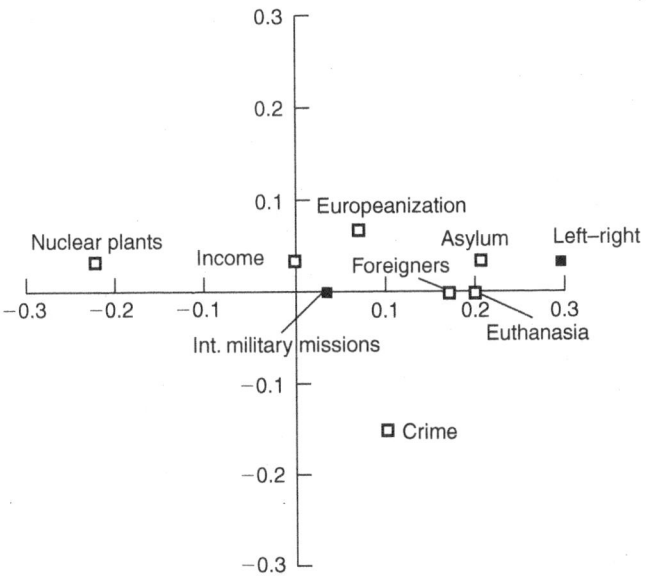

Figure 11.1e Membership interest association.

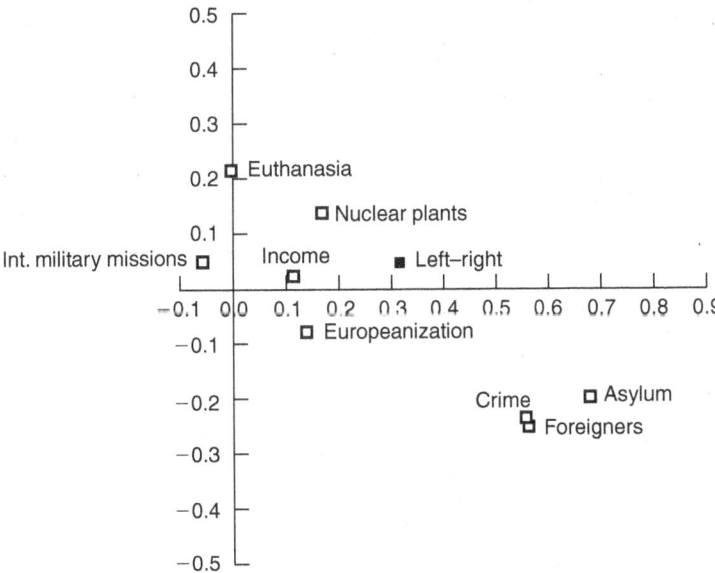

Figure 11.1f Membership activist association.

Notes
a Horizontal lines represent the relative frequencies of participation, comparing the participation rate of leftwing citizens (or policy preferences associated with leftwing preferences) to that of rightwing citizens. Vertical lines represent the relative frequencies of participation, comparing the participation rate of extremists to that of moderates.

First, we focus on the two most conventional, direct modes: voting and contacting an official. In line with hypothesis H1a, citizens with leftwing positions on asylum seekers are significantly more likely to have cast their vote at the previous election; citizens with leftwing positions on asylum seekers, foreigners, and European unification are significantly more likely to contact an official. However, there is no support for hypothesis H1a on the other policy dimensions: rather, those who have a leftwing position on nuclear plants, and (to a lesser extent) income differences are significantly less likely to vote or contact an official.

Second, demonstrating is done significantly more often by people with leftwing sentiments. This is most evident for citizens with leftwing positions on foreigners (3.5 times more likely than their rightwing counterparts), asylum seekers (3.5 times more likely), and crime (2.2 times more likely). In other words, in the last five years demonstrations in the Netherlands appear to have been dominated by citizens who want a less strict immigration, integration, and crime policy. There is no significant bias toward leftwing positions on the policy fields of euthanasia and European unification.

Third, we turn to the three modes of indirect political action. Civic action is undertaken significantly more often by leftwing citizens than rightwing citizens, along all policy dimensions except euthanasia, income differences, and nuclear plants. Membership of interest and activist associations, too, are dominated by citizens with leftwing preferences.[4] However, citizens with rightwing sentiments on nuclear plants are significantly more likely to be a member of interest associations. In summary, leftwing citizens are significantly more likely to participate than rightwing citizens along the various policy dimensions.[5] Generally, hypothesis H1a finds support, but not for all policy–activity combinations.

Extreme vs moderate

According to hypothesis H1b, extremists should be more likely to participate politically than moderates. The vertical axes of Figures 11.1a–f demonstrate the robustness of this hypothesis. The evidence is mixed at best. With regards to ideology, extremists are significantly more likely to engage in direct political action than moderates. However, the differences are not significant for indirect modes of political action.

Moreover, extremism on most of the policy dimensions does not stimulate participation either. Most differences are non-significant, and most of the significant differences are contrary to expectations. Citizens with extreme views on crime, foreigners, and European unification are not more, but less, likely to participate politically. The only consistent exception, where the empirical findings are in line with hypothesis H1b, is extremism on the issue of nuclear plants. Citizens with extreme preferences on nuclear plants are significantly more likely to demonstrate or to join an interest or an activist association. Nevertheless, hypothesis H1b should be rejected for the other policy fields.

Why, then, are extremists on crime, foreigners, and European unification *less* likely to participate politically? This finding is difficult to interpret when we understand the left–right scale solely as the overarching ideological dimension that encompasses all separate policy positions. Rather, these differences may be related to political sophistication: politically sophisticated citizens may be more likely to position themselves moderately on the policy dimensions, as well as more likely to participate politically. This underpins the need for multivariate analyses in the next section.

Direct vs indirect political action

According to hypothesis H2, participatory inequality should be larger for direct political action than for indirect political action. Figures 11.1a–f do not support that claim, however. The bias in direct political action toward leftwing citizens is not compensated by citizens' indirect political action (i.e. membership of civic action groups, interest associations, or activist associations). If anything, leftwing citizens are more consistently overrepresented in these indirect modes of political action. Similarly, there is no evidence that the inequality in participation rates between extremists and moderates on various policy fields is stronger for direct than indirect modes of political action. The only tentative support for hypothesis H2 involves the bias toward *ideological* extremists: ideological extremism has a significant positive effect on direct political participation, but no significant effect on indirect political participation.

Contrary to expectations, leftwing and extremist citizens are neither *more* nor *more consistently* overrepresented in direct political activities than in indirect political activities. Professional organizations are slightly (interest and activist associations) or strongly (civic action groups) dominated by citizens with leftwing preferences. Policy makers should acknowledge that these voices are consequently likely to be expressed and articulated more strongly and more often.

Results: multivariate tests

The bivariate analyses above show that direct and indirect political participation are unequal along ideological and political conflict lines. To assess whether the effects of ideology are explained by citizens' policy positions (as hypotheses H3a and H3b suggest), a multivariate test is required. We pit the ideological variables against the policy preferences and alternative (demographic) explanations of political participation. As the dependent variables in this study are dichotomous, binary logistic regression analysis is the most appropriate test. The regression models report the logit of participating politically. These models are carefully built up to avoid suppressed effects and multicollinearity problems.

Table 11.2 recapitulates the base model, in which citizens' direction and extremism on the ideological left–right scale explain the variance in participation. It provides estimates of the direct associations between ideological position and political participation, which we aim to explain in Table 11.3. Table 11.3 is an extension of Table 11.2 that also includes the direction and extremism

Table 11.2 Explaining six forms of participation by ideology, extremism, and perceived distance (log odds)

	Voting	Contacting	Demonstrating	Civic action	Interest organization	Activist organization
Ideology: left–right position	0.07 (0.05)	−0.02 (0.03)	**−0.24 (0.04)**	**−0.10 (0.05)**	**−0.08 (0.02)**	**−0.09 (0.02)**
Ideology: extremism	**0.30 (0.07)**	**0.12 (0.06)**	0.08 (0.07)	**0.17 (0.09)**	−0.02 (0.04)	−0.02 (0.04)
Net household income	**0.03 (0.02)**	0.02 (0.01)	0.01 (0.02)	0.02 (0.02)	**0.02 (0.01)**	**0.03 (0.01)**
Education level	**0.31 (0.08)**	**0.40 (0.08)**	**0.25 (0.09)**	**0.33 (0.12)**	**0.21 (0.05)**	**0.40 (0.04)**
Gender (ref.: male)	0.18 (0.16)	**−0.40 (0.14)**	0.13 (0.16)	−0.17 (0.22)	**−0.80 (0.10)**	**0.45 (0.09)**
Non-native Dutch	**−0.42 (0.16)**	**−0.36 (0.21)**	0.11 (0.18)	−0.53 (0.39)	−0.06 (0.14)	−0.19 (0.13)
Age	0.07 (0.02)	**0.14 (0.03)**	**0.08 (0.03)**	**0.14 (0.05)**	**0.15 (0.02)**	**0.06 (0.02)**
Age squared	0.00 (0.00)	−0.00 (0.00)	0.00 (0.00)	−0.00 (0.01)	−0.00 (0.00)	0.00 (0.00)
Religious denomination (ref.: none)						
• Roman-Catholic	−0.26 (0.20)	0.17 (0.17)	−0.12 (0.22)	0.37 (0.27)	0.18 (0.12)	−0.18 (0.12)
• Protestant Church of the Netherlands	0.45 (0.29)	−0.02 (0.21)	0.26 (0.24)	−0.24 (0.38)	**0.32 (0.14)**	0.14 (0.13)
• Other	−0.24 (0.34)	**0.95 (0.28)**	**0.64 (0.34)**	**0.83 (0.46)**	0.01 (0.24)	0.10 (0.22)
Dummy: missing values "Education level"	**−0.90 (0.33)**	−0.28 (0.30)	−0.14 (0.39)	−0.22 (0.48)	−0.30 (0.19)	**−0.54 (0.19)**
Dummy: missing values "Age"	−0.26 (0.66)	superfluous	superfluous	superfluous	superfluous	superfluous
Nagelkerke R^2	**0.15**	**0.10**	**0.10**	**0.07**	**0.13**	**0.14**

Notes
Binary logistic regression analysis.
Unstandardized coefficients, standard errors between brackets.
Bold figures are significant at $p<0.05$, 1-tailed.
N=2083.

Table 11.3 Explaining the ideology effects on six forms of participation by policy positions (log odds)

	Voting	Contacting	Demonstrating	Civic action	Interest organization	Activist organization
Left–right						
• Ideology	**0.10 (0.05)**	−0.04 (0.04)	**−0.11 (0.05)**	0.03 (0.06)	**−0.06 (0.03)**	−0.03 (0.02)
• Euthanasia	0.02 (0.06)	0.05 (0.05)	−0.05 (0.07)	−0.02 (0.09)	−0.04 (0.04)	0.05 (0.03)
• Income differences	−0.07 (0.06)	0.05 (0.06)	−0.14 (0.09)	−0.01 (0.10)	−0.06 (0.04)	0.01 (0.04)
• Asylum seekers	−0.05 (0.07)	0.03 (0.06)	**−0.21 (0.06)**	0.02 (0.08)	−0.02 (0.04)	**−0.08 (0.04)**
• Crime	0.13 (0.10)	0.07 (0.10)	0.02 (0.10)	**−0.22 (0.10)**	0.05 (0.07)	−0.06 (0.07)
• Nuclear plants	0.09 (0.06)	**0.09 (0.04)**	−0.03 (0.06)	−0.07 (0.07)	0.04 (0.03)	**−0.10 (0.03)**
• Foreigners	0.02 (0.07)	−0.04 (0.06)	**−0.17 (0.06)**	**−0.21 (0.09)**	0.02 (0.04)	**−0.10 (0.04)**
• European unification	−0.02 (0.05)	−0.05 (0.04)	0.08 (0.06)	−0.07 (0.06)	−0.01 (0.03)	−0.02 (0.03)
• International military missions	−0.02 (0.05)	−0.01 (0.05)	−0.03 (0.06)	−0.06 (0.07)	−0.00 (0.03)	**0.06 (0.03)**
Extremism						
• Ideology	**0.30 (0.07)**	**0.13 (0.06)**	0.09 (0.07)	0.15 (0.09)	−0.03 (0.04)	−0.01 (0.04)
• Euthanasia	−0.03 (0.11)	0.09 (0.09)	0.07 (0.11)	−0.04 (0.15)	0.00 (0.06)	**0.20 (0.06)**
• Income differences	0.03 (0.09)	0.06 (0.08)	−0.14 (0.12)	0.14 (0.15)	0.02 (0.06)	0.01 (0.06)
• Asylum seekers	0.07 (0.10)	0.01 (0.08)	0.10 (0.09)	0.11 (0.12)	0.07 (0.05)	−0.06 (0.05)
• Crime	**−0.38 (0.14)**	−0.15 (0.12)	−0.16 (0.12)	0.04 (0.14)	−0.11 (0.09)	0.01 (0.08)
• Nuclear plants	0.07 (0.09)	0.06 (0.07)	**0.16 (0.09)**	0.08 (0.12)	0.05 (0.05)	0.07 (0.05)
• Foreigners	−0.10 (0.10)	−0.12 (0.08)	**−0.17 (0.09)**	**−0.25 (0.13)**	0.03 (0.06)	−0.03 (0.06)
• European unification	−0.13 (0.09)	0.10 (0.07)	0.04 (0.09)	**0.21 (0.12)**	0.04 (0.05)	0.02 (0.05)
• International military missions	−0.09 (0.09)	0.02 (0.08)	−0.02 (0.09)	0.13 (0.12)	−0.04 (0.05)	0.01 (0.05)
Nagelkerke R^2	**0.17**	**0.11**	**0.16**	**0.12**	**0.13**	**0.18**
N	2510	2349	2349	2349	2349	2349

Notes
Binary logistic regression analysis.
Unstandardized coefficients, standard errors between brackets.
Bold figures are significant at p<0.05, 1-tailed.
These models are controlled for net household income, education level, gender, ethnicity, age, religious denomination.

measures of the eight policy dimensions. It allows us to see whether the original association between ideological position and political participation diminish after their inclusion.[6]

Sources of participatory inequality: ideological position

Table 11.2 displays the effects of ideological left–right position and ideological extremism on the six modes of political participation. It confirms most of the conclusions drawn from Figures 11.1a–f. In the Netherlands ideologically leftwing citizens are significantly more likely to take part in demonstrations (b=–0.24), and to be a member of a civic group (b=–0.10), an interest association (b=–0.08), and/or an activist association (b=–0.09). Ideological extremists are more likely than moderates to cast a vote (b=0.30), to contact officials (b=0.12), or to join a civic group (b=0.17).

Outcome vs process incentives

We tested hypotheses H3a and H3b (according to which the original effects of ideology are explained by policy positions) by comparing the b-values of ideological left–right position and ideological extremism of Table 11.2 to those in the expanded models of Table 11.3. This comparison shows that the effect of ideological left–right position is partly explained by respondents' policy positions. The original effect on civic action and activist association membership drops to non-significance, while the original effects on demonstrating and interest association membership become smaller (with 54 and 25 percent, respectively), although they remain significant. By contrast, the effect of ideological extremism is not explained by the inclusion of respondents' policy positions: only the b-value of extremism on civic action decreases (marginally, with 12 percent), while the other significant effects remain constant.

Overall, hypothesis H3a finds mixed support: the effects of ideological left–right position on political participation are to a large extent explained by policy positions, but the effects of ideological extremism are not.[7] Hypothesis H3b finds more consistent support. Policy positions (i.e. outcome incentives) are a better explanation of indirect than of direct political action. The effects of ideological left–right position on civic action and activist association membership[8] disappear largely when policy positions are included in the explanations.

Summary and discussion

This chapter started out from the assertion that participatory inequality is one of the major concerns in representative democracy (Lijphart 1998). When groups of citizens – especially citizens with differing ideological views or policy preferences – do not participate equally, some views are heard more strongly than others. In the end, such participatory inequalities might even lead to a bias in the governmental policy.

Empirical studies on participatory inequality focus primarily on conventional direct personal modes of political participation such as voting, contacting officials, campaigning, or taking part in a demonstration. These activities involve direct citizen engagement. However, not all citizens have the same resources or willingness to participate politically. Some citizens may decide to support professional organizations with political aims, in which professional activists engage in political activities on their behalf (Jordan and Maloney 2007). As such, these professional organizations may function as surrogates for citizens that do not want to engage in political activities directly. But is this the case? Does indirect participation through professional organizations counterbalance the dominance of leftwing and extreme citizens in direct political participation?

This chapter showed that there is little evidence that membership of civic action groups, interest organizations, or activist organizations counterbalances the overrepresentation of leftwing and ideologically extreme citizens in direct modes of political participation. Both direct and indirect participation are unequal across ideological and policy dimensions. Citizens with leftwing preferences are more likely to participate politically than citizens with rightwing preferences. There are also significant differences between extremists and moderates, but these are neither consistent nor in line with theoretical expectations. More importantly, the overrepresentation of leftwing citizens is even more consistent for indirect than direct political participation. In other words, the professional organizations do not counterbalance the ideological bias that favours leftwing and extremist citizens.

How then can we explain why leftwing citizens are more likely to participate politically than rightwing citizens? Theoretically, this chapter offered two mechanisms: *outcome* incentives and *process* incentives. Process incentives should matter less for indirect participation (as citizens do not really engage in political activities themselves, except for supporting their organization). Empirically, this chapter shows that outcome incentives do indeed explain to a large extent why leftwing citizens are more active, especially why they are more active in civic action groups and activist organizations.

Membership has more to do with outcome than with process incentives.

A new puzzle came up, however. The stimulating effect of an ideologically leftwing and ideologically extreme position is only partly explained by related policy positions. In other words, ideologically leftwing citizens are more likely to participate *not only* because they strive for leftwing policies. Outcome incentives (specific policy goals) only tell part of the story. Apparently, process incentives (the joy of engaging in political activities) matter as well as outcome incentives. Leftwing citizens are more likely to participate because the process of participation itself functions as an important incentive (Inglehart 1997). Yet, the causal direction of the relationship may be different from that expected. Political participation could very well be a characteristic that citizens identify with being leftwing – a characteristic next to other, more policy related characteristics. If that is the case, participation leads citizens to consider themselves as being leftwing, rather than being leftwing stimulating participation.

The overrepresentation of self-reported ideologically leftwing citizens might then have as much to do with subjective identities as actual policy positions: leftwing citizens consider political participation to be a part of their leftwing identity.

Notes

1 Participatory inequality is the extent to which social groups differ in their likelihood to participate politically. In this chapter I refer to participatory inequality as the extent to which groups with different ideological and policy positions differ in their likelihood to participate politically.
2 The theoretical distinction between these types of organizations by their primary aim has "significant, substantial, and theoretically relevant outcomes" (van der Meer et al. 2009b: 238): these different types of organizations are characterized by different repertoires of citizen involvement, by a different extent of involvement, and by a different social composition of members.
3 In principle, respondents with missing values are deleted listwise from the regression models. Therefore, the actual sample size differs per model. However, because two control variables (education and age) have a relatively large number of missing values, their missing values are substituted by the means and the additional inclusion of dummies (to compensate potential changes in the standard errors).
4 The overrepresentation of leftwing citizens in interest associations is significant with regards to ideology, euthanasia, asylum seekers, and foreigners. The overrepresentation of leftwing citizens in activist associations is significant with regards to ideology, asylum seekers, crime, nuclear plants, foreigners, and European unification.
5 Notable exceptions are shown along the policy fields of income redistribution (those who favor income redistribution are less likely to contact officials) and of nuclear plants (where the position associated with leftwing ideology – no more nuclear plants – are less likely to vote, to contact officials, or to be a member of an interest association).
6 Table 11.1 shows that the strength of the correlations of the policy positions with the ideological positions is not so strong as to fear multicollinearity problems. Nevertheless, I build up the models carefully to avoid such problems (see the concluding section of the chapter).
7 Table 11.3 also shows to what extent various policy positions are consistent determinants of political participation, taking each other and demographic characteristics into account. The models show that voting and contacting are hardly explained by citizens' policy preferences, while demographic characteristics matter more. By contrast, demonstrating and membership of activist associations are rather consistently related to policy preferences. This implies that we should distinguish theoretically between these forms of participation (conventional political action on the one hand, demonstrating and activism on the other hand) rather than between direct and indirect political participation. The former appear to be less consistently driven by policy concerns than the latter.
8 Activist associations had already been clearly linked to specific policy preferences in the survey: the questionnaire asked for membership of various associations that advocate leftwing positions, like human and animal rights, the environment, and peace. This might explain why specific leftwing policy positions play a large part in leftwing citizens' choice to get involved in activist associations.

12 The stability of individualized collective action
Results of a panel study among Belgian late adolescents

Ellen Quintelier and Marc Hooghe

Is individualized action different?

There seems to be a general consensus within political science that traditionally organized forms of political participation are losing ground in Western societies. In numerous countries, a structural decline of the membership base of political parties has been documented (Wattenberg and Dalton 2002). Traditional organizations like trade unions or church-related groups are equally trapped in a downward spiral. There is less consensus, however, on the question whether other forms of participation are replacing these traditional forms, and, if so, what are the consequences of this transformation. Jordan and Maloney (2007) have stated that professionalized forms of participation no longer rely on voluntary engagement, but increasingly can be seen as a result of the efforts of political entrepreneurs. Skocpol (2003) even argues that the professionalization of political participation limits the democratic potential of associations and interest groups. Interest groups largely rely on material resources, and they are no longer interested in bringing about mass participation. The end result might be that those who are well off in society further increase their ability to get their voice heard in political decision-making processes, while the underprivileged groups in society even have less voice than they used to have in the past.

Indeed, there is some ground for this concern. Empirical research has demonstrated quite convincingly that 'modern', non-institutionalized forms of participation are associated with stronger patterns of inequality, especially with regard to education level, than traditional, institutionalized forms of participation (Marien *et al.* 2010). Other researchers have expressed concern about the socializing impact of individualized forms of collective action. If we assume that socialization effects are mainly dependent on the interaction with like-minded others, one can expect that individualized action, or passive membership patterns will have a more limited impact on political attitudes and values (Putnam 2000). In this view, individualized political action is seen a superficial form of behaviour, that might be related to political preferences, but is inherently less 'political' than traditional forms of doing politics.

In this chapter, we do not wish to enter this normative debate, as we will not discuss the political or individual consequences of individualized collective action. Neither do we have any evidence about the crucial question of whether individualized political action is indeed able to bring about social or political change. Rather, our goal is to assess some empirical claims about individualized political participation. First of all, it remains to be investigated whether individualized participation indeed can be distinguished from traditional, organization based forms of participation. If individualized action really should be seen as a 'new' form of participation it remains to be investigated whether this attracts a new group of the population, or whether the same group that already used to participate, simply adds a new element to its participation repertoire.

Second, we want to assess whether those who are participating in individualized collective action are truly on the brink of social change. The expectation is that those participating in individualized action will have distinct socio-economic characteristics and background variables (Dalton 2008b). As is typical in the case of modernization processes, this kind of innovation too would probably be present first of all in specific groups of the population, before spreading out to the population as a whole.

Third, our aim is to address the criticism that individualized collective action is just an instantaneous and ephemeral phenomenon, not leading to any durable social ties. If this would be the case, we should be able to observe that individualized action is not stable over time, but can be seen as a direct and short response to specific social circumstances or mobilization efforts, without any enduring consequences.

In this study we focus on late adolescents (age 16 to 18) in Belgium. Adolescents are a good age group to study, since we can assume that they will belong to the first groups experimenting with innovative forms of social and political participation (Dalton 2008a; Bennett 2008). If this form of social change is present in Western European societies, we assume this will be most easily and most rapidly detected among adolescents and young age groups. We also know from previous research that their participation levels are already quite elevated, so there is sufficient variation to be studied (Quintelier 2008). A potential disadvantage of focusing on this age group, of course, is that they are not yet fully exposed to adult life experiences, like entering the labour market or having family responsibilities. The current analysis, therefore, does not allow us to make any assumptions about the way these participation patterns will be spread across an adult population.

Belgium also offers a good case study, since the participation levels in the country are close to the European average, as is documented by the results of the European Social Survey (Adam 2008). Furthermore, traditional associations like youth organizations are still strongly present in Belgium, so here too we have sufficient variation to study the differences between individualized and collective forms of participation.

Current changes in participatory behaviour

Individualized political action is being portrayed as a relatively new and increasingly popular form of participation. Citizens are expected to turn away from traditional, mass-membership based voluntary organizations in favour of more individual acts of participation (see van Deth and Maloney in this volume). Various reasons are invoked for this trend. First, one can observe a general feeling of dissatisfaction with traditional and hierarchical organizations. As individual self-expression is considered an increasingly important goal in contemporary societies, appreciation for this kind of mass based membership has declined (Dekker and Hooghe 2003; Hustinx 2005). To some extent, organizations have responded to this cultural change by adopting more horizontal organizational styles, providing more incentives for individual acts of participation and expression, but in practice these efforts have not led to a renewed appeal. Individualized acts of political participation allow citizens to express their opinions in a more self-directed manner, without having to pay attention to organizational instructions or strategies (Welzel et al. 2005). Second, the fragmentation of contemporary societies renders it increasingly difficult for voluntary associations to reach out to a large constituency. Traditional organizations in Western liberal democracies were built on fundamental cleavages within society, e.g. with regard to language, class position or religion. These kinds of all-encompassing cleavages have weakened, resulting in a stronger emphasis on small-scale, individualized identities (Giddens 1991). For organizations that are based on mass identities, like trade unions or women's associations, it becomes increasingly difficult to reach out to potential adherents. Third, it can be argued that life cycles and daily routines are becoming less standardized. Taking part in the activities of associations has become less self-evident for younger age cohorts that are confronted with flexible labour times and the difficult combination of labour and care responsibilities (Wajcman 2008). The traditional format of, for example, having meetings in the early evening or in the weekends, poses strong burdens on this age group. An act like political consumerism, on the other hand, can be performed at a moment of one's own choosing, and this kind of participation is therefore easier to reconcile with one's time planning than the organization based acts of participation. Some authors have argued that, mainly because of this flexible timing, individualized acts of participation are more likely to be practised by women than by men (Stolle et al. 2005).

For all these reasons, it can be expected that individualized acts of participation will be practised by a distinctive group of citizens. Based on the literature, we can expect that participants in individualized political action are younger, have higher education levels and they will be more strongly influenced by self-expressive and postmaterialist value patterns. Subsequently, it can also be expected that these are really two distinct forms of participation. The literature allows us to assume that there is a tension between mass based and individualized forms of participation. If the resistance against hierarchical organizations really is as strong as stated by some authors, we do assume that there is a distinctive group of citizens opting for individualized action. If one is motivated by self-expressive and postmaterialist value patterns, it makes little sense to go for the membership of a traditional organization, and instead one will opt for an individualized form of participation. If members of voluntary associations would just add some new acts to their already existing action repertoire, there would be no need for a strong theoretical distinction between both forms, as they apparently are just elements of one and the same action repertoire, practised by the same group of the population.

Furthermore, it is important to know whether individualized acts should be considered as full acts of participation. A number of authors are rather sceptical about the democratic potential of these individualized acts of participation (Putnam 2000). From a Tocquevillian perspective, it is argued that the interaction with fellow members is of crucial importance in explaining the socializing effects of voluntary participation. This interaction allows members to develop trust in others, to acquire the habit of collaborating with others, and to develop tolerance for opinions they do not agree with (Hooghe 2008). If there is no interaction at all, since the acts are being performed in a solitary manner, it is difficult to explain how socialization effects might occur. Individualized actions also run the risk of not being sustainable. The example of others, and the embeddedness in organizations is of crucial importance in explaining not just the mobilization into participation acts, but also the likelihood that the individual will remain committed to a social movement and its actions (Verhulst and Walgrave 2009). Again, it can be assumed that if there are no organizations ensuring repeated interaction and a reinforcement of motivation, this will lead to a weakened sustainability of participation. Indeed, with regard to some 'new' forms of participation, like the emotion-driven protest against acts of violence, it has been shown that this protest is not sustainable. While large groups might turn out for a demonstration, this kind of demonstration is usually quite spontaneous, without formal organizations that are responsible for organization and mobilization. As a result, these mobilizations can disappear just as quickly as they came into being, and in some instances these movements completely disappeared just a few weeks after their initial mobilization success (Hooghe and Deneckere 2003; Schinkel 2008). The resulting hypothesis therefore is that individualized political action is a once-only phenomenon, which is not sustained or stable over time.

The data of the Belgian Political Panel Survey (BPPS) allow us to test these research questions simultaneously. The BPPS was conducted among adolescents and we can assume that this age group is among the first to pick up new participation habits. First, the survey included an extended battery of participation acts, thus allowing us to make a distinction between various forms of participation. This way, it can be assessed whether the theoretical distinction between collective and individualized forms of participation can also be supported in an empirical manner. Second, the survey included extensive batteries with regard to attitudes and socio-economic background characteristics. If individualized participation is really preferred by young, highly educated and self-expressive segments of society, this should show up in the analysis. Third, and maybe most importantly for the current analysis, is the fact that the BPPS is a panel survey, with the same respondents being traced over a two-year period (2006 and 2008). If individualized action is indeed a more superficial phenomenon, the expectation is that this form of participation will be less stable throughout the life cycle, as individual participants are not being motivated by the presence of others to pursue their level of activity.

A panel survey among adolescents

For the current analysis, we rely on the results of the BPPS, 2006–08. These data are based on a two wave panel study among 16 and 18 year olds. In 2006, a representative survey was conducted among 6,330 16 year olds in Belgium, and the response analysis demonstrated that the survey was representative for language, school type, education track, gender and region. Based on written surveys completed by respondents in 112 schools, the study focused on adolescents' social and political attitudes and it contained questions about their background characteristics, political activities and political attitudes. To obtain a national random sample, all schools included in the survey were selected through a stratified sample, based on the location and type of the school. In each school, a minimum of 50 students was selected, representative of the tracks being offered in that school. In 2008, the respondents were surveyed again for a second wave, this time at the age of 18. While most of the initial respondents could still be reached in school, for those who had left or changed schools, alternative strategies had to be developed. Of the initial 112 schools, 109 participated again in the survey in 2008. In these schools, the same classes were resurveyed. This allowed re-interviewing more than 2,000 students. The other students were contacted through a mail survey. In total, 4,235 pupils (or 67 per cent) from the initial panel were resurveyed, in line with what we can expect for this kind of panel study. It has to be remembered that some adolescents might have filled in the questionnaire in 2006 out of the mistaken idea that participation was compulsory, and these participants did not fill the survey in again in 2008. Response analyses indicate that the data are still quite representative according to gender and educational track. As such, this dataset is ideally suited to test our main hypotheses. It allows us access to a total sample of 4,235 full panel respondents that were interviewed both in 2006 (age 16) and in 2008 (age 18). On average, the time interval is exactly two years, since in 2006 the average age was 15.7 and in 2008 this was 17.7 years (Hooghe et al. 2009).

Although it could be argued that late adolescents are not the best possible target population to test our hypotheses, a number of arguments can be advanced. First, to our knowledge, there are very few panel studies among adults including all the variables that are necessary to conduct the kind of analysis we conduct. Second, it can be argued that political attitudes are quite stable across the life cycle. If 18 year olds are already active in various kinds of associations and activities, it is very likely that they will continue this habit later in the life cycle (Galston 2001). Research among late adolescents, therefore, allows us already some glimpse into the future of participation patterns in Western societies. Third, we know from other research that young people at this age are already quite active, in various forms of engagement, so there is indeed sufficient behavioural variation to be analysed. Although they do not have the right to vote, they are active in almost all other forms of civic and political participation (Roller *et al.* 2006; Quintelier 2009). Finally, the literature allows us to assume that especially young people will be active in these 'new' forms of political participation, as they are not yet fully into the habit of participating in more traditional forms of organizational activity (Zukin *et al.* 2006). If our aim is to find a distinct group of citizens with a preference for individualized forms of political action, most likely it should be found among late adolescents and/or young adults.

Political participation: individualized and collective forms of participation

In the BPPS survey, political participation was measured by asking respondents how often they had participated during the last 12 months in a particular activity: never, sometimes or often. In designing the battery with participation items, we started from a broad approach, including acts that are considered as part of the political action repertoire in at least part of the literature. While there is an intensive ongoing debate about the exact delineation of the concept of participation (van Deth 2003), in the questionnaire we considered it as important to include a broad array of acts, which would allow us to make meaningful distinctions within this battery.

As can be seen from the frequencies in Table 12.1, respondents were indeed heavily involved in various acts, both in 2006 (age 16) and in 2008 (age 18). There was not that much difference between the scores in 2006 and 2008. In both years, donating money and signing petitions were the most frequently mentioned acts. Contacting public officials or being a member of a political party were acts that were mentioned by relatively few respondents. From the literature we derived the hypothesis that individualized and collective acts of participation should be empirically distinguished. Individual participation acts include all forms of activities that can be performed individually, contrasting them with collective group based forms of participation. Wearing a badge, signing a petition, contacting public officials, sending a political message, displaying a political message, donating money, boycotting and buycotting products are considered to be individualized political action since all of these actions are mostly being performed on an individual basis. Collective political participation, on the other hand, will be conceptualized as being a party member, participating in a protest march and attending a show with cultural content. These acts were chosen because they cannot be performed in an individual manner.

Both concepts were tested using a confirmatory factor analysis. Although both concepts do not have a perfect fit, they remain reliable enough to be used in the analysis.[1] In this regard it has to be remembered that this form of confirmatory factor analysis is relatively powerful with regard to attitudes, but is less robust in confirming the structure of behavioural items. While attitudes can be measured without paying attention to the context of the individual, participation behaviours are always dependent on the opportunities offered by the context of the individual.

Table 12.1 Frequency of participation acts (percentages)

	2006			2008			Correlation
	Never	Sometimes	Often	Never	Sometimes	Often	
Individualized participation							
Wearing a badge	84.4	13.6	2.0	81.7	15.8	2.5	0.693***
Signing a petition	58.9	39.2	1.9	54.9	42.8	2.2	0.282***
Contacting public officials	96.5	3.0	0.5	84.5	14.7	0.9	0.298***
Sending a political message	88.0	10.6	1.4	94.4	3.1	0.5	0.164***
Donating money	54.7	42.1	3.1	55.8	41.4	2.8	0.139***
Boycotting products	80.3	15.4	4.3	77.0	18.3	4.7	0.316***
Displaying message	95.6	3.7	0.7	83.6	14.6	1.8	0.388***
Buycotting products	79.9	16.6	3.5	74.0	21.6	4.4	0.070***
							0.314***
Collective participation							
Being a party member*	98.8	n.a.	1.2	98.5	n.a.	1.5	0.732***
Participating in a protest march	89.6	9.6	0.8	90.7	8.6	0.7	0.135***
Attending a show with political content	86.5	12.7	0.8	94.6	4.3	1.1	0.257***
							0.076***

Notes
Entries are frequencies of participation in that particular activity.
* Dummy variable: 0=no; 1=yes. Correlation is Kendall's Tau-b correlation between participation 2006 and 2008 (sign: *** p<0.001; ** p<0.01; * p<0.05; ns p>0.05).

Critics of the importance being attached to individualized action would argue that this kind of action is less persistent over time. The correlation between the 2006 and 2008 scores, however, does not confirm this notion. The Kendall's Tau-b correlations between individualized participation acts in 2006 and 2008 are roughly the same as for collective forms of political action. The strongest correlations can even be documented for two clearly individualized forms of action: boycotting and buycotting. This high correlation, therefore, already makes clear that political consumerism is not just a passing habit, but clearly continued over time. Displaying messages with a political content or attending political shows have the lowest correlation coefficients, so we can assume that both of these activities are related to specific campaigns and are of a more ephemeral nature.

The real test of continuity, however, is not based on individual items, but on the correlation between both measurements of the latent concepts. Individualized political participation proved to be a stable behavioural pattern: the standardized effect of individual political participation in 2006 on individual political participation in 2008 with autocorrelated errors is 0.693, which is highly similar to the standardized effect of 0.732 for collective political participation.[2] Therefore, it has to be concluded that although individual political participation is often considered to be less stable, the likelihood to participate in these activities in the future is similar for both type of activities. Even without the social pressure from fellow members, individualized patterns of political action are just as successfully continued over time as collective participation acts. Individualized forms of political participation therefore cannot be considered as instantaneous and superficial forms of behaviour.

Who participates how?

If we want to determine the background variables that have an effect on the likelihood of participating in individualized political action, we are confronted with the problem that there is of course an overlap between individualized and collective participation acts. Most respondents participating in one form of action also tend to be active in another way. In line with van Deth (in this volume), we created four distinct categories. The most straightforward category is composed of respondents who do not participate in any kind of political action (24 per cent of all respondents). This group can be labelled as passive citizens. A second group participates primordially in individualized acts of participants, while a third group specializes in collective forms of political action. Finally, we have a smaller fourth group (10 per cent of all respondents) that scores equally strong on both forms of participation, and we will refer to this group as the 'mixed' activists. In Table 12.2, we present the different types of participants. It is clear that more people engage in the individual forms of participation than the collective ones, although this largely depends on the activities that are considered in the questionnaire. These four types of participants will be used in the multinomial regression.

Table 12.2 Types of activists (number of activities)

		Collective				Total N
		0	1	2	3	
Individual	0	971	66	0	0	1,037
	1	1,438	324	5	0	1,767
	2	(577)	267	17	0	861
	3	(163)	124	17	1	305
	4	(49)	(50)	11	0	110
	5	(10)	(19)	6	0	35
	6	(2)	(6)	(2)	1	11
	7	(0)	(0)	(1)	0	1
	8	(0)	(0)	(0)	0	0
		3,210	856	59	2	4,127

Notes
No participation acts: passive citizens (italics); upper right corner (shaded): collectivist participants; lower left corner (figures between brackets): individualized participants; **bold**: middle group: mixed participation repertoire.
Entries are number of cases.

Determinants of individualized and collective political participation

In our effort to explain the determinants of participation behaviours, we will make use of the panel structure of the data. In the literature it is assumed that specific attitudes will lead to a preference for individualized political acts. However, in a cross-sectional observation, it is difficult to make any strong causal claims. For example, if we observed that participants in a specific form of action score significantly higher on self-expressive values, the question still remains whether this value pattern leads to this kind of participation repertoire, or whether the reverse causal order is more likely. Standard techniques of analysis do not allow us to solve this question.

Since we have access to panel data, however, the problem of causal order is significantly moderated. For all independent variables, the 2006 observation will be taken, while participation behaviour is measured in 2008. Self-evidently, this still does not solve all the problems, since measurements are related and an unobserved variable might still be responsible for the causal relation. Using the panel structure in this manner, however, already renders it more unlikely that participation effects in 2008 could have had an effect on attitudinal measurements in the year 2006.

In the analysis, we control for socio-economic status (measured by a factor score of current level of education, educational goal and the number of books at home), gender, citizenship status and religious denomination. We expect that respondents with a higher socio-economic status will participate more often in individualized forms of participation. Religious respondents are expected to have a preference for more traditional, and hence more organization based forms of participation. Women will be more likely to participate in individualized than collective forms of participation (Verba *et al.* 1995).

We should also expect, however, that individualized participation is related to a specific value pattern. First, it is expected that individualized acts are the expression of a postmaterialist and postmodern preference. The familiar postmaterialism scale, therefore, should have a positive effect on a preference for individualized political action. Individual participation is also a way to act as a global citizen and to become involved in global problems or in various forms of transnational activism. Therefore it is expected that respondents with a supranational identity (i.e. giving more importance to a world or European citizenship than to the adherence to the nation state), will be more strongly involved in individualized actions. Since this form of transnational identity is linked to low levels of ethnic and cultural prejudice, we equally assume that tolerance will have a positive relation with individualized acts. In this survey, tolerance was measured by using a thermometer question to ascertain how closely respondents felt to immigrants, Muslims and black people. Almost self-evidently, we expect that respondents who belong to various voluntary associations will be involved more strongly in collective action. It should be noted that this relation is not necessarily tautological, as the collective action battery does not include information about membership in a voluntary association. It is perfectly possible that respondents would participate in collective political participation acts without being a member of any voluntary association. Given the fact that individualized action depends more strongly on individual decisions, and less on collective routines, it is expected that individualized action will require more civic resources and skills (Verba *et al.* 1995). Political knowledge, efficacy and political interest, therefore, should have a positive effect on individualized political action.

Results: what are the differences?

The analysis will be performed in two steps. First, a logistic regression to predict the four types of political participation and, second, a multinomial regression to ascertain whether there are significant differences between the various participation modes. The logistic regression allows us to determine who belongs to one of the four categories of participants that we distinguished in Table 12.2, based on the measurement of the independent variables in the year 2006 (Table 12.3).

The first column presents the analysis for the passive citizens. Of all four models this model has the highest explained variance, indicating that this is the most distinctive group. Passive respondents are more likely to be male and to have a lower socio-economic status, but we do not observe an effect of religiosity or citizenship status. This group is also very distinctive by significantly lower scores on almost all the attitudinal variables we measured: postmaterialism, tolerance, political knowledge and political interest. Clearly, passive respondents

Table 12.3 Logistic regression for four types of participants

	Passive	Individual	Collective	Mixed
Gender (1 = male)	1.551***	0.743***	1.269ns	0.789ns
Belgian citizen	0.894ns	1.190ns	0.955ns	0.816ns
Socio-economic status	0.639***	1.284***	1.073ns	1.277**
Religious denomination				
Not religious (= ref.)				
Catholic	0.888ns	1.124ns	0.711ns	1.025ns
Other	0.783ns	1.246ns	0.856ns	0.911ns
Postmaterialism	0.704***	1.149*	1.082ns	1.126ns
Supranational identity	0.924ns	1.027ns	0.930ns	1.144*
Tolerance	0.775***	1.031ns	1.002ns	1.361***
N associations	0.771***	1.002ns	1.050ns	1.247***
Political knowledge	0.868***	1.017ns	1.056ns	1.137*
Political efficacy	0.970ns	0.971ns	1.011ns	1.109ns
Political interest	0.786***	1.053ns	1.021ns	1.213*
Constant	1.115ns	0.897ns	0.098***	0.037***
Nagelkerke R^2	17.5	3.5	0.9	10.0
Number of cases	3,205			

Notes
Entries are the result of a logistic regression, on belonging to one of these four categories. Entries are odds ratios and significances scores (sign: * $p<0.05$; ** $p<0.01$; *** $p<0.001$).

are a very distinctive category, and their attitudinal pattern does not seem to fit with the pattern that would generally be considered as an expression of a democratic civic culture.

A second group that is predicted is participants with a preference for individualized action. The explained variance of this model is rather low (3.5 per cent), therefore it is difficult to see this group as a distinctive set of participants. In line with our expectations, women and those with a higher socio-economic status engage more often in this kind of participation and there is a slight effect of postmaterialism. For all other indicators, however, the effect was non-significant. To make things worse for our analysis: the model for collective forms of participation is even less successful with 0.9 per cent explained variance and, almost self-evidently, no significant variables.

Finally, 'mixed' activists are somewhat more distinctive than individual and collective participants. Although mixed activists cannot be distinguished based on gender, citizenship and religious denomination, they have a higher socio-economic status than average. Furthermore, while it was expected that individual participants would adhere more strongly to a sense of supranational identity, this is more common among people who combine both forms of participation. Similarly, mixed activists are more tolerant, they are more often a member of a voluntary association and they have higher levels of political knowledge and interest.

To summarize the findings from Table 12.3: both individual and collective participants largely share the same background characteristics, and they are not particularly distinctive from the average respondent in this survey. The strongest difference seems to be between those who do not participate at all and those who used various participation modes. For individualized and collective action, there are no real apparent differences. In this regard, our survey material on Belgian adolescents is completely in line with the evidence from the European Social Survey (van Deth in this volume). One could argue therefore that there is no real reason to prefer collective action over individualized action, as both action repertoires are influenced by the same background variables and attitudinal pattern. If one wants to interpret these findings more pessimistically vis-à-vis contemporary developments in participatory behaviour, one could draw the conclusion that individualized participation is not some pioneering form of engagement that is only accessible to a very enlightened part of the population. There is no distinction between the variables leading to engagement in collective action and those leading to engagement in individualized action.

However, the logistic regression in Table 12.3 only tells part of the story. For every regression, those belonging to a specific category are compared simultaneously with the members of the three other categories. This analysis does not allow us to reach a firm conclusion about the difference between individualized and collective participants, or between individualized and mixed participants. To be able to make that comparison, we need a form of multinomial regression (reported in Table 12.4).

Table 12.4 Multinomial regression for different participation types

	Individual vs collective	Individual vs mixed	Collective vs mixed
Gender (1 = male)	1.404**	0.901ns	0.642**
Belgian citizen	0.885ns	0.781ns	0.882ns
Socio-economic status	0.950ns	1.145ns	1.205ns
Religious denomination			
Not religious (= ref.)			
Catholic	0.702ns	0.967ns	1.378ns
Other	0.791ns	0.844ns	1.066ns
Postmaterialism	1.009ns	1.064ns	1.054ns
Supranational identity	0.927ns	1.118ns	1.207*
Tolerance	0.987ns	1.308***	1.325***
N associations	1.044ns	1.218***	1.166**
Political knowledge	1.040ns	1.117*	1.074ns
Political efficacy	1.022ns	1.113ns	1.089ns
Political interest	0.995ns	1.169ns	1.174ns
Nagelkerke R^2	16.4		
Number of cases	3,205		

Notes
Entries are odds ratios and significances (sign: * $p<0.05$; ** $p<0.01$; *** $p<0.001$).

As could be expected from the results in Table 12.3, the differences between individualized and collective participants are quite small. The only significant difference is that men are more likely to participate in collective forms of participation. For all other determinants, there is no significant difference between individual and collective participants. As such, individualized participation does not seem to attract different groups of the population from collective forms of participation. Claims about individualized action being able to mobilize completely new segments of society are not supported by this analysis.

Subsequently, we compare individualized and collective participants with the mixed participants. Mixed participants are more tolerant, they have a higher level of political knowledge and on average they belong to more voluntary associations. It can also be observed that women tend to combine both forms of participation more often than men.

The main conclusion to be drawn from these two analyses, is that the most important difference we detected is one between those who do not participate at all, and those who participate. The analysis confirms quite clearly the importance of participation at the age of 18. Adolescents who do not participate are characterized by low levels of tolerance, a lack of political interest, a low level of political knowledge and a low socio-economic status. The fact that there is a time gap of two years between the measurement of the attitudes and the measurement of the participation behaviour might not solve all problems with regard to causality, but it does at least show quite convincingly that these patterns are stable over time. As such, the main research question still remains to determine why some people participate and others do not. *The precise form of participation clearly has less of an impact.* Basically we did not detect differences between individualized participants and collective participants. On the one hand this demonstrates that individualized participation is not something of a fringe phenomenon that is less relevant than the traditional, organization based forms of participation. One could rather argue the contrary because individualized acts are practised more often than collective acts. The analysis for the 'mixed' category, combining individualized and collective action, furthermore demonstrates that these forms of participation are not exclusive. Those who are most tolerant, and most active, tend to combine both forms of participation. As such, the most likely explanation for the pattern in our analysis is that individualized political action should not be regarded as a completely distinct phenomenon, but rather an addition to the political action repertoire of citizens. Citizens do not opt exclusively for one type of participation, but they combine, apparently in a flexible manner, various forms of participation, depending on circumstances and precise causes.

Conclusion

This analysis of recent Belgian survey data makes clear that individualized acts of political participation cannot be neglected if one wants to show the full picture of contemporary participation behaviour. Almost half of the participants in this survey reported that they had donated money or signed a petition during the previous 12 months. Not including individualized acts of participation, therefore, would lead to an incomplete view on participation behaviour. The question arises, of course, of whether one should consider these as full acts of political participation. One could argue that donating money is just an act of charity, while people often sign petitions just because they have been asked and just signing the appeal if often the easiest way to avoid being bothered about it. Buying fair trade products, too, often has been interpreted as just an individual consumer preference. Indeed, we should exercise caution. If we continue to expand the notion of political participation indefinitely, the concept may lose its meaning. Nevertheless, the current analysis shows that there are solid reasons to take individualized participation seriously and to consider it as part of the political action repertoire of contemporary citizens.

First, the sheer numbers of citizens engaging in these activities demonstrates that it is a widespread phenomenon. Second, and more importantly, the stability over time suggests that signing a petition, participating in political consumerism or donating money, is not just some form of whimsical behaviour. If people just ventured into political consumerism out of some sudden emotional urge, we would not observe the strong degree of stability over a two year period. This finding by itself is kind of puzzling, since we know from small-group research that the presence of like-minded others functions as a strong motivation to continue behavioural patterns (Verba 1961). Either this means that those participating in individualized acts do not need this kind of external motivation, or it could mean that there are informal networks reinforcing this behavioural preference. In some subcultural networks, political consumerism might be seen as self-evident and network members may experience social pressure to continue this form of participation in the future. A third argument could be that individualized acts of participation are associated with exactly the same kind of background characteristics as collective participation. Nobody would argue that taking part in a protest march or being a member of a political party should not be considered as full acts of political participation. The current analysis, however, demonstrates that exactly the same background characteristics are associated with, e.g. political consumerism. The only difference seems to be that while men prefer party activism, women – even at this age – have a preference for political consumerism. Again, this pattern does not provide any reason to exclude individualized acts from being considered as a normal act of political participation.

However, we should exercise some caution. It should be remembered that our study was based on a survey among adolescents. We do not know if our findings could be extrapolated to an adult population. Adults are more likely to be the target of institutionalized mobilization agents like trade unions and political parties. We know from other research that these traditional mobilization channels are gradually losing some of their impact in most Western societies. As such it could be argued or expected that if the current process of generational replacement continues in the same manner, the pattern found today among adolescents will gradually spread across the adult population.

Finally, one of the main findings of the Barnes and Kaase et al. (1979) volume on political action was that most people combine various acts of participation. Loyal party members also took part in demonstrations and other forms of unconventional political participation, without bothering too much about the theoretical distinction between conventional and unconventional participation. To some extent, we arrive at the same conclusion. A substantial proportion of the population simply mixes various participation acts. While the distinction between individualized and collective acts certainly is theoretically relevant and necessary to arrive at a full comprehension of participation behaviour and the normative implications for the quality of democracy – empirically both can be combined. While in some of the literature individualized participation is depicted as a *replacement* of collective action, the current analysis rather suggests it is *additional*. Individualized acts are being added on to existing participation repertoires. Theoretically this distinction is important. In some of the literature, the rise of individualized participation is seen as the result of resentment against organized collective action and hierarchical organizations. One can also observe, however, that while citizens remain a member of various associations, they also engage in individualized political action. The fact that participation patterns are cumulative, however, will only make it more difficult to disentangle any specific effects individualized actions might have, both on the societal and individual level.

Notes

1 For individualized political participation: Chi^2-value=426.191; 17 df; $p<0.001$; CFI=0.921; RMSEA=0.076; collective political participation: Chi^2-value=8.143; 1 df; $p<0.005$; CFI=0.961; RMSEA=0.041.
2 For individualized participation: $Chi^2=759.063$, df=70, $p<0.001$; RMSEA=0.049; CFI=0.919; N=4,019; for collective participation: $Chi^2=5.717$, df=4, $p<0.001$; RMSEA=0.010; CFI=0.997; N=4,088.

13 Youth participation from the top down

The perspectives of government and community sector decision makers in Australia

Ariadne Vromen[1]

Introduction

In recent years there has been an increase in the existence of formal youth participation programmes, as well as a growth in accompanying academic and practitioner critique. These programmes are ostensibly based on including the point of view of the subjects of policy making within the decision-making process, and are used to increase active citizenship and political engagement by young people. As yet there has been little examination of the usefulness of youth participation mechanisms for either the policy process or young people themselves. Scrutiny of the dominant ideas that underpin contemporary youth participation programmes shows that they exemplify the two themes of this book: the professionalization and formalization of youth participation, and the reliance on involvement of individual youth leaders and experts, rather than group representatives. This chapter analyses contemporary consultation type mechanisms used by Australian government and community sector organizations to include young people in decision making, and demonstrates how the individualized political actor is valorized.

Looking at actual practices of and discourses underneath youth participation programmes can help identify how the state has responded to new political constructions of youth. That is, a focus on the structural context within which the professionalization of youth participation occurs reveals whether the state actively enables or constrains citizen engagement. For example, has the state adapted to a changed context where issue based participation and individualized collective action have become the norm for young people? Or does it co-opt youth identities through its professionalized youth participation programmes? To resolve these quandaries the chapter is divided into three main sections. First, an overview of current scholarly debates on youth participation programmes. Second, a brief analysis of recent youth participation programmes used at the federal level in Australia as well as a survey of youth service providers on the consultation and participation mechanisms used to include young people in decision making. Third, analysis of focus groups with policy makers that investigates whether there is a disjuncture between the dominant discourse and practice of youth participation programmes.

Australia provides an appropriate case for analysis of youth participation because there is much contemporary debate about the disengagement of young people from the political process. To a large extent the debate has been hidden from the broader comparative context due to compulsory voting in Australia and high turnout rates of the general population. In other nations, especially the UK and USA, low turnout at elections by young people has created cause for concern and generated discussion on civic engagement and a democratic deficit (see for example, Furlong and Cartmel 2007: 121–37). Arguably Australia has seen a similar level of more generalized political disengagement when attitudes towards the formal political sphere are taken into account (Edwards 2007). Australia also has a government that is prepared to launch interventionist policy making to change young people's behaviours in general (see Bessant 2004; White and Wyn 2008). The questions being asked in Australia and the findings about the discourses that underpin current youth participation programmes will similarly apply to other national settings where governments have initiated new policies focused on increasing participation in society and decision making by marginalized subpopulations.

Youth participation

Conceptualizing young people's participation

Participation by young people tends to be conceptualized in three main ways, as shown in Table 13.1. First, as individualized actions that people do by themselves to try to influence political outcomes, which may or may not be part of a broader campaign, and may or may not be directed at the state. For example, Micheletti (2003: 25–34) has identified the rise of 'individualized collective action', which is engagement motivated both by self-interest and by the common good, is citizen led (rather than state institution or political process led) and occurs in a range of arenas. She highlights the growth of political consumerism

Table 13.1 Three levels of young people's participation in decision making

	Individual	*Collective*	*Consultation*
Actions	Electoral: e.g. voting, contacting the powerful (meetings, letters, emails, telephone), petitions (email and paper) Blogging Boycotts and buycotts Donating and volunteering	Group membership or ad hoc involvement: e.g. parties/unions, community groups, social movement organizations Protest Discussion boards and lists	Meetings: e.g. public or small group meetings Formal submissions Youth leadership positions, e.g. advisory groups, youth councillors

practices of boycotting and buycotting as part of this trend. Others have shown how these individualized actions increase young people's involvement in participation overall (Marien *et al.* 2010). These new individualized practices are contrasted both with traditional forms of collective action, such as pressure groups, political party or union membership, as well as with individual structurally based actions such as voting and contacting that are often found to be in decline among young people in most advanced democracies (see Dalton 2008a; Henn and Weinstein 2006; Print *et al.* 2004).

Second, participation can be understood as both traditional group or collectively based action, usually undertaken on a voluntary basis, which can influence government or general public opinion. However, there are also new forms of collective activity or community building that are often youth led and are precipitated by the Internet through interactive websites, discussion lists and social networking sites (see Bennett *et al.* 2009; Vromen 2008).

Third, there is consultation as participation when governments (and other organizations) choose to invite or include citizens within decision-making processes. Many of these are formalized top-down processes that rely on exclusive invitations and professionalized knowledge and expertise of participants. Some attribute the increasing use of consultation and participation strategies by governments as a response to the broader context of a democratic deficit, that is, a decline in citizen engagement in institutional politics (see Brooks 2009; Odegard 2007). Others see it as emblematic of a new wave of interactive and participatory policy making as it 'creates new channels for formerly excluded groups, but also stimulates individual citizens to participate in policy deliberation, thus bypassing the mediation via elected representatives or intermediary organizations' (Akkerman *et al.* 2004: 84).

Existing research has found that Australians, including young people, are generally 'joiners' (Passey and Lyons 2005: 78; Harris *et al.* 2007: 23). They either become members or are involved in community based activities for the common good or a shared interest, and are less likely to participate in traditional political organizations, such as political parties. However, most of the acts listed in the Table 13.1 are only legitimated, or recognized, as participation when they focus on citizen engagement with existing political institutions. Table 13.1 does not capture well informal or ad hoc participation activities that are arguably more related to contemporary young people's political experiences and preferences. Newer research emphasizes how young people's political participation reflects everyday practices and leads to a more individualized form of engagement. For example, new youth participation initiatives may attempt to harness everyday spaces where young people are acting and thinking politically, such as on the Internet, but also in their local or cultural communities, workplaces and social/peer groups (see Harris and Wyn 2009; Harris *et al.* 2010; Vinken and Diepstraten 2010). In particular, Bang (2005) celebrates the emergence of 'everyday makers' – a group that are young, favour ad hoc project specific involvement, mobilize around personally relevant issues rather than ideology, 'think globally act locally' and are not party oriented or state focused. For him, this provides the participants, new sites and practices for re-emergence of 'the politics of the ordinary'. The exemplars provided by Bang are of 'everyday makers' who focus on everyday local projects and issues to create political and social change. The 'everyday' participation idea resonates in other recent research such as 'structured lived experience' used to describe young English people's political participation and interaction with the state (Marsh *et al.* 2007); and by Harris *et al.* (2007, 24) who argue that it is incumbent on governments to actively 'create links between everyday and formal political spheres'.

The growth of government-led participation initiatives have also been addressed by Bang (2005). He argues that citizen politics now tends to occur inside the political system and within policy networks, rather than externally through civil society, and thus creates a new activist class of 'expert citizens'. Expert citizens are described by Bang as cooperative, networked, professionalized, well researched, expert communicators, 'part of and partnered with the state'; and without any overt ideological commitment. For Bang this is a new and exclusive elite republicanism, which could arguably be epitomized by many consultation approaches used by governments. He writes of: 'The core problem of exclusion at play here: how increasingly professional political deliberation, participation and cooperation uncouples citizenship from the politics of the ordinary, which is also at the heart of democracy' (2005: 173). Thus if Bang's argument about a tendency towards elitism is applied to new youth participation initiatives, concerns arise about the reliance on expert, 'professional young people' as youth representatives (see Bo'sher 2006; Odegard 2007: 292). As policy discourse continues to stress consultation mechanisms for political engagement there has been a corresponding emphasis on the 'management' of participation, rather than its autonomous growth through collective action and community building (see for example, Coleman 2007; Coleman and Blumler 2009). The potentially negative effect government-led consultation (as currently practised) can have on the recognition of young people's collective, community building has also been identified in Australia by White (2007). This shows that there is a strand of literature strongly critiquing the dilution of a notable state–society demarcation as spheres for political participation. That is, Coleman and White are both sceptical of state-fostered participation when it occurs at the expense of youth-led community building. This duality between state based interests in fostering the engagement of expert citizens in consultation and decision making, with a youth based preference for ad hoc, community oriented 'everyday making' is a tension for contemporary political participation and citizen engagement.

Existing research on implementation of youth participation programmes shows that there are two main outcomes of these approaches: socializing young people into social norms and roles; or facilitating young people to become active citizens. Within the socialization approach, youth participation is commonly used as an intervention strategy, including as a strategy for enhancing the benefits of other programmes and interventions, such as those aimed at employment, drug and alcohol rehabilitation, welfare recipients and so on. This means youth participation programmes are used as an intervention strategy promoting social development through youth transitions. For example, youth participation programmes are identified as a means of developing 'skills and confidence for future adult roles' (Macpherson 2008: 375). This approach has been particularly influential in the USA, and was also utilized in Australia at the federal government level through the Ausyouth strategy. In these programmes personal skills development and individual experience in decision-making processes are seen as fundamental to creating the necessary conditions for young people's transition to adulthood (see Bessant 2004: 390; Kirby et al. 2003: 9–14).

In active citizenship analyses there is a different emphasis on how youth participation programmes benefit young people through both individualized leadership experience, and the fostering of broader social outcomes. This means that the active citizenship approach does not focus solely on change in individual young people but argues that through participation and community development, or social capital type processes, young people are able to change policy making, organizations and society for the 'common good' (see Bessant 2003). Many active citizenship advocates critique most existing youth participation mechanisms, labelling them as tokenistic forms of participation for young people (Matthews 2001). Instead, there is emphasis on partnerships between younger and older people where power is often delegated to young people for decision making in areas relevant to their lives (see Wierenga 2003); and a focus on ensuring 'meaningful involvement' which includes: opinions being valued; timeliness; clarity of process; adequate training, feedback and resources; and allowing for young people to make mistakes (Nabben 2007: 31). Normative models of youth participation tend to have a common end point that focuses on partnership and power being shared between governments (or other powerful political actors) and young people (see for example, Shier 2001). Furthermore, most existing youth participation programmes are labelled as exclusive because they are utilized by only well-resourced young people who have been encouraged to become leaders within their communities. For example, Singer and Chandra-Shekeran (2006: 50) write that 'such processes exclude all but the most high achieving young people' and that more targeted, relevant and specialized youth participation programmes need to be created to include and engage refugee and migrant young people. These authors also critique the predominance of the socialization approach in existing youth participation policies with marginalized young people. That is, these groups tend to be treated as 'at risk' and in need of targeted intervention, and are less likely to be portrayed as having agency over decision making in their own lives. Others (Wierenga 2003: 14) show that while there has been a 'political push to include young people in *public decision-making*, due to economic and labour market changes increasing numbers of young people are actually being excluded from opportunities to make significant *decisions within their own lives*' (original emphasis). This echoes Bang's (2005) contention that 'everyday-maker' oriented policy and decision-making processes, based on young people's lived experience, could lead to better inclusion of young people (see also Matthews 2001; Edwards 2007).

Participation discourses

The previous section identified the current debates occurring in the literature on young people's political engagement and participation. This section attempts to place the debate about professionalization and individualization within youth participation programmes into a broader discursive context. Youth participation as a policy practice exists within a set of dominant ideas or discourses that favour particular conceptualizations of young people as well as certain approaches to their inclusion. Existing research on the use of consultation and participation strategies by government is a useful starting point for identifying discursive strategies used to legitimate these new political practices. Barnes *et al.* (2007) identified four main discourses in operation within the UK government-led consultation and participation agenda: 'empowered public' discourse, 'consuming public' discourse, 'stakeholder public' discourse and the 'responsible public' discourse. All four can be used to analyse Australian youth participation programmes, as they have been previously applied to a range of policy concerns including improvement in service and social outcomes, as well as a broad focus on democratic renewal (ibid.: 23).

The 'consuming public' discourse portrays individuals primarily through their experiences and expectations of the public services they use. The emergence of this discourse was seen as a conservative ideal whereby the state was no longer responsible for directly addressing social inequity through policy delivery but became the broker between consumer and service providers (ibid.: 13–15). This discursive construction of youth participation programmes would be applicable in debates about youth service standards or Citizen Charters that establish consumer expectations. The 'empowered public' discourse introduces a focus on diversity and social inclusion; and the introduction of government-led participation programmes is constructed as 'empower(ing) communities to enable them to act on their own behalves' (ibid.: 11). This discourse resonates with a youth socialization approach where youth participation enables individual young people through inclusion in professionalized youth participation programmes, rather than benefiting the broader policy process.

The 'stakeholder public' discourse's importance is twofold. First, it is based on the idea of the public (as individuals or groups) having a stake in good governance (ibid.: 15) and underlies the shift towards professionalization and the incorporation of knowledgeable, expert citizens within policy making. Second, it underpins calls for civic renewal of political institutions, communities and individuals to fit with consultation programmes that are implemented as a response to the perceived democratic deficit among young people. The 'responsible public' discourse reveals the alternative idealized pathway to a good society created by collective institutions and the state. It, instead, focuses on individual and group responsibility and is underpinned by communitarian ideals on the importance of family and civil society in fostering trust and reciprocity among social groups (ibid.: 19–20). When the four discourses are used to analyse youth participation programmes they conflict over the way they prioritize both the role of the state and the individual. That is, the 'empowered public' and 'stakeholder public' discourses have a central role for the collective shaping that allows the state to facilitate participation and leads to social change. These relationships are rarely a feature of the 'responsible' or 'consuming' public discourses that centre on individual roles and responsibilities. Barnes *et al.* (2007: 21) also point out that three of the four discourses have a universalizing approach while the 'empowered discourse' is deliberately aimed at marginalized social groups.

It is worthwhile evaluating the political participation of young people within the discursive context that it occurs. This does not mean that all participation results from opportunities that the political context provides. What it means is that prevailing, or dominant, discourse and political agendas shape how participation is recognized, legitimated and undertaken (see Bolzan 2003: 4–5). When governments choose to endorse youth participation programmes they regulate young people's behaviour into acceptable norms of political practice. They also simultaneously de-legitimate and undermine young people's participation that is seen as either challenging or external to state-led processes (such as, collective social movement activism). Barnes *et al.* (2007: 51) suggest that it is not appropriate to only look at official government discourses evident within the new participation agendas of government. But also the interaction with new citizen-led democratic spaces also need consideration in understanding how political discourses operate. Therefore our research looked towards both government and community organization based policy makers to see if they stressed different discourses and practices of youth participation.

Methodology and background to research

There are three research approaches adopted in the remainder of the chapter. First, a brief overview of youth participation policies in Australia. Second, a descriptive quantitative analysis from an original survey with service providers who implement youth participation programmes. Third, a qualitative analysis from focus groups conducted with senior policy makers in government and leading community organizations.

The existing literature on young people's participation often treats the young as homogeneous, having the same experiences and interactions with decision makers in their communities and government. This research project was predicated on the idea that there is no single understanding of being young and therefore generalizations about the universal social, economic and political experiences of young people are not useful. We instead sought to understand the relationship between political context and practice in youth participation programmes. Overall the methodology was broad based and multi-staged in an effort to investigate the views and practice of different stakeholders towards the participation of young people.

Four large focus groups were held with youth and diversity specific government and voluntary (or community) sector policy makers in four large state capital cities: Melbourne (Group 1), Adelaide (Group 2), Canberra (Group 3) and Perth (Group 4) in early 2007, with a total of 63 participants (60 per cent from government, and 40 per cent large community and advocacy organizations). Each discussion group ran for two hours and used a combination of large group discussion and smaller group exercises to elicit feedback on the key themes of the research. Focus groups were chosen as they provided a mechanism for engaging a cross-section of policy makers from a range of policy areas, and focus on qualitative debate, discussion and consensus rather than individuals' aggregated experiences. These discussions were unique in that analysis of the comprehensive notes taken at each meeting revealed the dominant discourse underpinning contemporary youth participation programmes.

A telephone survey was conducted with organizations that provide services to young people, and this complemented the qualitative approach of the focus groups by revealing the current extent to which youth participation mechanisms are being used. The survey included 101 service providers using a quota sample to ensure representation from both government and community based providers, and from all Australian states. There was no existing comprehensive list of Australian youth services from which to draw a random sample. The majority of organizations that participated were community based, service providing organizations (76 per cent), and were based in capital cities (72 per cent). This also reflects that 70 per cent of young people live in major cities, another 20 per cent live in inner regional areas and around 10 per cent live in outer regional or more remote areas (Australian Institute of Health and Welfare 2007: 6). The questionnaire examined how individual organizations approach and incorporate youth participation mechanisms in their service delivery. The questionnaire was a partial replication of a comparable survey undertaken in Ireland with 104 youth serving organizations (see National Youth Council of Ireland 2001). Analysis of this survey serves two purposes. First, it reveals the extent to which youth participation is used in service delivery in this select sample. Second, how everyday practice reveals the influence and implementation of dominant ideas of youth participation, or whether new ideas or counter discourses arise through practice.

Australian youth participation programmes

Youth participation programmes focus on how the capacities of young people can be enhanced through participatory experiences and ensure their transition toward 'full' and active citizenship (see Bessant 2004: 390). Professional skills development, experience in decision-making processes and a 'good work ethic', are fundamental features of these programmes for transforming young people into 'good citizens' (Kirby *et al.* 2003), and becoming 'the appropriate future leaders of the global citizenry' (Harris 2004: 77). Federal, state and local levels of government in Australia mainly use formalized youth advisory committees as youth participation mechanisms to input into youth policy. Young people have predominantly been treated in policy discourse as a marginalized group and participation programmes can be used to empower them. The shift to professionalization and formalization of these programmes is intrinsically tied in with the empowerment focus on leadership skills development. Therefore the 'empowering public' discourse has been the dominant idea underpinning the implementation of youth participation programmes. However, simultaneously and somewhat contradictorily, the 'responsible public' discourse also emerged through promotion of communitarian, non-state centred solutions to youth problems. That is, there was an increasing focus on mutual obligation in social policy delivery, and families and local communities were asked to address youth problems in society (McLelland 2002). Thus two ideas or discourses were at play. First, that young people needed individualized, empowering intervention to transition to responsible adulthood successfully. Second, that self-sufficiency was also important as successful transitions were no longer primarily in the realm of the welfare state, but relied instead on active responsibility taken by individuals, families and communities.[2]

At the federal level in Australia during the 11 year period of conservative government (1996–2007) there was a retreat from youth specific policy making, including first downgrading and then axing the Ministry for Youth, and an integration of youth concerns with other social policy 'problems'. There are two main features of youth participation programmes worth noting. First, the defunding of the Australian Youth Policy and Action Committee (AYPAC) and its replacement with the National Youth Roundtable. Second, the introduction of the government run National Youth Week.

The National Youth Roundtable was established in 1999 to replace AYPAC, which represented youth serving organizations in youth sector consultations with government (Sawer 2002). The Roundtable moved youth participation mechanisms away from advocacy and government interaction with youth serving organizations towards government-led consultation with 50 individual youth leaders biennially. Initially there was a separate Indigenous Youth roundtable structure but this was later combined with the broader Youth Roundtable. The young people discussed issues put on to the agenda mainly by the federal government and were expected to go back to their communities to consult or undertake small projects. The new youth participation progammme was critiqued as a shift to a top-down approach based on non-threatening communication and consultation mechanisms (Bessant 2004: 399) rather than a way of integrating young people's experiences into political decisions. There was little guarantee that the federal government would introduce policy issues and projects that were meaningful either to young people in general, or even to the young people selected for the Roundtable. There was also no broad policy commitment to implementing their views (see Bridgland Sorenson 2007). Some of the Roundtable participants actively campaigned for the reintroduction of a broader representative structure such as AYPAC (Bo'sher 2006: 340–5). The Roundtable advisory structure encapsulates the mix between a communitarian 'responsible public' discourse, with the individualized 'empowerment' discourse-individualization to take responsibility and become community leaders, rather than co-authors of government policy on young people.

Another key youth participation programme is the annual National Youth Week in April. National Youth Week was created by the conservative federal government in 2000 and remains an inter-governmental event, coordinated initially by the federal department for Family, Housing and Community Services and Indigenous Affairs (note that the oversight agency has now changed to the Department of Education, Employment and Workplace Relations). It consists of a broad range of youth specific events and was separate from formal participation initiatives such as the Roundtable. The national planning group is made up of a young person from each state (most were current members of a state based youth advisory council) who assist a staff member from each of the Commonwealth, state and territory governments and together they are involved in all aspects of planning, developing, implementing and promoting National Youth Week. Events include exhibitions, talent competitions, dance parties, gigs (e.g. band competitions), forums, arts and culture workshops, sporting activities (e.g. skating competitions) and other localized community events. These events are predominantly funded by state governments and run by local governments. It is difficult to determine what it means to emphasize that Youth Week events are 'run by and for young people' when in most states it is necessary that any funding is administered by an incorporated organization or a local council. Despite the direct involvement of young people 'on the ground' in Youth Week activities, it is primarily an example of a top-down model of youth participation that annually celebrates young people who are otherwise perceived to be marginalized from mainstream society thus representing the 'empowerment discourse' in youth participation. The remainder of the chapter will look at two ways these individualization discourses have been maintained and replicated through the professionalization and formalization of youth participation programmes. First, in the way youth participation policies are implemented through services aimed at young people. Second, through how senior policy makers believe and explain what youth participation policy achieves.

Participation and decision making for young people in service providing organizations

As explained above, formal and exclusive processes for youth participation, such as the use of non-representative roundtables or advisory councils, are the norm at the governmental level. However, our research found that service providers (as opposed to policy makers), and community based service providers especially, are much more flexible in their use of participation mechanisms, as shown in Table 13.2. The survey was used to gauge the extent to which service providers were already incorporating participation mechanisms to include young people in decision-making processes. The survey also differentiated among a range of participation mechanisms including both formal and informal approaches to participation. The most common methods used to engage young people in decision-making processes were informal chats, followed by formal participation processes of surveys and youth advisory groups.

While there are some similarities in the participation methods used by both government and community organizations to engage the input of young people

Table 13.2 Comparing participation mechanisms used by service providers to engage young people (in per cent)

Participation mechanism	All organizations (N = 98)	Government organizations (N = 22)	Community organizations (N = 75)
Informal chats	48	44	49
Youth advisory groups	46	61	41
Surveys	39	48	36
Youth forums/conferences	31	44	27
Individual interviews	26	22	28
Regular meetings	24	26	23
Young person sitting on board	16	13	17
Online technology	15	17	15
Public meetings	11	4	13

Notes
Other activities that less than 10 per cent of organizations used include: a suggestion box, activity based workshops, story writing, visual arts, drama, music or games.

(such as informal chats with service users), government organizations were far more likely to use formalized processes such as youth advisory groups, youth forums and surveys to engage the input of young people in decision making. This is probably attributable to two factors. First, that government organizations generally have more resources at their disposal for formalized and ongoing youth participation mechanisms. Second, as suggested earlier, youth advisory group structures have become the norm for the implementation of youth participation in Australia and elsewhere. It is also notable how few service providers (15 per cent) use online technologies such as feedback forms and discussion boards to create participation opportunities for young people.

Organizations were asked how often they involved young people in four categories of decision making:

1 *operational* – decision making with respect to the day-to-day provision of activities and services for young people by the organization;
2 *managerial* – decision making regarding overall management of the organization including allocation of resources, planning and evaluation;
3 *political* – decision making by the organization that relates to the public policy arena; and
4 *financial* – decision making relating to fundraising or other aspects of the organization's financial activities.

As can be seen in Table 13.3, organizations were most likely to involve young people in operational decision making (82 per cent said they did so either 'often' or 'sometimes'). There were similar responses with regards to involvement in managerial and political decisions (around half involving young people sometimes or often). Whereas organizations were least likely to involve young people

Table 13.3 Young people's involvements in types of decision-making processes (in per cent; n=91)

Frequency	Type of decision-making process			
	Operational	Managerial	Political	Financial
Never	7	20	16	24
Rarely	11	21	29	33
Sometimes	40	34	23	27
Often	42	22	26	12

in financial decision making (52 per cent said that they had either 'never' involved them or did so 'rarely'). These findings are interesting in that they suggest young people are seen to have the largest stake when it comes to the everyday service delivery provided by organizations, and least when it comes to financial activities. To some extent this is not surprising as young people are most likely to come into contact with the service dimension of the organization. However it also reveals that youth participation is rarely utilized through the whole of an organization from the top to bottom – i.e. from managerial and financial decisions to the operational everyday decisions.

Respondents were asked an open ended, multiple response question about the main purpose for engaging young people in decision making. Fifty-six per cent of surveyed organizations said that the main purpose for engaging young people's input in decision making and participation processes was to improve service delivery or policy/programme development. Other significant motivations were increasing organizational understanding of young people's perspectives and experiences (25 per cent) and ensuring that young people were able to exercise their right to be involved in decisions that affect them (23 per cent). When asked, 'who benefits from young people's involvement in decision making?' 75 per cent of surveyed organizations said that the young people involved in the decision-making processes benefited, 55 per cent said service users and 43 per cent said the organization benefited. These findings are interesting in that it has already been shown that a majority of the organizations surveyed state that the point of including young people is to improve the service, but a minority see that it is the organization that ultimately benefits from such inclusion. Instead it is the young people as either participants, or as clients/consumers of the services, that a majority perceives as benefiting from youth participation within organizations. This suggests the influence of the 'empowerment' (rather than 'stakeholder') discourse when it comes to implementing youth participation is dominant. The priority is to empower individual marginalized young people rather than foster overall good governance or benefit the policy process directly.

Youth participation discourses from policy makers within government and community

The focus groups revealed how policy makers within state government, federal government and large community based organizations see and understand youth participation. These qualitative, theme based results establish what the broad discourse is at this level of policy making. There was broad agreement on seeing youth participation as worthwhile, and that including young people in decision-making processes would improve the lives of young people in general. However, there was not a homogeneous view about whether top-down, formal and professionalized, or informal and more everyday mechanisms are more useful for the inclusion of young people. For example, the discussion group in Canberra was marked by widespread debate among the mainly federal government policy makers versus the territory government and community based counterparts about the superiority of using government-led top-down mechanisms for youth participation.

Two main themes emerged when group participants were questioned on the meaning of youth participation. The first reflected a top-down approach to participation that focuses on institutionalized processes led by formal decision-making bodies. For example, a government representative in Group Three stated that the only way participatory governance would become successful for young people was if it was structured and formally recognized. Another participant in Group Three argued that it needed to have the capacity to be part of a 'final decision-making' process. In Group One a government representative believed that formalization of participation processes could improve outcomes; their example was that in health organizations if people have a say it leads to positive health outcomes. A related viewpoint was offered by a community organization representative in Group One who maintained that for participation initiatives to be truly effective they need to reflect the governance structure of the auspicing organization, and that policy makers need to both ask and be convinced that it is appropriate to encourage participation.

The second theme revealed a more 'grassroots' understanding of participation and acknowledged that the needs of policy makers are not always aligned with the needs of participants and recognizes that minimal time and resources, and lack of youth ownership limit existing participation initiatives. Group participants from both government and community organizations articulated this theme and it is best identified as representative of an 'empowerment discourse' perspective. It focused on the importance of ownership by the young individuals who are involved in the participation process, included statements about the necessity to actively include and empower the subjects of decision making, and raised concerns about how to focus on specificity, diversity and representativeness. Thus while two themes emerged in our analysis, the theme most closely related to an 'empowerment' approach clearly dominated the discursive understandings of what youth participation is about and is for among Australian policy makers.

The government and community policy makers described young people generally as marginalized from decision making that was relevant to their lives. The identification of barriers to involving young people in decision making revealed the participants' perception of the complexities of the largely inflexible formal process of government-led youth participation in Australia. In examining the three main themes that emerged in discussion of barriers it is possible to identify the confluence of three discursive constructions of participation. Table 13.4 summarizes the themes that emerged in analysis and tentatively links them with discourses of participation from Barnes et al. (2007).

When Table 13.4 is coupled with the themes that emerged in the discussion of what constituted effective youth participation, the continuing dominance of the 'empowerment discourse' for youth participation policy makers emerges. However, other understandings remain, such as the youth focused problematic inherent to the 'responsible' citizenship discourse through a discussion of young people's limitation in fully engaging in youth participation initiatives, due to their lack of knowledge or time or commitment to the process. The third central theme on barriers to participation identified insufficient state–society linkage, and that communities and non-government organizations could be intermediaries between young people and the state. This is where the ideas underpinning a 'stakeholder discourse' focusing on democratic governance processes emerged.

To substantiate and analyse these themes further 'youth specific barriers' included issues of:

- young people's lack of knowledge of how participatory processes work;
- young people's cynicism about participation processes;
- life experience barriers, such as financial or time poverty.

For example, some participants discussed young people's inherent suspicion of government-led participation processes as a barrier, and a Group Two participant suggested that young people simply do not want to be involved in participation processes. Whereas a Group One participant stated that most young people did not want to get involved as they saw that the process was dominated by one group of young people: 'the university arts and law students', in other words, well-educated, middle class young people for whom ideals of citizenship and

Table 13.4 Identifying themes in youth participation discourses

Barriers to youth participation	Effective youth participation
Youth specific barriers (responsible)	Youth led (empowerment)
Ineffective networks and knowledge exchange between government, communities and young people (empowerment)	Creative and fun for young people (empowerment)
Organizational limitations and acting upon outcomes from participation processes (stakeholder)	Purposeful, providing feedback (empowerment/stakeholder)

responsibility resonate. Other group participants saw that cynicism was also borne of past involvements in consultation and participation exercises that did not demonstrate actual outcomes to the young people involved. A government representative in Group Four labelled this as 'consultation fatigue'.

Ineffective networks and knowledge exchange between government, communities and young people were identified as a barrier to sufficiently empowering marginalized young people. For example, there was an extensive discussion during Group Four on whether government, communities and young people were sufficiently connected through networks to be able to make participation work. One community organization representative pointed out that service providers were those who work most closely with young people but were not connected to high level policy makers within government. Another suggested that government agencies are not really aware of existing bodies of young people and therefore do not tap into them. A government representative in Group Four pointed out that networks and cooperation between government agencies that worked with young people were rare.

The third theme in the discussion of barriers involved an analysis of the existing limitations to implementing a democratic, 'stakeholder' focused approach to youth participation. Organizational limitations included:

- limited financial resources of community organizations and government agencies to establish effective participation processes;
- and the difficulties in changing institutions and sharing power, and thus the static, inflexible nature of institutions.

In the discussion of existing organizational limitations it was clear that most believed successful participation initiatives involved young people challenging decision makers and institutional structures to change. It was noted by Group One participants, however, that it was risky and difficult for organizational structures to change, or even share power, with young people. A representative from a Group Four community organization also pointed out that this barrier exists because government organizations do not fully recognize the power differential between them and young people, nor do they take it into account when planning and implementing consultative processes. When coupled with recognition of the difficulty government agencies have in acting upon outcomes from participation processes, it becomes apparent that the empowerment discourse underpinning youth participation policy makes it difficult to see beyond the focus on social equality for young people towards an ethic based on improving the policy process, as found in the 'stakeholder' discourse. Government representatives in Groups Two and Three suggested that there is a tendency for organizations to focus on the design and implementation of the participation process involving young people, rather than the follow through to meet the outcomes, objectives or intentions of participation. For example, one participant pointed out that participation is underutilized, as organizations simply do not know what to do with the outputs. Another argued that organizations might not want to consult with young people because it requires them to act on the outcomes of the consultation. Thus through questioning the use of outcomes from participation initiatives we start to see the emergence of a 'stakeholder' discourse that examines the potential effect on policy delivery and organizations, rather than solely on improvements made to the lives of young people.

Overall, it was mostly during the discussion of what effective youth participation practice ought to be that the groups largely articulated and maintained the 'empowerment' discourse, at the expense of a 'stakeholder', good governance discourse. Three main themes emerged as effective practice for involving marginalized young people in decision making. As noted in Table 13.4, these were that youth participation initiatives be:

- youth-led
- creative and fun
- purposeful and provide feedback.

Overall, group participants said that young people needed to have a sense of ownership of participation and decision-making processes both to sustain their own involvement and ensure an initiative's success. Many participants emphasized that a successful approach included 'going to where young people are' rather than always expecting them to come to agencies or organizations to participate. A Group Two community organization representative pointed out that decision makers going to young people's spaces could help ensure that a range of young people can be involved. Two other community organization representatives in Group Two focused on the importance of young people's existing networks and peer-to-peer mentoring, that could facilitate to 'break down the mistrust' of government agencies. Group Four participants stated that it was essential to make sure participation initiatives focused on 'young people's needs' and that organizations keep abreast of young people's issues 'as they change so quickly'. Thus the suggestion was for successful processes to lead to empowerment through being youth led: 'Let them consult with us and set the agenda.' It also became clear that many policy makers who had been involved in youth participation initiatives saw that a crucial dimension was that young people mainly found them to be worthwhile as a result of an everyday oriented fun or creative process. Group participants believed that best practice included using a range of informal participatory tools and creating opportunities for participants to be creative and have fun. A Group Two participant saw that by focusing on the fun aspect, such as through using a community arts process, it was possible to show marginalized young people 'what was in it for them'. Creative best practices identified included the use of multimedia such as video diaries, and the Internet to engage young people in participation.

The third best practice theme predominantly refers to how organizations incorporate participation initiatives. That is, for youth participation to be successful and effective, organizations need to have a long-term commitment to its success and a clear sense of purpose. For example, a community organization representative pointed out in Group One that participation is purposeful when it is linked with decisions that will have meaningful impacts on young people's everyday lives. This participant also stressed that often the best participation initiatives were 'very local'. Other group participants noted that best practice was also about ensuring that outcomes were clear to all those who were involved. For example, a Group Three participant pointed out that effective practices both ensure that participants believe their perspectives are listened to; and it is subsequently demonstrated how participants' ideas are incorporated into decision making. The idea of an 'effective feedback loop' to participants about the status and outcomes of their input was also emphasized by a government representative in Group Three.

It may seem incongruous in light of existing analyses of youth participation that most of the group participants – a majority of whom were from government agencies – saw best practice in an informal, everyday perspective to youth participation that would enable or empower young people. As was shown earlier in the chapter existing youth participation initiatives tend to be professionalized, formal and involve expert young people as youth representatives, not as community advocates or policy stakeholders. Part of the explanation for this outcome centres on the resilience of the empowerment discourse among decision makers, rather than a shift towards a good governance or 'stakeholder discourse', when youth participation in particular is under consideration. Young people are still primarily seen as disadvantaged and disenfranchised members of the broader community for whom participation can develop and enable their capacities. It is rare that participation initiatives are understood for what they are theoretically set up to be – consultation initiatives that use the perspectives of service and policy stakeholders with the intention of improving the policy process and delivering better outcomes. An explanation for why formalized youth participation processes, like youth advisory councils, remain dominant – and will do so despite the good will of elected federal and state ministers for youth – is less straightforward. It possibly lies in the power distance between young people and the rigid bureaucratic process from where youth participation initiatives are ultimately developed and implemented.

Youth participation futures

Despite the strong emphasis under the previous conservative federal government on individualized leadership development while portraying young people as at risk of marginalization, late 2008 saw the introduction of a new youth participation approach at the national level in Australia. What is now of interest to this chapter is whether a new policy approach represents a change in the dominant discourse underpinning the delivery of youth participation policy.

A minor policy platform of the successful Australian Labor Party in the 2007 federal election was the reintroduction of a federal Minister for Youth and disbanding of the National Youth Roundtable. Kate Ellis was appointed Minister and she has implemented the Australian Youth Forum (AYF). The AYF was launched in early October 2008, after a lengthy consultation process with young people and others involved in the youth sector. It has two dimensions. First, the embracing of ICT, ministerial outreach and large-scale public meetings coordinated by a ten-member youth advisory Steering Committee. The first Committee had six members who were representatives of youth-led non-government organizations (such as the National Union of Students, Oaktree Foundation and Vision Generation), while the remaining four members were individually selected by the Minister to represent diversity categories. These initial AYF members all had extensive youth leadership experience, and if not still in school all (except one indigenous woman) were at university. The Committee is closely run by the Youth Engagement Section, within the Office for Youth, within the federal Department for Education, Employment and Workplace Relations. Initial online forums were on body image, bullying and human rights, but there was very little involvement by young people on the online discussion boards. Of the approximately 1000 young people who attended the first simultaneous public forum (named youTHINK) most were university students or high achieving school students who found the youth participation initiative and discussion topics of 'violence and safety' and 'contributing to democracy' appealing. Future topics for the planned youTHINK events include climate change, affordability of education and war and peace. The Minister also explored ideas for outreach activities that can increase diversity and access 'disengaged' young people within AYF's initiatives; this includes going to remote indigenous communities. In late 2009 a 'National conversation' between the Minister and young people, was launched with the aim of establishing a National Strategy for Young People. It included an interactive website, online discussions hosted by a youth-serving non-government organization (the Inspire Foundation) and seven roundtables of young people at the national parliament. The 'conversation' has emphasized diversity categories of young people including regional and rural youth, and indigenous young people.

The second dimension of the AYF was the reintroduction of a funded national peak body, the Australian Youth Affairs Coalition (AYAC), for the youth sector generally to undertake both advocacy and research. The relationship between AYAC and AYF was only agreed upon officially in mid-2009 as there were some justifiable concerns on the part of AYAC about perception of independence and expectations of their advocacy role. Overall, it is the combination of these two factors and events within the AYF's approach (rather than relying on an individualized youth advisory structure alone) that may reveal a change in the dominant discourse underpinning Australian youth participation policy. I suspect that an overarching empowerment discourse, now unencumbered by notions of youth development and responsibility, is still primarily influential in the rollout of this approach. However, shared decision-making processes between young people, their representatives and powerful political actors at the federal level could yet lead to a shift away from a focus on the empowerment of marginalized young people to a more democratic and agency-centred 'stakeholder discourse'.

Conclusion

This chapter has shown that the Australian federal government's youth participation policy was influenced by a discourse on young people being enabled to become 'responsible' citizens, with a compatible discursive construction of marginalized young people needing 'empowerment' to be transformed into active citizens. These discourses are entrenched in the thinking of high level government and community decision makers, and shape youth participation policy practice in both community and government services. Focusing on the broader structural context within which youth participation occurs revealed that Australian governments actively shape and create the preferred forms of citizen engagement to be undertaken by individualized political actors.

The examination both of policy practices and of discourses of youth participation also identified how the state has responded to new political constructions of youth. These findings have general application to how we think about the youth participation agenda now being furthered in many advanced democracies. That is, under the guise of professionalization of involvement and ideas of youth empowerment there is a co-option of expert individual leaders into youth participation and consultation exercises that merely enable them to 'have their say'. In Australia there has been little systematic focus on issue based politics and community engagement that young people prefer to be involved in. Nor has there been an integration of new collective formations that young people use, such as through the Internet's social networking sites, to change policy delivery. Contemporary youth participation policies do not treat young people as active political agents with existing preferences derived from their lived experience. Future comparative work can identify whether this is, as I suspect, a common approach to the contemporary political construction and involvement of young people, or whether this is a distinctive approach of the Australian state. Until there is an intrinsic acceptance of the differences *among* young people, as well as an appreciation both of the commonalties and of the differences they have with older generations, young people's participation will not be imbued with the capacity to create political change and 'make a difference'.

Notes

1 I would like to acknowledge the funder of this research, the National Youth Affairs Research Scheme, a scheme jointly funded by Australian, state and territory governments; and Johanna Bell, Philippa Collin and the young people who worked on this project.
2 For a broader discussion than there is room for here on this type of individualization and neoliberalism for young people see Savelsberg and Martin-Giles (2008), Muncie (2006) and Harris (2004).

14 Conclusions

Professionalization and individualized political action

William A. Maloney and Jan W. van Deth

Democracy, organizations and participation

Democracy and participation are inseparable. By definition democracy implies the active and meaningful involvement of citizens. It is generally accepted that citizens' modes of participation should extend beyond the electoral arena and should be more frequent than the occasional vote. However, a vibrant and vital democracy does not require the active or passionate political engagement of each and every citizen all the time. What is needed is a willingness to participate and become actively involved every once in awhile. Accordingly, citizens' participatory repertoire should include activities such as voting, (active) membership of political organizations, taking part in campaigns, signing petitions etc. Based on the acknowledgement of this interdependence, ideas about democracy and participation are constantly attuned and in flux. Traditional and somewhat narrow definitions of representative democracy and electoral participation characterize much citizens' involvement beyond electoral politics as 'unconventional'. However, since at least the 1970s, these modes of participation have actually become part of the conventional repertoire of citizens' participation in many countries. In recent years some activities have expanded significantly, most notably, ethical shopping (boycotting and buycotting products) and cyber activism.

The starting point for this volume was based on a twofold observation of recent changes related to the junction of democracy and participation. First, the success and survival of organizations increasingly depends on their efficient and effective performance. Faced with the demands of quality, efficiency and accountability many organizations – in an increasingly competitive market – have chosen to replace the amateur volunteer with the technocratically trained professional. The ongoing process of professionalization has made many organizations more goal oriented and more 'successful'. However, it can lead to a diminution in the opportunities for citizens' involvement. In many cases citizens' involvement is reduced to the provision of financial support. In addition to this, new modes of participation such as boycotting products, ethical shopping or 'guerilla gardening' do not require any formal organization. These activities can be characterized as individualistic – any citizen can use these modes individually and in a disconnected manner. To be effective, it certainly helps that a large number of co-citizens behave similarly, but no organization, club, section or movement is required for an individual citizen to become politically active in these ways. In fact, in a world typified by ongoing individualization and privatization many new modes of participation appear to be exactly in line with changing citizens' political and social expectations and needs and priorities. Finally, the already blurred demarcation line between political and non-political modes of participation is becoming less visible.

The interesting aspect of these developments is that both processes can be seen as mutually reinforcing. The professionalization of organizational life relies strongly on the willingness of citizens to contract out participation to professionals and an increasing appetite for more individualized modes of participation. Both lead to increases in the professionalization of politics. Large numbers of citizens do not find political involvement attractive. Apparently, they are willing to embrace a marginal role in organized politics *because* professional politics functions more effectively without their direct involvement, and *because* their preferences have moved to more individualized modes of participation. In the introduction to this volume the professionalization and individualization processes were seen as being driven by four main factors: (i) shared interests (groups find financial supporters as opposed to members as an efficient way to mobilize), (ii) mobilization of bias (groups try to attract citizens engaged in individualized collective action), (iii) "the rise of the unelected" (groups tend to dominate decision-making processes relevant to their constituencies) and (iv) members as distraction (patronage means that many groups can operate effectively without the need to mobilize support among citizens). Which of these explanations and interpretations survives a confrontation with the empirical evidence?

The contributions herein have tried to bring together theoretical insights and empirical evidence on the contemporary trends of professionalization and the rise of individualized modes of participation in democratic systems. In this final chapter, we draw together the pieces of evidence from the various contributions to assess the empirical validity of the general expectations on professionalization and changing modes of participation. A closer examination of the four main explanations and interpretations (above and in Chapter 1) about the probable linkages between these two developments is required. Finally, we conclude with a brief discussion of these changing trends.

Changing democratic life

Professionalization

The first part of this volume contains six contributions on 'professionalization and democratic politics' dealing with discrete aspects of organizational life. All the analyses underline the changing ways in which associations function. While citizens' engagement remains important for the quality of democracy, many of the contributions have highlighted the trend towards replacing amateur volunteering activities by supporter-funded professional activities based on expert competences and professional training.

Two studies on political decision-making at the local level provided the first empirical corroboration of ongoing professionalization of civil society associations in their contacts with political authorities. The study presented by Matthias Freise on German associations in the health sector engaged in the so-called public–private partnerships (PPPs) with local authorities shows the development of an institutional framework that 'forces' voluntary associations to professionalize their activities. According to Freise the involvement of civil society actors in complex legal and financial arrangements related to PPPs exerts significant pressures on the day-to-day business of self-help groups to improve their activities. These organizations need to professionalize their activities in order to play a role in institutionalized arrangements with local authorities. Complex local arrangements and institutionalization are also key explanatory factors in Nicolas Maisetti's case study. He examined the intense competition among European cities for the European City of Culture nomination and the reasons for the success of the Marseille bid. He found that local politicians seemed to be constrained by the challenges of an international contest and that business leaders captured the process and played a leading role in Marseille. The final success of this 'entrepreneurial participation' was heavily dependent on the professional resources provided by business associations. As in the German case, institutionalization was crucial in Marseille. A transfer of responsibility taking from the political to the economic arena was institutionalized around the available managerial environment. It appears highly likely that neither local political engagement nor volunteering by citizens alone would have secured the City of Culture nomination – professionalism was pivotal.

These two local case studies clearly demonstrate the contextual pressures on organizations to professionalize their activities. In his analyses of British environmental associations Christopher Rootes goes one step further by assessing the impact of professionalization on the selection of specific forms of action at the local level. He finds strong support for his thesis that gradually professionalizing organizations opt for activities that do not embarrass their powerful interlocutors at the local level. Goals and actions aimed at national authorities frequently seek fundamental reforms and are campaign and/or protest based. At the local level most organizations seem to prefer a more accommodatory and practical approach. However, to sustain community organization and public commitment for action on climate change (over several decades), it appears that volunteering and citizen activities alone are insufficient. As with the previous two case studies (Freise and Maisetti) British environmental associations are under pressure to professionalize their activities to be effective in a highly complex context dealing with issues that cannot be solved in the short run.

While the first three studies emphasized the relevance of local activities for the professionalization of organizational life Sabine Saurugger considers the European level. Political participation through 'organized civil society' is expected to increase the quality of democracy at the national and international spheres. The sociological and political science literatures at the beginning of the twentieth century highlighted the accompanying processes of institutionalization, bureaucratization and professionalization among political organizations. Thus the expectation that the higher the level of involvement of organized civil society in decision-making processes at the European level the more effective and responsive the democratic decision-making process still awaits empirical corroboration.

The last two contributions to the first part of the volume emphasize the consequences of professionalization for the relationships between organizations and members/supporters. William A. Maloney deals with the opportunities that associations offer to increase the democratic involvement of citizens. In his view the rather limited use of these opportunities is largely unproblematic as long as associations offer participation rights to people who wish to be involved. Professionalized groups can enhance participation by improving internal democratic decision-making procedures, but also by being responsive to members' needs, and by offering participation rights along with financial support. His main argument, however, is that the professionalization of associational life as such does relatively little to enhance citizens' participation. In the last contribution to Part I of the volume Grant Jordan demonstrates how the consequences of professionalization are clearly visible in organizations' recruitment strategies. Jordan shows how these strategies have changed considerably in recent years. Conventional campaigns based on mailing and advertising are gradually being replaced by face-to-face contacting carried out by people employed by professional recruitment agencies. The job of recruiting supporters is contracted out to these companies that have a direct tangible (financial) stake. As a consequence, the main object of these campaigns is no longer to recruit active members or volunteers, but to enlist people as donors. Jordan is sceptical about the use of the large numbers of donors as robust indicators of 'participation' levels among the citizenry. His analyses show that professionalization implies changing recruitment strategies – and changing recruitment strategies means focussing on the passive donor rather than the active member.

Summarizing the results of the first part of this volume several conclusions can be formulated. First, professionalization appears to be a general process that can be documented in several very different circumstances. Usually the challenges, requirements and pressures provided by complex legal, political and organizational contexts seem to be a prime cause for this development. If groups want to be successful recruitment agencies and to influence policy outcomes they need to professionalize. Second, the institutionalization of procedures and cooperation with authorities make it very difficult for organizations to provide their clients with high quality products and services based on volunteering and 'amateur' activities. Third, professionalization implies changing participation opportunities for members as well as changing recruitment strategies. Although associations are open for members willing to play a more active role, professionalization moves the focus in recruitment strategies from members and volunteers towards donors and regular financial supporters.

New modes of participation

The second part of the volume deals with the changing nature of citizens' engagement patterns in democratic societies. The analyses show that participation patterns are indeed shifting and people are increasingly willing to support new forms of action. However, established modes of participation such as voting and demonstrating remain dominant and an unambiguous transformation towards more individualized modes has not occurred. While the research findings on professionalization relied mainly on case studies, the findings on citizen participation are generally based on survey data.

In the first contribution to this part of the volume Jan W. van Deth analyses the relationships between new modes of participation and so-called norms of citizenship using data from a number of representative samples. An increase in the use of individualized modes of political participation can be shown in many countries, but this increase is not accompanied by a substantive decrease in the use of other forms of action. Citizens using new modes of participation are not very enthusiastic about organized forms of participation or characterized by a relatively strong ethical/moral focus on global issues. The analysis, then, corroborates the idea that individualized modes of participation are based on a rejection of organized political life. Contrary to various claims presented the use of individualized modes of participation is not based on ethical or moral arguments.

Obviously, preferred modes of participation are closely related to the political and social environment of citizens. Two cross-national analyses of participation deal with contextual impacts using multilevel modelling. Starting from the well-known unequal distribution of engagement related to education and income Isabelle Stadelmann-Steffen shows that welfare states have the potential to act as a partial corrective to skewed participation. Using survey data and official statistics for OECD countries her analyses demonstrate the impact of social-economic determinants of social and political volunteering at the individual level, as well as the relevance of welfare state policies for citizens' involvement at the macro level. The results reject zero-sum game effects and highlight substantial differences across countries. The second contribution that examines the impact of contextual factors deals directly with widely used modes of political participation. Eline A. de Rooij's contribution focuses on cross-national differences in political participation and provides a detailed investigation of the attachments and motivations of citizens in various countries. In order to trace individual and contextual impacts on political participation she distinguishes between 'peripheral participants' and 'core participants'. The first group of citizens participate in a few political acts, which require little initiative or time. The second group invests more resources and engages in more time intensive activities. De Rooij finds that 'peripheral participants' are substantially less psychologically engaged with politics than 'core participants'. The differences, however, do not directly affect activity levels. Living in a more politicized context – such as in urban areas rather than in more remote areas or in cities where a variety of interest groups and social movements are active – increases the likelihood of participation. In a similar vein to Stadelmann-Steffen, de Rooij shows that contextual aspects are important, but not directly relevant for political mobilization. Contextual factors can modify relationships at the individual level, but do not compensate for conventional inequalities.

Inequality and compensatory mechanisms are the main topics of Tom W.G. van der Meer's contribution, which investigates issue preferences among Dutch citizens. He seeks to assess the extent to which voluntary associations offer an alternative form of participation for interests that are apparently underrepresented. Van der Meer discovers that people with leftwing orientations dominate every form of social and political action. The main explanation for this ideological bias is that leftwing citizens are more strongly motivated by 'outcome incentives' than others – i.e. their participation is purposive and directly aimed at influencing specific policy outcomes. Since people active in voluntary, non-political associations are also left leaning, civil society does not provide a counterbalance for this bias among political activists. The concepts of 'left' and 'right' have not lost their relevance for explaining political and social participation. Even today, leftwing orientations seem to be an unambiguous predictor of participation – irrespective of participatory modes.

The two last contributions to this volume focus on young citizens. This group is an especially interesting part of the population when we consider questions of social and political change. Younger people are presumed to be more open to new phenomena and to be more easily influenced by contemporary developments. Ellen Quintelier and Marc Hooghe present findings from a large panel study of Belgian adolescents' participatory habits. They discovered that individualized modes of participation are widely used by young people and are not a minority sport among this group. Furthermore, their analyses suggest that the choice of participatory modes is not taken on a whim, but can be seen as an extension of more conventional modes of protest and participation. Major differences can be observed between young people who are passive and those who are active – the differences between people using individualized modes of participation and other activists is negligible. Quintelier and Hooghe's results underline the popularity of individualized modes of participation among young people, which makes substantial increases in the use of these modes of participation likely in the near future. In the final contribution, Ariadne Vromen reports on Australian attempts to encourage young people to get involved in issue based policies and community projects. Within the context of a consultation-type mechanism the Australian government and local organizations offered young people opportunities to gain experiences within political decision-making processes. The results from these remarkable top-down initiatives are reassuring. Young people are certainly willing and able to participate if their limited experiences are not simply depicted as a shortcoming. Both chapters show that young citizens differ from the adult population in the way they use various modes of participation. Those already involved will use individualized forms of action as welcome extensions; those not involved can, with some positive encouragement, be mobilized.

Conclusions 237

The six contributions to the second part of the volume allow for several conclusions about changing modes of participation in democratic societies. First, individualized modes of participation are increasingly used and establish a regular part of the action repertoire, most notably by young people. Second, these new modes of participation do not replace existing forms of action, but can be seen as an extension to the participatory repertoire. Third, participation is still strongly biased by socio-economic background, motivations and leftwing orientations. Newer forms of participation do not seem to offer additional opportunities for a more balanced representation of interests. Finally, contextual factors are not directly relevant for political and social participation. Specific factors – i.e. welfare state measures, politicization, or top-down initiatives aimed at specific target groups – can offer opportunities for disadvantaged citizens.

Explaining professionalization and individualization

The professionalization of civil society organizations and changing modes of participation among citizenries are broadly supported by the empirical evidence presented in the various contributions to this volume. Both developments are characterized by their own causes, contexts and irregularities. Do the results presented in this volume allow us to go beyond the peculiarities of each development and to identify probable interdependencies? Linking them directly and causally would be a 'bridge too far' given our present understanding of social and political developments in democratic societies. Instead, we use the available evidence to assess the empirical validity of the four main explanations for possible relationships between professionalization and changing participation patterns.

i *Shared interests* (groups find financial supporters as opposed to members as an efficient way to mobilize).
  Jordan's analysis clearly illustrates that the move from conventional (direct) mailing and advertising to on-street recruitment further accentuates the mutation of groups from being membership based to supporter/donor based. In their contributions Jordan and Maloney note these recruitment procedures do not exclude the possibility of mobilizing active citizens. However, this is certainly not the main objective. Rootes' discussion of environmental groups in Britain shows that many of these groups have, in his words, 'given up even the pretence of being membership organizations and instead now count not their "members" but their "supporting donors" or "financial supporters"'. Finally, Maloney argues that there are reciprocal push and pull factors at work. So it is not simply that groups chase passive financial supporters, but that citizens don't seek active membership and are content to 'financially (and passively) support professionalized activism'. Turning to effective mobilization we see that groups increasingly do not (and do not need to) rely on active members. Maisetti's analyses show that Marseille's bid for the European Capital of Culture 2013 was dominated by business

organizations (relevant to the 'rise of the unelected' section below) and that mobilizing citizens was neither necessary to obtain additional resources nor needed to exert political pressure on local politicians. Maloney also makes a similar argument more generally. The conclusion from all these contributions is that professionalized groups find it relatively easy to mobilize parts of the population on a largely cash-cow basis – i.e. citizens provide the funds and the 'professionals' get on with influencing the policy.

ii *Mobilization of bias* (groups try to attract citizens engaged in individualized collective action).

Jordan demonstrates that professionalized associations target specific groups among the population and try to avoid certain biases (getting away from 'Dorothy Donor'). However, these recruitment strategies do not necessarily focus on citizens engaged in individualized collective action, but on groups that are most likely to be recruited as donors. Groups search as efficiently and economically as possible for a viable membership. However, the outcome of these recruitment strategies is indeed to strengthen financial support as a form of individualized collective action. Quintelier's and Hooghe's panel study of 16–18 year olds demonstrates that in 2006 (age 16) and 2008 (age 18) donating money and signing petitions were the most common participatory modes. They argue that individualized participation was not a fringe, but a widespread phenomenon and was utilized more frequently than collective modes. Their data points to strong stability over time and to the fact that individualized modes are being practised by the same type of participants who engage in collective acts. So these new modes of participation are likely to further accentuate the biases in political participation. Quintelier and Hooghe conclude that, 'individualized participation does not seem to attract different groups of the population from collective forms of participation. Claims about individualized action being able to mobilize completely new segments of society are not supported by this analysis.'

In a complementary analysis, van Deth's data show that the percentage of citizens who had boycotted a product grew significantly from the early 1970s, peaked in the late 1990s and has remained significantly higher than in the early 1970s. He argues that these results demonstrate that collective participatory modes are less attractive and that the prevalence of newer modes of participation among European citizens means that they have become part of the conventional repertoire. Van Deth also shows that people using individualized modes of participation are characterized by a lack of support for organized political life; that is, they do not consider involvement in political and social organizations important for democratic citizenship. This orientation makes it difficult for organizations to mobilize these citizens because they do not attach much importance to organized politics. Moreover, their relative low levels of support for ethical and moral considerations suggest that they have a relatively weak motivational base for active mobilization. Stadelmann-Steffen and de Rooij also uncovered some participatory bias, following the socio-economic standard model. Stadelmann-

Steffen's analysis clearly shows that a strong civil society is also a biased civil society with the overrepresentation of higher educational and income groups. While de Rooij finds that women, lower educated people and blue-collar workers were more likely to be 'peripheral' as opposed to 'core' participants. From a different perspective, van der Meer highlights the ideological biases in mobilizations. He shows that citizens with leftwing orientations dominate every mode of action and that it would be relatively easy for 'progressive' groups to recruit potential activists. Accordingly, the expansion of the modes of political action is likely to strengthen the mobilization of bias – i.e. increase support for leftwing policy goals. Van der Meer concludes that, 'Citizens with leftwing preferences are more likely to participate politically than citizens with rightwing preferences ... the professional organizations do not counterbalance the ideological bias that favours leftwing and extremist citizens.' Finally, the results presented by Vromen demonstrate how the barriers to young people's participation in Australia can be overcome and that given the right stimulus young citizens will participate.

iii '*The rise of the unelected*' (groups tend to dominate decision-making processes relevant for their constituency).

Freise's analyses on the developments of self-help groups in a regional context support this interpretation. In order to assure and improve a high level of help for their clients each group was willing to enter formal arrangements with local authorities. Once these arrangements were established professionalized procedures and activities increasingly replaced amateur activities. This process is even clearer in Maisetti's analyses of the Marseilles bid for European Capital of Culture 2013. He finds that organized business interests defined and constructed the bid and aimed to improve the image of their city in order to secure an attractive entrepreneurial environment in the future. The combined impact of a business dominated (bidding) process and the relative weakness of local public actors significantly limited citizen involvement.

In a similar way Rootes shows how British environmental organizations have been engaged in a process of institutionalization and professionalization over decades. Leading to the situation where many environmental organizations no longer rely on 'enthusiastic volunteers', but professionals. He notes that, professionalization facilitates 'effective lobbying and negotiation' and that environmental groups are increasingly likely to engage in lobbying rather than protest. Both Maloney and Jordan underline that professionalization has an impact on the internal functioning of associations. Jordan concluded that modern professionalized groups are elite dominated, engaged in professionalized lobbying and dependent upon spectator supporters with the occasional 'walk-on organizational roles – perhaps occasionally mobilized to "protest" with preprinted placards shoved in their hands, or more likely predrafted emails to forward.'

In conclusion, increasingly complex institutionalized arrangements stimulate greater professionalization. Volunteering and amateur activism appear, or at least are seen, to be less effective in delivering the outcomes that many groups seek.

iv *Members as distraction* (patronage allow groups to avoid the need to mobilize support among citizens).

Saurugger argues that the Ford Foundation's patronage programme that began in the 1950s was a crucial catalyst for the growth of patronage. It provided funding for many US public interest groups, reduced their reliance on membership subscriptions and stimulated the professionalization process. Maloney's figures on the financial resources of British associations underline the importance of patronage. Both Maloney and Saurugger point out that associations at the EU level depend largely on patronage from 'Brussels' and that this has the externality of decreasing the incentives to recruit members. Freise notes that in Germany a large part of self-help budgets are provided by public subsidies – in Münster most self-help groups received *circa* 80 to 90 per cent of their annual income from that source. These funding levels are seen as typical across Germany. Patronage is crucial at the local, regional, national and transnational levels. It enables many associations to avoid the time-consuming (and never-ending) process of recruiting members and regular donors. Maloney cites research by Cigler and Nownes (1995), Lowery (2007), Mahoney and Beckstrand (2008) and Hadden (2009) that demonstrates that patronage can have other side effects. It can have an impact on the shape of the public interest universe by funding professional rather than activist groups. Patronage may affect public interest groups' issue selection – it may be designed to appeal to issues of greatest concern to important patrons, more than supporters. Finally, it can also affect the goals and tactics of groups that are heavily reliant on funds from these sources for organizational survival – i.e. groups could become less challenging or contentious.

In conclusion, much patronage is aimed at levelling the playing field – i.e. providing funds to countervailing groups that lack the resources that business or professional associations possess. In addition to this, political institutions also provide patronage to organizations that may oppose them. Both these motivations are laudable and can be seen as bolstering democratic processes. However, while patronage succeeds in helping public interest groups compete more effectively, it also has some externalities that can be presented as less democratically enriching.

How benign is professionalized and individualized politics?

Our findings do not support the naive idea that professionalization and the rise of individualized political participation are causally linked. The two processes are linked but there is scant evidence of a causal relationship. The clearest evidence is provided by Jordan with his information about changing recruitment strategies. All other empirical evidence is mainly circumstantial, corroborating the plausibility of each of the four explanations considered. However, it is clear that both developments have been identified by the contributors throughout this volume in very different situations. The professionalization of representation has permeated many aspects of the political world – organizational recruitment, organizational maintenance, lobbying, rhetoric, etc. For example, Freise comments that self-help groups and health authorities in Germany used to refer to their clients as 'members', 'concerned persons' or 'customers'. They now use the label 'customers'. He argues that this is significant because it signals the transformation of amateur 'civil society participants to service providers with a customer base'. De Rooij, Jordan, Maloney and Rootes all note that many organizations mobilize a supporter base that is weakly ideologically predisposed and do so via a variety of sophisticated recruitment techniques. Accordingly, these supporters are stimulated by groups to provide financial contributions that fund professionalized representation. Individualized political participation is also omnipresent, as evidenced by the growth of ethical shopping, boycotting and buycotting. Professionalization and individualized political participation to a certain extent can be seen as compatible and contributing to the participatory repertoire of citizens. However, even though these developments can be presented as compatible the impact and affect question hangs in the air – i.e. compatibility does not necessarily imply that these developments are benign. To what extent can these developments be presented as democratically damaging or democratically enriching?

Skewed participation is an enduring democratic pathology. The rise of individualistic involvement creates opportunities to reduce participatory inequalities. However, the research conducted by the scholars in this volume found very little evidence of a more level participatory playing field. For example, van Deth while welcoming any reduction in participatory inequality found that citizens engaged in new and individualized modes of participation do not exhibit strong support for norms of citizenship.

There is also evidence of some more 'positive' findings. Both Stadelmann-Steffen and Vromen found that state intervention can have a positive impact on political inequality. Stadelmann-Steffen argued that an extensive welfare state and welfare state policy instruments 'can reduce social inequality in civic participation'. While Vromen demonstrated that well-designed policy interventions can encourage underrepresented and underactive groups to become more politically engaged. There are potentially wider democratic and societal benefits in transforming low participation groups into more active citizens. Quintelier and Hooghe found that the young people in their study who were politically disengaged exhibited 'low levels of tolerance, a lack of political interest, a low level of political knowledge and a low socio-economic status'.

As several chapters in this volume have shown, the increasing professionalization of many groups has a democratic cost. For example, Rootes highlights the case of Greenpeace which relies on frequent donations from 'their most committed supporters ... [and] makes no pretence of being a grassroots membership organization'. If groups choose to sacrifice or eschew internal democracy, partly in favour of organizational efficiency – this leaves them open to legitimacy questions. If members don't select leaders, debate and help shape policies and strategies or campaigning priorities then how can they claim to be the legitimate representatives of their supporters? This finding extends beyond the work in this volume. Barakso and Schaffer (2008: 205) concluded that, 'in an era when interest groups play a central role in terms of agenda setting and policymaking, both lawmakers and citizens have a reason to be concerned about who, precisely, is being represented by these organizations'.

Irrespective of the criticism that professionalized groups suffer from several democratic deficiencies, the contributions to this volume show that these organizations do have some democratically redeeming features. While direct democracy may be missing from the characteristics of many groups, as Schumpeter argued there remains 'an infinite wealth of possible forms in which the "people" may partake in the business of ruling or influence or control those who actually do the ruling' (1942: 247). Organizations that appear to lack responsive democratic mechanisms or who are unapologetically oligarchical can be seen as providing political and democratic linkage. Groups are (democratically) sensitive and responsive in a variety of ways, via market research, polls, surveys, focus groups, etc. While Rootes boldly argues that many NGOs can be seen as 'more accountable than political representatives elected for a term of years because the supporters of the former, unlike those of the latter, can turn off the tap or increase the flow of funds and support at any time'. Saurugger notes somewhat ironically that organizations seeking democratic reforms find that the best way to achieve such change may involve 'abandoning certain democratic and amateurish political practices'. Maloney cautions that democratic processes do not necessarily deliver civic or democratic outcomes. Finally, there is also a representation issue. Hayes (1986: 143) argued that while many citizen groups do not conform to the traditional membership based model, 'The continuing susceptibility of such large and diffuse constituencies to the free-rider problem suggest, however, that if alternative organizational forms had not emerged, most of these interests would remain unorganized today.'

Do these results suggest that democratic life is undergoing deep and persistent changes? Not much empirical evidence is presented here to robustly support such grand claims. Rather than claims about deepening rifts, the apparent 'end of democracy' or at least the arrival of the age of 'post-democracy'. Somewhat optimistically we may even speak of 'the best of all worlds'. Associations provide (democratic) products and services on the basis of professionalization and citizens are offered a variety of opportunities for participation – deep to shallow. Many citizens face the choice to participate if they want or pass on the offer if they don't want to get involved. Groups rely on support from members, supporters, donors and patrons and this support can also deliver beneficial democratic surrogacy to act on behalf of those who cannot participate or those who lack the necessary resources. The dual processes of professionalization and individualization may provide more opportunities for democracy than hoped for by many fashionable observers of democratic shrinkage and crisis.

References

Abbott, A. (1988) *The System of Professions: An Essay on the Division of Expert Labour*, Chicago, IL: University of Chicago Press.
Adam, F. (2008) 'Mapping Social Capital across Europe: Findings, Trends and Methodological Shortcomings of Cross-national Surveys', *Social Science Information*, 47(2): 159–186.
Addonizio, E.M., Green, D.P. and Glaser, J.M. (2007) 'Putting the Party back into Politics: An Experiment Testing whether Election Day Festivals increase Voter Turnout', *Political Science and Politics*, 40(4): 721–727.
Akkerman, T., Hajer, M. and Grin, J. (2004) 'The Interactive State: Democratisation from Above?' *Political Studies*, 52(1): 82–95.
Alliès, P., Roche, F. and Négrier, E. (1994) *Pratiques des échanges culturels internationaux*, Paris: La Documentation Française.
Almond, G.A. and Verba, S. (1963) *The Civic Culture. Political Attitudes and Democracy in Five Nations*, Princeton, NJ: Princeton University Press.
Andrew, C. and Goldsmith, M. (1998) 'From Local Government to Local Governance and Beyond?' *International Political Science Review*, 19(2): 101–117.
Arnstein, S.R. (1969) 'A Ladder of Citizen Participation', *Journal of the American Institute of Planners*, 35(4): 216–224.
Australian Institute of Health and Welfare (2007) 'Young Australians: Their Health and Wellbeing'. Online, available at: www.aihw.gov.au/publications/index.cfm/title/10451 (accessed 4 March 2011).
Bagnasco, A. and Le Galès, P. (eds) (1997) *Villes en Europe*, Paris: La Découverte.
Bailey, I., Hopkins, R. and Wilson, G. (2010) 'Some Things Old, Some Things New: The Spatial Representations and Politics of Change of the Peak Oil Relocalisation Movement', *Geoforum*, 41(4): 595–605.
Balme, R, Faure, A. and Mabileau, A. (eds) (1999) *Les Nouvelles Politiques locales: Dynamiques de l'action publique*, Paris: Presses de Sciences Po.
Bang, H. (2005) 'Among Everyday Makers and Expert Citizens', in J. Newman (ed.) *Remaking Governance: Peoples, Politics and the Public Sphere*, Bristol: Policy Press, 159–178.
Barasko, M. and Schaffner, B.F. (2008) 'Exit, Voice and Interest Group Governance', *American Political Research*, 36(2): 186–209.
Barber, B. (1971) *Superman and Common Men: Freedom, Anarchy, and the Revolution*, New York: Praeger.
Barnes, M., Newman, J. and Sullivan, H. (2007) *Power, Participation and Renewal: Case Studies in Public Participation*, Bristol: Policy Press.

Barnes, S.H., Kaase, M. with Allerbeck, K., Farah, B., Heunks, F., Inglehart, R., Jennings, M.K., Klingemann, H.D., Marsh, A. and Leopold Rosenmayr, L. (1979) *Political Action: Mass Participation in Five Western Democracies*, London: Sage.

Baumeister, R., Bratslavsky, E., Finkenauer, C. and Vohs, K.D. (2001) 'Bad is Stronger than Good', *Review of General Psychology*, 5(4): 323–370.

Bennett, W.L. (2008) 'Changing Citizenship in the Digital Age', in W.L. Bennett (ed.) *Civic Life Online: Learning How Digital Media can Engage Youth*, Cambridge, MA: MIT Press, 1–24.

Bennett, W.L., Wells, C. and Rank, A. (2009) 'Young Citizens and Civic Learning: Two Paradigms of Citizenship in the Digital Age', *Citizenship Studies*, 13(2): 105–120.

Berelson, B.R., Lazarsfeld, P.F. and McPhee, W.N. (1954) *Voting: A Study of Opinion Formation in a Presidential Campaign*, Chicago, IL: University of Chicago Press.

Berry, J. (1999) *The New Liberalism*, Washington, DC: Brookings Institution Press.

Berry, J.M. and Wilcox, C. (2009) *The Interest Group Society*, 5th edn, New York: Pearson and Longman.

Bessant, J. (2003) 'Youth Participation: A New Mode of Government', *Policy Studies*, 24(2): 87–100.

Bessant, J. (2004) 'Mixed Messages: Youth Participation and Democratic Process', *Australian Journal of Political Science*, 39(2): 387–405.

Beyers, J., Eising, R. and Maloney, W. (2008a) 'Researching Interest Group Politics in Europe and Elsewhere: Much We Study, Little We Know?' *West European Politics*, 31(6): 1103–1128.

Beyers, J., Eising, R. and Maloney, W. (2008b) 'The Politics of Organized Interests in Europe: Lessons from EU Studies and Comparative Politics', *West European Politics*, 31(6).

Blais, A. (2006) 'What Affects Voter Turnout?' *Annual Review of Political Science* 9: 111–125.

Boeßenecker, K.H. (2005) *Spitzenverbände der Freien Wohlfahrtspflege: Eine Einführung in Organisationsstrukturen und Handlungsfelder der deutschen Wohlfahrtsverbände*, München: Weinheim.

Boje, T.P. and Strandh, M. (2005) 'Different Worlds of Volunteering and Informal Care in Europe', Second Annual ESPAnet Conference, Fribourg.

Bolzan, N. (2003) '"Kids are Like That!" Community Attitudes to Young People', National Youth Affairs Research Scheme, FACS, Canberra. Online, available at: www.facs.gov.au/internet/facsinternet.nsf/aboutfacs/progams/youth-kids_that.htm (accessed 4 March 2011).

Bo'sher, L. (2006) 'Where are the Priorities? Where is the Action?' *Children, Youth and Environments*, 16(2): 338–347.

Bosso, C.J. (1995) 'The Color of Money: Environmental Groups and the Pathologies of Fund Raising', in A.J. Cigler and B.A. Loomis (eds) *Interest Group Politics*, 4th edn, Washington, DC: Congressional Quarterly Press, 101–130.

Bosso, C.J. (2003) 'Rethinking the Concept of Membership in Nature Advocacy Organizations', *Policy Studies Journal*, 31(3): 397–411.

Brady, H.E. (1999) 'Political Participation', in J.P. Robinson, P.R. Shaver and L.S. Wrightsman (eds) *Measures of Political Attitudes*, San Diego, CA: Academic Press, 737–801.

Brady, H.E., Verba, S. and Schlozman, K.L. (1995) 'Beyond SES: A Resource Model of Political Participation', *American Political Science Review*, 89: 271–294.

Brady, H.E., Schlozman, K.L. and Verba, S. (1999) 'Prospecting for Participants: Rational Expectations and the Recruitment of Political Activists', *American Political Science Review*, 93(1): 153–168.

Brandsen, T. (2008) 'The Third Sector and the Delivery of Public Services: An Evaluation of Different Meta-theoretical Perspectives', in S.P. Osborne (ed.) *The Third Sector in Europe: Prospects and Challenges*, London: Routledge, 105–117.

Bridgland Sorenson, J. (2007) 'The Secret Life of the National Youth Roundtable: Are We There Yet?' National Youth Conference Proceedings: Peer Reviewed Papers, Youth Affairs Council of Victoria, Melbourne, 69–77. Online, available at: www.yacvic.org.au/includes/pdfs_wordfiles/YACVic_ConfProceedings_Papers.pdf (accessed 4 March 2011).

Brooks, R. (2009) 'Young People and Political Participation: An Analysis of European Union Policies', *Sociological Research Online*, 14(1). Online, available at: www.socresonline.org.uk/14/1/7.html (accessed 4 March 2011).

Browne, W.J. and Draper, D. (2006) 'A Comparison of Bayesian and Likelihood-based Methods for Fitting Multilevel Models', *Bayesian Analysis*, 1(3): 473–514.

Brulle, R.J. (2010) 'From Environmental Campaigns to Advancing the Public Dialog: Environmental Communication for Civic Engagement', *Environmental Communication*, 4(1): 82–98.

Campbell, A. (1960) 'Surge and Decline: A Study of Electoral Change', *Public Opinion Quarterly*, 24(3): 397–418.

Campbell, A., Converse, P.E., Miller, W.E. and Stokes, D.E. (1960) *The American Voter*, New York: John Wiley & Sons.

Campbell, A., Converse, P.E., Miller, W.E. and Stokes, D.E. (1966) *Elections and the Political Order*, New York: John Wiley & Sons.

Castiglione, D., van Deth, J.W. and Wolleb, G. (eds) (2008) *The Handbook of Social Capital*, Oxford: Oxford University Press.

Castles, F.G. (2008) 'What Welfare States Do: A Disaggregated Expenditure Approach', *Journal of Social Policy*, 38(1): 45–62.

Cavaille, A. (2004) 'Au nom des femmes: Trajectoires sociales et carrières associatives au Lobby Européen des Femmes', communication presented at the workshop 'Société civile organisée et gouvernance européenne', IEP de Strasbourg, 21–23 June.

Chaskin, R.J. (2003) 'Fostering Neighborhood Democracy: Legitimacy and Accountability within Loosely Coupled Systems', *Nonprofit and Voluntary Sector Quarterly*, 32(2): 161–189.

Cigler, A.J. and Nownes, A.J. (1995) 'Public Interest Entrepreneurs and Group Patrons', in A.J. Cigler and B.A. Loomis (eds) *Interest Group Politics*, 4th edn, Washington, DC: Congressional Quarterly Press, 77–100.

Clarke, J., Newman, J., Smith, N., Vidler, E. and Westmarland, L. (2007) *Creating Citizen-Consumers: Changing Publics and Changing Public Services*, London: Sage.

Clark, J.D. (2001) 'Ethical Globalization: The Dilemmas and Challenges of Internationalizing Civil Society', in M. Edwards and J. Gaventa (eds) *Global Citizen Action*, Boulder, CO: Lynne Rienner Publishers, 17–28.

Cohen, J. and Arato, A. (1992) *Civil Society and Political Theory*, Cambridge, MA: MIT Press.

Cohen, S. (1973) *Folk Devils and Moral Panics*, St Albans: Paladin.

Coleman, S. (2007) 'Doing IT for Themselves: Management Versus Autonomy in Youth E-citizenship', in L. Bennett (ed.) *Civic Life Online: Learning How Digital Media Can Engage Youth*, Cambridge, MA: MIT Press, 189–206.

Coleman, S. and Blumler, J. (2009) *The Internet and Democratic Citizenship*, Cambridge: Cambridge University Press.
Conover, P., Searing, D. and Crewe, I. (2002) 'The Deliberative Potential of Political Discussion', *British Journal of Political Science*, 32(1): 21–62.
Converse, E. (1964) 'The Nature of Belief Systems in Mass Publics', in D. Apter (ed.) *Ideology and its Discontents*, Glencoe, IL: Macmillan.
Council of European Union (2009) *Decision Designation of European Capitals of Culture in 2013*, 2009/201/CE.
Cracknell, J. and Godwin, H. (2007) *Where the Green Grants Went 3: Patterns of UK Funding for Environmental and Conservation Work*, London: Environmental Funders Network.
Cracknell, J., Godwin, H. and Williams, H. (2009) *Where the Green Grants Went 4: Patterns of UK Funding for Environmental and Conservation Work*, London: Environmental Funders Network.
Crenson, M.A. and Ginsberg, B. (2002) *Downsizing Democracy: How America Sidelined its Citizens and Privatized its Public*, Baltimore, MD: John Hopkins University Press.
Curtis, J.E., Baer, D.E. and Grabb, E.G. (2001) 'Nations of Joiners: Explaining Voluntary Association Membership in Democratic Societies', *American Sociological Review*, 66(6): 783–805.
Dahlberg, L. (2005) 'Interaction between Voluntary and Statutory Social Service Provision in Sweden: A Matter of Welfare Pluralism, Substitution or Complementarity?' *Social Policy and Administration*, 39(7): 740–763.
Dalton, R. (2006) *Citizen Politics: Public Opinion and Political Parties in Advanced Industrial Democracies*, Washington, DC: CQ Press.
Dalton, R. (2008a) *The Good Citizen: How a Younger Generation is Reshaping American Politics*, Washington, DC: CQ Press.
Dalton, R. (2008b) 'Citizenship Norms and the Expansion of Political Participation', *Political Studies*, 56(1): 76–98.
Day, C.L. (1999) 'Grassroots Involvement in Interest Group Decision Making', *American Political Quarterly*, 27(2): 216–235.
Day, K.M. and Devlin, R.A. (1996) 'Volunteerism and Crowding Out: Canadian Econometric Evidence', *Canadian Journal of Economics*, 29(1): 37–53.
de Rijke, J., Gaiser, W. and Waechter, F. (2008) 'Political Orientation and Participation', in R. Spannring, G. Ogris and W. Gaiser (eds) *Youth and Political Participation in Europe: Results of the Comparative Study EUYOUPART*, Leverkusen: Budrich, 121–147.
Dearing, J. and Rogers, E. (1996) *Agenda Setting*, Thousand Oaks, CA: Sage.
Dees, J.G., Emerson, J. and Economy, P. (2001) *Enterprising Nonprofits: A Toolkit for Social Entrepreneurs*, New York: John Wiley & Sons.
Dekker, P. and Halmann, L. (2003) 'Volunteering and Values: An Introduction', in P. Dekker and L. Halmann (eds) *The Values of Volunteering: Cross-cultural Perspectives*, New York: Kluwer Academic/Plenum Publishers, 1–17.
Dekker, P. and Hooghe, M. (2003) 'De burger-nachtwaker: Naar een informalisering van de politieke participatie van de Nederlandse en Vlaamse bevolking', *Sociologische Gids*, 50(2): 156–181.
Denters, B. and van der Kolk, H. (2008) 'What Determines Citizens' Normative Conception of their Civic Duties', in H. Meulemann (ed.) *Social Capital in Europe: Similarity of Countries and Diversity of People?* Leiden/Boston, MA: Brill, 135–157.
Denters, B., Gabriel, O. and Torcal, M. (2007) 'Norms of Good Citizenship', in J.W. van

Deth, J.R. Montero and A. Westholm (eds) *Citizenship and Involvement in Europe: A Comparative Analysis*, London: Routledge, 88–108.
Dijkzeul, D. and Gordenker, L. (2003) 'Cures and Conclusions', in D. Dijkzeul and Y. Beigbeder (eds) *Rethinking International Organizations: Pathologies and Promise*, Oxford, New York: Berghahn Books, 311–336.
Doherty, B. (2006) 'Friends of the Earth International: Negotiating a Transnational Identity', *Environmental Politics*, 15(5): 860–880.
Donzel, A. (ed.) (2001) *Métropolisation, gouvernance et citoyenneté dans la région urbaine marseillaise*, Paris: Maisonneuve et Larose.
Donzel, A. (2005) 'Marseille, une Métropole duale?' *Faire Savoir*, 5: 13–19.
Downs, A. (1957) *An Economic Theory of Democracy*, New York: Harper & Row.
Duch, R. (1998) 'Participation in the New Democracies of Central and Eastern Europe: Cultural Versus Rational Choice Explanations', in S.H. Barnes and J. Simon (eds) *The Postcommunist Citizen*, Budapest: Erasmus Foundation and Institute for Political Science of the Hungarian Academy of Sciences, 195–229.
Eberwein, W. and Saurugger, S. (2009) 'The Professionalization of NGOs: An Obstacle to Global Participatory Democracy?' chapter presented at the ISA Convention in New York, 15–18 February.
Edwards, K. (2007) 'From Deficit to Disenfranchisement: Reframing Youth Electoral Participation', *Journal of Youth Studies*, 10(5): 539–555.
Eliasoph, N. (1998) *Avoiding Politics: How Americans Produce Apathy in Everyday Life*, Cambridge: Cambridge University Press.
Elster, J. (1998) 'A Plea for Mechanism', in P. Hedström and R. Swedberg (eds) *Social Mechanism: An Analytical Approach to Social Theory*, Cambridge: Cambridge University Press, 45–73.
Erikson, R. and Goldthorpe, J.H. (1992) *The Constant Flux: A Study of Class Mobility in Industrial Countries*, Oxford: Clarendon Press.
Euchner, C.E. (1996) *Extraordinary Politics: How Protest and Dissent are Changing American Democracy*, Boulder, CO: Westview Press.
Evans, D. (1997) *A History of Nature Conservation in Britain*, 2nd edn, London: Routledge.
Evans, T. (2009) 'Stopping the Poor getting Poorer: The Establishment and Professionalization of Poverty NGOs, 1945–75', in N. Crowson, M. Hilton and J. McKay (eds) *NGOs in Contemporary Britain*, Basingstoke: Palgrave, 147–163.
Evers, A. (2005) 'Mixed Welfare Systems and Hybrid Organizations: Changes in the Governance and Provision of Social Services', *International Journal of Public Administration*, 28(9–10): 736–748.
Favell, A. (2007) 'The Sociology of EU Politics', in K.E. Joergensen, M. Pollack and B. Rosamond (eds) *The Handbook of EU Politics*, London: Sage, 122–137.
Finsveen, E.M. and van Oorschot, W. (2007) 'How does the Welfare State affect Social Capital? A Literature Study', paper prepared for the ECPR Joint Sessions, Workshop Social Capital, the State and Diversity, Helsinki, May.
Fiorina, M.P. (1999) 'Extreme Voice: A Dark Side of Civic Engagement', in Theda Skocpol and Morris P. Fiorina (eds) *Civic Engagement in American Democracy*, Washington, DC: Brookings Institution Press, 395–425.
Fisher, D.R. (2006) *Activism Inc.: How the Outsourcing of Grassroots campaigns is Strangling Progressive Politics in America*, Stanford, CA: Stanford University Press.
Flinders, M. (2005) 'The Politics of Public–Private Partnerships', *British Journal of Politics and International Relations*, 7(2): 543–567.

Forsé, M. (2008) 'Définir et analyser les réseaux sociaux-les enjeux de l'analyse structurale', *Informations sociales*, 147(3): 10–19.

Franklin, M.N. (2004) *Voting Turnout and the Dynamics of Electoral Competition in Established Democracies since 1945*, Cambridge: Cambridge University Press.

Friedman, S. (2003) 'The State, Civil Society and Social Policy: Setting a Research Agenda', *Politikon*, 30(1): 3–25.

Fuchs, D. and Klingemann, H.D. (1990) 'The Left–Right Schema', in M.K. Jennings, J.W. van Deth, S.H. Barnes, D. Fuchs, F.J. Heunks, H.D. Klingemann, and J.J.A. Thomassen (eds) *Continuities in Political Action: A Longitudinal Study of Political Orientations in Three Western Democracies*, Berlin: Walter de Gruyter, 203–234.

Furlong, A. and Cartmel, F. (2007) *Young People and Social Change: New Perspectives*, 2nd edn, Berkshire: Open University Press.

Galston, W. (2001) 'Political Knowledge, Political Engagement, and Civic Education', *Annual Review of Political Science*, 4: 217–234.

Gaskin, K. and Smith, J.D. (1997) *A New Civil Europe? A Study of the Extent and Role of Volunteering*, London: National Center for Volunteering in Britain.

Gaskin, K., Smith, J.D. and Paulwitz, I. (1996) *Ein neues bürgerliches Europa: Eine Untersuchung zur Verbreitung und Rolle von Volunteering in zehn Ländern*, Freiburg im Breisgau: Lambertus.

Gaudin, J.-C. (2008) *Marseille Capitale européenne de la culture en 2013*. Online, available at: www.jeanclaudegaudin.net/v3_jcg/index.php?option=com_content&view=article&id=1028:marseille-capitale-europeenne-de-la-culture-en-2013-&catid=8:actualite-marseille&Itemid=47 (accessed 16 June 2010).

Gerber, A.S., Green, D.P. and Larimer, C.W. (2008) 'Social Pressure and Voter Turnout: Evidence from a Large-scale Field Experiment', *American Political Science Review*, 102(1): 33–48.

Giddens, A. (1991) *Modernity and Self-Identity: Self and Society in the Late Modern Age*, Cambridge: Polity Press.

Gobin, C. (1997) *L'Europe syndicale: entre désir et réalité*, Bruxelles: Ed. Labor.

Grande, E. (2002) 'Post-National Democracy in Europe', in M.T. Greven and L.W. Pauly (eds) *Democracy Beyond the State? The European Dilemma and the Emerging Global Order*, Lanham, MD: Rowman & Littlefield, 115–138.

Granovetter, M. (1973) 'The Strength of Weak Ties', *American Journal of Sociology*, 91(6): 1360–1380.

Granovetter, M. (1983) 'The Strength of Weak Ties: A Network Theory Revisited', *Sociological Theory*, 1(2): 201–233.

Grant, W. (2003) 'Pressure Politics: The Challenge for Democracy', *Parliamentary Affairs*, 56(2): 297–308.

Green, D.P. and Smith, J.K. (2003) 'Professionalization of Campaigns and the Secret History of Collective Action Problems', *Journal of Theoretical Politics*, 15(3), 321–339.

Greenwood, J. (2002) *Inside the EU Business Associations*, Basingstoke: Palgrave.

Greenwood, J. (2007) 'Review Article: Organized Civil Society and Democratic Legitimacy in the European Union', *British Journal of Political Science*, 37(2): 333–357.

Gross, M.L. (1997) *Ethics and Activism: The Theory and Practice of Political Morality*, Cambridge: Cambridge University Press.

Guérini, J.-N. (2008) 'Marseille-Provence capitale européenne de la culture en 2013: une bonne nouvelle pour tous les habitants des Bouches-du-Rhôn'. Online, available at: www.jn-guerini.fr/2008/09/16/marseille-provence-capitale-europeenne-de-la-culture-

en-2013-une-bonne-nouvelle-pour-tous-les-habitants-des-bouches-du-rhone-%C2%BB/ (accessed 16 June 2010).
Guillet, M. and Galli, C. (eds) (1996) *Marseille XXè: un destin culturel*, Lyon: Éditions Via Valeriano.
Guiraudon, V. (2001) 'Weak Weapons of the Weak? Transnational Mobilization around Migration in the European Union', in D. Imig and S. Tarrow (eds) *Contentious Europeans: Protest and Polity in an Emerging Polity*, London: Rowman & Littlefield, 163–186.
Hadden, J. (2009) 'Two Worlds of European Collective Action? Civil Society Spillover(s) in European Climate Change Networks', Paper presented at 'Bringing Civil Society In: The European Union and the Rise of Representative Democracy' Conference, Robert Schuman Centre for Advanced Studies, European University Institute, Centre d'études européennes de Science Po Paris, Florence, 13–14 March.
Haezewindt, P. (2003) 'Investing in Each Other and the Community: The Role of Social Capital', in C. Summerfield and P. Babb (eds) *Social Trends* 33, London: Stationery Office for Office of National Statistics, 19–27.
Hale, S. (2008) *The New Politics of Climate Change: Why We are Failing and How We will Succeed*, London: Green Alliance.
Hannigan, J. (1995) *Environmental Sociology: A Social Constructionist Perspective*, London: Routledge.
Hansen, J.M. (1985) 'The Political Economy of Group Membership', *American Political Science Review*, 79(1): 79–96.
Harris, A. (2004) *Future Girl: Young Women in the Twenty-first Century*, New York: Routledge.
Harris, A. and Wyn, J. (2009) 'Young People's Politics and the Micro-Territories of the Local', *Australian Journal of Political Science*, 44(2): 327–344.
Harris, A., Wyn, J. and Younes, S. (2007) 'Young People and Citizenship: An Everyday Perspective', *Youth Studies Australia*, 26(3): 19–27.
Harris, A., Wyn, J. and Younes, S. (2010) 'Beyond Apathetic or Activist Youth: "Ordinary" Young People and Contemporary Forms of Participation', *Young: Nordic Journal of Youth Research*, 18(1): 9–32.
Harrison, R., Newholm, T. and Shaw, D. (eds) (2005) *The Ethical Consumer*, London: Sage.
Hay, C. (2007) *Why We Hate Politics*, Cambridge: Polity Press.
Hay, C. and Stoker, G. (2009) 'Revitalising Politics: Have We Lost the Plot?' *Representation*, 45(3): 225–236.
Hay, C., Stoker, G. and Williamson, A. (2008) 'Revitalising Politics: Have We Lost the Plot?' Online, available at: revitalisingpolitics.files.wordpress.com/2008/09/revitalizing-politics-position-paper.pdf (accessed 14 August 2010).
Hayes, M.T. (1986) 'The New Group Universe', in A.J. Cigler and B. Loomis (eds) *Interest Group Politics*, 2nd edn, Washington, DC: Congressional Quarterly Press, 133–145.
Hedström, P. and Swedberg, R. (1996) 'Rational Choice, Empirical Research, and the Sociological Tradition', *European Sociological Review*, 12(2): 127–146.
Henn, M. and Weinstein, M. (2006) 'Young People and Political (In)Activism: Why don't Young People Vote?' *Policy and Politics*, 34(3): 517–534.
Her Majesty's Inspectorate of Constabulary (2009) *Adapting to Protest: Nurturing the British Model of Policing*, London: Her Majesty's Inspectorate of Constabulary.
Hibbing, J.R. and Theiss-Morse, E. (2002) *Stealth Democracy: Americans' Beliefs about How Government should Work*, Cambridge: Cambridge University Press.

Himmelweit, H., Humphreys, P. and Jaegar, M. (1981) *How Voters Decide*, Milton Keynes: Open University Press.

Hirschman, A.O. (1970) *Exit, Voice and Loyalty: Responses to Decline in Firms, Organizations and States*, Cambridge, MA: Harvard University Press.

Hogg, D. (2006) *A Changing Climate for Energy from Waste? Final Report for Friends of the Earth*, Bristol: Eunomia Research & Consulting Ltd.

Hooghe, M. (2008) 'Voluntary Associations and Socialization', in D. Castiglione, J.W. van Deth and G. Wolleb (eds) *The Handbook of Social Capital*, Oxford: Oxford University Press, 568–593.

Hooghe, M. and Dejaeghere, Y. (2007) 'Does the "Monitorial Citizen" Exist? An Empirical Investigation into the Occurrence of Postmodern Forms of Citizenship in the Nordic Countries', *Scandinavian Political Studies*, 30(2): 249–271.

Hooghe, M. and Deneckere, G. (2003) 'La Marche blanche de Belgique (Octobre 1996): un mouvement de masse spectaculaire, mais éphémère', *Le Mouvement Social*, 202: 153–164.

Hooghe, M., Quintelier, E., Claes, E. and Dejaeghere, Y. (2009) *The Belgian Political Panel Survey 2006–2008, Technical report*, Leuven: K. U. Leuven.

Hustinx, L. (2005) 'Weakening Organisational Ties? A Classification of Styles of Volunteering in the Flemish Red Cross', *Social Service Review*, 79(4): 624–652.

Hyden, G. (1997) 'Civil Society, Social Capital and Development: Dissection of a Complex Discourse', *Studies in Comparative International Development*, 32(1): 3–30.

IDEA (2010) 'Voter Turnout, Country View'. Online, available at: www.idea.int/vt (accessed 24 June 2010).

Imig, D. (1994) 'Advocacy by Proxy: The Children's Lobby in American Politics', Paper prepared for the Annual meeting of the American Political Science Association, New York.

Imig, D. and Tarrow, S. (eds) (2001) *Contentious Europeans: Protest and Polity in an Emerging Polity*, London: Rowman & Littlefield.

Inglehart, R. (1997) *Modernization and Postmodernization: Cultural, Economic, and Political Change in 43 Societies*, Princeton, NJ: Princeton University Press.

Inglehart, R. and Catterberg, G. (2002) 'Trends in Political Action: The Developmental Trend and the Post-honeymoon Decline', *International Journal of Comparative Sociology*, 43(3–5): 300–316.

Janoski, T. (1998) *Citizenship and Civil Society: A Framework of Rights and Obligations in Liberal, Traditional, and Social Democratic Regimes*, Cambridge: Cambridge University Press.

Johnson, E. (1995) 'How Environmental Groups Recruit Members: Does the Logic Still Hold Up?' Paper presented at the Annual Meeting of the American Political Science Association, Chicago, 2 September.

Jones, K. (1997) 'Multilevel Approaches to Modelling Contextuality: From Nuisance to Substance in the Analysis of Voting Behaviour', in G.P. Westert and R.N. Verhoeff (eds) *Places and People: Multilevel Modelling in Geographical Research*, Utrecht: KNAG/Netherlands Geographical Studies, 19–43.

Jordan, G. (2007) 'Policy without Learning: Double Devolution and Abuse of the Deliberative Idea', *Public Policy and Administration*, 22(1): 48–73.

Jordan, G. and Maloney, W.A. (1997) *The Protest Business: Mobilizing Campaign Groups*, Manchester: Manchester University Press.

Jordan, G. and Maloney, W.A. (2006) 'Letting George Do It: Accounting for Low Participation Rates?' *Journal of Elections, Public Opinion and Parties*, 16(2): 115–139.

Jordan, G. and Maloney, W.A. (2007) *Democracy and Interest Groups: Enhancing Participation?* Basingstoke: Palgrave Macmillan.

Jordan, G. and Maloney, W.A. (2009) 'The Business of Building Group Membership: Recruitment as Disengagement?' in C. McGrath (ed.) *Interest Groups and Lobbying, in the United States, and Comparative Perspectives*, Lewiston, NY: Edwin Mellen Press, 329–355.

Jordan, G., Maloney, W.A. and McLaughlin, A. (1994a) 'Collective Action and the Public Interest Problem: Drawing a Line Under Olson?' in P. Dunleavy and J. Stanyer (eds) *Contemporary Political Studies 1994: Proceedings of the Political Studies Association's 1994 Annual Conference*, Queens University, Belfast: UK Political Studies Association 1994, 519–534.

Jordan, G., Maloney, W.A. and McLaughlin, A. (1994b) 'Interest Groups: A Marketing Perspective on Membership', in P. Dunleavy and J. Stanyer (eds) *Contemporary Political Studies 1994: Proceedings of the Political Studies Association's 1994 Annual Conference*, Queens University, Belfast: UK Political Studies Association 1994, 545–560.

Jowell, R. and the Central Co-ordinating Team (2003) *European Social Survey 2002/2003: Technical Report*, London: Centre for Comparative Social Surveys.

Kaase, M. (1989) 'Mass Participation', in M.K. Jennings, J.W. van Deth, S.H. Barnes, D. Fuchs, F.J. Heunks, R. Inglehart, M. Kaase, H.D. Klingemann and J.J.A. Thomassen (eds) *Continuities in Political Action: A Longitudinal Study of Political Orientations in Three Western Democracies*, Berlin: Walter de Gruyter, 22–66.

Katz, R. and Mair, P. (1995) 'Changing Models of Party Organization and Party Democracy: The Emergence of the Cartel Party', *Party Politics*, 1(1): 5–28.

Katz, R.S. (1997) *Democracy and Elections*, New York: Oxford University Press.

Kääriäinen, J. and Lehtonen, H. (2006) 'The Variety of Social Capital in Welfare State Regimes: A Comparative Study of 21 Countries', *European Societies*, 8(1): 27–57.

Kirby, P., Lanyon, C., Cronin, K. and Sinclair, R. (2003) *Building a Culture of Participation Involving Children and Young People in Policy, Service Planning, Delivery and Evaluation: A Handbook*, London: Department for Education and Skills. Online, available at: www.dfes.gov.uk/listeningtolearn/downloads/BuildingaCultureofParticipation%5Bhandbook%5D.pdf (accessed 4 March 2011).

Knoke, D. (1986) 'Associations and Interest Groups', *American Sociological Review*, 12(1): 1–21.

Kohler-Koch, B., Bath, V. and Quittkat, C. (2008) 'Civil Society Organizations under the Impact of the European Commission's Consultation Regime', Chapter presented at the Connex Final Conference, Mannheim, 7–8 March.

Korpi, W. and Palme, J. (1998) 'The Paradox of Redistribution and Strategies of Equality: Welfare State Institutions, Inequality, and Poverty in the Western Countries', *American Sociological Review*, 63(5): 661–687.

Kriesi, H. (1993) *Political Mobilization and Social Change: The Dutch Case in Comparative Perspective*, Brookfield: Avebury.

Kriesi, H. (2008) 'Political Mobilisation, Political Participation and the Power of the Vote', *West European Politics*, 31(1–2): 147–168.

Kriesi, H. and Koopmans, R. (eds) (1995) *The Politics of New Social Movements in Western Europe: A Comparative Analysis*, Minneapolis, MN: University of Minnesota Press.

Künemund, H. and Rein, M. (1999) 'There is More to Receiving than Needing: Theoretical Arguments and Empirical Explorations of Crowding In and Crowding Out', *Ageing and Society*, 19(1): 93–121.

Lahusen, C. (2004) 'Joining the Cocktail-Circuit: Social Movement Organizations at the EU', *Mobilization*, 9(1): 55–71.

Lamb, R. (1996) *Promising the Earth*, London and New York: Routledge.

Lane, R.E. (1959) *Political Life: Why and How People Get Involved in Politics*, New York: The Free Press.

Langevin, P. and Chouraqui, E. (eds) (2000) *Aire métropolitaine marseillaise, encore un effort*, La Tour d'Aigues: Éditions de l'Aube.

Lansley, J. (1996) 'Membership Participation and Ideology in Large Voluntary Organizations: The Case of the National Trust', *Voluntas*, 7(3): 221–240.

Larsen, C.A. (2007) 'How Welfare Regimes Generate and Erode Social Capital: The Impact of Underclass Phenomena', *Comparative Politics*, 40(1): 83–102.

Lascoumes, P. and Le Galès, P. (2007) 'From the Nature of Instruments to the Sociology of Public Policy Instrumentation', *Governance*, 20(1): 1–21.

Laver, M. and Budge, I. (1992) *Party Policy and Government Coalitions*, London: Macmillan Press.

Laver, M. and Hunt, W.B. (1992) *Policy and Party Competition*, New York: Routledge.

Le Galès, P. (1995) 'Du Gouvernement urbain à la gouvernance urbaine', *Revue française de science politique*, 45(1): 57–95.

Le Grand, J. (1982) *The Strategy of Equality: Redistribution and the Social Services*, London: George Allen and Unwin.

Lelieveldt, H., Astudillo, J. and Stevenson, L. (2007) 'The Spectrum of Associational Activities', in W.A. Maloney and S. Roßteutscher (eds) *Social Capital and Associations in European Democracies: A Comparative Analysis*, Oxford: Routledge, 81–95.

Lijphart, A. (1998) 'The Problem of Low and Unequal Voter Turnout: And What We Can Do About It', *Political Science Series*, 54: 1–13.

Lipset, S.M., Lazarsfeld, P., Barton, A. and Linz, J. (1954) 'The Psychology of Voting: An Analysis of Political Behaviour', in G. Lindzey (ed.) *Handbook of Social Psychology*, Cambridge, MA: Addison-Wesley, 1124–1175.

Lorentzen, H. and Hustinx, L. (2007) 'Civil Involvement and Modernization', *Journal of Civil Society*, 3(2): 101–118.

Lorig, W. (2008) 'Modernisierungsdesigns für die öffentliche Verwaltung: New Public Management und Public Governance', in W. Lorig (ed.) *Moderne Verwaltung in der Bürgergesellschaft: Entwicklungslinien der Verwaltungsmodernisierung in Deutschland*, Baden-Baden: Nomos, 29–51.

Lorrain, D. and Stoker, G. (eds) (1997) *The Privatization of Urban Services in Europe*, London: Pinter.

Lowe, P. and Morrison, D. (1984) 'Bad News or Good News: Environmental Politics and the Mass Media', *Sociological Review*, 32(1): 75–90.

Lowery, D. (2007) 'Why do Organized Interests Lobby? A Multi-goal, Multi-context Theory of Lobbying?' *Polity*, 39(1): 29–54.

McLelland, A. (2002) 'Mutual Obligation and the Welfare Responsibilities of Government', *Australian Journal of Social Issues*, 37(3): 209–224.

Macnaghten, P. and Urry, J. (1998) *Contested Natures*, London: Sage.

Macpherson, S. (2008) 'Reaching the Top of the Ladder? Locating the Voices of Excluded Young People within the Participation Debate', *Policy and Politics*, 36(2): 361–379.

Mahoney, C. and Beckstrand, M.J. (2008) 'Following the Money: EU Funding of Civil Society Organizations', Chapter prepared for presentation at Cornell University's Center for European Studies, EU Research Workshop, Ithaca, NY, 25 October.

Mair, P. (2006) 'Polity Scepticism, Party Failings, and the Challenge to European Democracy', Uhlenbeck Lecture 24, Wassenaar: NIAS.

Maloney, W.A. (1999) 'Contracting Out the Participation Function: Social Capital and Checkbook Participation', in J.W. van Deth, M. Maraffi, K. Newton and P. Whiteley (eds) *Social Capital and European Democracy*, London: Routledge, 108–119.

Maloney, W.A. (2007) 'The Professionalization of Representation: Biasing Participation', in D. de Bièvre, W.A. Maloney and B. Kohler-Koch (eds) *Connex Report Series*, Mannheim: Connex, 69–95.

Maloney, W.A. (2008) 'Interest Groups, Social Capital, and Democratic Politics', in D. Castiglione, J.W. van Deth and G. Wolleb (eds) *The Handbook of Social Capital*, Oxford: Oxford University Press, 303–326.

Maloney, W.A. (2009) 'Interest Groups and the Revitalization of Democracry: Are We Expecting too Much?' *Representation*, 45(3): 277–287.

Maloney, W.A. and Roßteutscher, S. (2005) 'Welfare through Organizations', in S. Roßteutscher (ed.) *Democracy and the Role of Associations*, London: Routledge, 89–112.

Maloney, W.A. and Roßteutscher, S. (2007) 'Assessing the Significance of Associational Concerns: Leisure, Politics and Markets', in W.A. Maloney and S. Roßteutscher (eds) *Social Capital and Associations in European Democracies: A Comparative Analysis*, Oxford: Routledge, 52–78.

Maloney, W.A. and van Deth, J.W. (eds) (2008) *Civil Society and Governance in Europe: From National to International Linkages*, Cheltenham: Edward Elgar.

Manin, B. (1997) *The Principles of Representative Government*, Cambridge: Cambridge University Press.

March, J.G. and Olsen, J.P. (1998) 'The Institutional Dynamics of International Political Orders', *International Organization*, 52(4): 943–969.

Marien, S., Hooghe, M. and Quintelier, E. (2010) 'Inequalities in Non-institutionalised Forms of Political Participation: A Multi-level Analysis of 25 Countries', *Political Studies*, 58(1): 187–213.

Marks, G. and McAdam, D. (1996) 'Social Movements and the Changing Structure of Political Opportunity in the European Union', *West European Politics*, 19(2): 249–278.

Marseilles City Hall (2001) 'Marseille 2002–2012: La Culture au cœur du débat', Direction Générale des affaires culturelles, Cultural Policy Master Plan.

Marseilles City Hall (2008a) 'Visite d'une délégation du jury', Secretary General, Press Release.

Marseilles City Hall (2008b) 'Marseille Capitale européenne de la culture 2013: une délégation spéciale de fonctions est attribuée à M. Muselier', Secretary General, Press Release.

Marseilles-Provence 2013 Association (2008a) 'Marseilles-Provence 2013, Capitale européenne de la culture', Application form.

Marseilles-Provence 2013 Association (2008b) 'Economic Personalities Invited to Meet the Jury of the European Capital of Culture in 2003 on September 3rd in Marseilles', Press Release.

Marseilles-Provence Chamber of Commerce and Industry (2005) 'Marseille-Provence dans le Top 20 des métropoles européennes', *Contact*, 1: 1–16.

Marseilles-Provence Chamber of Commerce and Industry (2007a) 'Marseille-Provence Capitale européenne de la culture', *Cahiers du Top 20*, 1: 1–8.

Marseilles-Provence Chamber of Commerce and Industry (2007b) 'Proposition de Charte des entreprises soutenant Marseille-Provence 2013', Press Release.

Marseilles-Provence Chamber of Commerce and Industry (2008a) 'Benchmark sur la positionnement de Marseille-Provence', *Cahiers du Top 20*, 2: 1–8.

Marseilles-Provence Chamber of Commerce and Industry (2008b) 'Les Vrais atouts de Marseille Provence', *Cahiers du Top 20*, 4: 1–8.

Marseilles-Provence Chamber of Commerce and Industry (2008c) 'Attractivité du territoire: la CCI Marseille-Provence au coeur de l'action', Press Release.

Marseilles-Provence Chamber of Commerce and Industry (2008d) 'Tous les Députés du territoire derrière Marseille-Provence 2013', Press Release.

Marseilles-Provence Chamber of Commerce and Industry (2008e) 'La Victoire d'une méthode', Press Release.

Marsh, A. and Kaase, M. (1979) 'Background of Political Action', in S.H. Barnes, M. Kaase, K. Allerbeck, B.G. Farah, F. Heunks, R. Inglehart, M.K. Jennings, H.D. Klingemann, A. Marsh and L. Rosenmayr (eds) *Political Action: Mass Participation in Five Western Democracies*, Beverly Hills, CA: Sage, 97–136.

Marsh, D., O'Toole, T. and Jones, S. (2007) *Young People and Politics in the UK: Apathy or Alienation?* Basingstoke: Palgrave Macmillan.

Marshall, T.H. and T. Bottomore (eds) (1950) *Citizenship and Social Class*, London: Pluto Press.

Martens, K. (2005) *NGOs and the United Nations: Institutionalization, Professionalization and Adaptation*, Basingstoke: Palgrave.

Martens, K. (2006) *Nichtregierungsorganisationen (NGOs)*, Wiesbaden: Verlag für Sozialwissenschaften.

Martens, K. (2009) 'Explaining Societal Activism by Intra-organizational Factors: Professionalized Representation of Human Rights NGOs at UN Level', in C. McGrath (ed.) *Interest Groups and Lobbying, Vol. 1 The United States, and Comparative Studies*, Lewiston, NY: Edwin Mellen Press, 225–244.

Martin, I. and van Deth, J.W. (2007) 'Political Involvement', in J.W. van Deth, J.R. Montero and A. Westholm (eds) *Citizenship and Involvement in European Democracies: A Comparative Analysis*, London: Routledge, 303–333.

Matthews, H. (2001) 'Citizenship, Youth Councils and Young People's Participation', *Journal of Youth Studies*, 4(3): 299–318.

Mattina, C. (2004a) 'Mutations des resources clientélaires et construction des notabilités politiques à Marseille', *Politix*, 17(67): 129–155.

Mattina, C. (2004b) 'L'intermédiation politique des présidents de comités d'intérêt de quartier: le territoire de la notabilité', in P. Fournier and S. Mazzella (eds) *Marseille entre ville et port: Les destins de la rue de la République*, Paris: La Découverte, 82–96.

Mécènes du Sud (2008) 'Les Mécènes et la fondation de l'association'. Online, available at: www.mecenesdusud.fr (accessed 16 June 2010).

Meyer, D. and Tarrow, S. (1998) 'A Movement Society: Contentious Politics for a New Century', in D. Meyer and S. Tarrow (eds) *The Social Movement Society: Contentious Politics for a New Century*, Lanham, MD: Rowman & Littlefield, 1–28.

Micheletti, M. (2003) *Political Virtue and Shopping: Individuals, Consumerism and Collective Action*, New York: Palgrave Macmillan.

Micheletti, M. and McFarland, A. (eds) (2011) *Creative Participation: Responsibility-taking in the Political World*, Boulder, CO: Paradigm.

Micheletti, M. and Stolle, D. (2007) 'Mobilizing Consumers to take Responsibility for Global Social Justice', *Annals, AAPSS* (May): 157–175.

Micheletti, M., Follesdal, A. and Stolle, D. (eds) (2003) *Politics, Products, and Markets:*

Exploring Political Consumerism Past and Present, New Brunswick, NJ: Transaction Press.
Michels, R. ([1914] 1959) *Les parties politiques: Essais sur les tendances oligarchiques des démocraties*, Paris: Flammarion.
Michels, R. ([1915] 1959) *Political Parties: A Sociological Study of the Oligarchical Tendencies of Modern Democracy*, New York: Dover.
Middendorp, C.P. (1978) *Progressiveness and Conservatism: The Fundamental Dimensions of Ideological Controversy and their Relationship to Social Class*, The Hague: Mouton.
Milbrath, L.W. (1965) *Political Participation: How and Why do People get Involved in Politics?* Chicago, IL: Rand McNally & Company.
Miller. M.K. (2009) 'Membership has its Privileges: How Voluntary Groups Exacerbate the Participatory Bias', *Political Research Quarterly*, 63(2): 356–372.
Ministry of Culture and Communication (2008) 'Marseille, Capitale européenne de la culture 2013', Press Release.
Minkoff, D., Aisenbrey, S. and Agnone, J. (2008) 'Organizational Diversity in the U.S. Advocacy Sector', *Social Problems*, 55(4): 525–548.
Mitchell, D. (2005) 'The S.U.V. Model of Citizenship: Floating Bubbles, Buffer Zones, and the Rise of the "Purely Atomic" Individual', *Political Geography*, 24(1): 77–100.
Mitlin, D. (2008) 'With and Beyond the State: Co-production as a Route to Political Influence, Power and Transformation for Grassroots Organizations', *Environment and Urbanization*, 20(2): 339–360.
Moore, K. (1996) 'Organizing Integrity: American Science and the Creation of Public Interest Organizations, 1955–1975', *American Journal of Sociology*, 101(6): 1592–1627.
Möller-Bock, M. (2007) *Selbsthilfeförderung durch die Bundesländer in Deutschland im Jahr 2007*, Berlin: NAKOS.
Muller, P. (2007) 'La Synthèse d'un politiste: six questions en suspens', in A. Faure and E. Négrier (eds) *Les Politi-ques publiques à l'épreuve de l'action locale: Critiques de la territorialisation*, Paris: L'Harmattan.
Muncie, J. (2006) 'Governing Young People: Coherence and Contradiction in Contemporary Youth Justice', *Critical Social Policy*, 26(4): 770–793.
Mundo, P. (1992) *Interest Groups: Cases and Characteristics*, Chicago, IL: Nelson Hall.
Nabben, R. (2007) 'The Victorian Local Government Youth Charter: Opportunities and Dilemmas', *Youth Studies Australia*, 26(2): 27–34.
Nagel, J. (1987) *Participation*, Upper Saddle River: NJ: Prentice-Hall.
National Youth Council of Ireland (2001) 'Taking the Initiative: Ireland'. Online, available at: http://cypi.carnegieuktrust.org.uk/files/IrelandFullreport_000.pdf (accessed 4 March 2011).
Négrier, E. (1999) 'The Changing Role of French Local Government', *West European Politics*, 22(4): 120–140.
Négrier, E. (2005) *La Question métropolitaine: les politiques à l'épreuve du changement d'échelle territoriale*, Grenoble: Presses Universitaires de Grenoble.
Negrine, R. (2008) *The Transformation of Political Communication*, Basingstoke: Palgrave.
Norris, P. (1999) 'Conclusions: The Growth of Critical Citizens and its Consequences', in P. Norris (ed.) *Critical Citizens: Global Support for Democratic Governance*, Oxford: Oxford University Press, 257–271.
Norris, P. (2002) *Democratic Phoenix: Reinventing Political Activism*, Cambridge: Cambridge University Press.

Nownes, A.J. and Neeley, G. (1996) 'Public Interest Group Entrepreneurship and Theories of Group Mobilization', *Political Research Quarterly*, 49(1): 119–146.
Odegard, G. (2007) 'Political Socialization and Influence at the Mercy of Politicians', *Young: Nordic Journal of Youth Research*, 15(3): 273–297.
OECD (2007) *Social Expenditures, 1980–2003: Interpretative Guide of SOCX*. Online, available at: http://stats.oecd.org/OECDStatDownloadFiles/OECDSOCX2007 Interpretative-Guide_En.pdf (accessed 11 November 2008).
Offerlé, M. (2009) *Sociologie des organization patronales*, Paris: La Découverte.
Olive, M. and Oppenheim, J.-P. (2001) 'La Communauté urbaine de Marseille, un fragment métropolitain', in E. Négrier and F. Baraize (eds) *L'Invention politique de l'agglomération*, Paris: L'Harmattan, 31–66.
Olson, M. (1965) *The Logic of Collective Action*, Cambridge, MA: Harvard University Press.
Olson, M. (1971) *The Logic of Collective Action* (2nd edn), Cambridge, MA: Harvard University Press.
Oppen, M. and Sack, D. (2008) 'Governance und Performanz: Motive, Formen und Effekte lokaler Public Private Partnerships', in G.F. Schuppert and M. Zürn (eds) *Governance in einer sich wandelnden Welt*, Wiesbaden: VS Verlag, 259–281.
Osborne, S.P. (ed.) (2008) *The Third Sector in Europe: Prospects and Challenges*, London: Routledge.
Ostrogorski, M. ([1912] 1993) *La démocratie et l'organisation des partis politiques*, Paris: Calman-Levy (Fayard 1993).
Pammett, J.H. (2009) 'Participation and the Good Citizen', in J. DeBardeleben and J.H. Pammett (eds) *Activating the Citizen: Dilemmas of Participation in Europe and Canada*, Basingstoke: Palgrave, 197–213.
Panebianco, A. (1988) *Political Parties: Organization and Power*, Cambridge: Cambridge University Press.
Passey, A. and Lyons, M. (2005) 'Voluntary Associations and Political Participation', in S. Wilson, G. Meagher, R. Gibson, D. Denemark and M. Western (eds) *Australian Social Attitudes*, Sydney: UNSW Press, 62–81.
Pattie, C., Seyd, P. and Whiteley, P. (2004) *Citizenship in Britain: Values, Participation and Democracy*, Cambridge: Cambridge University Press.
Paxton, P. (2002) 'Social Capital and Democracy: An Interdependent Relationship', *American Sociological Review*, 67(2): 254–277.
Pestoff, V. (2010) 'Relationship between Volunteering and Co-production in Europe', Paper presented at ISTR 9th International Conference in Istanbul, July.
Pestoff, V. and Brandsen, T. (eds) (2008) *Co-production: The Third Sector and the Delivery of Public Services*, London: Routledge.
Pevehouse, J.C. (2005) *Democracy from Above: Regional Organizations and Democratization*, Cambridge: Cambridge University Press.
Pinker, S. (2002) *The Blank Slate: The Modern Denial of Human Nature*, London: Penguin.
Pinson, G. and Sala Pala, V. (2007) 'Peut-on vraiment se passer de l'entretien en sociologie de l'action publique?' *Revue française de science politique*, 57(5): 555–597.
Pinson, G. (2006) 'Projets de ville et gouvernance urbaine, pluralisation des espaces politiques et recomposition d'une action collective dans les villes européennes', *Revue française de science politique*, 56(4): 619–651.
Pinson, G. (2009) *Gouverner par projet: Urbanisme et gouvernance des villes européennes*, Paris: Presses de Sciences Po.

Plows, A. (2006) 'Blackwood Roads Protest 2004: An Emerging (Re)cycle of UK Eco-action?' *Environmental Politics*, 15(3): 462–472.
Poppelaars, C. (2009) *Steering a Course Between Friends and Foes: Why Bureaucrats Interact with Interest Groups*, Delft: Eburon.
Price, S. (2011) 'How the Environmental Movement influenced Climate Change Debates and Action in Britain between 1987 and 2008', PhD thesis, School of Social Policy, Sociology and Social Research, University of Kent, Canterbury.
Print, M., Saha, L. and Edwards, K. (2004) 'Youth Electoral Study Report 1: Enrolment and Voting'. Online, available at: www.aec.gov.au/About_AEC/Publications/youth_study/youth_study_1/index.htm (accessed 15 December 2010).
Putnam, R.D (1995) 'Bowling Alone: America's Declining Social Capital', *Journal of Democracy*, 6(1): 65–78.
Putnam, R.D. (2000) *Bowling Alone: The Collapse and Revival of American Community*, New York: Simon & Schuster.
Putnam, R.D., Leonardi, R. and Nanetti, R. (1993) *Making Democracy Work: Civic Traditions in Modern Italy*, Princeton, NJ: Princeton University Press.
Quintelier, E. (2008) 'Who is Politically Active: The Athlete, the Scouts Member or the Environmental Activist? Young People, Voluntary Engagement and Political Participation', *Acta Sociologica*, 51(4): 355–370.
Quintelier, E. (2009) 'Political Participation in Late Adolescence: Political Socialization Patterns in the Belgian Political Panel Survey', PhD Dissertation, University of Leuven, Leuven.
Rabe-Hesketh, S. and Skrondal, A. (2006) 'Multilevel Modelling of Complex Survey Data', *Journal of the Royal Statistical Society*, 169(4): 805–827.
Rawcliffe, P. (1998) *Environmental Pressure Groups in Transition*, Manchester: Manchester University Press.
Richardson, J.J. (1995) 'The Market for Political Activism: Interest Groups as a Challenge to Political Parties', *West European Politics*, 18(1): 116–139.
Robert, R. (2004) 'Reform der Kommunalfinanzen zwischen Flickschusterei und großem Wurf', in R. Robert and P. Kevenhörster (eds) *Kommunen in Not: Aufgaben- und Finanzverwaltung in Deutschland*, Münster: Waxmann, 19–73.
Roller, E., Brettschneider, F. and van Deth, J.W. (eds) (2006) *Jugend und Politik: 'Voll normal!' Der Beitrag der politischen Soziologie zur Jugendforschung*, Wiesbaden: VS Verlag für Sozialwissenschaften.
Roncayolo, M. (1990) *L'Imaginaire de Marseille: port, ville, pôle*, Marseille: Editions de la Chambre de Commerce de Marseille.
Ronit, K. and Schneider, V. (2000) *Private Organizations in Global Politics*, London: Routledge.
Rootes, C. (2003a) 'Britain', in C. Rootes (ed.) *Environmental Protest in Western Europe*, Oxford: Oxford University Press, 20–58.
Rootes, C. (2003b) 'The Resurgence of Protest and the Revitalization of British Democracy', in P. Ibarra (ed.) *Social Movements and Democracy*, New York: Palgrave Macmillan, 137–168.
Rootes, C. (2005) 'A Limited Transnationalization? The British Environmental Movement', in D. della Porta and S. Tarrow (eds) *Transnational Protest and Global Activism*, Lanham, MD: Rowman & Littlefield, 21–43.
Rootes, C. (2006) 'Facing South? British Environmental Movement Organizations and the Challenge of Globalization', *Environmental Politics*, 15(5): 768–786.

Rootes, C. (2007) 'Acting Locally: The Character, Contexts and Significance of Local Environmental Mobilizations', *Environmental Politics*, 16(5): 722–741.

Rootes, C. (2009a) 'Environmentalism: Environmental NGOs and the Environmental Movement in England', in N. Crowson, M. Hilton and J. McKay (eds) *NGOs in Contemporary Britain: Non-state Actors in Society and Politics since 1945*, Basingstoke: Palgrave Macmillan, 201–221.

Rootes, C. (2009b) 'More Acted upon than Acting? Campaigns against Waste Incinerators in England', *Environmental Politics*, 18(6): 869–895.

Rootes, C. (2012) 'From Local Conflict to National Issue: When and How Environmental Campaigns Succeed in Transcending the Local', *Social Movement Studies*, 11(3) [forthcoming].

Rosamond, B. (2007) 'The Political Sciences of European Integration: Disciplinary History and EU Studies', in K.E. Jorgensen, M.A. Pollack and B. Rosamond (eds) *Handbook of European Union Politics*, London: Sage, 7–30.

Rose, R. (2009) 'Bottom Up, Civil Society and Top Down Models of Representing Europeans', Paper presented at 'Bringing Civil Society In: The European Union and the Rise of Representative Democracy' Conference, Robert Schuman Centre for Advanced Studies, European University Institute, Centre d'études européennes de Science Po Paris, Florence, 13–14 March.

Rosenstone, S.J. and Hansen, J.M. (1993) *Mobilization, Participation, and Democracy in America*, New York: Macmillan.

Rossi, F. and della Porta, D. (2009) 'Social Movement, Trade Unions and Advocacy Networks', in C. Haerpfer, P. Bernhagen, R. Inglehart and C. Welzel (eds) *Democratization*, Oxford: Oxford University Press, 172–186.

Roßteutscher, S. (2004) 'Die Rückkehr der Tugend?' in J.W. van Deth (ed.) *Deutschland in Europa*, Wiesbaden: VS-Verlag, 175–200.

Rothstein, B. (2001) 'Social Capital and the Social Democratic Welfare State', *Politics and Society*, 29(2): 207–241.

Royal Society for the Protection of Birds (RSPB) (2004) 'Introducing the RSBP'. Online, available at: www.rspb.org.uk/Images/Introducing%20the%20RSPBtcm5-58645.pdf (accessed 20 July 2006).

Rozenblat, C. and Cicille, P. (2003) *Les Villes européennes: Analyse comparative*, Paris: La Documentation Française.

Rucht, D. (1996) 'The Impact of National Contexts on Social Movement Structures: A Cross-movement and Cross-national Comparison', in D. McAdam, J.D. McCarthy and M.N. Zald (eds) *Comparative Perspectives on Social Movements: Political Opportunities, Mobilizing Structures, and Cultural Framings*, Cambridge: Cambridge University Press, 185–204.

Rucht, D. (2007) 'The Spread of Protest Politics', in R.J. Dalton and H.D. Klingemann (eds) *The Oxford Handbook of Political Behavior*, Oxford: Oxford University Press, 708–723.

Rucht, D., Lattert, B. and Rink, D. (1997) *Soziale Bewegugen auf dem Weg zur Institutionalisierung*, Frankfurt: Campus.

Ruiter, S. and De Graf, N.D. (2006) 'National Context, Religiosity, and Volunteering: Results from 53 Countries', *American Sociological Review*, 71(2): 191–210.

Sack, D. (2009a) 'Zwischen Usurpation und Synergie: Motive, Formen und Entwicklungsprozesse von Public Private Partnership', *Zeitschrift für Sozialreform*, 55(3): 211–230.

Sack, D. (2009b) *Governance und Politics: Die Institutionalisierung öffentlich-privater Partnerschaften in Deutschland*, Baden-Baden: Nomos.

Salamon, L.M. and Sokolowski, W.S. (2003) 'Institutional Roots of Volunteering', in P. Dekker and L. Halman (eds) *The Values of Volunteering: Cross-cultural Perspectives*, New York: Kluwer Academic/Plenum Publishers, 71–90.

Salisbury, R.H. (1992) *Interest and Institutions: Substance and Structure in American Politics*, Pittsburgh, PA: University of Pittsburgh Press.

Sanchez-Salgado, R. (2007) *Comment l'Europe construit la société civile*, Paris: Dalloz.

Sanchez-Salgado, R. (2009) 'How the EU Creates its Own Protest', Paper presented at 'Bringing Civil Society In: The European Union and the Rise of Representative Democracy' Conference, Robert Schuman Centre for Advanced Studies, European University Institute, Centre d'études européennes de Science Po Paris, Florence, 13–14 March.

Sanders, L. (1997) 'Against Deliberation', *Political Theory*, 25(3): 347–376.

Sani, G. and Sartori, G. (1983) 'Polarization, Fragmentation and Competition in Western Democracy', in H. Daalder and P. Mair (eds) *Western European Party Systems: Continuity and Change*, London: Sage, 307–340.

Sanmarco, P. (2000) *Marseille Capitale?* Aix-en-Provence: Edisud.

Sartori, G. (1976) *Parties and Party Systems*, Cambridge: Cambridge University Press.

Saunders, C. (2007) 'The Local and the National: Relationships between Local and National Environmental Organizations in London', *Environmental Politics*, 15(5): 724–764.

Saunders, C. (2008) 'The Stop Climate Chaos Coalition: Climate Change as a Development Issue', *Third World Quarterly*, 29(8): 1509–1526.

Saunders, C. and Price, S. (2009) 'One Person's Eu-topia, Another's Hell: Climate Camp as a Heterotopia', *Environmental Politics*, 18(1): 117–122.

Saurugger, S. (2006) 'The Professionalisation of Interest Representation: A Problem for the Participation of Civil Society in EU Governance?' in S. Smismans (ed.) *European Governance and Civil Society*, Cheltenham: Edward Elgar, 260–276.

Saurugger, S. (2007) 'Democratic Misfit? Conceptions of Civil Society Participation in France and the European Union', *Political Studies*, 55(2): 384–404.

Saurugger, S. (2008) 'Interest Groups and Democracy in the European Union', *West European Politics*, 31(6): 1274–1291.

Saurugger, S. (2010) 'The Social Construction of the Participatory Turn: The Emergence of a Norm in the European Union', *European Journal of Political Research*, 49(4): 471–495.

Savelsberg, H. and Martin-Giles, B. (2008) 'Young People on the Margins: Australian Studies of Social Exclusion', *Journal of Youth Studies*, 11(1): 17–31.

Savitch, H. and Kantor, P. (2002) *Cities in the International Marketplace: The Political Economy of Urban Development in North America and Western Europe*, Princeton, NJ: Princeton University Press.

Sawer, M. (2002) 'Governing for the Mainstream: Implications for Community Representation', *Australian Journal of Public Administration*, 61(1): 39–49.

Scheepers, P. and Te Grotenhuis, M. (2005) 'Who Cares for the Poor in Europe? Micro and Macro Determinants for Alleviating Poverty in 15 European Countries', *European Sociological Review*, 21(5): 453–465.

Schier, S. (2001) *By Invitation Only: The Rise of Exclusive Politics in the United States*, Pittsburgh, PA: University of Pittsburgh Press.

Schinkel, W. (2008) 'Contexts of Anxiety: The Moral Panic over "Senseless Violence" in the Netherlands', *Current Sociology*, 56(5): 735–756.

Schlozman, K.L., Verba, S. and Brady, H.E. (1999) 'Civic Participation and the Equality

Problem', in T. Skocpol and M.P. Fiorina (eds) *Civic Engagement in American Democracy*, Washington, DC: Brookings Institution, 427–460.

Schmid, G. (1984) 'The Political Economy of Labor Market Discrimination: A Theoretical and Comparative Analysis of Sex Discrimination', in G. Schmid and R. Weitzel (eds) *Sex Discrimination and Equal Opportunity: The Labour Market and Employment Policy*, Aldershot: Gower Publishing Company, 264–308.

Schumpeter, J.A. (1942) *Capitalism, Socialism and Democracy*, New York: Harper & Brothers.

Scott, A. (1998) *Regions and the World Economy: The Coming Shape of Global Production, Competition and Political Order*, Oxford: Oxford University Press.

Scruggs, L. and Allan, J. (2006) 'Welfare-state Decommodification in 18 OECD Countries: A Replication and Revision', *Journal of European Social Policy*, 16(1): 55–72.

Shaiko, R.G. (1991) 'More Bang for the Buck: The New Era of Full-Service Public Interest Organizations', in A.J. Cigler and B.A. Loomis (eds) *Interest Group Politics*, 3rd edn, Washington, DC: Congressional Quarterly Press, 109–130.

Shier, H. (2001) 'Pathways to Participation: Openings, Opportunities and Obligations. A New Model for Enhancing Children's Participation in Decision-making, in line with Article 12.1 of the United Nations Convention on the Rights of the Child', *Children and Society*, 15(2): 107–117.

Shingles, R.D. (1981) 'Black Consciousness and Political Participation: The Missing Link', *American Political Science Review*, 75(1): 76–91.

Shirky, C. (2008) *Here Comes Everybody: The Power of Organizing without Organizations*, New York: Penguin.

Siméant, J. (2005) 'What is Going Global? The Internationalization of French NGOs', *Review of International Political Economy*, 12(5): 851–883.

Siméant, J. and Dauvin, P. (2002) *Le travail humanitaire: les acteurs des ONG, du siège au terrain*, Paris: Presses de Sciences Po.

Singer, E. and Chandra-Shekeran, K. (2006) 'Leading Themselves: Refugee Youth Participation – Learning and Challenges', *Just Policy*, 39: 49–53.

Skocpol, T. (1999). 'How Americans became Civic', in T. Skocpol, and M.P. Fiorina (eds) *Civic Engagement in American Democracy*. New York: Russell Sage Foundation, 27–80.

Skocpol, T. (2003) *Diminished Democracy: From Membership to Management in American Civic Life*, Norman, OK: University of Oklahoma Press.

Snijders, T.A.B. and Bosker, R.J. (2004) *Multilevel Analysis: An Introduction to Basic and Advanced Multilevel Modelling*, London: Sage.

Snow, D.A, Zurcher, L.A. Jr and Ekland-Olson, S. (1980) 'Social Networks and Social Movements: A Microstructural Approach to Differential Recruitment', *American Sociological Review*, 45(5): 787–801.

Solt, F. (2008) 'Economic Inequality and Democratic Political Engagement', *American Journal of Political Science*, 52(1): 48–60.

Stadelmann-Steffen, I. (2011) Social Volunteering in Welfare States: Where Crowding out should Occur, *Political Studies*, 59(1): 135–155.

Staggenborg, S. (1997) 'The Consequences of Professionalization and Formalization in the Pro-choice Movement', in D. McAdam and D.A. Snow (eds) *Social Movements: Readings on their Emergence, Mobilization, and Dynamics*, Los Angeles, CA: Roxbury, 421–439.

Steenbergen, M.R. and Jones, B.S. (2002) 'Modelling Multilevel Data Structures', *American Journal of Political Science*, 46(1): 218–237.

Steffek, J., Kissling, C. and Nanz, P. (2007) *Civil Society Participation in European and Global Governance: A Cure for the Democratic Deficit?* Basingstoke: Palgrave Macmillan.
Stoker, G. (1998) 'Governance as Theory: Five Propositions', *International Social Science Journal*, 50(155): 17–28.
Stoker, G. (2006a) *Why Politics Matters*, Basingstoke: Palgrave Macmillan.
Stoker, G. (2006b) 'Politics in Mass Democracies: Destined to Disappoint?' *Representation*, 42(3): 181–194.
Stolle, D., Hooghe, M. and Micheletti, M. (2005) 'Politics in the Supermarket: Political Consumerism as a Form of Political Participation', *International Political Science Review*, 26(3): 245–269.
Stone, D. (1996) *Capturing the Political Imagination: Think Tanks and the Policy Process*, London: Frank Cass.
Streeck, W. and Schmitter, P. (1999) 'The Organization of Business Interests: Studying the Associative Action of Business in Advanced Industrial Societies', *MPIfG Discussion Chapter* 99/1, Köln: Max-Planck-Institut für Gesellschaftsforschung.
Streeck, W., Grote, J., Schneider, V. and Visser, J. (eds) (2006) *Governing Interests*, London and New York: Routledge.
Strolovitch, D.Z. (2006) 'Do Interest Groups Represent the Disadvantaged? Advocacy at the Intersection of Race, Class and Gender', *Journal of Politics*, 68(4): 894–910.
Strømsnes, K., Selle P. and Grunstad, G. (2009) 'Environmentalism Between State and Local Community: Why Greenpeace Failed in Norway', *Environmental Politics*, 18(3): 391–407.
Sudbery, I. (2003) 'Bridging the Legitimacy Gap in the EU: Can Civil Society help to bring the Union Closer to its Citizens?' *Collegium*, 26: 75–95.
Szerszynski, B. (1991) *Environmentalism, the Mass Media and Public Opinion*, Lancaster: Lancaster University.
Theiss-Morse, E. (1993) 'Conceptualisations of Good Citizenship and Political Participation', *Political Behavior*, 15(4): 355–380.
Theiss-Morse, E. and Hibbing, J.R. (2005) 'Citizenship and Civic Engagement', *American Review of Political Science*, 8: 227–249.
Teorell, J., Sum, P. and Tobiasen, M. (2007) 'Participation and Political Equality: An Assessment of Large-Scale Democracy', in J.W. van Deth, J.R. Montero and A. Westholm (eds) *Citizenship and Involvement in European Democracies: A Comparative Analysis*, London: Routledge, 384–414.
Tocqueville, A. de (1835 [1969]) *Democracy in America*, edited by J.P. Mayer, New York: Harper Perennial.
Topf, R. (1995) 'Beyond Electoral Participation', in H.D. Klingemann and D. Fuchs (eds) *Citizens and the State*, Oxford: Oxford University Press, 52–91.
UNDP (2004) 'Human Development Report'. Online, available at: http://hdr.undp.org/en/reports/global/hdr2004 (accessed 24 June 2010).
Union of International Associations (2004) 'Yearbook of International Organizations: Guide to Civil Society Networks'. Online, available at: www.uia.be (accessed 24 June 2010).
van der Brug, W. (1997) *Where's the Party? Voters' Perceptions of Party Positions*, Amsterdam: Thesis.
van der Eijk, C. and Niemöller, B. (1983) *Electoral Change in the Netherlands: Empirical Results and Methods of Measurement*, Amsterdam: CT Press.
van der Heijden, H. (1997) 'Political Opportunity Structure and the Institutionalisation of the Environmental Movement', *Environmental Politics*, 6(4): 25–50.

van der Meer, T.W.G., van Deth, J.W. and Scheepers, P.L. (2009a) 'The Politicized Participant: Ideology and Political Action in 20 Democracies', *Comparative Political Studies*, 42(11): 1426–1457.

van der Meer, T.W.G, te Grotenhuis, M. and Scheepers, P.L. (2009b) 'Three Types of Voluntary Associations in Comparative Perspective: Applying a Typology of Associations to Associational Involvement Research in 21 European Countries', *Journal of Civil Society*, 5(3): 227–241.

van Deth, J.W. (ed.) (1997) *Private Groups and Public Life: Social Participation, Voluntary Associations, and Political Involvement in Representative Democracies*, London: Routledge.

van Deth, J.W. (2001) 'Studying Political Participation: Towards a Theory of Everything?' Paper delivered at the Joint Sessions of Workshops of the European Consortium for Political Research, Grenoble, 6–11 April.

van Deth, J.W. (2003) 'Vergleichende politische Partizipationsforschung', in D. Berg-Schlosser and F. Müller-Rommel (eds) *Vergleichende Politikwissenschaft*, Opladen: Leske and Budrich, 167–187.

van Deth, J.W. (2007a) 'Norms of Citizenship', in R.J. Dalton and H.D. Klingemann (eds) *The Oxford Handbook of Political Behaviour*, Oxford: Oxford University Press, 402–417.

van Deth, J.W. (2007b) 'Creative Participation: Creative Democracy?' Paper prepared for delivery at the third Karlstad Seminar on Studying Political Action, Karlstad (Sweden), 18–20 October.

van Deth, J.W. (2009) 'The "Good European Citizen": Congruence and Consequences of Different Points of View', *European Political Science*, 8(2): 175–189.

van Deth, J.W. (2010) 'Is Creative Participation Good for Democracy?' in M. Micheletti and A.S. McFarland (eds) *Creative Participation: Responsibility-taking in the Political World*, Boulder, CO: Paradigm, 148–172.

van Deth, J.W. and Zmerli, S. (eds) (2010) 'Civicness, Equality, and Democracy: A "Dark Side" of Social Capital?' Special Issue of the *American Behavioral Scientist*, 53(5): 631–639.

van Oorschot, W. and Arts, W. (2005) 'The Social Capital of European Welfare States: The Crowding Out Hypothesis Revisited', *Journal of European Social Policy*, 15(1): 5–26.

Vauzelle, M. (2008) 'Marseille-Provence sera capitale européenne de la culture 2013'. Online, available at: http://michelvauzelle.regionpaca.fr/index.php/tag/culture/ (accessed 16 June 2010).

Verba, S. (1961) *Small Groups and Political Behavior: A Study of Leadership*, Princeton, NJ: Princeton University Press.

Verba, S. (2006) 'Fairness, Equality and Democracy: Three Big Words', *Social Research*, 73(2): 499–540.

Verba, S. and Nie, N.H. (1972) *Participation in America: Political Democracy and Social Equality*, New York: Harper & Row.

Verba, S., Nie, N.H. and Kim, J.-O. (1971) *The Modes of Democratic Participation: A Cross-national Comparison*, Beverly Hills, CA: Sage.

Verba, S., Nie, N.H. and Kim, J.-O. (1978) *Participation and Political Equality: A Seven-nation Comparison*, Cambridge: Cambridge University Press.

Verba, S., Schlozman, K.L. and Brady, H. (1995) *Voice and Equality: Civic Voluntarism in American Politics*, Cambridge, MA: Harvard University Press.

Verhulst, J. and Walgrave, S. (2009) 'The First Time is the Hardest? A Cross-national

and Cross-issue Comparison of First-time Protest Participants', *Political Behaviour*, 31(3): 455–484.
Viard, J. (ed.) (1994) *La Métropole inachevée: Les ferments d'une démarche de prospective partagée*, La Tour d'Aigues: Éditions de l'Aube.
Vibert, F. (2007) *The Rise of the Unelected. Democracy and the New Separation of Powers*, Cambridge: Cambridge University Press.
Vinken, H. and Diepstraten, I. (2010) 'Buy Nothing Day in Japan: Individualizing Life Courses and Forms of Engagement', *Young: Nordic Journal of Youth Research*, 18(1): 55–76.
Visier, C. (2005) 'La Méditerranée, d'une idéologie militante à une vulgate consensuelle', *Sciences de la société*, 65: 145–163.
Vromen, A. (2008) 'Building Virtual Spaces: Young People, Participation and the Internet', *Australian Journal of Political Science*, 43(1): 79–97.
Wajcman, J. (2008) 'Life in the Fast Lane? Towards a Sociology of Technology and Time', *British Journal of Sociology*, 59(1): 56–77.
Walker, J. (1991) *Mobilizing Interest Groups in America: Patrons, Professions and Social Movements*, Ann Arbor, MI: University of Michigan Press.
Walzer, M. (1992) 'The Civil Society Argument', in C. Mouffe (ed.) *Dimensions of Radical Democracy: Pluralism, Citizenship, Community*, London: Verso, 89–107.
Warleigh, A. (2001) 'Europeanizing Civil Society: NGOs as Agents of Political Sozialisation', *Journal of Common Market Studies*, 39(4): 619–639.
Warren, M.E. (1996) 'What Should We Expect from More Democracy?' *Political Theory*, 24(2): 241–270.
Warren, M.E. (2001) *Democracy and Association*, Princeton, NJ: Princeton University Press.
Wattenberg, M. and Dalton, R. (eds) (2002) *Parties Without Partisans: Political Change in Advanced Industrial Democracies*, Oxford: Oxford University Press.
Webb, P. (1994) 'Party Organizational Change in Britain: The Iron Law of Centralization?' in R.S. Katz and P. Mair (eds) *How Parties Organize*, London: Sage, 109–133.
Weber, M. (1963) *Le savant et le politique*, Paris: Plon.
Weisbrod, B. (1978) *The Voluntary Independent Sector*, Lexington, MA: Lexington Books.
Welzel, C., Inglehart, R. and Deutsch, F. (2005) 'Social Capital, Voluntary Associations and Collective Action: Which Aspects of Social Capital have the Greatest "Civic" payoff?' *Journal of Civil Society*, 1(2): 121–146.
White, R. (2007) 'Paradoxes of Youth Participation: Political Activism and Youth Disenchantment', in L. Saha, M. Print and K. Edwards (eds) *Youth and Political Participation*, Rotterdam: Sense Publishers, 65–78.
White, R. and Wyn, J. (2008) *Youth and Society: Exploring the Dynamics of Youth Experience*, 2nd edn, Melbourne: Oxford University Press.
Whiteley, P.F. and Seyd, P. (2002) *High-intensity Participation: The Dynamics of Party Activism in Britain*, Ann Arbor, MI: University of Michigan Press.
Wierenga, A. (2003) 'Sharing a New Story: Young People in Decision-making', The Foundation for Young Australians and the Australian Youth Research Centre, University of Melbourne. Online, available at: www.youngaustralians.org/library/items/2008/05/207932-upload-00001.pdf (accessed 4 March 2011).
Wilson, J. (2000) 'Volunteering', *Annual Review of Sociology*, 26: 215–240.
Wilson, J. and Musick, M. (1997) 'Who Cares? Toward an Integrated Theory of Volunteer Work', *American Sociological Review*, 62(5): 694–713.

World Bank (2006) 'World Development Indicators Database'. Online, available at: http://devdata.worldbank.org/data-query (accessed on 24 June 2010).

Zald, M.N. and McCarthy, J.D. (eds) ([1987] 1994a) *Social Movements in an Organizational Society: Collected Essays*, New Brunswick: Transaction Publishers.

Zald, M.N. and McCarthy, J.D. ([1987] 1994b) 'Resource Mobilization and Social Movements: A Partial Theory', in N.Z. Mayer and J.D. McCarthy (eds) *Social Movements in an Organizational Society: Collected Essays*, New Brunswick: Transaction Publishers, 15–42.

Zalio, P.-P. (1999) *Les Grandes familles de Marseille au XXe siècle: Enquête sur l'identité économique d'un territoire portuaire*, Paris: Belin.

Zalio, P.-P. (2004) 'D'impossibles notables: Les grandes familles de Marseille face à la politique (1860–1970)', *Politix*, 16(65): 93–118.

Zimmer, A. and Freise, M. (2008) 'Bringing Society Back In: Civil Society, Social Capital and the Third Sector', in W.A. Maloney and J.W. van Deth (eds) *Civil Society and Governance in Europe: From National to International Linkages*, Cheltenham: Edward Elgar, 19–42.

Zimmer, A., Appel, A., Dittrich, C., Lange, C., Sittermann, B., Stallmann, F. and Kendall, J. (2009) 'Germany: On the Social Policy Centrality of the Free Welfare Associations', in J. Kendall (ed.) *Handbook on Third Sector Policy in Europe: Multi-level Processes and Organized Civil Society*, Cheltenham: Edward Elgar, 21–42.

Zimmer, A., Gärtner, J., Priller, E., Rawert, P., Sachße, C., Strachwitz, R.G. and Walz, R. (2004) 'The Legacy of Subsidiarity: The Nonprofit Sector in Germany', in A. Zimmer and E. Priller (eds) *Future of Civil Society: Making Central European Nonprofit-Organizations Work*, Wiesbaden: VS Verlag, 681–711.

Zukin, C., Keeter, S., Andolina, M., Jenkins, K. and Delli Carpini, M.X. (2006) *A New Engagement? Political Participation, Civic Life, and the Changing American Citizen*, Oxford: Oxford University Press.

Index

Page numbers in *italics* denote tables, those in **bold** denote figures.

activation 159
activism 126, 130, 134–5, 136
age 170
airports, environmental activism 58–9
AirportWatch 58
Australia *see* youth participation study
Australian Youth Affairs Coalition (AYAC) 229
Australian Youth Forum (AYF) 228–9
Australian Youth Policy and Action Committee (AYPAC) 220
autonomy 25–6, 78

Bang, H. 214–15
behavioural stability 204
Belgian Political Panel Survey (BPPS) 200–1
Belgium **123**, **125**, **128**, **131**, **143**, 166, 198, 201
boycotting 118–19, 121–2, 124–6, 132, 134, 135
budget deficits 25
business interests, and civil society 78
business leaders, social networks of 33
business-organized mobilization 39
buycotting 132, 134, 135

Camp for Climate Action 55–6, 58
Campaign against Climate Change 54–5, 59
canvassing 105–8
Carbon Rationing Action Groups (CRAGs) 59–60
career opportunities, civil society 75
career patterns, civil society 81
Chamber of Commerce 28
chequebook participation 2, 77, 85–6, 88, 94, 109, 116, 159, 179
chuggers 107–8
citizens, welfare co-production 15

citizenship 2, 116, 126–35, 169
City of Culture *see* Marseilles
civic engagement 139–41, 141–2, 146–7, **147**, 153–4
civic trinity 1
civil society 3–4, 64, 69–70, 82; *see also* EU civil society
civil society organizations (CSOs) 15–16, 20–2, 26, 69–70; *see also* EU civil society
climate change 53–60, 63, 66
Climate Change Act (UK) 61
Climate Outreach and Information Network (COIN) 60
collective mobilization 44
collectivism 127, 132, 134, 136, 204
consultation 214–15, 226–7
consumerism, political 124
consuming public discourse 217–18
contact, with members 92–3
contracting out 116, 178–9
convergence, environmental activism 65–7
cooperation, pressures on 15–16
COP6 54
crowding in 144
crowding out 142, 143–4
cultural actors, Marseilles-Provence 2013 39–40
cultural territory building, Marseilles 43
culture, and metropolitanization 30–2
customers, use of term 21

DATAR report 30, 35
decentralization, Marseilles 32
democracy 1, 69–70, 82, 231; *see also* European democracy; participation
democratic deficit, and professionalization 45
depoliticization, Marseilles bid 36
direct mail 104–5, 106, 109
discourses of participation 217–18

Index

domestication of CSOs 20–2, 26
donations, fundraising and membership 106–8
donations, types of 107
door-to-door recruitment (D2D) 105–6, 107
Dorothy Donors 105

economic development 166
education 152–3, 157, 159, 170
Ellis, Kate 228–9
empowered public discourse 217–18, 220
entrepreneurial institutionalization, Marseilles 34–5
environmental activism: airports 58–9; British movement in context 47–53; civil society 64; climate camps 55–6, 58; climate change 53–60; context and overview 46–7; convergence 65–7; growth areas 48–9; institutionalization 46–7, 48–53; leading ENGOs *50–1*; levels of campaigning 49–50, 64–5; local action 63; local campaigns 56–9; local level climate action 59–60; membership of ENGOs *49*; and the political agenda 65; pressure groups 65–6; professionalization 47, 64; protest and participation 64–5, 66–7; public mobilization 61–3; public support 47; renewable energy 63; roads 56–7; social justice 66; waste 57–8
environmental protest 52–3
ethical/moral considerations 126–32
EU civil society: activists and professionals 77–8; career opportunities 75; career patterns 81; conceptual approaches 70–9; context and overview 69–70; efficiency and influence 79; funding and patronage 80; organizational structures 75–8, 79–81; power relations 79–80; professionalization of representation 72–4; social actors 81; social capital hypothesis 71–2; social movements and interest groups 74–9; summary and conclusions 82; *see also* civil society; civil society organizations (CSOs)
Euromediterraneanism 41–2
Europe, peripheral and core participants 160–3, **163**
European Capital of Culture 42, 43; *see also* Marseilles; Marseilles-Provence 2013
European democracy 84–6; *see also* democracy
everyday makers 214

fragmentation, of society 199
free-riding 103–4, 105
free welfare associations 15, 17
freelancers, use of 22

Friends of the Earth 52–4, 61–6
funding and support 76, 89–90
fundraising, membership and donations 106–8

gender 134, 169–70
Germany, state principles 15
governance: and business mobilization 36–9; change of approach 26; Healthy House 19–20; Marséilles-Provence 2013 38–9
governments, support for groups 89
Greening Campaign 60
Greenpeace 49–50, 53, 64
group construction, of individual preferences 99–102
group-induced participation 99–102

Healthy House 19–22, 25–6

ideology 87, 178–9; and policy preferences 180–1; and political participation 181
income sources, UK campaign groups *89*
individual preferences, group construction of 99–102
individualization 67, 115, 126–7, 129, 132, 134–5, 204, 231–2; as benign 240–2; explanations of 237–40; political participation **119**; and professionalization 3–7
individualized collective action 197–8
inequality 178–9, 191–6, 197; along policy lines **187–9**
information, access and selection 103
institutionalization, environmental activism 46–7, 48–53
interest groups: competing goals 87; functions 85; government support 89; internal democracy 93; membership 166; organizational structures 87; participation 86–92; patronage 88–91; professionalization 85–6; and social movements 74–9; summary and conclusions 94–5; as surrogates 94
internationalization 44, 75
Internet 129, 132, 134

Jordan, G. 99

Latarjet, B. 27, 28, 36–7, 38
left-right position, and policy preferences *185*
legitimacy, of local politics 26
Lille, as reference for Marseilles bid 31
local politics, legitimacy of 26
low income, effects on volunteering *152*

major issues, and mobilization 164–5
marginalization 39–40, 225–6

Marseilles: business-organized mobilization 39; collective action 28; common strategic identity 31; context and overview 27–9; control by business 38; cultural policy and politics 30–2; 'Cultural Policy Master Plan' 36; cultural territory building 43; culture and promotion 29; data sources 29; as declining city 29–30; depoliticization of bid 36; entrepreneurial institutionalization 34–5; Euromediterraneanism 41–2; family businesses 34–5; image of 31; nature of politics 41; political economy of culture 40–1; primacy of economics 28; roles of actors in bid 28; Top 20 Ambition Club 35; trajectory of bid 32–5; urban governance and business mobilization 36–9
Marseilles-Provence 2013 41; governance 38–9; internationalization 44; marginalization of cultural actors 39–40; summary and conclusions 43–5
Marseilles-Provence Chamber of Commerce and Industry (MPCCI) 31, 32, 33, 34, 35, 37, 44
Marshall, T.H. 116
Mécènes du Sud 32–3, 35
media 102–3, 164
members, contact with 92–3
membership, donations and fundraising 106–8
metropolitanization, and culture 30–2
mobilization 101–2, 157, 158–60, 164–5, 166, 171, 174
Münster 17–22, 25–6
Muselier, R. 41–2

naming and shaming strategy 22
National Trust 97
National Youth Roundtable (Australia) 220
National Youth Week (Australia) 220–1
neo-liberalism 15
new public management 25
nuclear power 63

Olson, M. 99–101
on-street recruitment (F2F) 105–6, 107, 109
opinions, shaping 102–4
opportunity 169
organization, participation as 115–17
organizational modernization, and supply side professionalization 98–106
outsourcing activism 116, 178–9

participants 133–4; antecedents **130–1**; characteristics of 133–4, **133**; core 159, 160, 160–3, 168–9, 174–5; Europe **163**; *see also* peripheral participants

participation: choice of 84–5; and democracy 231; desirable mode 97; determinants of form 126–32; enhancing 92–4; group-induced 99–102; ideology, extremism and distance **192–3**; low levels 86–92; modes of –2, 126–32, 135–6, 231–2, 235–7; typology **127**, **128**; as organization 115–17
push/pull factors 86–7; resources for 168–70
participation and protest 64–5, 66–7
participatory behaviour, changes in 199–201
participatory inequality *see* inequality
passivity 4–7
patronage 88–91
peripheral participants **164**, **165**; context and overview 157–8; Europe 160–3, **163**; by mobilization **167**; mobilization of 158–60; prevalence 164–74; summary and conclusions 174–5; *see also* core participants
Pfister, J. 27, 34, 35, 38
policy making, professionalization 91–2
policy preferences 181; and left-right position *185*
political activity, ease of 115–16
political agenda, and environmental activism 65
political consumerism 124
political engagement, measuring 169
political participation: costs of 161; differentiation 161–2; expansion 117–22; explorative structure of **125**; individualization **119**; modes of 117–22, **120–1**, **123**; new modes 122–6; typology **162**
political spaces, professional structuring 72–3
political volunteering 141–2, **143**, 145–6; effects of low income *152*; and welfare state policy *147*
politicization, of self-help groups 24
privatization 16
proactive targeting 104–6
professionalization: as benign 240–2; civil society organizations (CSOs) 20; and democratic deficit 45; enhancing participation 92–4; environmental activism 64; EU civil society *see* separate heading; explanations of 237–40; growth of 2–3; and individualization 3–7; interest groups 85–6; of policy making 91–2; of representation 71–4; for self-help groups 22–5; summary and conclusions 232–4; *see also* supply side professionalization
professionalization, environmental activism 47
prospecting 108
protest and participation 64–5, 66–7
public action, territorialization of 31

Index 267

Index

public–private partnerships (PPPs) 16, 19–24
Putnam, R. 98

rational choice 100–1
renewable energy 63
representation, professionalization of 71–4
research questions 7–11
responsibility-taking 130, 135–6
responsible public discourse 217–18, 220
Richardson, J.J. 99
Rising Tide 54
roads, environmental activism 56–7
RSPB 97

Sarkozy, N. 42
self-help groups, Germany 16–18, 22–5
Skocpol, T. 99
social capital hypothesis, and professionalized civil society 71–2
social movements and interest groups 74–9
social networks, of business leaders 33
social volunteering 141–2, **143**, 144–5, 146; effects of low income *152*; and welfare state policy *147*
socio-economic development 159, 171
socio-economic status (SES) model of participation 168
stakeholder public discourse 217–18
Stop Climate Chaos 54–5
supplier–customer relationships 116
supply side professionalization: context and overview 97–8; group-induced participation 99–102; membership, donations and fundraising 106–8; and organizational modernization 98–106; proactive targeting 104–6; shaping opinions 99–102; summary and conclusions 109–10; *see also* professionalization
supply side, role in securing support 97–8
surrogacy 94, 179
sustainable development 53–4

targeting, proactive 104–6
territorialization, of public action 31
Top 20 Ambition Club 35, 38
Transition Towns network 59, 66
trust 169, 170–1

UK campaign groups, income sources *89*
Union for Mediterranean (UfM) 42
urbanization 165, 171

volunteering 141–2, **143**, 144–6, *152*; welfare state effects *150*; and welfare state policy *147*

waste, environmental activism 57–8
welfare services, co-production 15
welfare state effects: context and overview 139–41; data and method 146–8; empirical findings 148–53; political volunteering 145–6, *150*; social volunteering 144–5, *150*; summary and conclusions 153–4; theoretical accounts 142–6
welfare state policy: and civic engagement **147**; and political volunteering *147*; and social volunteering *147*

young people, voting 213
youth participation programmes 215–16, 219–21
youth participation study 219–21; conceptualizing participation 213–16; context and overview 212–13; discourses of participation 217–18; future developments 228–9; involvement in decision-making *223*; levels of participation *213*; methodology and background 218–29; participation mechanisms *222*; policy makers' discourses 224–8; service providing organizations 221–3; summary and conclusions 230–1; themes in discourses *225*; *see also* adolescents study